AIR MONOPOLY

AIR
MONOPOLY

How Robert Milton's Air Canada Won – and Lost –
Control of Canada's Skies

KEITH McARTHUR

M&S

For Laura
For Dad

National Library of Canada Cataloguing in Publication

McArthur, Keith
Air monopoly : how Robert Milton's Air Canada won and lost control
of Canada's skies / Keith McArthur.

Includes bibliographical references and index.
ISBN 0-7710-5688-5

1. Air Canada – History. 2. Milton, Robert A. I. Title.

HE9815.A93M34 2004   387.7'06'571   C2003-905671-6

We acknowledge the financial support of the Government of Canada through the Book Publishing Industry Development Program and that of the Government of Ontario through the Ontario Media Development Corporation's Ontario Book Initiative. We further acknowledge the support of the Canada Council for the Arts and the Ontario Arts Council for our publishing program.

Typeset in Bembo by M&S, Toronto
Printed and bound in Canada

This book is printed on acid-free paper that is
100% ancient forest friendly (100% post-consumer recycled)

McClelland & Stewart Ltd.
The Canadian Publishers
481 University Avenue
Toronto, Ontario
M5G 2E9
www.mcclelland.com

1 2 3 4 5   08 07 06 05 04

CONTENTS

THE RED TEAM
Trans-Canada Air Lines — Air Canada

MONTIE BREWER: Hired away from United Airlines in 2002, Brewer oversaw scheduling, marketing, and new business ventures.

PAUL BROTTO: With a reputation as a cost-cutter, Brotto has held key positions under various CEOs.

LAMAR DURRETT: The "gentleman" CEO ran Air Canada from 1996 to 1999, including the single most profitable year in the airline's history.

RUPERT DUCHESNE: Hired to replace Robert Milton as vice-president of marketing, Duchesne later became president of Aeroplan.

HOLLIS HARRIS: After holding senior executive posts at Delta and Continental, Robert Milton's mentor was recruited to replace Claude Taylor as CEO in 1992.

GORDON McGREGOR: President of Trans-Canada Air Lines and Air Canada from 1948 to 1968.

ROBERT MILTON: Named Air Canada's CEO in 1999, Milton presided over the airline during the most tumultuous period in the history of aviation.

ROB PETERSON: Worked his way from the loading ramp to the job of chief financial officer.

DOUG PORT: A former journalist who oversaw government affairs, public relations, and customer service at Air Canada.

ROB REID: The vice-president in charge of Air Canada's day-of-flight operations.

CALIN ROVINESCU: A Stikeman Elliott lawyer who took a big cut in pay to work as Robert Milton's right-hand man.

STEVE SMITH: His varied career at the Red Team was interrupted between 1999 and 2000 when he became president and chief executive officer of WestJet Airlines.

CLAUDE TAYLOR: Worked for four and a half decades at Air Canada, including twenty-seven years as chairman or chief executive officer, before stepping down in 1993.

THE BLUE TEAM
*Western Canada Airways – Canadian Airways – Canadian Pacific
Airlines – CP Air – Pacific Western Airlines – Wardair – Nordair – Eastern
Provincial Airlines – Canadian Airlines International*

RUSSELL BAKER: The founder of Pacific Western Airlines.

KEVIN BENSON: The final president and CEO of Canadian Airlines
before it was taken over by Air Canada in 2000.

DON CARTY: The Canadian-born chairman and CEO of American
Airlines. Carty was president of CP Air when PWA acquired it in 1987.

DOUG CARTY: Don's little brother was a key player during the final
months of Canadian Airlines, where he worked closely with Kevin
Benson as chief financial officer.

GRANT McCONACHIE: The flamboyant entrepreneur ran Canadian
Pacific Airlines from 1947 until his death in 1965

JAMES RICHARDSON: The father of commercial aviation in Canada,
Richardson founded Western Canada Airways, one of the forerunners
to Canadian Airlines, in 1926.

GERRY SCHWARTZ: Onex Corporation's president and CEO, who
fronted the plan to buy and merge Air Canada with Canadian Airlines
in 1999.

MAX WARD: Launched Wardair in 1953 as a bush charter airline based
in Yellowknife, then built it into a major scheduled airline.

THE NEW TEAM
WestJet Airlines – Canada 3000 – Royal Airlines – Greyhound Air –
CanJet Airlines – Roots Air – Jetsgo

CLIVE BEDDOE: The real-estate developer who provided the seed money for WestJet Airlines, bringing the low-cost model to Canada.

DON BELL: WestJet's co-chief operating officer specializing in customer service and one of its four founders.

RICHARD BRANSON: The flashy British billionaire behind Virgin Atlantic Airways.

JOHN GILMORE: A former Air Canada lawyer who helped develop CanJet Airlines.

MARK HILL: WestJet's aggressive vice-president for strategic planning, who wrote the airline's business plan.

DICK HUISMAN: The flying Dutchman who envisioned Greyhound Air as part of a coordinated system of passenger transportation.

ANGUS KINNEAR: The charming but moody Brit behind Canada 3000.

MICHEL LEBLANC: A perennial figure in the airline industry, Leblanc has founded various airlines, including Intair, Royal, and Jetsgo.

JOHN LECKY: The wealthy former Olympic rower who invested some of his inheritance to launch Canada 3000 in 1988.

TIM MORGAN: Another of WestJet's founders, Morgan oversees flight operations and shares the job of chief operating officer with Don Bell.

DAVID NEELEMAN: The guru of low-cost airlines, whose name and reputation helped WestJet raise its start-up capital before he founded JetBlue.

RUSS PAYSON: The CEO of Skyservice Airlines, who deviated from his risk-averse strategy just once – to launch Roots Air.

KEN ROWE: One of the richest men in Atlantic Canada, Rowe used his personal wealth to launch CanJet Airlines – twice.

TED SHETZEN: The garrulous ideas man behind Roots Air.

MARK WINDERS: The chief operating officer of CanJet Airlines.

TEAM OTTAWA

DAVID COLLENETTE: The minister of transport watched the airline industry for Jean Chrétien from 1997 to 2003.

KONRAD VON FINCKENSTEIN: The federal commissioner of competition from 1997 to 2003.

BRUCE HOOD: The outspoken former NHL referee appointed to be the country's first air-travel complaints commissioner.

C.D. HOWE: Known as the "minister of everything," Howe was the country's first transport minister and the driving force behind Trans-Canada Air Lines.

JOHN MANLEY: As industry minister in 1999, Manley worked closely with David Collenette on the airline competition file.

PROLOGUE

A monopoly is only a bad thing for the customer if it is abused. If the airline can be depended on to be forward-thinking, to be progressive, not to impose higher tariffs than necessary, then this is the cheapest way the service can be given.[1]
— Gordon McGregor, Air Canada's president from 1948 to 1968

An 80-per-cent market share is a curse.[2]
— Robert Milton, Air Canada's president from 1999

*W*arren Buffett, the billionaire investor known as the Oracle of Omaha, likes to say that the global airline industry has shown a net loss since Orville Wright made his first flight on December 17, 1903. "If there had been a capitalist down there at Kitty Hawk," Buffett has said more than once, "he should have shot down Orville and saved us a lot of money."[3] Since the U.S. airline industry was deregulated in 1978, some of the most prominent names in aviation have vanished: carriers like Pan American Airlines, Eastern Airlines, and Braniff International Airways. In Canada, Wardair, Canadian Airlines, and Canada 3000 have also disappeared, through either acquisition or bankruptcy.

A century after the Wright brothers' first flight, the commercial airline business is in critical condition. Between 2001 and 2003, Air Canada has piled up more than $3 billion in losses, several times more than it had realized in profits since it was founded as Trans-Canada Air Lines in 1937. Discount carriers like WestJet and Southwest and JetBlue are posting consistent profits, but doing so at the expense of the traditional industry giants. Air Canada and United Airlines have been forced to file for court-ordered bankruptcy protection, wiping out their existing shareholders, and desperately trying to stay alive by slashing operating costs and settling debts at a fraction of face value.

Passenger air travel is a business where equipment is expensive and most employees are unionized, where inventory is spoiled every time a flight takes off with unsold seats, where the bottom line is extremely vulnerable to the economy and the price of fuel, and where competition – when it exists – is cutthroat. It is a business where losses are more common than profits and the vast majority of new start-ups fail. Everyone who fantasizes about starting an airline knows the risks. Yet there are always entrepreneurs eager to send them aloft and investors willing to gamble on the adventure. They are driven by the very human aspiration to succeed where others have failed. In 1903, the Wright brothers pursued a dream – as old as humanity – to conquer the skies against impossible odds. The same dream has inspired airline operators like Robert Milton ever since.

"The business model is broken," Milton declared in 2003. "Air Canada and our people need to embrace a culture change and a new way of doing business." The airline's president and chief executive officer regarded himself as the right man to reinvent the industry. With chubby pink cheeks and short, tousled black hair, Milton could look almost cherubic – not what one would expect from Canada's most notorious CEO. But his blunt, baritone voice, with its hint of an American accent, betrayed his true nature. Milton had no veneer; what you saw was what you got. He didn't like to charm or mince words, but he might try to win over his opposition with strong argument and rhetoric. Somewhat like a TV evangelist, he came across as a man who truly believed only he knew what was best. His unrelenting confidence in his own abilities was perhaps his greatest strength. In its extreme form – when it emerged as self-righteousness or arrogance – it was also his worst flaw.

In this he was little different from other industry legends, people like James Richardson or Grant McConachie in Canada and Juan Trippe or Bob Crandall in the United States. The airline business has always attracted large egos. Perhaps it is because the struggle to make money in the industry – like the act of flying itself – is one that defies the known laws of nature and calls a select few. Since 1937, CEOs from the world's largest airlines have gathered regularly at luxury resorts and ranches to participate in an exclusive club known as the Conquistadores del Cielo – the Conquerors of the Skies. Milton has attended many times. "There's something about this glamorous, sexy business," Roots Air's Ted Shetzen has said. "Airplanes are bigger than Porsches for a lot of guys."[4]

In a business run by egomaniacs, nothing should be more satisfying than a monopoly. Economic theory holds that monopolies are absolute; they exist only when a single firm controls 100 per cent of the supply of a given product. But economists will also use the more subjective concept of "monopoly power," which can exist even when there is more than one firm in a market. In simple terms, a firm's monopoly power represents its ability to raise prices due to the absence of effective competition. While Air Canada has never had an absolute monopoly in the Canadian domestic market, it has enjoyed unprecedented monopoly power, as well as very real monopolies on dozens of individual routes. In the summer of 2000, more than half of Canada's two hundred busiest routes were the exclusive domain of Air Canada or one of its subsidiaries.[5] Dominance equals power in any industry, but this is especially true in the airline business, where customers will pay a premium for frequent service. There is a proven correlation between market share and profitability. Supremacy, the theory goes, is key to success in the airline business. When he won control of Canada's skies in 2000, Robert Milton dreamed of global expansion and bountiful profits. What he got was something else altogether.

I

The Red Team and the Blue Team

The word "Monopoly" had been thrown in the teeth of Air Canada from the beginning. It was never quite that, but came pretty close to it, and as if the idea of a monopoly were not sufficiently unpopular with the average customer, we had the added stigma of being a government monopoly.[1]

> – Gordon McGregor, president of
> Trans-Canada Air Lines/Air Canada, 1948–68

Actually, Gordon and I are good personal friends. The only flaw in our relationship is that I envy him. I would envy anyone who can eliminate his competition by the simple device of losing money, and the more money he loses, the more secure his monopoly.[2]

> – Grant McConachie,
> president of Canadian Pacific Airlines, 1947–65

*T*hey were almost immortal; certainly, they were brave. At the end of the First World War, after waging war in primitive flying machines made of wood, cloth, and wire, Canadian flying aces like Billy Bishop and Raymond Collishaw returned home and infected a generation of their countrymen with the aviation obsession. Younger pilots hoped to make their fortunes as barnstormers and wingwalkers, risking their lives for entertainment with daring aerial stunts. Others became pioneers in Canada's fledgling airline industry, gambling everything as pilots and entrepreneurs while ferrying furs, mining supplies, and mail. Almost an act of God-defiance, flying challenged the known laws of nature. And it was solitary work, attracting driven personalities and outsized egos. As their successors would never forget, it takes a healthy dose of hubris to fly close to the sun.

In the early twentieth century, two such individuals – the visionary business titan James Richardson and the powerful cabinet minister C.D. Howe – put the stamp of their personalities on the companies that would become Air Canada and Canadian Airlines.

Richardson was heir to a Kingston, Ontario, grain dynasty founded by his grandfather. It was the largest private company in Canada when Richardson moved the business to Winnipeg in 1923. Three years later, he formed Western Canada Airways with an HS-2L waterplane, a Fokker Universal landplane, and an investment of $200,000. Richardson conceived the airline as a means to reach untapped mineral resources in northern Ontario, but it delivered much more than that. By 1930, WCA was the world's largest air-cargo company, flying north with miners and their supplies and returning south with furs and fish. WCA's success allowed Richardson to snap up other airlines that were struggling financially, and in 1930 it attracted the interest of the country's twin transportation giants, Canadian Pacific Railway and the government-owned Canadian National Railway. While Richardson remained the controlling shareholder, each railway invested $250,000 in the airline, which was renamed Canadian Airways. By the mid-1930s, Canadian had secured lucrative government contracts to transport mail throughout Canada and into the United States and to the Magdalen Islands. Richardson had dreams of extending his reach much farther, turning Canadian Airways into an overseas operator like Imperial Airways in Britain, Pan American World Airways in the United States, or Deutsche Luft Hansa in Germany.

If Richardson was the father of private aviation in Canada, his counterpart in public enterprise was Clarence Decatur Howe, Canada's first federal transport minister. Howe was born in Waltham, Massachusetts, but moved to Halifax in 1908 to teach at Dalhousie University, before founding a thriving grain-elevator business. Average in build and looks, but with piercing dark eyes, Howe was one of the richest men in the

House of Commons when William Lyon Mackenzie King made him minister of canals and railways in 1935.

The previous prime minister, R.B. Bennett, had taken some preliminary steps towards founding a national airline but abandoned the idea during the Depression. Bennett had even cancelled air-mail contracts in those years, fearing that Prairie farmers would fume if they saw government-financed planes flying over their dusty, barren fields. As a result, Canada lagged behind other countries in civil aviation when King's Liberals were returned to power in 1935. Within a month of taking office, King promised to establish a national airline that would fly between Montreal and Vancouver. He envisioned a state-sanctioned public-private monopoly – initially for the purpose of transporting mail, but eventually for passenger service as well. While there might be room for some government involvement, King didn't want Trans-Canada Air Lines to be a Crown corporation. The prime minister intended to involve the two railways in the project to eliminate overlap and to ensure that mail and passengers flowed easily between rail and air. "This means neither government ownership outright, nor private ownership outright, but part private, part public with government control," King wrote.

Howe was given the task of delivering on King's vision, an assignment he would come to relish. He flew across the United States on different airlines, making detailed notes about runway lighting and weather services, and cozying up to industry legends like Pan Am's Juan Trippe, Eastern Airlines' Eddie Rickenbacker, and American Airlines' C.R. Smith. His research time in the United States must have been a welcome relief from the intense lobbying of aviation companies at home, all vying for a chance to become the government's chosen instrument for air services.

James Richardson did everything he could to make sure Canadian Airways was picked for the job, sending emissaries to Ottawa and penning letters to Howe and King. Howe signalled that he liked Richardson's chances. "Every consideration will be given to the past experience of Canadian Airways when plans for new services are being developed," Howe wrote him in a letter dated February 12, 1936. "I consider it important that our two national railways be represented on the directorate of whatever Company will dominate the aviation future of Canada, and I feel you are fortunately situated in that regard."[3] A mutual friend later told Richardson that Howe viewed Canadian Airways as the only company in the running. That was good enough for Richardson, who bought aircraft, hired pilots, and drew up a detailed route system in anticipation of the government's announcement. He even maintained unprofitable air-mail routes in order to stay in the government's good books.

When the transport minister tabled his airline bill in 1937, however, there was no mention of Canadian Airways or James Richardson. Instead, a new airline was to be created, one jointly owned by the country's two railways and controlled by the federal government. The bill allowed Ottawa to appoint two-thirds of the directors – one-third through direct appointments and another third through its control of Canadian National Railway. Richardson was aghast, and so was Canadian Pacific Railway, which was expected to assume half the risk for just one-third the board votes. CPR officials asked that they be excluded from the scheme. Howe offered Richardson a chance to buy shares in the airline, but Richardson politely declined. His wish was to see Canadian Airways become the government's official choice for air travel, not to hold a minority interest in a separate airline. Thereafter, Trans-Canada Air Lines, as it was christened, was a government airline – a subsidiary of Canadian National Railways – despite King's wishes that it be a public-private partnership. That was fine with Howe, who responded to charges that TCA represented a step towards socialism by saying, "That's not public enterprise, that's my enterprise."[4]

Trans-Canada Air Lines made its first flight – sort of – on July 30, 1937. The flight was little more than a publicity stunt and a near disaster. Howe had promised the prime minister that the airline would be operating by July. It wasn't, but Howe figured a dawn-to-dusk flight between Montreal and Vancouver would demonstrate that the airline was at least ready to stimulate interest in passenger air travel. TCA didn't yet have planes or pilots of its own – the airline would not be capable of regular transcontinental service for another two years – so the inaugural mission was flown in a Department of Transport Lockheed 12A. Howe was one of the flight's few passengers, along with officials from Canadian National Railway and Lockheed. The minister wore a jacket and tie, not the leather coat and goggles that Canadians had come to expect of aviators, as if to signal that aviation in Canada had come of age, that it was a sophisticated adventure rather than a dangerous expedition.

TCA's maiden flight was anything but reassuring. The pilot went out for a test flight early that morning but circled back and returned the plane to its hangar because visibility was so limited. Despite the poor conditions, however, the publicity exercise went ahead. Howe and company ran into a heavy thunderstorm soon after taking off from Montreal's St. Hubert Airport. The Lockheed made its first fuel stop near North Bay, but missed the next stop because of thick fog. When it landed in the clear near Sioux Lookout, the plane was minutes away from running out of gas. The weary travellers arrived in Vancouver seventeen hours and ten minutes after their departure from Montreal. There is no clear answer as to why the decision was made to set out in stormy weather but, according to one account, it was Howe who insisted that the show must go on, overruling the pilot's belief that it was too dangerous. This version was penned by none other than James Richardson, whose resentment still smouldered. He claimed to have heard the whole story from the flight crew. "If their gas had given out just before they got to Sioux Lookout they would have been written off," Richardson wrote in a letter to his friend Edward Beatty, president of CPR. "It was altogether just a fool piece of business and something that could only be gotten away with the odd time."

Richardson died in 1939, two years after Trans-Canada Air Lines' publicity flight. In 1941, Beatty proposed to Howe that the government and CPR jointly buy Richardson's stake in Canadian Airways and merge it with TCA. Howe thought a merger was a good idea, but the timing was wrong for a government preoccupied with the Second World War. As a result, CPR unilaterally bought Richardson's stake, then combined several smaller airlines with Canadian Airways under the name Canadian Pacific

Airlines. The ownership and the name on the fuselage changed once again, but Richardson's spirit would live on for decades in the tension between private aviation interests and the government airline.

The Trans-Canada Air Lines Act established a clear hierarchy for the country's air carriers. There was TCA and there was everybody else. TCA was granted a transcontinental monopoly on east-west travel between Vancouver and Halifax. Other airlines could apply to the Department of Transport for the right to serve north-south feeder routes, which they would typically get only if TCA didn't want them. Canadian Pacific Airlines was loath to accept its second-tier status; Richardson's successors wanted access to TCA's mainline routes, and appeared to have the support of the Canadian people, who remained skeptical about public ownership in areas that could be handled by private enterprise. Canadian carriers were not yet flying to foreign locales, but CPA also wanted equal access to international routes when the time came.

However, Prime Minister King rebuffed CPA's efforts to break the TCA monopoly. He delivered a strongly worded statement to the House of Commons on April 2, 1943, in which he maintained that there was no place for competition in the airline industry. "The government sees no good reason for changing its policy that Trans-Canada Air Lines is the sole Canadian agency which may operate international air services. Within Canada, Trans-Canada Air Lines will continue to operate all transcontinental systems, and such other services of a mainline character as may from time to time be designated by the government."

Canada's first initiatives in international air travel came in July 1943, with the formation of the Canadian Government Trans-Atlantic Service, a federal-government body designed to carry troops and officials across the Atlantic during wartime.[5] There were already philosophical disagreements between nations concerning the conduct of the postwar civil-aviation industry. The United States was the dominant force in air travel, and Washington believed its carriers would benefit from an open and competitive regime in which every airline had the freedom to land in or fly through any country's airspace. But Britain, whose commercial industry had been stunted by the war effort, wanted to protect the special access its Imperial Airways enjoyed to Canada and other Commonwealth countries. (Such debates over protectionist air policies predated the airplane. As early as the 1870s, there were diplomatic discussions in Europe about whether a country had sovereignty over its skies, or whether hot-air balloons could roam freely like ships on the seas.)

In 1944, a thousand delegates from forty-four countries met in Chicago to hammer out the safety and economic rules that would govern the postwar industry. Canada's delegate, Trans-Canada Air Lines president Herbert Symington, tried to find common ground between the positions of Britain and the United States. But with no consensus the U.S. proposal for an open market failed. The result was a heavily regulated environment in which nations were required to negotiate complex bilateral agreements before their carriers could serve international destinations.

The Chicago convention agreed on a series of access rights or "freedoms" that could be extended by one state to another through bilateral agreements, from the most basic "first freedom" to fly through another nation's airspace without landing, to the "fifth freedom" to carry passengers or cargo between two foreign states. None of the original five freedoms contemplated the possibility that a country might allow a foreign airline to fly between two of its own cities.[6] Decades later, little has changed. Allowing foreigners to supply goods and services is taken for granted in most other industries, but the idea is considered extremely radical in domestic aviation. The concept is known as *cabotage*, a French term referring to coastal trading in one country by ships registered in another, and it is almost non-existent in the airline world. In fact, the U.S. Congress, in a reversal of its position of sixty years ago, has passed laws that prevent the president from negotiating bilateral agreements that would allow it.

Most of the international agreements governing aviation stipulate that an airline designated to serve a foreign country must be "substantially owned and effectively controlled" by the government or by its citizens. In extraordinary circumstances, such as a war, a country could revoke the freedoms. Consequently, most countries limit foreign ownership in their airlines to 49 per cent, leaving majority ownership in the hands of their citizens. Canada and the United States go further, restricting foreigners to just 25 per cent of the voting shares in an airline. Traditionally, such restrictions have been applied to all airlines, whether they serve international routes or not.

The decisions made in 1944 led to the notion and the creation of national flag-carriers. Every country wanted its own flag-carrier to exercise the rights obtained by its government through bilateral negotiations. A nation might be able to do without independent sources of power or food or clean water, but it needed an airline. The flag-carrier airlines stirred nationalistic sentiments like no other business. In 1947, only four developing countries had their own international carriers; by 1977 the number had climbed to eighty-two.[7] While some of the world's flag-carriers operated as highly efficient and profitable airlines, most did not. Many required millions of dollars in government aid to stay afloat, as well as artificial barriers to protect them from any real competition.[8] In Canada, these barriers kept competitors away from TCA's lucrative transcontinental and international routes.

Canadian Pacific Airlines would likely have remained a mouse to TCA's elephant forever if not for Grant McConachie, an aggressive young executive who took advantage of a government airline afraid to take risks. Born in Alberta in 1909, George William Grant McConachie earned his private pilot's licence at age twenty, and four years later started a small airline to carry passengers and mail between Edmonton and Whitehorse. His company was one of many acquired by CPR during the Second World War. By the time he was thirty-seven, in 1947, McConachie was president of Canadian Pacific Airlines.

A few months later, TCA likewise appointed a new president who would have a major impact on its development. Also a pilot, Gordon McGregor had won the Distinguished Flying Cross during the war – the same medal that had been presented to Charles Lindbergh after his solo flight across the Atlantic. McGregor joined TCA in 1945 as general traffic manager and was promoted to president three years later.

Beyond the fact that both were pilots, the two men could not have been more different. McConachie was a flamboyant entrepreneur, willing to leap first and look later. McGregor was cautious and plain-spoken, never making a move without detailed analysis. Or, as the *Ottawa Journal* once put it, "McGregor worries about balancing the books while McConachie concentrates on expansion and pizzazz."[9] McGregor's conservatism may have been related to a warning Howe gave him when he got the job: "You keep out of the taxpayer's pocket and I'll keep out of your hair."[10] Or perhaps McConachie was more willing to take risks because Canadian Pacific Airlines had little to lose and everything to gain. The opposite was true of TCA.

McGregor's cautious nature led him to make a decision his successors at TCA and Air Canada would regret for decades. He turned down a chance to provide air service to Australia and Asia, because he believed the routes could not be profitable. McConachie, by contrast, jumped at the opportunity. C.D. Howe was in no hurry to help CPA, but he feared that a foreign airline might take over the routes if a Canadian carrier didn't claim them. He reversed the previous position that TCA would be Canada's only international carrier and granted the routes to CPA, with the stipulation that CPA buy some Canadian-made North Star aircraft. The Australia service, which was launched in July 1949, did not make money for two decades. Few observers expected the Tokyo route to do any better. But when the Korean War broke out in 1949, CPA was paid to transport troops to Asia and the route suddenly became a cash cow. "Jesus Christ," McGregor declared. "Only McConachie could be that lucky."[11] More significantly, Howe had set a precedent by awarding international-route rights to a secondary carrier. Within a decade, Canadian Pacific Airways had secured rights to destinations on most continents, flying south to Mexico City and Lima, Peru, and east to Amsterdam, Madrid, and Lisbon.

In 1957, the Liberals were swept from office by John Diefenbaker's Conservatives, who looked less favourably on TCA's privileged position and had campaigned on the notion of increased competition. TCA got off to a bad start with the Tory leader when it lost his luggage on a flight from Prince Albert to Ottawa, causing Diefenbaker to "jump up and down like a little kid," according to Clark Davey, a *Globe and Mail* reporter who witnessed the scene. "Don't they know who I am? I'm the new prime minister!" Diefenbaker shouted.[12] The episode foreshadowed a testy relationship between TCA and the Conservative government. Transport minister George Hees soon signalled that he would permit competition wherever two carriers could operate a route economically. A year later, the government awarded CPA the right to operate one return flight each day between Vancouver and Montreal, with stops in Winnipeg and Toronto. It wasn't much, but after two decades as the government's "chosen instrument," TCA's monopoly on the east-west trunk routes had finally been cracked.

Gordon McGregor wanted it restored. In 1960, the TCA president put forward a proposal to merge the two airlines. The plan would have eliminated competition on domestic routes and allowed TCA access to CPA's lucrative international routes. Despite Diefenbaker's earlier push for more competition, the government supported the proposal. But McConachie dismissed it out of hand, preferring to fight for more international routes and a bigger slice of the domestic market. In his memoirs, McGregor expressed regret that the marriage could not be arranged. "The advantages to the country and the industry both in terms of airline service and economics were recognized to be potentially immense," he wrote. "With only one main line and international carrier, bilateral and traffic pool agreements could have been negotiated from strength, and wasteful competition in international routes eliminated, enabling Canada to compete more vigorously with foreign flag carriers."[13]

The Diefenbaker government shot down McGregor on a separate proposal he was floating to have the airline's name changed to Air Canada, a moniker that worked equally well in English or French. The name *Trans-Canada Air Lines* was not bilingual, and its French translation, *Les Lignes aériennes Trans-Canada*, was cumbersome. The company's board was set to adopt the Air Canada brand and had planned an elaborate public-relations campaign to explain the change to employees. But when Diefenbaker caught wind of their intentions, he had George Hees lean on McGregor to keep the Trans-Canada label. Diefenbaker didn't want to appear to be pandering to Quebec.

It would take a change in government – and four years – before Parliament voted to rename the airline. The new name was introduced as a private member's bill by a young Jean Chrétien, who would later refer to it as his first major victory in Parliament. Chrétien stood in the House of Commons on March 3, 1964, to argue for a more inclusive name for the country's flag-carrier. Not only was the old name unilingual, Chrétien argued, it was inaccurate. While the airline had been created to provide transportation from Halifax to Vancouver, it had become much more than that, with "routes that touch many parts of the world." With no opposition from Prime Minister Lester B. Pearson or transport minister Jack Pickersgill, the bill became law and the company's corporate name was officially changed to Air Canada on January 1, 1965.

By the time Canadian Pacific Airlines went through a similar rebranding in 1968 – changing its name to CP Air and repainting its aircraft bright orange, befitting the spirit of the 1960s – the airline had established itself as a competitive domestic alternative to Air Canada. The year before, Pickersgill had granted the airline a second transcontinental route and had said that, over time, its share of the transcontinental market could grow to 25 per cent. The airline had become a strong player on international routes as well. In 1964, Pickersgill had divided the world between the two airlines, giving CPA Asia, Australia, South America, southeast Europe, and Amsterdam. Air Canada got the Caribbean and the rest of Europe, including Great Britain. Africa and the United States were excluded from the designations. In effect, the division of routes did little more than reaffirm the status quo, but by making it official, Pickersgill was able to stave off Air Canada's efforts to fly into Asia and Canadian Pacific's push to get into London.

But CP Air wasn't the only airline pushing for a slice of Air Canada's pie. Airlines such as Wardair, Nordair, Eastern Provincial Airlines, and

Pacific Western Airlines were also chafing under a regulatory environment that limited them to regional and charter routes.

Pacific Western Airlines began life in 1946 as Central British Columbia Airways, and grew quickly by purchasing other regional airlines. By the time it changed names in 1953, founder Russell Baker had ambitious goals for his carrier. "I want PWA to become the first or second-largest airline in Canada and for it to extend right across the world," he said.[14] Like McConachie, Baker was a former bush pilot who had dreamed of flying planes since he was a young boy. He was just sixteen when he started doing stunt flying – barnstorming – on the Prairies. Baker and McConachie were good friends and close allies. On family vacations together they plotted ways to break down Air Canada's monopoly. By 1974, PWA was the country's largest regional airline and Canada's third-largest carrier overall. Through cargo services and charter flights, PWA was operating in more than fifty countries.

Max Ward likewise had lofty goals for Wardair, which he launched in 1953 as a bush charter airline based in Yellowknife. Growing up in Edmonton, Ward had been entranced by the bush pilots passing through town with news of their exploits. "My whole idea of adventure, of living, was tied up in the notion of joining their ranks some day in a magnificent flying machine. My boyhood was spent building toy airplanes out of boxwood, which I got from a butterbox factory near our home, or from ingenious materials in a Meccano set."[15] Using cargo planes purchased from TCA, Wardair grew quickly in northern Canada. But by the early 1960s, there was no room left to grow in the north and the federal government refused Ward's repeated requests for southern routes.

PWA and Wardair were not content to remain in their established regional markets, but Ottawa had little interest in allowing the scrappy airlines to achieve their grand ambitions. Allocations for the scheduled routes that mattered went to Air Canada first and CP Air second; there was no third. Instead, PWA and Wardair grew by focusing on areas that were less heavily regulated by government, securing charter licences to fly the domestic and international routes they coveted. There was a catch: an airline could fly a charter route only if the entire aircraft was filled with members of the same club or organization. As Max Ward wrote in his autobiography, the so-called affinity rules led to some imaginative circumventions of the regulations. "We flew the Alberta Judo Club, whose members included little old ladies in wheelchairs; canoe clubs turned up with members who had never seen a paddle; and card-carrying mountaineers from the bald prairie put down their money and took the flight."[16] Over time, the government eased the affinity restrictions, allowing charter airlines to sell to anyone as long as the tickets were booked far enough in advance. The new charter rules also allowed Air Canada and CP Air to sell deeply discounted seats on scheduled flights for the first time.

But Max Ward wanted more. The solution, he believed, lay in deregulation.

Jimmy Carter was elected president of the United States in 1976 on the promise of a more efficient, less burdensome federal government. Although he was a Democrat, Carter could see that the public had grown suspicious of free-spending, interventionist politicians. As an expedient first step to demonstrate his sincerity, Carter urged Congress to reduce federal regulation of the commercial airline industry. All U.S. airlines were privately owned – unlike the situation in most other countries – but they were heavily regulated by government nonetheless. And the policies in Washington were a lot like those in Canada: competition was generally frowned on, and the government regulated fares in such a way as to make sure that the big airlines neither made too much money nor went bankrupt. As a result, U.S. airlines had little incentive to reduce their costs. There was no need for an airline to take a strike in order to keep labour costs down; airline wages increased steadily and so did airfares. As one observer put it, the airlines were like chess players "required to clear their moves in advance with an arbiter committed to taking the contestants to a draw."[17] By the time Carter took office, there was a general perception that excessive regulation of airlines was keeping fares artificially high. New entrants like Southwest Airlines, which avoided federal regulations by operating inside the borders of a single state, had been able to reduce fares significantly. The public believed that the cost of air travel would fall across the country if the government allowed more airline competition. Carter's Democratic Party rival, Senator Ted Kennedy, led the push for deregulation in the Congress and, in 1978, Carter put his signature on the Airline Deregulation Act. "For the first time in decades," Carter said, "we have deregulated a major industry."[18]

Airfares fell dramatically with deregulation, but only at the bottom end of the market. Passengers paying full fare saw steady increases as airlines learned that business travellers (or their employers) were willing to pay a hefty premium for the convenience of on-demand travel. The up charge could be used to subsidize fares for the budget-minded. Dozens of airlines were born out of deregulation and dozens died because of it. Between 1979 and 2001, 137 U.S. carriers filed for bankruptcy.[19] The slow-moving, high-cost carriers that had done so well in a protected, regulated environment had trouble keeping up in the new climate. Some of the most revered names in the business disappeared, including Pan Am, Eastern Airlines, and Braniff. But then some of the lean, mean upstarts that gave the established airlines so much grief soon found that they couldn't make sustainable profits over the long term. When discount airlines like People Express and Air Florida closed their doors, fares crept up once again.

Twenty-five years later, there is still debate about the wisdom of deregulation. In his 1995 book, *Hard Landing*, Thomas Petzinger, Jr., concluded that it would be wrong to think of deregulation in terms of success or failure. "Deregulation was a massive exercise in the redistribution of wealth, a zero-sum game in which not billions but trillions of dollars in money, assets, time, convenience, service, and pure human toil shifted among many groups of people, from one economic sector to another." Deregulation, Petzinger wrote, was neither good nor bad, but it was inevitable.[20]

Watching developments south of the border, Claude Taylor could see that deregulation of the Canadian airline industry was also inevitable. Taylor had started as a passenger ticket agent with Trans-Canada Air

Lines in 1949 and worked his way through the ranks until he was appointed president of Air Canada in 1974. Despite having grown up inside its bureaucratic culture, Taylor believed that the airline would be stronger if it were owned by private shareholders and had greater access to investment capital. His push for change led to the 1977 Air Canada Act, which made the airline a stand-alone Crown corporation, separate from Canadian National Railway. At Taylor's insistence, the act also introduced a concept C.D. Howe had never intended for Air Canada – profit. Over a long night of negotiations, Taylor and government officials hammered out wording that directed the airline to "have due regard to sound business principles and, in particular, the contemplation of profit." It was a peculiar directive, modest and considered, but it opened the door to the revolutionary possibility of privatization.

Claude Taylor's Air Canada did more than contemplate profit. The airline made $20 million in 1977 and $40 million in 1978, allowing him to have the audacity to suggest that Air Canada was ready to fly on its own without government protection. "There is place for two trans-continental airlines in Canada," Taylor said in early 1979, "and there is place for the regional carriers. But to what extent the regulators in Ottawa will permit more competition is unknown and the change in style may be slow in coming."[21] But change was anything but slow. In March that year, transport minister Otto Lang announced that the government cap that limited CP Air to 25 per cent of the market would be eliminated altogether. It wasn't deregulation – not yet – but rather a shift from one privileged airline to two. By choosing his words carefully and signalling that there was room in the marketplace for *two* transcontinental carriers, Taylor had invited not open competition but a duopoly, and that's exactly what Lang had given him.

Max Ward continued to lobby for deregulation, sensing that consumers wanted it and its promise of increased competition and lower airfares. He believed that any Canadian carrier should be allowed to fly any domestic route, and wanted Wardair to be eligible for international routes without the burden of the charter rules. But Ward was one of the few airline executives to support the idea. PWA officials had concerns that deregulation would lead not to more competition, but to concentration of smaller airlines and eventually to a monopoly. Even CP Air, which had been the aggressive underdog for four decades, was nervous about deregulation. The carrier now enjoyed a privileged status in Canada, which it would lose if the market were opened up further. CP Air was dealt a major blow in 1985 when Ottawa granted Wardair the rights to become the second scheduled Canadian carrier to fly to England and France – routes CP Air had coveted since Richardson's day.

Despite the industry opposition, however, the Liberals unveiled their prosaically titled "New Canadian Air Policy" in 1984, ending the Air Canada/CP Air duopoly. The government did away with distinctions between national and regional carriers, allowing any carrier to apply for any route. Government regulators would still approve route applications, but the legislation called for the phasing out of their role in setting airfares. The Progressive Conservative government of Brian Mulroney carried deregulation even further in 1987, moving out of the business of deciding which airlines would fly which routes. Under this new legislation, it was no longer necessary for a carrier to show that its service was required by "public convenience and necessity." As long as an airline could meet basic safety and financial requirements, it could operate any domestic route. A decade had passed since the U.S. government had deregulated its industry overnight; now Canada had done the same, in the country's usual measured and stately way.

In reality, "deregulation" is a misnomer. In the early twenty-first century, air travel remains one of the most heavily regulated industries in the world. The vast majority of the world's airlines, for example, are still prohibited from flying within Canada's borders. In order to operate domestic flights in Canada, an airline must show that at least 75 per cent of its voting shares are owned by Canadians. While globalization has become an unquestioned fact of life in almost every other industry, nations remain highly protective of their airlines. Governments employ scores of taxpayer-funded negotiators who do nothing but frame treaties governing which foreign airlines can land on their turf, how often, and in which cities. In 1995, Canada negotiated a so-called open-skies agreement with the United States, but this too was limited. The agreement allowed any airline from either country to fly any trans-border route. But the domestic market remained the exclusive domain of each country's own carriers.

Air Canada expressed varying degrees of opposition to deregulation over the years. Claude Taylor, who was the airline's CEO and later chairman, says that he was never personally opposed to deregulation, expecting that it would make Air Canada a stronger competitor. More importantly, he believed that deregulation was a prerequisite to his real goal: the privatization of Air Canada. Taylor felt that five decades of government ownership had made the airline lethargic and complacent. Its productivity had fallen behind that of competitors in Canada and south of the border, and major decisions couldn't be made quickly because they needed approval at several levels. Taylor knew that in business, management was supposed to work for the shareholder, but he was never sure who Air Canada's "shareholder" was. Was it the taxpayer, the travelling public, the transport minister, or the federal Treasury Board?[22]

Individual members of parliament sometimes behaved as if Air Canada were responsible directly to them. In 1978, for example, Air Canada's schedulers decided to eliminate a 10:50 p.m. flight from Ottawa to Toronto because there weren't enough passengers to make the flight financially viable. The flight was a favourite of Toronto-area MPs, who used it on Thursday nights to return to their ridings for the weekend. The evening parliamentary session usually finished with a 9:45 vote, so once the 10:50 flight was cancelled, MPs were stuck in Ottawa until Friday morning. One of the disgruntled parliamentarians was David Collenette, then vice-chair of the House of Commons standing committee on transportation issues. Collenette urged his fellow MPs to sign a petition, then put in a call to Claude Taylor's office suggesting that the 10:50 flight be reinstated. It was.[23]

Taylor found a sympathetic ear to his pleas for privatization in Brian Mulroney. Soon after becoming prime minister in 1984, Mulroney delivered some brilliant political doublespeak on the issue, stating emphatically that the Canadian Broadcasting Corporation and Air Canada were "not for sale," then hinting that he might be willing to change his mind. There may, he said, "be some persuasive arguments in the case of Air Canada that some people can make in regard to the disposition of equity. I'll take a look at it. But Canada needs a national airline."[24] Taylor redoubled his lobbying efforts.

The public appeared to support Air Canada's privatization, so the political case was strong. The economic case was even stronger. As a Crown corporation, Air Canada had not been replacing its planes as quickly as large airlines in the United States. Taylor believed Air Canada needed $3-billion worth of new aircraft in order to stay competitive. While some could be financed through debt, the rest would be paid for by the company's shareholder: the federal government. Taylor must have delivered the "persuasive arguments" Mulroney was looking for. In late 1988, the government sold 43 per cent of Air Canada to the public at eight dollars a share, raising about $240 million to pay down Air Canada's debt. In order to prevent a takeover, the privatization act limited any single shareholder from owning more than 10 per cent of Air Canada's shares, a condition that would become important a decade later. The shares quickly fell below the offering price, but rebounded in January 1989 when a wave of consolidation reduced the number of Canadian carriers fighting for passengers. Later that year, the government sold the rest of Air Canada at twelve dollars a share. This time the government raised nearly $500 million – money that went to government coffers to reward taxpayers for their investment in the national airline. After the privatization, the federal government's involvement in Air Canada was limited to the same regulatory role it performed for other carriers, including overseeing safety regulations and negotiating international-route rights.

Air Canada's earliest shareholders were a disparate group. Thousands of Canadians who knew little about investing took the chance to invest in Canada's airline. The equity offering also attracted interest from powerful investment funds in the United States and Britain, as well as Quebec's giant provincial pension fund, the Caisse de dépôt et placement du Québec.

PWA president Rhys Eyton feared that regional carriers would lose their traditional role in a deregulated world, in an anticipated wave of consolidation. He believed PWA had to be acquired or had to grow very fast. Eyton first offered PWA to Air Canada and to CP Air, but was rebuffed by both. So Eyton changed tack; he stopped looking for a buyer, and started looking for something to buy. CP Ltd., the conglomerate that owned an airline, a railway, and a hotel chain, was happy to sell CP Air, which had been a chronic money loser, despite its position as the second-largest national carrier. So PWA acquired CP Air in 1987 for $300 million. The deal was so counterintuitive that one CP Air flight attendant suggested that the canary had swallowed the cat.[25] After all, PWA had just acquired an airline that was about five times its size with an established international-route network.

Some analysts described the deal as a win–win, but others were concerned that PWA had instantly transformed itself from a lean, mean operation to a bloated beast with a high debt-load. At first, PWA promised that the two airlines would be operated separately. But within a year, the airlines had been merged under the new name Canadian Airlines International. The corporate parent continued to be known as PWA. The acquisition was particularly challenging for employees, especially those coming from CP Air, which had recently acquired Nordair and Eastern Provincial Airlines. Old loyalties and competing cultures lived on among workers who continued to identify themselves by the colours of their former planes – blue for PWA, orange for CP Air, and yellow for Nordair.[26] But over time, employees would come to embrace Canadian Airlines' signature blue[27] – especially when pitted against Air Canada's aptly provocative red. While there had been intense competition and rivalry between the government airline and its competitors for decades, the creation of Canadian Airlines International meant that, for the first time, Canadian consumers had a choice between two airlines of roughly the same size. PWA reported revenue of $1.9 billion for 1987; Air Canada's was $3 billion.

Holding company PWA wasn't finished with its growth spurt. In January 1989, it acquired Wardair for about $250 million. Estimates put

Air Canada's share of the domestic market at about 52 per cent, with PWA taking the remaining 48 per cent through Canadian Airlines and Wardair. At first investors pushed up the price of PWA shares, assuming the acquisition would eliminate the fare wars that had hurt its bottom line. But after crunching the numbers, analysts suggested that PWA probably paid too much for Wardair. Yes, Wardair was loved by its customers and respected by its competitors. But its rapid expansion had made profitability hard to achieve. And the deal added another $700 million in debt to PWA's balance sheet, which was already weakened by its acquisition of CP Air. Once again, the acquirer said it had no intention of merging the two airlines. This time, the pledge lasted less than a year and, in 1990, the Wardair name disappeared when it was absorbed by Canadian Airlines. The Blue Team's roster was complete.

The late 1980s had been kind to Canada's airlines. As long as the good times continued, the Blue Team was poised for profitability, and was in a position to overtake Air Canada – the Red Team – as the country's largest airline. But if anything went wrong, on top of all that debt, the consequences could be devastating. The list of external threats in the airline business is long: economic downturn, higher fuel prices, new taxes, too many seats offered by competitors, not to mention war. Any one of these factors would have been enough to hurt Canadian Airlines, but when they all happened at once, they were disastrous. By the time Iraq invaded Kuwait in early August, 1990, Canada's economy had already fallen into a recession. The war that followed created major problems for airlines; not only were passengers afraid to travel, but turmoil in the Middle East raised their fuel bills to nearly double. Then, in early 1991, the federal government introduced the Goods and Services Tax, which drove up airfares still further. Both airlines had ordered new planes in the late 1980s, when passenger volumes were surging; now neither could fill its seats.

In a high-stakes game of chicken, the companies slashed fares in an effort to minimize losses, but such cutthroat competition soon threatened to put both airlines out of business. The Red Team and the Blue Team entered into their most serious round of merger talks to date, just as Claude Taylor moved out of the CEO's office at Air Canada's Montreal headquarters to make room for Hollis Harris, an American airline veteran with years of experience at Delta and Continental.

Within months of his arrival, Harris had imported the two men who would be his successors: Lamar Durrett, a southern gentleman who had lived for years in Harris's shadow, and Robert Milton, an unknown hotshot with something to prove.

2

THE PLANE-SPOTTER

Maybe people have a problem that I say it as I see it. If people don't like that, too bad.[1]

— Robert Milton, chief executive officer, Air Canada

Robert Aaron Milton walked into his bedroom and carefully started packing a small suitcase with some of his clothes. He was four years old, upset with his parents, and ready to move out of his Hong Kong home.

"Where do you think you're going?" his father asked.

"I'm going to Indonesia on Garuda Indonesia Airways," Robert replied earnestly. Other kids ran away from home; young Robert Milton intended to fly.

It would not be an exaggeration to say that the future Air Canada chief had been in training for the job since 1963, the year his father accepted a position in Hong Kong and relocated the family from the United States. Robert was just three years old. Those first long-haul flights – to Hawaii on United Airlines and on to Asia on Pan Am – were magical to him. He was soon begging anyone who would listen to take him to the Hong Kong airport. "If I was around on the weekend and looked like I was relaxing too much, he'd be on me," Robert's father recalls. David Milton generally obliged his son's passion; he, too, had made regular visits to the airport as a boy growing up in Miami.

The family moved regularly, as David's work, first for the U.S. State Department and later for multinational corporations like Ralston Purina, took him around the world – from Boston to New York to the suburbs of Washington, D.C., then on to Hong Kong, England, Belgium, and Singapore. Although Robert was born in the United States, he grew up with little sense of national allegiance. His parents refused to send him and his two younger sisters to American schools in Europe and Asia; instead he attended the local British or international school, where he joined a cosmopolitan student body. At first, Robert missed burgers at McDonald's and baseball on TV, but as he grew older he came to appreciate his international upbringing and the fact that his father was constantly jetting off on business trips. David returned home with specification sheets of the latest aircraft he had flown, with aircraft models and every kind of airline memorabilia.

When Robert announced at age eight that he wanted to be a pilot, David gave him some fatherly advice. Commercial pilots, he explained, are no different from bus drivers; they don't fly where they want, just where the company tells them to go. Instead of becoming a professional pilot, he declared, Robert should find a job that he liked and make enough money to buy his own plane. Then he could earn a private pilot's licence and fly wherever he wished.

If Robert had a second love, it was baseball. Every Saturday night, he fell asleep listening to the crackling sound of a Major League Baseball game broadcast over the U.S. Armed Forces Radio Network. But as he grew older, Robert's interest in the Yankees waned as his obsession with aviation grew. "He wasn't a child with a wide range of interests," his father recalls. "It was airlines, aircraft, aviation, baseball broadly, and the New York Jets football team specifically."

At first, it was the aircraft themselves that captured Robert's imagination – those big, beautiful machines that seemed to defy nature, departing from the familiar to touch down at the exotic. Over time, he became enamoured of the business of aviation. Before he reached his teens, he could astound his parents with an almost uncanny knowledge of the world's airlines – who flew what, where, and when. He studied their schedules to understand how they deployed their planes; whenever he flew, he tried to figure out if he would be on the same aircraft for the return leg of his journey. He wrote fan letters to airline CEOs asking for brochures and photographs, and at the library he devoured weekly issues of *Flight International* magazine, reading about the larger-than-life men who ran the airline industry and about their expensive toys.

Robert especially loved the giant Boeing 747, which entered service when he was ten years old. He spent hours with a calculator computing passenger and cargo payloads and the amount of fuel required in different types of weather. On a trip to the United States, his father arranged to take him to the Boeing plant in Seattle where the 747s were manufactured. "He was absolutely fascinated and in awe," David Milton recalls. Robert made it a personal goal to fly on a 747 with every airline in the world that had one in its fleet. He would give up that dream only when tiny airlines in dangerous countries started to acquire the planes.

Robert's best friend at high school in Singapore was Doug Green, a boy whose passion for aviation rivalled his own. They routinely spent two days a week plane-spotting at the Singapore airport, watching aircraft take off and land, recording their registration numbers with the help of binoculars, and snapping photographs for submission to aviation magazines. "It was a rivalry between us," says Green, who is now a training pilot with British Airways. "If one of us happened to be at the airport when the other wasn't and an unusual aircraft came in, we couldn't wait to tell the other what we'd seen."

One hot, sunny day, the boys spent forty minutes hiking through the jungle with their photography equipment to a location on the far side of the airport closer to the runways. They stretched out on the ground to watch aircraft movements, listening to a small radio that picked up air-traffic-control transmissions – an illegal act in Singapore. Doug quickly buried the radio when he saw a police car approaching around the perimeter of the airport. The police hauled the teenagers into the station, where the commanding officer demanded that they explain themselves. The boys didn't want to admit that they had been recording aircraft registration numbers for fear they would be suspected of spying. "We just like taking pictures of planes," Robert said. "It's a hobby."

Satisfied that they were not a threat to national security, the officer told them they were free to go. A grateful Green made for the door, but not Milton. Leaving aside the illegal radio, he let it be known that an injustice had been done.

"He demanded that we be driven back to the exact spot where we had been picked up," Green recalls. Robert's chutzpah didn't get him anywhere with the police. But it had a profound impact on Green, who came to admire his friend's single-minded determination to pursue his goals, regardless of the obstacles – or the authorities – in his way. "He was always very ambitious," Green says. "He never seemed to have any doubts about achieving what he set out to achieve."

Milton was elected class president and became editor of the school yearbook, but academics were not his priority. Some high-school acquaintances remember Robert as an individual destined for success; others recall him as middling, an average student, somewhat popular, sort of generous, who could turn any assignment into an exposition on the airline industry. In his senior year he was close to an Italian girl whose father was an Alitalia pilot. Not surprisingly, his entry in the 1977–78 school yearbook cites Alitalia as the world's best airline and lists his goals: photographing planes, becoming a pilot, taking an "eternal" honeymoon with Karen Giambalvo. Robert never would become a pilot – or marry a pilot's daughter. He claims it was Giambalvo who wrote the yearbook entry as a lark after he left Singapore for college. But he did meet his future bride in Singapore. At the time, he didn't pay much attention to his sister's friend, Lizanne Lietzan, who was five years his junior. But fifteen years later, they would wed in Atlanta.

Aviation even played a role in Robert's choice of university. David Milton says his son chose Georgia Institute of Technology partly because it was his alma mater, but mostly because Atlanta had a busy airport, irresistible to the seasoned plane-spotter. Robert took an airline-related job while at college, sorting packages for DHL Worldwide Express, an international courier company. But he was not particularly happy at Georgia Tech. It was primarily an engineering school, and Robert's interests were in business and a liberal-arts education.

Worried that he might drop out, David offered to buy his son a car as a graduation present – an incentive to encourage him to finish.

"What kind of car?" Robert asked.

David Milton considered for a moment. "Well, not a Rolls-Royce."

"How about a Jag?"[2]

Milton senior shook his head in disbelief. If his father had offered to buy him a car, he would not have been picky, but Robert wasn't so reticent. For him, everything was a negotiation. At the time, a new Jaguar was selling for about $25,000 U.S. That was a fair price, David decided, to keep his son in school. A Jag it was.

Robert went on to finish his degree, but he wasn't done negotiating. When he graduated from Georgia Tech, he had a proposition for his father. "Dad," he said, "will you give me the cash instead of the car?" He had a plan to lease a Piper Seneca airplane and use it to fly mail and other small packages on behalf of DHL, the company where he worked part-time. DHL would give him a chance to operate a route if he could find a plane and a pilot. After considering his son's sales pitch, David Milton agreed to forget the car and fork over the cash. The episode suggested that his son would make a very clever businessman, able to make the most of every opportunity.

David Milton likes to think that he may be partly responsible for Robert's dogged persistence. Father and son had played squash together since Robert was a boy and David always refused to give him an easy victory. They played in sets of five, and for years the score at the end never changed: 5-love for David. The lopsided wins angered young Robert and frustrated his mother, who begged David to allow his son an occasional triumph. By the time he was in high school, Robert was winning the odd game, though losing the sets 1-4 or 2-3. Then, when he was eighteen, Robert beat his father 5-love. "That's it, Dad," he said defiantly, "I'm never playing with you again." But a satisfied Milton senior felt he had taught his son a valuable lesson in how to pursue a goal and feel genuine pride in achieving it.

Milton co-founded a company in Atlanta with Mario Rosario, a school friend from Singapore. They named their new airline Midnite Express, borrowing the title of a 1978 film about an American drug smuggler who is imprisoned in Turkey after boarding an airplane with two kilograms of hashish. Years later, Milton would be embarrassed by the name, but at the time it was all pretty cool. Just twenty-three years old, he was doing exactly what he had dreamed of his whole life – running his own airline. It was fun, but it was also stressful. Milton could be cranky and demanding of employees, including his childhood friend Doug Green, who drove a truck for the airline.[3] Workers felt the pressure to work long and hard.

Milton was developing a reputation for bullheadedness that would stick. But despite the tough exterior, he displayed a commitment to social-justice issues. He did volunteer work in poor Atlanta neighbourhoods, and still sports a scar where he was stabbed in the face after chasing down a purse-snatcher at an Atlanta Braves baseball game. It was also out of compassion that Milton became a vegetarian in the early eighties. He and Lizanne visited a sheep farm on a trip to New Zealand. Minutes after watching his wife feed baby lambs from a bottle, Milton was served a plate of glistening lamb shanks. He never ate meat again.

Midnite Express was never properly capitalized, but Milton always managed to find the money for another plane. The fleet grew to ten, then twenty, then twenty-five aircraft, transporting small packages for DHL and other courier companies. Green worried that his friend had bitten off more than he could chew. David Milton also wondered where the project – and his minority investment – were going, but he had confidence that his son would succeed. "There was no idea of what we were trying to get to," Milton admitted later. "The whole thing was crazy. But it was *important* and it was an adventure." He says Midnite Express was a well-run operation that never managed to make much of a profit. He sold the airline's routes and assets to a division of US Airways in 1988.

Milton took it easy for a while, travelling in Australia for a year, then doing charity work in Atlanta with Lizanne, who had helped found Hands on Atlanta, a non-profit agency promoting volunteerism. He set up shop as a consultant and did work for some small cargo operators and for British Aerospace. Life slowed down. In 1991, his father invited him to a Georgia Tech alumni dinner. Milton didn't really want to be there, but went along as a favour to his dad. There he met Joel Cowan, who was starting up an aviation consulting company – Eagle Air Holdings – with Hollis Harris, the recently fired chairman of Continental Airlines. Harris was a legend in the airline industry, someone Robert had admired from afar for years. Harris had spent most of his career at Delta Air Lines, working his way up to the number-two spot before being lured away to take the top job at Continental Airlines in 1990. Continental was in rough shape when he arrived, but the Gulf War pushed the airline into even deeper trouble. It was forced to file for Chapter 11 bankruptcy protection on Harris's watch. Despite the bankruptcy filing, Harris insisted on growing the airline to avoid service cutbacks or layoffs. Two days before his ouster, he asked Continental employees to pray to save the airline. "God will show us a way to survive, just as he showed us the way to victory in the gulf war."[4]

Milton impressed Joel Cowan as a polite and outgoing young man with an encyclopedic knowledge of all things aeronautical. He arranged for Milton and Harris to meet, knowing the two were a match. "There was a love affair immediately between Hollis and Robert," Cowan recalls. In Milton's mind, an introduction to Hollis Harris was the equivalent of another man's introduction to Julia Roberts.[5] They shared a passion for the minutiae of airplane design and technology, such questions as the merits of a Pratt & Whitney JT9D aircraft engine versus a Boeing CF6. "I just wanted to suck out information," Milton recalls. "It was so exciting."

While continuing with consulting work for British Aerospace, Milton joined Harris at Eagle Air Holdings. It was a tiny group – just Cowan, Harris, Milton, and Lamar Durrett, another former Delta executive who had followed Harris to Continental only to be fired along with him. Although they called themselves consultants, they were primarily interested in setting up new airline ventures. They drafted a business plan for a discount airline to be based in Atlanta. Written largely by Milton, it envisioned a low-cost carrier, with a small first-class section. The city had been desperate for a new carrier since Eastern Airlines had stopped flying in early 1991, giving Delta Air Lines a 90-per-cent market share out of Atlanta's Hartsfield Airport. Joel Cowan took the proposal to politicians and potential investors, arguing that Delta's near monopoly in Atlanta would drive up the cost of air travel for its citizens and generally make Atlanta an expensive place to do business. Milton also worked with Cowan on another plan to establish a cargo airline that would connect Europe and Asia through Russia. But Eagle Air was having difficulty raising money for both enterprises in the midst of a recession. Then the call came from Montreal.

Claude Taylor had given more than four decades of his life to Air Canada, and the sixty-seven-year-old chairman and chief executive officer was ready to retire. But identifying his successor was proving to be a challenge. He had given the CEO title to Pierre Jeanniot, another Air Canada lifer, back in 1984, only to reclaim it on Jeanniot's abrupt departure in 1990. He had offered the job to Don Carty, the former president of CP Air, but Air Canada had not been able to offer terms that would entice Carty to leave his current post at American Airlines.[6] In 1992, when the company's directors couldn't find a qualified Canadian to run the country's flag-carrier, they did the unthinkable. They offered the top job at Canada's national airline to an American.

Hollis Harris was intrigued by the invitation, because of the merger talks under way between Air Canada and Canadian Airlines. Air Canada's search committee had told him their merger was almost a done deal. He asked Milton to research the state of the Canadian industry and was given a report that portrayed a desperate situation, much like the environment that existed in the U.S. Between 1990 and 1992, Air Canada and Canadian Airlines each lost more money than they had made in their respective histories. Canadian was in particularly rough shape, with a heavy debt-load after the three-way merger of PWA, Canadian Pacific, and Wardair. Milton's brief concluded that the two airlines had to merge, and he added some recommendations as to how to achieve their consolidation.

Harris said he would take the CEO position, provided he was also offered the chairmanship of Air Canada's board, a post commonly held by airline CEOs in the United States, but not in Canada, where the jobs are usually separate. Taylor agreed to step down from the chairmanship after a few months, but emphasized that one of Harris's priorities should be to groom a Canadian to take over from him.

The media reacted sharply to Harris's appointment. The *Globe and Mail* quipped that the "first phase in Air Canada's so-called 'made-in-Canada solution'" to the industry's problems was to hire an American.[7] Air Canada's board of directors seemed to anticipate the backlash. The press release announcing his appointment emphasized that Harris and his wife would make their home in Montreal. Harris didn't mind. "I knew the board wanted a Canadian when they ended up with me," he recalled. "That just made my challenge bigger." As it happened, a greater challenge awaited him in the attempt to finalize a deal with Canadian Airlines. The merger was not as certain as he had been led to believe.

Officials at PWA, Canadian Airlines' parent, had been searching for a solution to their financial woes for the past two years, looking for concessions from creditors and employee groups or cash injections from the federal government. Air Canada had expressed interest in buying Canadian's international routes and had dangled the merger option. But to PWA's board of directors, a deal with Air Canada was a deal with the devil – it was the last resort. Instead, PWA had pursued a partnership with AMR Corporation, parent of American Airlines, that would have brought in enough cash to keep Canadian Airlines afloat. Under the deal, AMR would have acquired a one-third interest in PWA, including 25 per cent of the company's voting shares – the maximum allowed by a foreign investor under federal law.

Air Canada officials saw this deal with AMR as a dangerous proposition – one that would breathe life into a vulnerable competitor and that had to be stopped at all costs. Ironically, it was Air Canada's new made-in-the-U.S.A. CEO who played the Red Team's trump card, appealing to nationalist and anti-American sentiments. Like Air Canada, Canadian Airlines had become a symbol of national pride, displaying the maple leaf at destinations not served by Air Canada. "I just think, from a perception standpoint, it is not acceptable to the people of Canada for a non-Canadian airline to be their flag carrier. The Canadian people are proud people,"[8] Harris opined in his thick Georgia drawl.

That argument carried weight with the federal government, which had mixed feelings about the AMR-PWA alliance. The deal would preserve competition where a PWA–Air Canada deal would not, but what government would want to be accused of allowing one of its airlines to fall, in effect, into foreign hands? Ottawa preyed on PWA's financial weakness – and its need for government assistance – to draw the airline away from its talks with AMR. The government turned down a new request from PWA for loan guarantees, and it attached a condition to an earlier promise to help PWA by paying $150 million for three of its jets. The Department of National Defence would buy the aircraft only if PWA broke off talks with AMR and pursued a deal with Air Canada. With no other alternatives, PWA officials crawled back to Air Canada and reluctantly agreed to a merger.

"This is a historic day for the Canadian airline industry," a beaming Hollis Harris told a press conference on September 9, 1992. "I'm very pleased." It was a classic understatement. Air Canada had been pushing for a merger with Canadian Airlines for the past twelve months and the country's second-largest carrier had finally surrendered. The consolidation, Harris explained, was good for everyone; not only would shareholders benefit, but so would consumers, who could look forward to stable, competitive airfares. The merger would mean a little pain for the airline's employees, but he projected just six thousand job losses – not the ten thousand that had been rumoured in the press. The two airlines, Harris added, would continue to operate separately.

The folks at PWA didn't paint quite so rosy a picture. Yes, PWA's board had voted unanimously to accept Air Canada's offer, which would give its shareholders a 40-per-cent interest in the merged company and protect the interests of most of its employees. But they weren't going to pretend to be happy about the end of the airline that had been built by aviation icons like James Richardson, Grant McConachie, Russell Baker, and Max Ward. Asked if he was personally satisfied with the deal, PWA chairman Rhys Eyton answered philosophically, if somewhat cryptically: "Once you've made a decision, you've made a commitment."9

Public reaction was mixed, with concerns raised about a lack of competition, debilitating job losses, and the elimination of air service to small communities. Financial analysts and newspaper columnists dubbed the proposed mega-carrier Air Monopoly, or Mapleflot (after the Russian carrier Aeroflot). Liberal transport critic John Manley called the deal "the worst of all possible worlds: an unregulated, privately owned monopoly."

Then, barely a month after the tentative merger deal was announced, Air Canada's board, led by former president Claude Taylor, overruled Hollis Harris on the details of the proposal. Taylor says the parties couldn't agree on precise financial terms, but officials for the Blue Team wondered if something more sinister was at play. "It became clear," Canadian Airlines president Kevin Jenkins later recalled, "that the Air Canada board believed that the merger was not financeable and that in any event, Canadian Airlines would not survive past the first quarter of 1993, so why go through all of this when they could soon have [its assets and international routes] for nothing."10 In November 1992, PWA filed a $1-billion lawsuit against Air Canada alleging predatory pricing practices and suggesting that Air Canada had no intention of concluding a merger.

Tempers at PWA became further inflamed a year later when PWA resumed talks with AMR, only to have Air Canada try once again to buy PWA's international routes. Air Canada's $1 billion offer comprised $200 million in cash, plus $800 million in debt and lease payments on eight aircraft. The folks at PWA viewed the offer as a political manoeuvre designed to encourage the government to block any PWA–AMR deal. Rhys Eyton called it part of a "diabolical plot to kill Canadian" and took aim at both Air Canada and its president. "I've had enough of the arrogance of a former Crown corporation, of a gunslinger that arrives up from Georgia to tell us how to organize our Canadian structure."

Air Canada officials proclaimed their innocence, but there is evidence to suggest that Air Canada's primary interest in tabling proposals was indeed to block a deal with AMR. Days after Harris arrived in Canada to become Air Canada's new president, his executive assistant R.R. Thomson, had advised him, "Don't walk away from the PWA merger because as long as we express interest, it helps prevent an AMR/PWA deal." A month later, Air Canada's corporate secretary advised the strategic-issues committee that the airline should "continue its strategy of slowing down/denying the AMR deal."[11] One manifestation of that strategy was Air Canada's appeal to the courts in November 1992, to prevent Canadian Airlines' withdrawal from Gemini, a computer-reservations company jointly owned by the two carriers. AMR had insisted that Canadian transfer its reservations system to its own Sabre division as part of the price of its investment. American Airlines had little interest in simply owning a share in Canada's second-largest carrier, one that hadn't made money in years. It had only a marginal interest in Canadian's international routes. First and foremost it wanted a lucrative contract for Sabre, and PWA was willing to pay more than the market rate for the service in order to secure an equity investment from AMR.[12] However, the new Liberal government wasn't pleased with Air Canada's legal footwork. If the Red Team wasn't willing to consummate a merger, it shouldn't stand in the way of the only option that would keep the country's second-largest airline out of bankruptcy.

After some preliminary court victories for Canadian, Air Canada dropped the litigation in January 1994. As a reward, Ottawa designated Air Canada the second carrier to Japan, and allowed it to launch service to Osaka. But PWA wasn't home free yet. AMR insisted on a major debt restructuring in which PWA's creditors agreed to forgive more than $700 million in debts in exchange for shares. Its employees agreed to accept reduced salaries over four years in exchange for stock. The airline's previous shareholders saw the value of their shares diluted significantly as new shares were handed out to AMR, creditors, and employees. But PWA had been saved — at least for the moment.

Meanwhile, Air Canada was developing partnerships of its own with U.S. carriers. In 1992, Air Canada acquired a one-third interest in Continental Airlines and signed a major marketing agreement with

United Airlines. The investment in Continental – Hollis Harris's former employer – resulted in a significant financial benefit: Air Canada made a gain of more than $350 million U.S. on an initial investment of about $55 million U.S.

With the merger talks on hold, Hollis Harris turned his full attention to Air Canada's internal problems. He likes to point out that Air Canada was losing $1.5 million a day when he arrived. He needed to make some serious moves fast, and his first was to enlist familiar help. He hired Lamar Durrett as vice-president of technical services in May 1992, and brought in Robert Milton as a consultant a couple of months later. Milton's initial task was to study Air Canada's cargo operations. He found that the airline was chartering cargo jets while its own cargo planes sat idle. Staffers claimed it was cheaper; Milton crunched the numbers and disagreed. The charter jets were returned.[13] Harris credits Milton with saving millions through the move. Over lunch one day, Milton asked Harris if he could go on commission, getting a cut of whatever cost savings he brought to the airline. "Robert," Harris replied, "when I go on commission you can go on commission."

The new consultant didn't always get his way. Milton noticed that certain cargo flights were consistently half an hour late. Air Canada was accustomed to loading its cargo aircraft one package at a time. Milton insisted that the cargo be pre-loaded onto pallets, a procedure he believed would improve on-time performance. When cargo officials reluctantly agreed to try it, the flights started running two hours late. "What they were demonstrating to me was 'We do it this way, so don't tell us to do it that way,'" Milton recalls. "We went back to bulk-loaded airplanes." Milton admits he may have made some enemies with his initiatives in cargo, but says he has no regrets about shaking things up.

More feathers were ruffled when Harris turned him loose on the passenger side of the airline. Milton intended to boost the airline's productivity by 5 per cent over the summer months, but when he pitched the idea to other executives, they told him it couldn't be done. If he added 5-per-cent more flights to the airline's schedule, he would incur 5-per-cent more expense. Milton won Harris's approval for an unheard-of deception. He distributed phony flight schedules to the operations people, schedules they used to prepare for the summer traffic. But the schedule that went up for sale to the public offered 5-per-cent more flights. The crew schedulers scrambled to fill all the extra shifts with a limited component of staff. "The operations people were livid," Milton remembers. "The schedule was coming at them and they didn't have the people."[14] But the plan worked: Air Canada met the increased demand with the same staff generating 5-per-cent more revenue without any increase in costs. The move helped Air Canada in 1994 post its biggest profit to date, though there are still senior personnel at Air Canada who hold a grudge against Milton for his subterfuge.

The attitude of the American whiz kid rubbed some veterans the wrong way, but Milton didn't have to worry. The favouritism Harris showed to his loyal lieutenants, Durrett and Milton, was apparent even to those outside the company. After a shareholders' meeting, one of the corporate directors told Harris that he had been slipped a note from a shareholder concerned that the CEO was indulging Robert Milton because he was his son-in-law.[15] The false rumour that they were somehow related circulated for months at Air Canada's Montreal offices.

Managers who have worked with both men say they take a similar approach to decision-making. They might canvass the opinions of those around them, but once they have made up their minds, they are immovable. One Air Canada executive described Hollis Harris as "a dictator in the best sense of the word."

His campaign to bring back the Lockheed TriStar illustrates Harris's bullheaded determination.[16] Air Canada had parked three of the aircraft in the Arizona desert because they had been plagued with minor but costly operational problems. Harris was partial to the planes; he'd had dozens of them in his fleet at Delta. "There's no problem with these aircraft," he told his executives. "They work fine if you know what you're doing." Harris commissioned internal studies on the question of whether to reinstate the TriStars; every report answered with an emphatic "No."

Other managers weren't giving Harris the answer he wanted, so he asked Milton to give it a try. Milton reluctantly prepared a one-page summary of routes appropriate to the TriStars, picking safe routes where almost any aircraft would be able to turn a profit.

Harris walked into the next executive meeting holding Milton's brief high in the air. "Robert's finally given me an evaluation that says the right thing to do is bring back the TriStars," Harris said defiantly. "I want to know who supports me on this." Harris looked around the room. Nobody raised a hand, not even Robert Milton. Harris made a show of tallying the vote. "Seventeen to one," Harris concluded. "I've faced worse odds in my life. The TriStars are coming back." By operating the aircraft on a limited number of routes, the plan worked; Milton made sure of it.

Harris sums up his managerial style this way: Listen carefully to the people around you, but don't rely on their support. "I've never been afraid to make a decision, even when I didn't have a full consensus." Working closely with Hollis Harris for half a decade likely reinforced the same natural tendencies in Robert Milton.

If Milton was like Harris, Lamar Durrett was his opposite. While Harris and Milton worked from instinct and damn-the-opposition, Durrett was a careful consensus-builder, who liked to get everybody on side before acting. The word most commonly used to describe Durrett is "gentleman." It is both a compliment to his personal style and an explanation of his managerial shortcomings. "Lamar operates best in a world of gentleman's agreements where everybody is totally above-board, because he is very much like that," says Priscille LeBlanc, Air Canada's director of corporate communications. Rupert Duchesne, who replaced Robert Milton as vice-president of marketing in 1996, compares Milton and Lamar Durrett this way: "Robert is 'just do it.' Use intelligence, a modicum of analysis, and a good hunch . . . and see if it works. Lamar was an organizer, a structurer, very cautious, not a risk-taker. Just complete opposites."

Air Canada's board of directors had to choose between these opposites in February 1996, when Hollis Harris announced that he was leaving Air Canada earlier than expected. Harris cites three reasons for his departure. First, he had an opportunity to become involved in an airline start-up in Long Beach, California. Second, Air Canada's fortunes had turned around, and Harris thought it was best to leave while the prospects were sunny. And third, he wanted his old friend Lamar Durrett to have a shot at running the company. "I'd hired him and mentored him and he deserved the opportunity," Harris says. "If I stayed for another five years, his age might become a factor. The board might find it more difficult to put him in when he was past sixty."

The board was split into three factions.[17] Some agreed with Harris that it was time to give Durrett his chance. Others wanted to conduct a formal executive search. And some thought it was time to hand the reins to Robert Milton, the thirty-six-year-old prodigy who had already won the respect of influential people on the board of directors and within the company. Some managers had taken to calling him "Number 99." Like Wayne Gretzky, Milton's abilities in a high-pressure game were acknowledged as superior to all those who had played before him.

Harris warned his fellow directors that they risked offending, and losing, both Durrett and Milton if they looked outside the company for his replacement. And he managed to convince them that it wasn't yet Robert Milton's moment. Milton was good, but he needed experience and seasoning. Time would provide both. On February 22, 1996, Lamar Durrett was named CEO of Air Canada. Harris continued as executive chairman until July 1996, when Winnipeg businessman Jack Fraser was named non-executive chairman.

Durrett's appointment elicited another round of groans from the Canadian press. Wasn't there anybody in Canada who could do the job? Did we really need another American, another *Georgian*? Despite their shared backgrounds, however, there were profound differences in Harris's and Durrett's attitudes towards Canada. Harris made no secret of the fact that he saw himself as a temporary visitor, a mercenary who would return to the United States once the job of fixing Air Canada was done. Durrett took French lessons when he arrived and eventually applied for Canadian citizenship. He bought a home in Montreal's Westmount neighbourhood and a chalet in the Laurentians. He even became a hockey fan.

But Durrett was doomed to work in Harris's shadow. The gentleman CEO tried to carve out his own niche, laying accolades on Harris for planning change while noting that executing it can be more difficult. At first, Durrett appeared to execute well: in 1997, Air Canada posted a profit of $427 million – its biggest ever. But in 1998, the airline reported a $16-million loss, partly because of a two-week pilots' strike that reduced the bottom line by $155 million. Although the directors had endorsed management's handling of the strike, some blamed Durrett for failing to deliver value to shareholders. Many wondered if it wasn't time to see what Robert Milton could do.

In early 1999, Canadian Airlines was on the verge of bankruptcy. Again.

The carrier had emerged from its first restructuring in 1994 with a more manageable debt-load and a solid partnership with American Airlines, only to find that its operating costs remained too high. In 1996, Canadian tried to improve its operating profitability by persuading employees to take further pay cuts and by shifting aircraft away from short, money-losing routes and into a schedule more closely tied to that of American Airlines. At first these changes appeared to do the trick. In 1997, Canadian eked out a small profit for the first time in almost a decade.

But in late 1998, the surging economic growth of the previous few years came to an end. As the domestic economy slowed, so too did passenger traffic. Worse still was the troubled Asian economy: Canadian's prized Asian routes suddenly failed to make money. At the same time, its natural market in Western Canada was being eroded by the rapid growth of WestJet Airlines, a Calgary-based discount carrier that had launched service in 1996. These were supposed to be the two stable pillars on which Canadian could build a recovery; now its traditional strengths were undermined. The Air Canada pilots' strike should have been just what Canadian needed to get its finances in order. Instead, the strike took a brutal toll on both carriers when Air Canada slashed fares after the shutdown to win back market share. Canadian Airlines lost $138 million in 1998.

In January 1999, Canadian Airlines' CEO Kevin Benson went to his board of directors to tell them what they did not want to hear: Canadian Airlines was not going to make it. The airline wasn't in immediate danger of running out of cash, but the former accountant warned that, unless the Canadian airline industry underwent a major restructuring, the day of reckoning would soon come.

Kevin Edgar Benson immigrated to Canada from South Africa in 1977 to work at Edper Investments, a company controlled by Edgar and Peter Bronfman. He took a job in Edper's real-estate division as a protegé of Edper's executive vice-president Jack Cockwell, another accountant from South Africa, and worked his way through the organization to become president of Trizec Corporation in the late 1980s. His timing could not have been worse – or better. The early 1990s saw a massive meltdown of Canada's commercial real-estate market, resulting in the bankruptcy of Bramalea, a Trizec subsidiary. Yet while other real-estate companies failed, Trizec prevailed. Benson worked closely with creditors, designing a restructuring plan that kept Trizec alive. Benson left Trizec in 1994 when the company was sold to Horsham Corporation, but his reputation was made.

Benson set up a consulting firm in Calgary and expected to relax. Instead, he accepted a job as chief financial officer of Canadian Airlines. Nine months later, he took over as CEO from Kevin Jenkins. He didn't know a lot about airlines, but he had proven at Trizec that he was a wizard with corporate finance. He also happened to be an amateur pilot, which went with his love of all things fast. He was an avid skier and part owner of an Indy racing team. Benson is described by former colleagues as gracious, patient, and humble. Despite his average height and build, he possesses a commanding presence, enhanced by piercing blue eyes and a ready smile.

When Benson briefed his board of directors in early 1999 about Canadian's precarious financial state, he acknowledged he didn't have a lot of options. He couldn't go back to the airline's employees and creditors and ask them to bleed again; they had already given plenty in the last two restructurings. The federal government had no appetite for another bailout of a broken airline. And although American Airlines had been supportive of Canadian's efforts to right itself, Benson knew he would have a hard time justifying their further investment in Canada's number-two airline.

Canadian needed capital, but there was a more fundamental problem to be faced: there were too many airline seats and not enough passengers. Benson had to accept that the Canadian market could not support two major full-service carriers. Fierce competition had reduced fares to the point at which Canadian Airlines no longer made economic sense as a stand-alone airline. If there was any hope for Canadian, it lay in the fact that Air Canada was also suffering. Perhaps the Red Team would be willing to take another look at a merger, Benson reasoned. Canadian's board of directors authorized Benson to initiate another round of merger talks. These discussions would be different from those of 1992. Back then, Canadian was trying to do a deal with either Air Canada or American Airlines. This time, Benson knew, a deal would have to involve both carriers, since American was Canadian's largest shareholder.

On February 4, 1999, Benson met quietly with American Airlines president Don Carty and with Air Canada's CEO Lamar Durrett and chairman Jack Fraser. The meeting took place in Miami, where many of the world's airline executives and analysts had gathered for the annual Goldman Sachs & Co. airline-investment conference.

"You're struggling," Benson told Durrett, "and we're in trouble. Maybe we can bring our forces together."[18] Air Canada agreed to explore the possibility, hiring lawyers and investment bankers to study options the three carriers could consider.

With cotton-white hair, Carty looked much older than his fifty-three years. Born in Toronto and raised in Montreal, Carty's list of accomplishments was as impressive as Benson's. After spending time at Air Canada and Americana Hotels, Carty became a vice-president of American Airlines when he was thirty-three. He returned to Canada in 1985 to become CEO of CP Air until it was acquired by PWA, then returned to American Airlines, where he became president in 1995 and chairman in 1998. His younger brother Doug was the chief financial officer at Canadian Airlines.

Doug Carty led the team looking into the merger for Canadian Airlines. As they crunched the numbers, he was encouraged to see how easy it would be to take two money-losing airlines and turn them into a winner. Both were flying similar domestic schedules, operating half-empty planes that left for the same destinations at about the same times. Carty's team calculated that, by merging the carriers, flights – and costs – could be reduced by about 10 per cent, without anything close to a 10-per-cent drop in revenue. If you didn't need to compete, you wouldn't have so many empty seats. It was an easy home run. A merger would save Canadian Airlines and it would benefit the shareholders of Air Canada, who would see some consistent profits at last.

The CEOs of the three airlines met again in Toronto on February 11, 1999, where they agreed on the general structure of the merged airline. They set out an aggressive timetable for an agreement, culminating in a public announcement on March 15. It was in everybody's interest to move briskly, before news of their merger talks leaked out. Air Canada worried about the reactions of its international airline partners, United Airlines and Lufthansa, if they heard it was thinking of abandoning them for a partnership with American Airlines. Canadian Airlines fretted that talk of its wobbly financial position could hurt its bookings. And American Airlines was wary of being drawn into another politically charged debate about U.S. involvement in the Canadian airline industry.

The demand for secrecy collided with the need for smooth relations with the government. The airlines feared that government officials would be less than discreet in advance of any agreement. If they left the government out of the loop, however, they might not win the necessary support. The federal government was dealing with two controversial bank-merger proposals at the time, and the scuttlebutt was that Ottawa was poised to disallow them. The banks had made a strategic error in not involving Ottawa in the process early enough. Not wanting to make the same mistake, the airlines decided to encourage federal involvement, while stressing that any leak would likely kill a potential deal.

In early March, the three airlines knew an agreement wouldn't be finalized by March 15, but talks were progressing well and the time was right to brief transport minister David Collenette. They agreed that Kevin Benson should be the first to approach the minister. The two enjoyed a good working relationship, and Collenette was aware of Canadian's precarious situation. Benson met with Collenette on March 12, where he presented the minister with a document cleverly titled "A New National Dream." Collenette was a railway buff and would surely have caught the reference to *The National Dream*, Pierre Berton's monumental opus about Canadian Pacific Railway, the transportation company that helped build a country.

The document painted a picture of an industry in crisis – Air Canada with little chance of generating an acceptable return on capital and Canadian Airlines "at risk of running unacceptably low on cash in the near future." It presented the merger as a good thing for Canada. Yes, there would be job losses in the short term, but over time a merged airline would expand, resulting in an *increase* in jobs. It would strengthen airport hubs in Toronto, Vancouver, and Montreal, and result in larger planes serving small communities.

"There is a unique opportunity for the Government of Canada to shape the future of Canada's airline industry through the creation of a strong national carrier that serves Canadians from coast to coast, and stimulates jobs and economic growth in all regions of the country. The new airline will truly be Canada's flagship carrier, and will symbolize excellence around the world," the document promised. Collenette, who had concluded twenty years earlier that Canada was not large enough to sustain two flag-carriers, was pleased that Air Canada appeared willing to participate in a solution that might forestall a bankruptcy. But he gave no indication of the government's formal position. And because confidentiality was paramount, the document was not widely distributed among Transport bureaucrats.

The three airlines continued to talk and quickly came to terms on the broad features of a merged airline. The carrier would employ about 35,000 workers, resulting in the loss of 6,500 jobs. It would retire 70 older and smaller aircraft, 26 from Air Canada and 44 from Canadian. And Air Canada would pay about $122 million for Canadian Airlines.

On the surface, it looked like a steal. Of course, Air Canada would be acquiring debts along with assets. These debts were not insignificant, especially since Canadian's weakened financial position meant that it had less favourable terms from creditors.

Agreeing to a plan that met the needs of Canadian Airlines was easy. It was more difficult to come to terms that satisfied both American Airlines and Air Canada. American was willing to give up its lucrative services agreement with Canadian, but insisted that the merged carrier be part of the oneworldglobal airline alliance, a marketing partnership that included British Airways and Cathay Pacific Airways of Hong Kong. Air Canada was a member of the rival Star Alliance, which counted United Airlines and Germany's Lufthansa among its partners. These global alliances, through which airlines co-marketed services and swapped passengers, were developed in the 1990s as an alternative to international mergers, a corporate practice that is forbidden in the airline industry because of foreign-ownership restrictions. They help generate hundreds of millions of dollars in revenues for their members every year. To the executives in Calgary and Fort Worth, oneworld seemed a better fit, since more Canadians travelled to Britain than to Germany. But Air Canada's negotiators wanted to stick with Star Alliance, an arrangement that boosted its revenues by close to $500 million annually. They believed switching alliances would cost them money.

While the people in Calgary were optimistic that the airlines would be able to smooth over their differences, AMR chairman Don Carty had less faith in the process. Lamar Durrett seemed committed, but Carty was never sure that the Air Canada executives under him shared the same enthusiasm. "I had the feeling that we'd sit and talk and Lamar would go back, ask his people to run some numbers, and they would beset him with data just to convince him that we were wrong."

The talks continued in secrecy on March 25, 1999, when the three CEOs met in Chicago. AMR and Canadian presented Air Canada with a formal proposal. Air Canada rejected it the next day, saying it was about $2 billion too expensive: Air Canada would have to switch alliances and assume too much debt. Air Canada countered with the suggestion that the $2-billion gap could be closed, in part, if Canadian Airlines undertook one final debt-restructuring.

"Their view was that the only way this transaction could work was through debt-restructuring," Doug Carty recalled. "Our view was, 'Let's go look at the model. That's not the case.'"

Carty reviewed the $2-billion discrepancy with president Kevin Benson. It seemed clear the parties were not going to meet across this divide. American Airlines felt it was already giving as much as it could, and Air Canada had little incentive to make concessions to an opponent on the brink of bankruptcy. Benson and Carty knew that, to many outsiders, it appeared Canadian Airlines had already survived far longer than it should have. Was it possible, they wondered now, for the lucky airline to throw one final Hail Mary pass that would allow it to save thousands of jobs and get something for its shareholders instead of being forced into bankruptcy? Benson thought it was possible. His thesis was simple: Air Canada believed a financial restructuring was necessary; he wanted to prove that it wasn't, and the way to do so was to find a third-party investor who shared his view.

"If they're not going to do a deal with us, we've got to find another financial investor. Then we'll take it back to Air Canada," Benson said, "or we'll take them over."[19]

When Robert Milton's daughter was born in 1996, he asked Lamar Durrett to be her godfather. Although their personalities and their management styles were radically different, they shared an affectionate mutual respect.

But Milton knew that Durrett wasn't going to be around forever. In 1999, he made a play for the succession.[20] Armed with a job offer from Montreal-based transportation giant Bombardier Inc., Milton asked Air Canada's board of directors for a commitment that he would eventually replace Durrett. "I was happy to stay and report to Lamar," Milton explained later, "but I wasn't happy to stay and report to Lamar if I wasn't sure I'd be the next CEO."[21] Executives at other companies have been punished for such boldness, but it paid off for Milton. The directors assured him that, when Durrett left, he would be appointed CEO. To mollify him until then, they promoted him to president, effective May 1999. Durrett remained CEO and was named vice-chairman of the airline.

A few weeks later, Milton was paraded before the country's top airline analysts, the influential corporate researchers who study a company's prospects and make recommendations to investors. In the course of a surprisingly frank meeting, Milton told them that his boss had been stripped of the president's title because he had been unable to create shareholder value.[22] He boldly promised that things would change under his command. Labour relations would improve, costs would come down, but above all, Air Canada would start looking after shareholders as well as customers and employees. (After reporting a $16-million loss for 1998, Air Canada had managed to squeeze out a tiny profit of $3 million in the first quarter of 1999 thanks to savvy investments. But the company's shares were still mired around the $6 mark, $2 below the price at which they'd debuted more than a decade earlier.) Some analysts were skeptical, but Milton's confidence − or was it arrogance? − left most feeling optimistic about the company's prospects.

Milton had good reason to be confident; his universe was unfolding exactly as it should, at work and at home. If his string of luck continued, he could be CEO of a major international airline before he turned forty − an impressive accomplishment by any standard. His wife, Lizanne, had recently given birth to a beautiful baby boy, their second child and first son. Milton liked to say that his aspirations in life had never been to stay small, and here he was, surpassing even his own ambitious goals.

Occupying the CEO's chair at a merged airline was a goal still to be realized. The talks with Canadian had gone off the rails for the time being, but Milton knew this messy duopoly couldn't go on forever: Canadian Airlines would disappear sooner or later, whether through merger or bankruptcy. With the board's promise that he was next in line for the CEO's office, Milton was prepared to wait.

At the end of May, a battered Lamar Durrett gathered his executives together for a briefing on the stalled talks with Canadian and American

Airlines. He told his colleagues that he didn't think it would be long before Canadian and American came begging for a merger on something close to Air Canada's terms.[23] After all, he reasoned, American Airlines had just two options: either it could spend $1 billion to pay off Canadian's debt so it could survive as an independent airline or it could spend the same to reach an agreement with Air Canada. Wouldn't it make more sense to choose the latter and be part of a merged carrier? Heads nodded around the table. But one executive, Paul Brotto, wasn't so sure.

There was in fact another option for American Airlines, and a less expensive one, he suggested. With Air Canada's stock trading at six dollars a share, American could buy half the company and control Air Canada for a lot less than a billion dollars. Federal law prevented foreign investors from owning more than 25 per cent of a Canadian airline, but Brotto wondered if there couldn't be some way American could indirectly acquire Air Canada shares. Nobody thought much of this speculation until a few weeks later, when his colleagues noticed unusual activity in the trading of the company's shares. Somebody was quietly acquiring huge blocks of Air Canada stock.

3

Project Peacock

We were very deliberate. We said if we start down this road, one of two things will happen. We will either get this deal done or Air Canada will buy Canadian. Those are the only two possible outcomes – both of those are better than what we've got on the table.[1]

– Don Carty, chairman and CEO, AMR Corp.

*F*riday the thirteenth, it was. At a hastily called press conference late in the afternoon of August 13, 1999, transport minister David Collenette and industry minister John Manley announced that they were invoking Section 47 of the Canada Transportation Act, thereby suspending Canada's antitrust laws so that Air Canada and Canadian Airlines could freely discuss ways to fix the country's broken airline industry. The act was designed to prevent collusion, to prohibit the carriers from fixing prices or carving up the country's routes. But by limiting what they could say to each other, these provisions had become an obstacle to finding a solution that would prevent a bankruptcy at Canadian Airlines. "What we're trying to do is facilitate the restructuring process that we believe needs to occur – and indeed the two major airlines believe needs to occur," Collenette said.

Reporters – who tend to be suspicious of any announcement made late on a Friday afternoon – had a lot of questions. Would Collenette approve a merger of the two airlines if such a proposal were put forward? Would he allow the carriers to divide the country's domestic routes between them? Several times, the minister resorted to a single, well-rehearsed line: "We are not going to speculate on where this process will lead us." As defence minister during the 1996 Somalia crisis, Collenette had become quite skilled at responding to questions by saying very little. But he did emphasize that *both* airlines had asked the government to invoke Section 47.

The federal cabinet can implement Section 47 only when it believes "an extraordinary disruption" is imminent in the country's transportation system and when a failure to suspend competition laws would be "contrary to the interests of users and operators of the national transportation system." In this instance, it was allowing Air Canada and Canadian to discuss fares, routes – even the specifics of a merger – without worrying that such discussions would be deemed anti-competitive.

The decision had been made just a few hours earlier by Collenette and Manley, in consultation with officials from the Departments of Transport, Industry, Justice, and the Privy Council Office.[2] Prime Minister Jean Chrétien had delegated authority over the issue to the two ministers after prolonged debate failed to produce a consensus at the cabinet table. There was agreement on one position: taxpayers should provide no more money to Canadian Airlines. The Calgary-based carrier had received government assistance on two occasions over the past decade, but this time a publicly funded rescue wasn't in the cards. The debate at Cabinet had come down to whether it was preferable for Ottawa to stand back and let Canadian Airlines go bankrupt or to become involved in seeking some better solution. Collenette, a self-professed interventionist, leaned towards government involvement. The main sticking point, however, hadn't been about policy but about optics. How would the decision play, cabinet ministers wondered, when it emerged that a powerful Liberal stood to gain enormously from the merger deal that might result from restructuring discussions?[3]

Collenette had known since June 25, when he met with Kevin Benson, that Liberal fundraiser Gerry Schwartz was involved in a proposal to buy and merge Canada's two major airlines. As the chairman and founder of Onex Corporation, Schwartz was one of the country's most powerful businessmen and one with impeccable Liberal connections. Schwartz had been the party's top fundraiser for a decade, and his wife,

Heather Reisman, was Ontario co-director of Paul Martin's first leadership bid. On a rainy night in 1995, the couple had hosted a $1,000-a-plate Liberal fundraiser at their Toronto mansion, where the guests included Prime Minister Jean Chrétien and most of his Ontario ministers. In the 1997 election, Onex had made donations to several leading Liberal candidates, including the prime minister, Paul Martin, Allan Rock, and Sheila Copps. Collenette had known Schwartz through Liberal Party circles for fifteen years and, when he was defence minister, had helped arrange a thrill ride for Schwartz on a CF-18 fighter jet.

Suspending the competition laws for Gerry Schwartz was a politically risky move, even if Collenette believed it was the right decision for the country's transportation system. Ottawa insiders hemmed and hawed for weeks but, by August 13, it became obvious that news of the takeover plan had leaked out. That morning, an anonymous fax containing surprisingly accurate details of the proposed deal was sent to some of the country's biggest investment firms. "AMR/American Airlines and Onex to create a new company," the fax trumpeted.[4] Manley and Collenette called an urgent meeting with a small team of officials to weigh the pros and cons of invoking Section 47. The main pro was Kevin Benson's warning that Canadian Airlines would run out of cash by February. Since there was no time for a formal merger review by the Competition Bureau, Benson argued, Section 47 was necessary to save sixteen thousand jobs and prevent tens of thousands of passengers from being stranded. The big "con" was the potential political fallout from Gerry Schwartz's central role in the scheme.

"At one point I thought we weren't going to do it," Collenette said later. "But then we came to the conclusion that we had to bite that bullet. We could not be worried about political criticism if we believed substantively that it was the right process to follow to try to get to a solution."[5]

The first responses to the ministers' announcement from the airlines were puzzling, considering that Canadian was actively plotting a hostile acquisition of Air Canada. Air Canada vice-president Doug Port expressed his airline's opinion that a merger of the two was necessary, while Canadian Airlines CEO Kevin Benson bluffed brilliantly, saying the suspension of competition rules would not necessarily result in a merger. Benson said Canadian's request for a suspension of the competition laws was aimed at attracting investors, not merging with its Montreal-based rival. "If you limited every date to one that would lead to a fifty-year marriage, you wouldn't have been on too many dates in your life," Benson told the *Globe and Mail*.[6]

Benson's comments offered little reassurance to Robert Milton, who had been named Air Canada's CEO five days earlier. The rumours about Canadian Airlines working with American Airlines on a bid for Air Canada were so consistent and specific that, when American Airlines CEO Don Carty called to congratulate Milton on his appointment, Milton had asked when the takeover offer was coming. "Ah, well," Carty laughed, "we're looking at all our alternatives."[7] Weeks before the competition rules were suspended, Milton had heard the name of his adversary for the first time when a Montreal stockbroker warned his contacts at Air Canada that corporate raider Gerry Schwartz would be the front man for the bid.

When Gerald Wilfred Schwartz identifies an objective, he almost always achieves it. Schwartz and Heather Reisman are among the most powerful of Canadian power couples. They host dinner parties for international leaders and statesmen, donate generously to numerous social causes, travel by personal jet, and drive rare antique cars. Gerry's calls are returned by presidents and prime ministers, billionaire business titans and Hollywood starlets. But by 1999 one achievement had eluded Schwartz: a major, high-profile takeover. Schwartz desperately wanted to own a household brand that would bring Onex Corporation the recognition it deserved. In 1995, he had lost a well-publicized battle for beer giant John Labatt Ltd. and its baseball team, the Toronto Blue Jays. Onex had spent five months preparing a $2.3-billion offer, only to be outbid by Interbrew SA of Belgium. Schwartz felt the loss deeply and personally. "We cared about it so much," he told the *Globe and Mail* five months later. "I'm still living with the hurt." Now he was taking a run at another prominent Canadian institution. The plan was to buy and merge Canada's two major airlines, and this time the stakes were enormous. Schwartz knew that, if he missed again, he might forever wear a reputation as the guy who couldn't close the big deal.

Schwartz was born in 1941 into a middle-class Jewish home in Winnipeg. His father, Andy, owned an auto-parts business along with his brothers. His mother, Lillian, the first female Jewish lawyer in Canada, became deaf at Gerry's birth and was often sick. The family lived with Gerry's grandmother, who collected money on street corners for social-ist causes and invited left-wing speakers to their home. Schwartz spent his youth working for his father, then took commerce and law degrees at the University of Manitoba. After graduating, he pestered Israel (Izzy) Asper, one of Winnipeg's top tax lawyers, until Asper gave him a job as an articling student. "A bit pushy, I thought, but his determination intrigued me," Asper once observed.[8] In 1968, Schwartz moved his family to Boston, where he attended Harvard Business School, and where he came into contact with Bernie Cornfeld, the legendary mutual-fund king who founded Investors Overseas Services. Cornfeld took to Schwartz immediately and offered him a job. Schwartz left his wife and kids in Boston and spent the summer of 1969 at Cornfeld's Geneva villa. He hated the fast-paced party life and returned to Boston at the end of the summer. The timing was fortuitous. In 1970, Cornfeld's empire crum-bled, landing him in a Swiss jail for eleven months before fraud charges against him were dropped.

After finishing his M.B.A., Schwartz got a job at Bear Stearns on Wall Street, where he worked with Henry Kravis and other young financial wizards who were pioneering the art of leveraged buyouts. LBOs are financed by borrowing against the assets of a takeover target, meaning that investors can make impressive returns using little of their own money. Schwartz soaked up all the knowledge he could, then returned to Canada to establish a merchant bank with his old boss, Izzy Asper.

They co-founded CanWest Capital Corporation in 1977, acquiring companies like Monarch Life Assurance and Global TV before they had a personal falling-out in 1983. In the meantime, Schwartz had met the love of his life. Heather Reisman, a former social worker, discovered that Schwartz had a soft centre inside a hard, cerebral shell. They married in 1982, shortly before Schwartz moved to Toronto to seek his fortune.

Using $2 million of his own money and $48 million from others, Schwartz founded Onex Corporation in 1984. Its assets had grown to $2 billion when he took the company public three years later, and stood at over $6 billion in 1999. Despite the company's unquestioned success, Schwartz was criticized in the early years for a personal compensation package that seemed out of whack with Onex's early share performance. Schwartz fired back at critics who questioned his pay, blaming it on a desire by Canadians "to bring successful people down. If I earn a $4-million bonus, that's a lifetime's income for most people, and they like to read that I'm a jerk for having done that. It makes them feel better."9

Schwartz and his tiny team of executives look for deals with significant upside potential, sniffing them out with rigorous financial analysis. For every opportunity they pursue, dozens more are rejected. Their patience pays off for Onex investors and especially for Schwartz himself, who owns about 20 per cent of the company, but controls over 60 per cent of its votes. Schwartz's group uses a variation on the traditional leveraged buyout model. Like other LBO firms, Onex minimizes its own equity investment in acquisition targets, but instead of flipping companies quickly, Onex builds them over time, sometimes using them as vehicles to consolidate a number of enterprises. The company has made billions investing in industries most people don't care about, such as car parts (Automotive Industries), rail cars (Johnstown America), and airline food (Sky Chefs, a catering company that serves some of the world's largest airlines). BC Sugar and Beatrice Foods are better-known concerns, although the company's greatest success was its 1996 purchase of a chunk of Celestica, a computer-parts manufacturer, from IBM Canada. Celestica helped raise Schwartz's reputation in financial circles, but he remained unknown to most Canadians.

When Canadian Airlines chief Kevin Benson approached him in early May 1999 with a plan to buy and merge the country's two main air carriers, Schwartz was keen. Onex had looked into Canadian Airlines in 1996, and again in early 1999. Both times, Schwartz's team concluded that it made no sense to invest in the country's second-largest airline when there seemed to be room in Canada for only one full-service carrier. But investing in a merged airline was different altogether. It was the type of investment opportunity Schwartz liked – the kind in which he couldn't lose. Schwartz knew that he could acquire a toehold investment in Air Canada shares ahead of his offer. Since those shares would rise in value when he went public with his proposal, Onex would gain on its investment even if it lost the takeover bid. Between June 15 and July 23, Onex acquired $43 million in Air Canada shares through AirCo, the company it established for the purposes of its merger offer. By late August, it had purchased 3.1 per cent of the voting shares, at prices ranging from $5.81 to $6.85, and 6.6 per cent of the non-voting shares, at prices ranging from $4.79 to $7.30.

"Hi. This is Gerry Schwartz."

It was the call that Robert Milton had been dreading. A story connecting Schwartz to Air Canada had already appeared on the front page of the *Globe and Mail*. Now it was Tuesday, August 24, and the Toronto Stock Exchange had halted sales of Air Canada's shares at the opening bell. Sales of shares in Canadian Airlines and Onex had also been halted. That could mean only one thing – a hostile takeover. Now the culprit was on the other end of the telephone line.

"Do you know why I'm calling you?" Schwartz said.

"To try to poach the Cara contract?" Milton joked, trying to be light. Onex's Sky Chefs was a major competitor of Cara Operations Limited, the Toronto-based food-services company that was Air Canada's main supplier. But the call was not about airplane food. Schwartz confirmed what Milton suspected: Onex and American Airlines were about to launch a hostile bid to buy and merge Canada's two largest airlines.

Schwartz explained that he was making the announcement in Montreal because he hoped to meet with Milton later in the day. Milton said he would listen to his announcement and get back to him.[10]

As soon as Milton hung up, another call was patched through. It was Jurgen Weber, CEO of Lufthansa. Before calling Milton, Schwartz had placed a courtesy call to Weber, alerting him to the imminent bid. Weber was incensed. Lufthansa had just purchased 14 per cent of Sky Chefs from Onex for $405 million – money Schwartz would now use to snatch Air Canada out of Lufthansa's Star Alliance and into American Airlines' rival oneworld alliance. He told Milton that Lufthansa would do whatever was necessary to keep Air Canada in Star Alliance. This was precisely the support a fledgling CEO needed. But Milton had no time to chat; his officials were yelling at him to get into the corporate boardroom. Schwartz's press conference had begun.

"I have come to Montreal today to announce a plan formulated by Onex," Schwartz began, "which will create a single, Canadian-controlled, national airline. This is a good deal for Canada and for all Canadians."

Many of Milton's most trusted advisors were already at the boardroom table, including chief financial officer Rob Peterson and senior vice-president of business development Paul Brotto. Calin Rovinescu, a corporate lawyer from Stikeman Elliott, was also there. Milton had a lot of respect for Rovinescu, who had been heavily involved in previous merger talks with Canadian Airlines and AMR. Rovinescu was much like Milton in temperament. He called it as he saw it and didn't tolerate nonsense from anyone. He spent his holidays climbing mountains and kept a framed pickaxe mounted behind his desk.

They watched the press conference on a large projection TV at the front of the room. Schwartz's plan involved buying both Air Canada and Canadian Airlines and merging them into a single airline controlled by Onex. The merger, Schwartz explained, would help eliminate the irrational competition that had resulted in years of red ink for both carriers. Schwartz pointed out that, in the eleven years since Air Canada went public, its share price had not risen a nickel. In fact, he noted, Air Canada's share price had fallen from $8, when it first started trading in 1988, to $6.50 on August 12, the day before the government announced that it was suspending the country's competition laws. (That announcement had caused Air Canada's stock price to soar.)

As Schwartz spoke, Milton skimmed the details from the Onex press release, which had just been made available over the Internet. He didn't like what he saw. American Airlines' parent, AMR Corporation, would own 14.9 per cent of the merged carrier, which would join oneworld alliance, just as Jurgen Weber had feared. Worse, it looked as if Schwartz was trying to steal Air Canada from its shareholders. He was offering $8.25 a share — twenty-five cents below its closing value the day before — in a combination of cash and stock in the merged company. Schwartz called it a $5.7-billion deal, referring to the enterprise value of the two airlines: $1.8 billion in equity plus $3.9 billion in debt. But in reality, Onex's equity investment was limited to $250 million of its own money. Through a complicated arrangement, Onex was borrowing $225 million from AMR for an additional equity stake, for which Onex would own 31 per cent of the shares in the new Air Canada. The press release also noted that Onex would eliminate about five thousand jobs, roughly 10 per cent of the workers at the merged company. The job cuts would occur "primarily through normal attrition and voluntary severance agreements."

Schwartz continued to speak at the podium, but he didn't look entirely comfortable. Trim and expensively suited, with just enough grey in his frizzy black hair, Schwartz was an imposing figure. But the cheerful and charming personality known to his intimates was missing on public occasions. His delivery was wooden, some might say insincere. He wasn't just reading his speech, he *sounded* like he was reading his speech. A friend once described him as a man who carried himself with "the impeccable posture of a hand puppet."[11] While Gerry Schwartz was well known on Bay Street, this was the first time most Canadians had ever heard of him. And his performance didn't play well on Main Street.

"I invite Air Canada and Canadian to join us," Schwartz concluded. "Together we can create a great Canadian success story."

Schwartz's aide then opened the floor to reporters. The first question, from *Globe and Mail* reporter Konrad Yakabuski, went for the jugular. Was it in anticipation of the Onex proposal that the federal government had suspended the competition rules? Choosing his words carefully, Schwartz said he believed the decision to invoke Section 47 was not "specifically" related to the Onex bid, but rather "the tremendous uncertainty being created in the marketplace by the financial difficulties of Canadian – also the financial results of Air Canada." Schwartz added that Onex did not have "a specific plan formulated" before the government suspended the competition rules. These comments might have been true in a literal sense, since Onex hadn't finalized the details with AMR before the Friday the thirteenth announcement. But the government clearly knew – and was responding to – Onex's proposal to buy and merge the two carriers. Schwartz went on to acknowledge that Onex had been in "detailed talks" with AMR for four to six weeks.

Now that he had put aside his prepared text, Schwartz seemed more at ease. He answered questions about Star Alliance (oneworld is better), the job cuts (mostly through attrition), seat sales (they would continue), the magnitude of the potential cost savings (in the hundreds of millions of dollars), and Schwartz's contact with Air Canada. (In addition to Milton, he had spoken that morning with chairman Jack Fraser: "Jack is a long-time friend of mine. We both lived in Winnipeg for many years and were friends there.")

Towards the end of the forty-minute press conference came the question that was most personally relevant to Robert Milton and his colleagues. Who would run the merged company? Schwartz's response was ambiguous. "We are fortunate that there are excellent chief executives at both companies. Kevin Benson at Canadian Airlines and the recently appointed Rob Milton, who is a real crackerjack at operations. I think we've got a great opportunity to meld this team together."

The crackerjack was livid. Air Canada's future was finally in Robert Milton's hands, and now Gerry Schwartz was trying to snatch the company away from him and his shareholders. Milton's instinct was to stand up and fight. But Rovinescu and other senior executives convinced him to sit tight and say little. "The toughest part in the first thirty days was keeping Robert buttoned down," recalled Paul Brotto. "He wanted to attack and we said, 'No, no. Keep your powder dry. Let's get ourselves organized.'" Fending off the Onex bid would demand all the finesse the Red Team could muster, and Milton's colleagues knew they couldn't allow their boss's short fuse to get them into trouble.

Instead of putting Milton behind a podium or making him available for interviews, Air Canada issued a terse press release, saying the Onex proposal appeared to transfer value from Air Canada to Onex, Canadian, and American Airlines. "It is difficult to see in the Onex proposal any benefit for Air Canada shareholders or employees," the statement said. "The formal proposal has not been received by Air Canada. When received, it will be reviewed in detail with Air Canada's external advisors."

Robert Milton wasn't the only one who didn't like Gerry Schwartz's proposal. Transport minister David Collenette also felt his gorge rise as he read the Onex press release. Collenette was prepared for the firestorm that would erupt after the media and opposition parties realized that Section 47 had been invoked – at least in part – for a businessman with Liberal connections. But when he saw the details of the Onex proposal for the first time, Collenette was disturbed by the extent of AMR's involvement.[12] In addition to investing $275 million to own 14.9 per cent of the shares in the merged airline, AMR was also lending money to Onex and to the merged airline. And while AMR was described as a "passive" investor, its Sabre reservations system would take over the information-technology functions for the merged carrier, which would result in Canadian jobs being transferred to the United States.

None of this sat well with Collenette, one of the most ardent Canadian nationalists in Chrétien's Cabinet. He had never been very comfortable with free trade, and had opposed the government's decision to privatize Air Canada a decade earlier. Collenette saw the airline as a proud symbol of the nation, as much a part of Canada as the maple leaf or the beaver. The Onex proposal – with its heavy dependence on American Airlines – spelled the end of that vision in Collenette's view. "This was basically a hostile takeover, with a proposal that certainly went against my philosophical grain as a Canadian nationalist. I couldn't believe Gerry had done that. He looked at it from a business point of view. . . . But from a political point of view, I saw this as cleaning out Air Canada and it becoming American Airlines North."

Over the next few weeks, all sides would embrace the maple leaf in an effort to convince politicians, employees, and consumers that their position was the best for Canada. Ironically, the public-relations battle pitted Don Carty, the Canadian-born chairman and CEO of American Airlines, against Robert Milton, the American-born president of Air Canada. When Carty gave a rare press conference in Toronto, surrounded by twelve red-and-white Canadian standards, he disparaged Milton as "an American CEO who is wrapping himself in the Canadian flag." And both Milton and Schwartz mused emotionally about the pride they felt whenever they saw the maple-leaf logo on an Air Canada plane at some far-flung airport.

Mergers and acquisitions; breaking up companies or pushing them together; secret talks; backroom deals; legal battles; proxy fights; hostile takeovers.

This is the fun stuff, the sacred essence that makes the day-to-day banality of corporate Canada bearable, the high that transforms pimply M.B.A.s into grey-haired pros, stirs the passions of jaded financial journalists, buys yachts for investment bankers and cottages for corporate lawyers. These are the trials that can destroy a young CEO's future or make him a titan of the business world. This is the heart of Bay Street, the soul of Onex.

Hatching a big deal is serious sport, and naming it is part of the play. Canadian Airlines' effort to right its sinking ship in 1992 was labelled "Project Iceberg." When Air Canada studied a potential merger with Canadian Airlines in 1996, they called their analysis "Project Zeppelin." The 1999 talks between Air Canada, Canadian Airlines, and AMR were known as "Project Champlain." Canadian's subsequent attempt to do an end run on Air Canada was "Project Tornado." And Onex's cunning plan to dominate Canada's airline industry was given the moniker "Project Peacock."

Project Peacock — an exotic thing of beauty. It was the ultimate hostile bid, because it was a bid that only Onex could win. Faced with an unfriendly takeover attempt, the acquisition target will usually seek a "white knight" investor to fund a counter-bid, resulting in a bidding war. Gerry Schwartz had lost Labatt this way in 1995. He wasn't about to lose again; he wanted to make sure that his takeover target was cornered. Air Canada's ability to find a white knight was limited by the fact that Onex had the support of AMR, the holding company that owned American Airlines and one-third of Canadian Airlines. Without AMR on side, it would be next to impossible to put together a deal to merge the two airlines. And without merging the two airlines, it would be very difficult to come up with an offer that would be as attractive to Air Canada's shareholders as the one Onex was proposing. Milton could complain that the Onex bid didn't reflect the true value of Air Canada, but if he couldn't come up with a richer offer, he was trapped.

"It's hard to believe that there would be a better solution, because of our relationship with American Airlines," Schwartz had taunted at his press conference. "But be that as it may, if somebody else has a better plan, please put it forward."

If there was one flaw in Project Peacock, it was that, under the Air Canada Public Participation Act, no individual or institution was allowed to own more than 10 per cent of the company's voting shares. The limit had been established at the time of Air Canada's privatization in the late 1980s and was designed to ensure that large blocks of shares did not fall into the hands of a small number of shareholders. The 10-per-cent cap also acted as a protective shield for Air Canada's board of directors and management. Since no one could own more than 10 per cent of the shares, no one could force out those running the company. And no one could amass a substantial shareholding to launch a hostile takeover.

The Onex proposal created a corporate entity named Airline Industry Revitalization Co. Inc., or AirCo, which would own 100 per cent of the shares of both Air Canada and Canadian. Onex would own 31 per cent of AirCo. On the surface, Onex's position appeared to be a clear violation of the 10-per-cent limit. But Onex had an answer. Although AirCo was offering to buy Air Canada's voting shares, it would never actually own them. Instead, these shares would be "transformed" into a special class of non-voting shares between the time they were sold by the shareholders and the time they were acquired by AirCo. The federal government would then be asked to abolish the 10-per-cent limit. Once it did so, the AirCo shares would revert to voting status. Onex wanted to appoint its own people to the merged airline's board right away, thereby ensuring its control of the company. But without any voting shares, Onex could not elect directors. Instead, it made its bid conditional on Air Canada's shareholders voting for a slate of Onex directors. The process was clever but messy. AMR officials had their own name for it: they called it "Frankie" – short for Frankenstein.

Onex had hired a phalanx of high-priced lawyers to help formulate this complex manoeuvre. They estimated that, if Air Canada's shareholders voted for the proposal, the government would surely scrap the 10-per-cent cap in favour of saving Canadian Airlines. Further, the lawyers assured Schwartz that their creativity in circumventing the ownership restrictions would likely stand up to legal challenge. Calin Rovinescu, Air Canada's top legal advisor, questioned that presumption. He set to work on a court challenge, seeking to have the Onex bid declared illegal because it violated the Air Canada Public Participation Act.

On the operations front, Robert Milton's first move was to split his executive team in two. Half of his vice-presidents were instructed to ignore the Onex threat and focus on running the airline. The others were pulled out of their regular jobs to work full-time on Air Canada's response to the Onex bid. Working with thirty-nine-year-old Milton on the defence team were Rob Peterson, forty-eight, the Winnipeg-born chief financial officer, who had worked his way up from the loading ramp to the executive suite; Paul Brotto, forty-eight, a Venetian cabinet-maker's son whose gift for problem-solving had made him a valued resource for several Air Canada CEOs; Doug Port, fifty-six, a former journalist from Scotland, who handled government affairs and public relations; and Rupert Duchesne, forty, a one-time consultant in Britain, whom Milton had hired as his replacement as vice-president of marketing. While the vice-presidents on the defence team were all older than Milton, they were all younger than Gerry Schwartz, who at fifty-seven was seen to hold the advantage of age and experience. They worked closely with Rovinescu and a team of advisors from BMO Nesbitt Burns and Goldman Sachs.

Milton approached every conflict with a corporate competitor as an epic battle of good against evil, and this was no exception. His close-knit group cheerfully regarded themselves as underdogs in a David-and-Goliath struggle: the new CEO and his youthful band versus the considerable might of AMR, Canadian Airlines, Onex, and perhaps even the federal government. He sincerely believed that a wrong had been done when Ottawa suspended the competition laws, and he was determined to see justice prevail. Air Canada's initial reaction to the Section 47 order had been favourable, but that view quickly turned to suspicion once Onex surfaced. Milton vehemently disagreed with the government's claim that both airlines had requested the order; Air Canada certainly did not intend to open itself up to a hostile bid. He was concerned too that Air Canada workers would lose their jobs under an Onex merger, and he worried that the airline would become little more than a puppet company controlled by AMR chairman Don Carty out of Fort Worth, Texas. There was also, as Milton saw it, a bitter financial reality: when Air Canada's bean-counters studied the numbers in the Onex bid, they concluded that shareholders were being offered significantly less than their shares were worth. The Red Team resistance fighters needed to find a way out of the Onex ambush, and they didn't have a lot of options.

On September 20, Rovinescu filed a motion with the Quebec Superior Court, arguing that the Onex bid was illegal, since it violated the 10-per-cent ownership limit. But a win in court would represent a Pyrrhic victory unless it was accompanied by an alternative plan to reward the company's owners. Just as Schwartz had anticipated, Onex's bid had unearthed a tremendous amount of value for Air Canada's shareholders. By mid-September, Air Canada stock was trading at around $10 a share, compared with $6.50 before the government suspended competition laws. By defeating the Onex bid in court without offering a substitute proposition, Milton's team would send Air Canada's shares back down to the $7 mark or lower. Shareholders wouldn't stand for that from any CEO.

Any alternative plan would require a pile of cash, but Air Canada couldn't raise funds by the usual method.[13] The airline couldn't seek out an investor to mount a counter-bid, since any such rescuer would demand a major ownership stake in the company. After contending that the Onex bid was illegal because it placed more than 10 per cent of the merged company's ownership in a single shareholder's hands, Air Canada could hardly propose to do the same. Project Peacock had Milton's team stumped.

"What we need is a gift. A big gift," Rob Peterson said.[14]

It was a throwaway line, the kind uttered when there's nothing left to say. But the executives who gathered daily in Air Canada's boardroom were desperate enough to seize on the idea and play with it. They certainly needed a gift, but from whom? From everyone who had a vested interest in seeing the Onex plan fail: Air Canada's employees; the airlines in the Star Alliance; Canadian Imperial Bank of Commerce, which risked losing the Aerogold VISA card; and Cara Operations, which would lose a major customer if Onex handed the catering contract to rival Sky Chefs.

The defence team approached the stakeholders on its list one by one. While the unions offered moral support – workers pinned anti-Onex buttons to their uniforms – they weren't interested in contributing the contract concessions that management wanted.

Air Canada had better luck with the other parties on the wish list. Cara gave favourable terms for a ten-year extension of a contract it didn't want to lose. United Airlines and Lufthansa – Air Canada's two main allies in Star Alliance – came through with undertakings worth hundreds of millions of dollars in exchange for a commitment from Air Canada that it would remain in the alliance until 2009. The two carriers agreed to guarantee $312 million in new debt, and they acquired 7 per cent of Air Canada's shares for $232.5 million. United Airlines also agreed to pay for three aircraft Air Canada had ordered but could no longer afford, freeing up another $188 million. Under the deal, Air Canada would lease back the jets from United over the next decade. The arrangements with Lufthansa and United included a serious disincentive for Gerry Schwartz. If anyone acquired more than 25 per cent of Air Canada's stock or tried to break the ten-year contract during the first year, the airline would have to pay $250 million in damages.

It was significant money – more than $700 million – but it wasn't enough. Milton arranged a dinner meeting with CIBC chairman John Hunkin and their respective advisors at Le Latini, one of Montreal's best Italian restaurants. Milton knew that the Aerogold VISA card was extremely profitable for CIBC and he wanted Hunkin to understand that his bank would likely lose the contract – perhaps to Royal Bank, which was involved in the Onex bid – if Onex came out the winner. Paul Brotto remembers the conversation going something like this:

Milton: We've got a great relationship. Thank you for coming. We need your help.
Hunkin: We're here to help.
Milton: We need $200 million from you.
Hunkin: We'd be happy to loan you $200 million.
Milton: You don't seem to understand. We need a gift.
Hunkin: Oh! You mean interest-free?
Milton: No, a gift.

"They finally got the message," Brotto jokes. "They didn't stay for dessert."

But CIBC did agree to assist, paying a one-time service charge of $200 million for an extension of the Aerogold VISA contract until December 31, 2009. In exchange, Air Canada provided CIBC with 4.4 million warrants to buy Air Canada shares for between $24 and $28 over the next five years. If Air Canada's shares rose above this mark – and in 1999 most analysts expected that they would – the warrants would be a generous bonus to thank CIBC for coming to Air Canada's aid.[15]

It took seven weeks for the defence team to line up financing and prepare their counter-offer. They worked brutally long days, seven days a week. While Gerry Schwartz criss-crossed the country through September and October to sell his scheme, Robert Milton was holed up at Air Canada's Montreal headquarters. Milton kept such a low profile during those weeks that Onex officials jokingly asked each other, "Where's Waldo?"

By mid-October, Milton's group had put together a war chest of $930 million – a sum roughly equivalent to the amount that Onex and AMR were putting on the table.

On Tuesday, October 19 – fifty-six days after Schwartz's announcement – Robert Milton rose at Montreal's elegant Le Windsor conference hall to unveil the alternative. "Air Canada's strategy throughout this period has been very simple: we have chosen to listen and think before acting," Milton began. "Having listened, we went to work. Today, we are pleased to present Air Canada's plan for the future."

Milton outlined his own design for mastery of Canada's airline industry, beginning with the purchase of Canadian Airlines. The proposal seemed to offer something for everybody. Employees were told that there would be only 2,500 job cuts, compared to 5,000 in the Onex plan, and no Air Canada workers would lose their jobs, since all the cuts would be made at Canadian. Small communities were promised that they wouldn't lose service. Canadian Airlines' shareholders would receive $2 per share, matching the Onex offer. And for Air Canada's shareholders? If they stayed with Milton's team, they would be handsomely rewarded. Air Canada offered to buy back 35 per cent of its shares at $12 a piece, well above the $9 to $10 range they reached in the weeks following the Onex bid. In effect, the share buyback was a legal bribe, with money passing from United, Lufthansa, and CIBC to Air Canada's shareholders.

Milton also had something for consumers. While Schwartz wanted to merge Air Canada and Canadian, Milton pledged to keep both airlines alive. "Air Canada and Canadian will not be merged," the press release stated emphatically. "The airlines will operate as separate entities, providing choice and distinct brands." Furthermore, Canadian Airlines would maintain its own management team, a separate board of directors, and a head office in Calgary.

There was even a surprise element to Milton's bid. He promised not two airlines in the Air Canada stable, but three: Air Canada, Canadian Airlines, and a new low-fare carrier to operate out of John C. Munro International Airport in Hamilton, Ontario. Milton knew that large international carriers such as Delta Air Lines, U.S. Air, and British Airways had started up discount subsidiaries to deal with low-fare competitors. Milton saw an opportunity to do the same in Canada to compete with WestJet. It was good politics, too. A low-cost carrier based in Hamilton was likely to win the support of two influential members of parliament from Hamilton: Sheila Copps, the deputy prime minister, and Stan Keyes, chairman of the all-party parliamentary transport committee.

Milton pitched the discount airline as a vehicle to enhance competition, but journalists attending the press conference were skeptical. "If I were a consumer listening to this," one reporter told Milton, "I would think that we're going from a competitive environment in Canada . . . to a monopoly which is not only controlling two airlines now, but a third which you are going to create."

Milton went to great lengths to emphasize that, if he won the takeover battle, the government's wish would be his command. He said he would welcome "the involvement and scrutiny" of the federal Competition Bureau and the "input" of transport minister David Collenette. "In creating the configuration of the industry that we are advocating, we believe that it is pro-competitive. But in any circumstance, we are totally of the mind that we will fully co-operate with the Competition Bureau and the regulators of this country to determine an outcome that is fully beneficial to the consumers."

Prime Minister Chrétien responded to Air Canada's announcement by repeating comments he had made in the past: that this was an issue for shareholders, not the government, to decide. But Collenette took the opportunity to strut, saying Air Canada's bid showed that the government had done the right thing in suspending the competition laws. That move had resulted in not one, but two options for shareholders of Air Canada and Canadian Airlines.

At an afternoon press conference on Parliament Hill that same day, Onex vice-president Nigel Wright charged that Air Canada's bid involved too much money from U.S. investors and, possibly, violated the 10-percent limit on share ownership. These were the precise accusations that Air Canada had been throwing at the Onex bid for weeks. Wright – a former advisor and speech writer for Prime Minister Brian Mulroney – even suggested that Onex might go to court to have Air Canada's bid declared illegal, again mimicking Air Canada. He suggested, however, that from a public-relations perspective, it wasn't a bad thing to have another proposal on the table.

"The news today is that we have a second offer," Wright said. "It's been a little bit like being the only duck in duck-hunting season around here for the last little while. And I'm pleased to have another duck along."

4

DOGFIGHT

There was a real possibility we were going to lose. This was that kind of defining moment for Air Canada. If we lost, you could only assume that the entire management team would have either resigned or been fired.[1]
   – Calin Rovinescu, future executive vice-president, Air Canada

On the morning of Saturday, September 18, 1999, Gerry Schwartz woke up to read a troubling public-opinion poll on the front page of the *Globe and Mail*. According to pollster Angus Reid, 68 per cent of Canadians surveyed supported a merger of Air Canada and Canadian Airlines, but only 42 per cent approved of the Onex plan. The response was particularly disturbing given that, at the time of the survey, the Onex bid was alone on the table; Air Canada's counter-bid would not be announced for another month. Further, only 43 per cent of Canadians regarded Onex as "trustworthy" and two-thirds believed Schwartz had received an "inappropriate" level of support from his friends in government. "Onex has not been able to build the kind of psychological bridge of trust that is required in these kinds of deals," said Reid. "They've still got a lot of work to do in terms of telling Canadians who they are and what they are about."[2]

The federal government was doing its own canvassing of public opinion, as were Air Canada, Onex, and American Airlines. All were collecting similar information. While Canadians weren't opposed to a merger in theory, they were concerned about the nature of the carrier that would result. Respondents said they didn't want workers to lose jobs, they didn't want Americans to take over the Canadian airline industry, and they didn't want the merged airline to raise prices, reduce frequencies, or eliminate service to small communities. In other words, a merger was okay as long as nothing else changed.

Onex should have had a clear advantage in the public-relations war. Schwartz had aligned himself with the underdog, rescuing Canadian Airlines from big, bad Air Canada, which was still perceived as an arrogant Crown corporation more than a decade after its privatization. Canadian seemed to have won the affection of the country's citizens, even if it didn't get their bookings. The Calgary-based carrier had likewise become the favourite in Ottawa's power circles. CEO Kevin Benson had registered as a lobbyist, and government officials say Canadian did a much better job of keeping the government informed about its financial health and prospects than did its Montreal-based rival. The carrier's government-relations strategy went beyond communication to scratching backs – doing favours for the people who could do favours for it. "If there was an empty seat, why wouldn't you upgrade somebody who was important to you, whether it was the premier of Alberta or a federal cabinet minister?" asked Jeff Angel, Canadian's former director of corporate communications. At terminals across the country, Canadian Airlines employees met politicians at their cars, boarding passes in hand, ready to whisk them through security. "We really made an effort to show them that we were a great company and that great people worked for this company," Angel said. "To me that's just smart politics, smart business."

Dancing attendance on politicians was anathema to the folks in Montreal, and especially to Robert Milton, who has been accused by federal officials of performing miserably in the government-relations department. In Milton's view, Canadian Airlines was good at lobbying because it had to be. "Air Canada was making record profits before the hostile takeover attempt. We were on a roll. Canadian was failing," Milton said later. "What's the point of great government relations if it's just to subsidize something that's not working?"3

Once his company became a takeover target, however, Milton was forced to leap into the government-relations act. He had been nearly invisible for the eight weeks since Schwartz unveiled Onex's plan; now he had his own bid to sell, and he made a handful of public appearances before editorial boards and parliamentary committees. Part of Milton's sales pitch was that Air Canada's goal was to save its Western rival, not to destroy it.

"I want to make very clear our statement to members of this committee and to Canadians generally that we are absolutely committed to reviving and rebuilding Canadian Airlines," Milton told the House of Commons standing committee on transport on October 27. "Indeed, this is a key part of our plan. Some would have you believe that we intend to shut down Canadian – or that Canadian's creditors will begin seizing the company's aircraft – as soon as any deal with Air Canada is concluded. Nothing could be further from the truth. Such scare-mongering is not helpful in the context of the profoundly important debate that is now under way. And it is not fair to Canadian's employees, many of whom are understandably worried about their future. They are hard-working people, and I do not believe it is right to play politics with them and their families. Simply put, we are committed to returning the airline to financial health and profitability and to operating the company as a distinct brand. Anyone who tells you otherwise is not telling the truth."

It would be hard to imagine a less ambiguous statement, but Reform Party MP Val Meredith pressed for confirmation. "As I understand it, from what you've said, if your merger deal went through, your commitment to Canadian Airlines would be to keep them functioning over a long period of time. Is that understanding correct?"

"Absolutely," Milton replied. "As emphatically and categorically as I can state it, it is a long-term proposition. We look to protect the interests of the employees of Canadian Airlines and to build that franchise, long term, by rejuvenating it, re-fleeting it, and really letting it achieve its full potential."

Both sides hired government-relations firms and ad agencies to present their proposals to politicians and the public. Before launching its hostile bid, Onex was able to lock up several of the country's top lobbying firms, including Capital Hill Group, Global Public Affairs Inc., and Earnscliffe Strategy Group, which employed Michael Robinson, one-time advisor to finance minister Paul Martin. Schwartz later brought in his friend Paul Pellegrini, president of Toronto's Sussex Strategy Group, and Bill Fox, former press secretary to Prime Minister Brian Mulroney. Canadian Airlines and American Airlines used Global Public Affairs, and Wallding International Inc., the government-relations firm run by former Liberal cabinet minister David Dingwall. Air Canada hired GPC Canada and Hugh Riopelle, a seventy-one-year-old former Air Canada lobbyist, who had set up his own government-relations firm after retiring from the airline.

Their strategies included the usual lobbying of MPs and government officials, as well as unusual and expensive advertising campaigns that played out in the country's newspapers. On behalf of Onex, Bill Fox booked full-page ads in newspapers across the country asking, "How many Canadians does it take to change an airline?" The copy sought to assure the average Canadian that the merged airline would provide better service, offering more flights at more convenient times. Another ad tried to correct the belief – held by more than half of respondents surveyed in an Onex/American Airlines poll – that Onex was an American firm. This dangerous notion warranted double-page ads: "Who are you guys anyway?" demanded the headline on the first page. The second page replied that Onex was one of Canada's ten largest companies, "owned and run by Canadians and headquartered in *Canada*."

There were Onex ads designed specifically for shareholders, focusing on questions of trust and value. One pointed out that, if an investor had bought $1,000 worth of shares in each of Air Canada and Onex in 1988, the former investment would have fallen to $813, while the latter would have risen to $9,446. "Who do you trust to create shareholder value?" was the question. An Air Canada ad responded that the company's results in the first nine months of 1999 had been the best in the airline's history.

Air Canada knew from its polling that two themes resonated strongly with the public. Canadians were fearful of American control of the Canadian airline industry, and they were suspicious of Gerry Schwartz's

Liberal connections. Air Canada invoked these concerns at every opportunity. "We did very careful surveys to understand where the public's perceptions were and where the triggers were," said Rupert Duchesne, a member of the Air Canada defence team. "And we pulled them very carefully."

It was inevitable that the contest would descend to mudslinging. When Schwartz promised to buy jets from Montreal-based Bombardier, Air Canada spin doctors made sure reporters knew that his personal jet, a Gulfstream II, was made by the U.S. giant General Dynamics. When Onex bashed Air Canada for trying to delay a shareholder vote on the takeover bid, raising the issue of shareholder rights, Air Canada reminded observers that Schwartz had structured Onex in such a way that he owned some 20 per cent of the shares but controlled more than 60 per cent of the votes. The fine points of the debate were often lost on the public. For many it simply came down to which of the CEOs made people feel better about themselves and the future.

It proved to be a difficult time for the Onex chief, and it showed. "The things that Gerry did throughout that period were completely alien and unpleasant to him. He doesn't like doing media interviews particularly. He doesn't feel comfortable on a platform," according to one insider. "He will try too hard to be likeable, and he comes across as sort of smarmy." Advisors who got to know Schwartz as he went across the country in September and October nevertheless found the serious businessman to have a fun-loving, even silly, side. Gerry's penchant for regional cuisine caused the Onex team to fall behind schedule more than once. After unveiling his bid at Montreal's Château Champlain, Schwartz directed his driver to Deli Snowdon for a round of smoked-meat sandwiches for the troops. After meeting with Premier Gary Doer in Winnipeg, Schwartz took his aides to C. Kelekis, a Winnipeg diner on North Main Street, where he ordered a dozen hot dogs. They gobbled down two dogs each before heading to a meeting with the editorial board of the *Winnipeg Free Press*. After the meeting, the group stopped at Salisbury House for its trademark Nip burgers and pie. In the minivan en route to the airport, some executives had to unbutton their pants:

everybody was feeling extremely full – except Gerry. "We didn't go to Junior's for chili dogs!" he exclaimed.

After Air Canada unveiled its counter-bid, its executives conducted similar promotional tours aimed at selling the plan to the pension and mutual funds that owned Air Canada stock. "We'd go to our shareholders and say our deal is the best for the following reasons," chief financial officer Rob Peterson recalls. "And then Gerry and his team would arrive to tell them his deal was the best. And then we'd visit them again and explain why Gerry was wrong."

Milton and Schwartz were also fighting for the hearts and minds of the airlines' employees. Pilots, flight attendants, and customer-service agents on Canadian Airlines' Blue Team lined up behind Schwartz, while members of Air Canada's Red Team wholeheartedly supported Milton. The unions representing these workers were in an awkward spot. Three unions – the Canadian Auto Workers (CAW), the Canadian Union of Public Employees (CUPE), and the International Association of Machinists and Aerospace Workers (IAM) – acted for large numbers of workers at both airlines. The leadership at two of these organizations chose to remain neutral during the takeover battle rather than alienate whole segments of their membership. The other dove head first into the melee.

Basil (Buzz) Hargrove never did shy away from a fight. Back in 1996, the last time Canadian Airlines had been on the brink of bankruptcy, Hargrove angered Canadian Airlines employees by refusing a wage cut for the customer-sales-and-service workers he represented as president of the CAW. The airline's position was that, without the rollback, the company would go under. Tensions were high, and rumours circulated among the pilots and mechanics that Hargrove wanted to see Canadian fail, because its demise would benefit the workers he represented at Air Canada. One Canadian Airlines pilot was enraged enough to post Hargrove's home address on a Web site, urging Canadian's employees to send Buzz a message. The address, however, was out of date – Hargrove hadn't lived there for six years. "My daughters and granddaughters were living there with my former wife, and in broad daylight they came and slashed the tires on three cars sitting in the driveway," Hargrove recalled.

"They threatened to bomb the house. The Durham police spent two weeks protecting my family." In the end, Hargrove recommended the pay cuts to his members after the federal government threatened to force a membership vote on the proposal.

Hargrove was raised in hardscrabble rural New Brunswick, the sixth of ten children. While his dad was off logging in the bush, Hargrove helped his mother work a potato farm. He dropped out of school in grade ten and spent much of his youth drinking and drifting across the country from one blue-collar job to another. He went to work at the Chrysler plant in Windsor, Ontario, in 1964, and was union shop steward a year later. In 1992, Hargrove was elected president of the Canadian Auto Workers.

Despite its name, the union today represents workers in some fifteen different industries, including fisheries, hospitality, and mining. Hargrove says airlines are the toughest employers. "It is probably the most classic example of dog-eat-dog capitalism that we have experienced in any sector," Hargrove says. He blames deregulation, saying it is now impossible for most airlines to make a profit. "It's been horrific," he says. "The workers in this industry have gone through some of the worst scenarios of any group of workers that I've experienced."

Hargrove worried that airline employees would face layoffs and forced relocations under Onex's proposal to buy and merge Air Canada and Canadian Airlines. Indeed, he made it clear early on that he did not support a merger of any kind. Yes, the airline industry was crippled by years of cut-throat competition, but the CAW believed the federal government could fix the problem by buying part of Canadian Airlines, re-regulating the industry, and forcing both carriers to shrink. If a merger was unavoidable, however, Hargrove was determined to influence the outcome.

He met with Schwartz, then Milton, trying to play one against the other for job guarantees, early-retirement incentives, and a commitment that his members would not be relocated. At first, neither Schwartz nor Milton were willing to deal, but Hargrove found that Schwartz delivered a more palatable no. "Schwartz is a much nicer person. I found him to be a very honest, very decent, very straightforward person," Hargrove recalls. "Milton was arrogant, very aloof, a bit of a dictator . . . 'I know best and you guys should just agree and go along.'"4 The perception was reinforced when Hargrove invited the two CEOs to explain their plans to the union leadership at both airlines. While Schwartz showed up in person to take the heat from Air Canada representatives, Milton sent vice-presidents in his place.

Circumstances eventually brought Hargrove and Schwartz together in an astounding alliance. Hammered in the media for his Liberal ties and his involvement with American Airlines, the Onex chairman was desperate for a friend and ally. He contacted Hargrove to say that he was prepared to negotiate. Schwartz would agree to some of the CAW's demands if Hargrove would publicly endorse the Onex plan. The union boss had no problem endorsing the Onex bid, although he intended to give Air Canada a chance to agree to the same conditions. Hargrove hoped to extract improvements to the workers' contracts no matter who won the takeover battle.

Schwartz pledged not to lay off or relocate any CAW members until March 2002, and he committed to hundreds of millions of dollars in early-retirement packages. Hargrove says Schwartz offered the same terms to CUPE and the IAM in return for their support. "They wanted the same deal desperately, but they wouldn't go public, so it was never signed," Hargrove says. Hargrove asked for the same concessions from Air Canada, but the airline had no interest in opening up its contracts to win an endorsement from the CAW. With his employees virtually unanimous in their opposition to Onex, Milton didn't need to court their unions' leadership.

At a joint press conference on November 1, Hargrove gave his blessing to the Onex proposal. Schwartz used the occasion to get personal, charging that Milton had "shown immaturity" in his response to the Onex bid. He said Milton would have a job at the merged airline "on the operational side," the first clear indication that Milton would be demoted if Onex won the dogfight.

Hargrove, meanwhile, claimed that he had the "overwhelming support" of his members in his decision to back Onex. His Air Canada brothers and sisters — who had been wearing anti-Onex buttons for weeks – vehemently disagreed. Tom Freeman, the head of the CAW's Air Canada component, called Hargrove's comments "totally premature." Instead of lending Schwartz the positive spin he badly needed, Hargrove's endorsement caused a schism in the CAW and sent Air Canada's workers rallying to Milton's side. Busloads of Air Canada employees held a protest at the CAW's Toronto headquarters, where they chanted, "Robert Milton, he's our man. If he can't do it, no one can!" They wore "Buzz off" buttons, and some spoke of pulling out of the CAW altogether.

Hargrove says he accepts criticism as a fundamental part of the job, but years later, it's clear he still feels his strategy was misunderstood. "Nobody ever did get the position right, because nobody wanted to listen," Hargrove says. "All I did was bargain an agreement that, if this group of investors led by Onex won, then this was the agreement. It was still subject to the ratification of the members." But it wasn't the details of the deal that caused tempers to flare. It was his public embrace of Onex. Buzz had underestimated his members' enduring corporate allegiances. "I never could get my head around who owned the airline being important," Hargrove said. "The loyalty of the employees to their brand was absolutely incredible."

Hours after the Schwartz–Hargrove press conference, Air Canada released its own letter to union heads, guaranteeing that no employees at either airline would be involuntarily laid off as a result of the merger, and promising that the proposed low-fare carrier would not be used to erode working conditions, wages, or benefits at Air Canada or Canadian Airlines.

If Gerry Schwartz was the black king – the King of Clubs – using power and connections and American dollars to win the day, and Robert Milton was the red king – the King of Hearts – playing on national sentiments to keep Schwartz at bay, what role was there for transport minister David Collenette? It seemed to the media that he was the Joker.

During the fall of 1999, the balding, bespectacled minister was repeatedly lampooned by columnists, editorial cartoonists, and the CBC television satire *This Hour Has 22 Minutes*. Some charged that Collenette had suspended competition laws as a favour to his pal, Gerry Schwartz. One cartoon from Montreal's *La Presse* showed Schwartz sitting on a stool with his hand in the back of a tiny Collenette puppet. Schwartz says, "And I haven't even moved my lips," while the Collenette dummy chants "Onex, Onex, Onex, Onex."[5] Others complained that the minister should have let natural market forces prevail and allowed Canadian Airlines to fail, rather than open the door to a merger. Terence Corcoran, a columnist with the *National Post*, compared him to Mr. Magoo, refusing to admit that his vision was failing. "With the ideological nearsightedness of a cartoon character," Corcoran wrote, "Transport Minister David Collenette is bumbling his way into air transport pandemonium."

It wasn't the first time Collenette had been at the centre of controversy. As defence minister in 1996, Collenette had faced repeated calls for his resignation in the midst of an inquiry into the activities of the Canadian Airborne Regiment in Somalia. While the scandal dated back to the previous Progressive Conservative government, critics demanded Collenette take ministerial responsibility for documents that disappeared on his watch and for his choice of chief of defence staff Jean Boyle. He was as surprised as anyone when he was forced to resign suddenly before the inquiry had concluded. His departure wasn't related to the Somalia affair, but to a letter sent by his office to the Immigration Board, asking for special consideration in a case involving a constituent – a clear conflict of interest. Collenette had signed the letter without paying attention to what he was signing. "I was trapped," Collenette said later. "It was a bullshit reason to resign, and I was really mad about doing it."[6] Nonetheless, dealing with crises was what David Collenette loved most about politics. He was a true political animal for whom waging the battle was as important – and usually more fun – than the outcome.

Collenette was born in 1946 near London's Marylebone, an area of railway freight yards that had been heavily bombed in the war. He remembers playing in the craters made by bombs dropped from German planes. By the time he was six he was studying subway route maps, riding the London Underground by himself, and fascinated by the trains that rolled through his neighbourhood. Collenette also believes that growing up in London – where politics was played out daily in the class system – helped shape his early interest in party politics. Current events were discussed regularly at the dinner table, and there was no shortage of opinions. His maternal grandfather, who drove a garbage truck, was active in his union and a great supporter of the Labour Party. His maternal grandmother was a Scot and remained an advocate of the unpopular Liberal Party. Collenette's grandparents on his father's side were staunch Anglicans and Tories.

Collenette's family moved when he was eleven as part of a massive wave of immigration to Canada. His father travelled on a Canadian Pacific ship, but Collenette and his mother flew a Pan Am Clipper into New York City. They had tickets on Trans-Canada Air Lines for the connection to Toronto, but there was a mechanical problem with the plane, so they were transferred to a combination passenger/freight plane for a turbulent trip over Lake Ontario.

Collenette's parents voted for John Diefenbaker in the 1958 election, believing the pro-monarchy Tories best represented the interests of expatriate Brits. But by the next federal vote, Diefenbaker was out of favour and they shifted to the Liberal Party. So did their son. When Diefenbaker visited East York Collegiate Institute during the 1962 election campaign, young Collenette organized a group of fellow students to heckle the prime minister from the balcony, a moment captured on the front page of the next day's *Toronto Telegram*.

Collenette was smitten by party politics and he has been involved in every election since 1962, first as a supporter, then as a senior Liberal Party official or candidate. He was elected for the first time in 1974, lost his seat in 1979, and was re-elected in 1980. Three years later, Prime Minister Pierre Trudeau made him minister of state for multiculturalism, a junior cabinet post. Collenette lost his seat again when Brian Mulroney swept the Liberals out of office in 1984. But thirteen months at the cabinet table was enough to establish a lifelong friendship with a future prime minister. Collenette's wife, Penny, whom he met at a Liberal Christmas party in 1972, worked as director of volunteers for Jean Chrétien's first run at the leadership, a campaign that was lost to

John Turner. When Chrétien's time came in 1993, the Collenettes were rewarded. Penny became the prime minister's director of appointments and David was offered a job in Cabinet.

"So, David, what would you want?" the prime minister asked him, apparently prepared to grant any wish.

Collenette didn't need to think twice. His childhood passion for trains and subways had grown into a general love of anything to do with transportation. He understood how Canada's history was intertwined with transportation systems, with road, rail, and air travel. "I'd really like Transport," he said. "I think it's a great portfolio."

Chrétien shook his head. "How about Defence?"

"I really like Transport."

"How about Defence?" the prime minister offered again.[7]

Chrétien wanted someone in Transport who could shrink the department and make drastic changes – not a transportation buff like Collenette. He convinced Collenette that his love of history made him an ideal candidate for Defence. Despite the Somalia affair and his untimely 1996 resignation, Collenette enjoyed his time in that portfolio. He did his penance out of Cabinet, and then in 1997 Chrétien finally appointed him transport minister.

Collenette dreamed of reviving passenger rail services in Canada, but he was also intrigued by the crisis he could see developing in the airline industry. The government had injected more than $50 million into Canadian Airlines the previous year, because it couldn't afford to deal with a bankruptcy before a federal election. Collenette knew that the Canadian Airlines problem would soon need fixing once and for all. He regarded the suspension of competition laws on August 13 as the first step in that process.

Central to the charge that Collenette had done a favour for Schwartz was the question of who had requested the Section 47 order. Air Canada has always said it was a Canadian Airlines initiative, while Collenette and his officials insist both airlines requested the order. The truth lies somewhere in between. It was Canadian Airlines CEO Kevin Benson who first raised the idea with the minister on March 12, when he presented his

"New National Dream" white paper. The paper noted that a Section 47 order was "crucial" because of the "unique circumstances" faced by both airlines. Air Canada's top executives had signed off on the document before it went to the minister and, at a separate meeting with Transport officials two weeks later, Air Canada vice-president Doug Port discussed the possibility of invoking Section 47 to facilitate a friendly merger.

It was only after talks broke down between the airlines that a difference of opinion emerged on Section 47. Officials at Canadian still wanted the order so they could do their deal with Schwartz. Officials at Air Canada no longer saw the need for a suspension of the competition rules. In late June, Air Canada gave Canadian the excuse it needed to renew requests for the Section 47 order when it made an unsolicited offer to buy Canadian Airlines' international routes and inventory for $525 million. Air Canada would also have assumed $1.4 billion of Canadian's debt and leases on aircraft operated on international routes, and taken on hundreds of Canadian Airlines employees to run the flights. Canadian would have become a domestic feeder for the oneworld alliance. Kevin Benson wasn't interested. Canadian had put all its eggs into the Onex basket, but it kept talks open with Air Canada so that it wouldn't oppose the petition for a Section 47 order. Kevin Benson made a written request on August 9, 1999, which Collenette signed four days later.

Collenette has said that the airline crisis was more difficult for him personally than the Somalia inquiry; he knew he would be held accountable for the repercussions of the Section 47 order. Peter Gregg, the minister's director of communications during the airline-merger debate, remembers it as a painful period. "He was hated across this country, because he was seen as the meddler, screwing up the nation's airline system, removing competition, allowing Air Canada to run roughshod. Getting on a plane with the guy in those days was terrible because the [Air Canada] staff would either yell at him or stare him down."

Ironically, one of the safest places for the minister was the House of Commons. The airline debate rarely came up in question period, largely because the Reform Party knew its support base in British Columbia and Alberta favoured the Onex proposal. But following question period, the media would be lying in wait. Would Collenette eliminate the 10-per-cent cap on individual share ownership? Would the Competition Bureau have final approval of any merger? How would the minister ensure competition if the two airlines merged? Collenette gave few real answers to such questions, sticking instead to his rehearsed lines: The government of Canada had no preconceived notion of who the owner of the merged airlines should be. It was up to shareholders to decide which bid would prevail.

An indication of Collenette's interventionist leanings came at the end of September when he met with provincial transport ministers in Saint John, New Brunswick. He again refused to say whether ownership limits would be lifted or whether a merger would be subject to the review of the Competition Bureau. But he did declare that the federal government had a "very critical role" to play in assessing any merger. "The market is functioning but the market alone will not decide what is in the best interests of Canadians," he said. Collenette laid out five criteria any merger would have to meet: consumer protection, service to small communities, respect for the rights of employees, fostering of competition, and Canadian control of the merged carrier. Some observers noted that these comments appeared at odds with those made earlier in the day by his boss, Prime Minister Jean Chrétien, who continued to insist the outcome was in the hands of Air Canada's shareholders.

On October 26, Collenette put some flesh on these ideas when he appeared before the transport committees of the Senate and the House of Commons. He tabled a policy statement that cast the imminent merger as a positive development for Canada. A merged carrier, the document stated, would "be a major competitor in the world airline industry, ensuring effective international service to Canadians." Instead of two carriers flying half-empty planes, a single airline would redeploy aircraft, resulting in "a more efficient use of resources and lower costs." The minister's document bore striking similarities to "A New National Dream," the proposal Kevin Benson had presented to Collenette seven months earlier.

In addition, the minister finally answered some of the most persistent questions. Yes, any merger would be subject to the review of the federal commissioner of competition. And if Air Canada's shareholders voted for the Onex proposal, the government might be willing to lift the limit on individual share ownership: "The government is prepared to consider increasing the limit to a new level, to be decided following input from Parliamentarians, if such a measure contributes to achieving a healthy, Canadian-controlled airline industry."

Few of the combatants in the takeover battle got much sleep on the night of Thursday, November 4. With a shareholder vote scheduled for Monday, executives at both Onex and Air Canada worked through the night preparing for one final round of bidding. Milton and Schwartz had been hastily raising the stakes in the weeks previous. Onex had sweetened its share offer to $13 from $8.25, while Air Canada's had increased to $16 from $12. The bids could not be compared dollar for dollar, since Air Canada proposed to buy back only 35 per cent of its shares, and Onex's offer would be paid out in a combination of cash and stock. Each side claimed its offer was best for shareholders, but analysts and institutional investors weren't sure. There was pressure on both to make the choice a clear one.

It was Onex's turn to bid, but Milton wanted to be ready with a trump as soon as Schwartz showed his hand. Finding the cash to do so wouldn't be easy. Air Canada had already squeezed its friends at United Airlines, Lufthansa, and CIBC, and had scrounged every dollar available from its treasury. Now it was time to turn to its largest shareholder, the Caisse de dépôt et placement du Québec. The airline was reluctant to do a deal with the Caisse unless it was absolutely necessary; the pension fund had historic ties to Quebec's nationalist movement and was known to drive a hard bargain. It was an unlikely ally for Canada's flag-carrier. But rumours of a substantially richer offer coming from Onex left Air Canada with little choice. Calin Rovinescu and Rob Peterson negotiated around the clock with Caisse officials. They finalized a deal early on Friday, November 6, which gave them a $150-million loan and an option to take another $150 million. The agreement allowed the Caisse to convert the debt into Air Canada shares at a favourable rate, provided the airline's shares appreciated significantly after the merger.

Hours later, Gerry Schwartz held a conference call with analysts and reporters to unveil his third and final bid. He was offering $17.50 per share – more than double the price proposed ten and a half weeks earlier. Shareholders were guaranteed to receive at least $6.55 per share in cash, 73 cents per share higher than Air Canada's last offer. "It's simple," Schwartz said. "Our plan offers more cash and gives investors better airline stock." The bid was conditional on Onex being relieved of penalties for breaking the long-term contract Air Canada had recently signed with United and Lufthansa. Despite this fine print, the Onex offer appeared seductive enough to persuade some of Air Canada's largest institutional shareholders to support Onex at the shareholders' meeting.

Now that Milton's team knew what they were dealing with, they put the finishing touches on their own final bid. At the same time, they anticipated the Quebec court's ruling due that day on their motion to have Onex's bid declared illegal, a ruling that no one could predict with certainty. Most observers figured the Quebec ruling might be ambiguous, giving neither side a clear victory. In fact, on Friday afternoon, Mr. Justice André Wery of the Quebec Superior Court came down strongly on Air Canada's side, noting that, though Onex's mechanism for getting around the Air Canada Public Participation Act was "arguably an ingenious one," its underlying legal conclusion was specious. In short, he wrote, the Onex bid was illegal.

The court decision struck a serious blow to the Onex campaign, but Gerry Schwartz was not without options. He could appeal the ruling. He could lobby the federal government to scrap the 10-per-cent limit on individual share ownership. He could reconfigure his model so that AirCo would never own more than 10 per cent of the shares. But Schwartz did none of these things; instead, he capitulated. The takeover king had been upping the ante for weeks – raising the bids, making promises, putting his personal credibility on the line – but the time had come to fold his hand.

At a hastily assembled press conference late Friday afternoon at

Onex's head office in downtown Toronto, Schwartz read from a prepared statement. He looked grim but calm, freshly shaven and wearing a crisp mauve shirt. "Onex is disappointed in the Quebec court's conclusion that shareholders cannot accept our offer," said Schwartz. "Naturally, we will respect that decision and accordingly have instructed our counsel that our offers and our resolutions at next Monday's shareholders' meeting be immediately withdrawn."[8] He did not answer questions about whether Onex might be willing to make another bid in the future. The war was suddenly over. Air Canada's trump bid was moot and the shareholders' meeting scheduled for Monday was cancelled.

Schwartz's unexpected retreat deprived Air Canada's young CEO of his first major victory. Yes, Air Canada had won the court battle, thanks to Calin Rovinescu's legal work, and Air Canada appeared to be winning the public-relations war. But the contest was supposed to have been decided at the shareholders' meeting. In the end, Milton was denied the dramatic showdown he so desperately wanted.

"It was a bittersweet moment for Robert," Rovinescu admitted. "We were fighting the mother of all takeover battles. We had just lined up all our big guns to level Onex – and they pull out. It meant that Robert could not prove to the world that we had beaten them."[9] Nevertheless, the champagne flowed freely at Air Canada's Montreal headquarters that night. To other members of the Red Team, it was a clear win, and celebrations quickly spread across the company. Laura Cooke, manager of media relations for Central Canada, sipped red wine as she fielded media calls from her desk at the Air Canada Centre.

With Schwartz out of the picture, Milton had some tough choices to make. He wasn't the one who had initiated this takeover fight; would he be the one to finish it? He avoided any suspense by announcing at once that Air Canada would honour its commitment to reward shareholders by buying back 35 per cent of its stock at $16 a share. And if American Airlines and Canadian Airlines were willing, Air Canada would proceed with its plan to buy the Blue Team and merge it with the Red Team. He felt he owed it to shareholders and to Canadians to follow through on his promises, even though his rival had quit the field. "Your word is your word," Milton explained later. But it went beyond that: Milton genuinely believed that acquiring Canadian Airlines was the right thing to do for Air Canada, that merging the two carriers would boost profits by hundreds of millions of dollars a year.

At Canadian Airlines, the prospects were grim. Having lost its best hope, the carrier issued a simple press release, expressing "disappointment" in Schwartz's decision to withdraw. In fact, Canadian and American Airlines executives felt abandoned. "We thought there were a couple more rounds there," Doug Carty said. "It was a tough couple of days . . . Onex had left and wished us well and it wasn't like our predictions about running out of cash were any rosier at that point."

The management and board of directors at Canadian Airlines searched desperately for any option that could save them from accepting Air Canada's $2-a-share proposition. They held a secret meeting with members of the oneworld alliance. American Airlines was still eager, and British Airways did not dismiss the possibility of helping out, but the others, among them Iberia and Cathay Pacific, weren't willing to sink their shareholders' money into something they saw as American Airlines' problem. In the end, Canadian's board grudgingly recommended that shareholders tender their shares to Air Canada.

It's never pleasant to be acquired; clearly, most managers and hundreds of non-unionized staff would lose their jobs as a result of the takeover. But it was better than bankruptcy. Canadian executives said later that the outcome was an acceptable Plan B, since they managed to secure some return for shareholders, save thousands of jobs, and finally get Air Canada to agree to a merger deal. "At the end of the day, we won. We got Air Canada to buy a bankrupt company. I think that's one hell of a feat," a former executive says. "Kevin Benson deserved to be CEO of the year in 1999."

That honour eluded Benson, but he would feel some satisfaction early the next year when the Official Airline Guide named Canadian Airlines the best airline in North America – a coveted honour in the industry. Despite everything Canadian had endured as it scrambled to avoid collapse, the Blue Team had provided better customer service than industry titans like United Airlines and American Airlines. Certainly better than Air Canada.

Onex's attempt to merge Air Canada and Canadian Airlines was one of the most expensive takeover battles in Canadian corporate history. Air Canada spent $43 million on advertising, legal counsel, banking, and lobbyist services to fend off the attack. Onex has never revealed its precise costs, but the tab has been estimated at well in excess of $50 million. In keeping with Schwartz's calculation going in, however, Onex covered most of its expenses by selling its Air Canada shares for considerably more than it had paid back in the summer, when it was establishing a toehold in the company. In a regulatory filing early in 2000, Onex pegged its net "costs related to potential mergers" in 1999 at less than $6 million.

Even so, friends say Gerry Schwartz regards the Air Canada episode as the most difficult experience of his professional life. When he grants interviews, which he does sparingly, he asks that the matter remain off the agenda. But in a 2001 interview with the *National Post Business Magazine*, he admitted that the loss of Air Canada was extremely painful, especially as it came on the heels of his failure to win the 1995 bidding war for John Labatt Ltd. "Air Canada was a much bigger loss than usual because it had so much publicity and we had so many people involved. It took a little longer to lick our wounds."[10]

So why did Gerry lose? He wasn't talking, but the pundits at Air Canada were happy to offer their views. They said Schwartz misjudged the significance of the 10-per-cent cap on individual share ownership and underestimated the lengths to which United Airlines and Lufthansa would go to keep Air Canada in the Star Alliance. They also claimed that the Onex team didn't play the public-relations game to their advantage. Polling showed that Onex could have won over the public by defining the debate as one about the arrogance of a former Crown corporation. Instead, they allowed Air Canada to play on fears of the Americans taking control of Canada's skies.

Robert Milton says the sheer dedication of Air Canada's defence team triumphed over the experienced hands at Onex. The Red Team was fighting for its survival and, as Milton likes to frame it, for a higher cause.

"Modestly speaking, I think it was a group of very capable people hitting on all cylinders, but ultimately what do I think helped us to prevail? The fact that we were on the side of right. You can fight so much more effectively when you're telling the truth and when you're battling for something just. And you know, that's what we were doing. The power of that conviction is worth a lot."[11]

According to Milton, Schwartz's biggest mistake was launching a hostile bid instead of trying to negotiate with Air Canada. "If Gerry had [used] his traditional method of coming in the front door and offering a fair price, I think he would have gotten it," Milton said. Schwartz had an entry through his friendship with Air Canada chairman Jack Fraser, after all, and Milton suggested that they could have worked together to find a way around the 10-per-cent cap and to determine which airline alliance made the most sense. Ironically, Schwartz has acknowledged that attempting a hostile takeover, rather than negotiating, cost him Labatt.

The office of the federal commissioner of competition is in a government building on the Quebec side of the National Capital Region. From his window on the twenty-first floor, Konrad von Finckenstein could look across to the Parliament Buildings on the other side of a provincial border and the Ottawa River. During the fall of 1999, he was more distant than usual. The imposition of the Section 47 order in mid-August meant that he was temporarily off the airline file. Instead of actively evaluating the two competing merger proposals, von Finckenstein sat powerless on the sidelines, confined to a purely advisory role.

At six-foot-four, von Finckenstein is a commanding figure, but he speaks softly in a thick German accent. He was born in Malchow, Germany, in 1945, just after the country's unconditional surrender to the Allies. His mother became a parliamentarian in the postwar administration, then a diplomat for East Germany. She was posted to Canada when Konrad was sixteen years old. With politics in his blood, it was natural that he should study political science at Carleton University, and then take a degree in law at Queen's University. After working for several years in the Department of Justice in trade and commercial law and serving as chief legal advisor to the 1987 free-trade negotiations, he was named commissioner of competition in 1997.

The commissioner liked to see himself as his own man, operating at arm's length from the federal government and its political imperatives. He knew he had no choice but to accept David Collenette's decision to suspend the competition rules, but he was determined that he would continue to champion their intended effect. "I made it quite clear that, notwithstanding the fact that there is suspension, the Cabinet should not throw competition overboard," von Finckenstein said.

Days after Schwartz unveiled his initial bid, von Finckenstein sent a twenty-seven-page letter to Collenette, warning that a merger would lead to "very significant" competition concerns. He outlined an assortment of measures to minimize those concerns: force the merged carrier to give up some of its prime takeoff and landing slots at Toronto's Lester B. Pearson International Airport; require it to sell its frequent-flyer points to competitors; and make it easier for Canada's charter airlines to provide international service. But these remedies would have only a marginal effect, the commissioner said. In order to promote real competition, the government should make the necessary regulatory changes to allow for increased foreign ownership and competition in the Canadian industry. He suggested that foreign investors be permitted to own up to 49 per cent of the voting shares in a Canadian airline, well above the existing 25 per cent limit. He recommended that carriers from the United States or overseas be allowed to establish airlines that would operate only within Canada. While these would be foreign-owned subsidiaries, they would be required to employ Canadians and to register their aircraft in Canada. His recommendations might have gone even further, but Collenette had specifically said he didn't want to hear any proposals about allowing foreign airlines to travel between Canadian cities, the forbidden cabotage.

Von Finckenstein's regulatory powers were restored in mid-November when the ninety-day suspension period quietly expired, a week after Onex pulled its proposal. Collenette had indicated earlier that any merger would require the approval of both Transport Canada and the Competition

Bureau. Finally, von Finckenstein could sink his teeth into the deal. When his officials studied the details, they saw immediately that Canadian Airlines could not survive beyond the end of the year. The airline had an unmanageable debt-load, bookings had plunged through the autumn, and there was little cash coming in. Von Finckenstein had just two options: he could allow Canadian to go bankrupt and see its assets recycled through bankruptcy court, or he could approve the merger. Neither option would be good for competition, but von Finckenstein decided the latter would be the lesser of two evils. It seemed inevitable that Air Canada would acquire Canadian's assets either way. By negotiating a merger, von Finckenstein hoped to extract some concessions that might bridle Air Canada's dominance.[12]

In presenting Air Canada's alternative to the Onex proposal on October 19, Milton had promised that he would "fully co-operate" with the Competition Bureau and other regulators to ensure that his vision benefited consumers. But just three days after Schwartz's withdrawal, Milton warned a Senate transport committee that government regulators could scuttle the merger if they interfered too heavily. "I'm not willing, and I think it would be inappropriate and unreasonable for you to suggest that I be willing, to accept anything that they say," Milton said.

Negotiations between von Finckenstein and Milton commenced in mid-November. They were tense discussions, coloured by brinkmanship on both sides. The commissioner threatened to block the merger unless Air Canada met Ottawa's terms, while Milton delivered ultimatums to pressure the government to concede to his. "The threat that was clearly hanging over the negotiations was: 'We'll let [Canadian Airlines] go bankrupt. Thousands of Canadians won't be home for Christmas. Thousands of employees will be out of jobs. And it will all be your fault,'" von Finckenstein recalls. He described Milton as a tough negotiator, "blunt and blustery."

Meanwhile, Transport Canada was engaged in separate bargaining with Milton's team. With Collenette quarterbacking behind the scenes, deputy transport minister Margaret Bloodworth secured guarantees that there would be no layoffs or employee relocations for a minimum of two years and that Air Canada would continue to serve small communities for at least three years. Collenette wanted more, and he sensed that Air Canada desired the merger as much as he did. "This was their new Jerusalem. I figured we could get more out of them, because they would not have easily given up on that dream," Collenette said later.

The big prize for the minister would be Air Canada's agreement to sell its regional carriers – Air Ontario, Air BC, Air Nova, and Canadian Regional – thereby creating instant competition. He expected investors would come forward to buy the regionals and use them to build a significant domestic competitor. But Air Canada resisted, again threatening to allow Canadian Airlines to go bankrupt. Collenette was tempted to call Air Canada's bluff, but the prime minister and his cabinet colleagues urged him to quit while he was ahead. "Cooler heads prevailed," Collenette admitted.[13] Air Canada accepted a compromise, keeping its own regional carriers but putting Canadian Regional, acquired as part of the merger, on the block. In the end, Air Canada kept all of its regional carriers when no one was willing to pay fair market value for Canadian Regional.

On December 21, Air Canada received approval from Collenette and von Finckenstein to go ahead with its merger plan. No one was entirely happy with the deal, but everyone could live with it. Air Canada agreed to make some of its prime landing slots at Pearson International Airport available to its competitors and to offer its Aeroplan frequent-flyer points program to its smallest rivals. Milton had pushed hard for permission to launch a low-fare carrier, but he was willing to keep the proposed discounter out of Eastern Canada for a year, allowing potential new carriers a chance to establish themselves. Milton was so confident of the ultimate benefits of the merger that these concessions did not seem onerous. He had what he needed to move ahead with Air Canada's $92-million bid for Canadian Airlines and for a $1.1-billion stock buyback from its own shareholders.

Von Finckenstein was plainly peeved by the ministerial decision to invoke Section 47 in advance of the Onex bid, but he stops short of saying the politicians made a mistake. In the end, the competition commissioner ruled on the fate of the merger, raising the question whether the Section 47 order – which gave Collenette so much grief – had served any purpose after all. Von Finckenstein insists he would have had a stronger hand if he had been able to negotiate with Onex and Air Canada when both proposals were on the table – and when Canadian Airlines wasn't so close to bankruptcy. "Obviously the weaker they are, the more difficult it is for us to impose meaningful conditions," he said.

By the time Air Canada's takeover bid expired on December 23, 1999 – with 82 per cent of Canadian's shareholders having accepted the offer – Canadian Airlines was essentially bankrupt. There wasn't enough cash on hand to meet the Christmas payroll, so Air Canada advanced $30 million to Canadian in exchange for its landing slots at Tokyo's Narita Airport. Air Canada executives had coveted the profitable Asian route for decades. Now that they controlled a near-collapsed Canadian Airlines, they finally secured the jewel in its international network.

Collenette revealed the rest of the government's response to Air Canada's near monopoly in February 2000, when he tabled Bill C-26, "legislation to protect the public interest during the period of airline restructuring." The bill was designed to prevent Air Canada from over-charging on routes where there was no alternative carrier and from using its dominance to squeeze smaller competitors out of the market. It gave unprecedented powers to the commissioner of competition, who could unilaterally order Air Canada to raise its fares temporarily if he believed the airline was being predatory in its pricing – that is, sustaining losses on certain routes in order to put its rivals out of business. The bill also gave the Canadian Transportation Agency the ability to regulate fares on monopoly routes and to address a wide range of consumer complaints.

Critics wondered why Collenette was suddenly so wary of the monopoly he had helped create. If there wasn't room in the market for two national airlines before, why was the minister now so keen to foster competition to that end? As usual, Collenette stuck to his lines. "The government will not tolerate price-gouging," he said. "Our overriding objective is to ensure that we effectively protect consumers from any abuse by a dominant carrier."[14]

At a news conference following introduction of the bill, Collenette mused about allowing foreign carriers to fly Canadian routes within eighteen to twenty-four months if domestic carriers couldn't provide enough competition to Air Canada. "If we have to let the Americans in – if that's the only way that we can get competition – then we'll let the Americans in," Collenette declared. It was a remarkable statement from a nationalist minister who at one time had not been comfortable with even the privatization of Air Canada.

For now, Collenette was content to put his hopes in the few new and expanding Canadian carriers who were rushing to fill the competition gap. Canada 3000, Royal Airlines, and WestJet had all announced plans to grow more quickly in the wake of Air Canada's acquisition of Canadian Airlines. There were new players, too: Roots Air at the luxury end of the market and CanJet on the discount side. Business plans were in development for a number of regional start-ups, among them Alberta's Capital City Air, Manitoba's Great Plains, and Regional Airlines Holdings and London Air in Ontario. Even the notorious Sir Richard Branson was considering a new domestic airline in Canada.[15]

5

FOOLS RUSH IN

Nobody likes competition. Air Canada hates competition. WestJet hates competition. And most importantly, the new entrants don't know how to be competitive, because they end up being kamikazes.[1]

> — Ted Shetzen, executive vice-president, Roots Air

Sir Richard Branson, the flashy British billionaire behind a music and aviation empire, is widely regarded as a marketing genius with more limited abilities when it comes to formulating well-researched business plans. In his 1998 autobiography, *Losing My Virginity*, the self-described "adventure capitalist" boasts that he can make up his mind about a business venture in about thirty seconds. "I rely far more on gut instinct than researching huge amounts of statistics," Branson writes.

Before making the decision in 1984 to launch Virgin Atlantic Airways – using the profits that were pouring into Virgin Music from the sale of Culture Club records – Sir Richard made full use of his thirty seconds. The airline he had in mind would fly to New York from London's Gatwick Airport, the route that had been served by Sir Freddie Laker's Skytrain service until it went out of business in 1982. Branson put in a call to People Express, the only airline offering cheap fares across the Atlantic at that time. The line was constantly busy, which Branson took as a sure sign that it made sense to pump British pounds into the typically unprofitable and unpredictable airline business. He reasoned that People Express was either so poorly managed that it would be an easy target, or there was so much demand for its services that there was room for competition. Nevertheless, he took the extraordinary precaution of making two more calls; better to be safe than sorry. He dialled directory assistance and found a phone number for Boeing in Seattle. At Boeing he tracked down a salesperson who said they would be willing to grant him a short-term, twelve-month lease on a 747. Branson could reduce his exposure to one year just in case – despite all the time he had spent researching the industry – the project ended in failure. Somehow, it didn't.[2]

Virgin Atlantic soon made itself famous for offering business-class travellers such extras as in-flight massages and manicures and for providing each customer in coach with his or her choice of movie on a personal video screen. As the airline grew, it added destinations around the world, checking them off one by one from a list of the most-travelled routes out of London. By 2000, Virgin Atlantic was serving more than twenty cities, including Shanghai, Cape Town, and San Francisco. Although Toronto was one of the top ten destinations out of London, Virgin executives had steered clear of it. Even David Tait, Virgin Atlantic's vice-president for North America and a former Torontonian who had worked at Wardair, saw the city as a dud. He tried to persuade Branson that the route was a money-loser: there was the weak Canadian dollar and it would be hard to steal passengers from Air Canada, which picked up 40 per cent of its passengers from other Canadian cities. Branson was not convinced.[3]

He announced Virgin Atlantic's Canadian debut at a splashy press conference in Toronto in November 2000. With scruffy flaxen hair and a face full of beard, Branson looked every bit the music-business tycoon when he arrived by helicopter, accompanied by two leggy flight attendants, one a blonde, the other a brown-haired Minnie Driver look-alike. Each gave him a peck on the cheek for the cameras. It was a typically cheeky event, the kind that Branson did best. His daring attempts to break speed and distance records by hot-air balloon and boat had already secured his reputation as a flamboyant publicity hog.

Branson donned hockey skates and joined the Etobicoke Dolphins, a local girls hockey team dressed in Virgin Atlantic jerseys.[4] First Sir Richard, then the Dolphins, took turns shooting a puck through the legs of a cardboard goalie draped in an Air Canada jersey. Branson was adopting the role of spunky underdog, just as in Britain, Virgin had positioned itself as a David against British Airways' Goliath.

The stunt was brilliant, but Sir Richard came across as poorly prepared. Asked which airline he had flown to Toronto, Branson scrambled to remember which one had prevailed in the bidding war – was it Air Canada or Canadian Airlines? "Canadian Airlines from New York," he said, then laughed and corrected his answer to Air Canada. In response to another question about low-cost carriers, he was able to recall the name of WestJet Airlines because he had it inscribed on his hand in ink. A Radio-Canada reporter stumped him by asking if Virgin would offer bilingual services on its flights into Canada. "I should have been briefed," Branson quipped as he kept on grinning. Then, the light bulb almost materializing over his head, he sputtered, "Of course! We're in Canada! Of course we'll have –" An associate interrupted to explain that Virgin would likely ask its French-speaking flight attendants to work the London–Toronto route.

Branson declared that Virgin Atlantic would initiate daily service between London and Toronto the following spring, using a Boeing 747 aircraft. He said he might eventually put an Airbus A380 "superjumbo" jet on the route. That elephantine aircraft was still on the drawing board, but Branson mused about fitting the giant planes with casinos, on-board Jacuzzis, and sleeping compartments with double beds. Branson estimated it could take four or five years for the Toronto route to become profitable, but he said he would be "deeply disappointed" if Virgin wasn't flying into Vancouver within three years.

Sir Richard did his best to play up the notion that his airline would compete with Air Canada – even though it would operate only a single route where Air Canada already faced several competitors, including British Airways and Canada 3000. But in a series of interviews after the press conference, Branson confided that he had bigger plans for Canada. If the government allowed it, he would launch a new airline within the country's borders to challenge Air Canada's dominance on domestic routes. It was hard to tell if Branson was serious, or simply serving up another juicy sound bite. Either way, the possibility of a new domestic carrier guaranteed Branson's Toronto appearance front-page play in the *Globe and Mail* and the *National Post*. "We'd definitely give it a go if we could get permission," Branson said. "I think once we've shown the benefits of Virgin Atlantic to the Canadian government, they may open up Canada to allow Virgin to fly internally."

If Sir Richard was sincere about the proposal, he had good reason to be optimistic. The previous spring, transport minister David Collenette had encouraged the Virgin team to go to work on plans for a new Canadian domestic carrier similar to Virgin Blue, the discount airline Branson had recently launched in Australia.[5] In June 1999, Australia had modified its rules to remove the foreign-ownership restrictions on domestic carriers.

From a transportation perspective, there is perhaps no other country more similar to Canada. Each has a relatively small population spread across an enormous land mass. Canada's population is concentrated along the U.S. border; Australia's is generally confined to its outlying coastal areas. The distance between cities makes efficient air travel a necessity in both countries, while a small population base makes it less economical. Australian economists were long perplexed by the absence of price competition. And like their counterparts in Ottawa, Australian politicians had wrestled with airline mergers and the problem of how to ensure competition after the bankruptcy of a major carrier.

Australia embraced deregulation around the same time as Canada did. In 1990, the government got out of the business of approving routes and fares and left those decisions to the open market. But the market was still heavily segmented. The sole international carrier, Qantas, wasn't allowed to serve domestic routes, while Ansett Australia and Australian Airlines couldn't fly internationally. Compass Airlines, the most promising carrier arising out of deregulation, grew quickly, carving out 12 per cent of the domestic market within a year. Compass brought down fares at the low end of the market, as Australian Airlines and Ansett matched its lowest prices. Then, days before Christmas 1991, Compass failed spectacularly, after the government refused a bailout, stranding 125,000 passengers. The

Trade Practices Commission – Australia's equivalent of the Competition Bureau – investigated, but found no indications of predatory pricing by Ansett or Australian. The commission concluded that Compass failed because of shortcomings in its entry strategy and poor management. The airline made a brief resurgence the following year before disappearing for good. The same year, the government allowed Qantas to move into the domestic market by acquiring Australian Airlines, resulting in a comfortable duopoly that lasted for most of the decade.

So comfortable was it, in fact, that Qantas shares plunged 15 per cent on November 29, 1999, when Sir Richard announced plans to take advantage of the looser ownership rules and set up his own airline in that country. The airline was named Virgin Blue because of its red planes: Australians refer to redheads as "blueys." The airline launched service on August 31, 2000, with just two routes, Brisbane to Sydney and Brisbane to Melbourne. Three months later, Branson was in Toronto, saying that he wanted to do something similar in Canada.

Now that Branson had gone public with his intention of launching a Virgin Canada airline, however, David Collenette was not so encouraging. He dismissed Branson's proposal, suggesting that foreign airlines would hurt the made-in-Canada competition that was slowly developing. "The airline industry is a very fragile industry," he said. Governments around the world had protected their domestic airlines for six decades, and Collenette wasn't about to abandon that policy just because Air Canada suddenly owned four-fifths of the domestic passenger market.

"At the moment, the transport minister doesn't favour the extra competition," Branson said mischievously during a visit to Toronto in early 2001. "But our offer is still open if he changes his mind." The British High Commission got into the act, claiming that the cost of blocking foreign competitors was higher airfares for Canadians. But the more Branson lobbied, the stronger the government's resistance. And if their exchanges generated ongoing publicity for Virgin's Toronto–London service, so much the better.

As early as 1994, John Gilmore had approached potential investors with a plan to start a discount airline in Canada, a dream he called CanJet.[6] South of the border, discounters were all the rage – airlines like Dallas-based Southwest and Atlanta-based ValuJet were putting bums in seats with low fares and an irreverent attitude. They were filling their planes with VFRs – Visiting Friends and Relatives – people who previously would have driven cars, taken the bus, or stayed at home. By offering radically lower fares, these upstarts were rewriting the economics of the airline industry, posting healthy profits while traditional full-service airlines were struggling.

Gilmore, a former Air Canada lawyer, believed the Canadian market was ripe for a discounter of its own. There had been modest interest from potential investors, including Toronto's Deluce family, which had invested in the regional Air Ontario and Canada 3000, a charter operation. Bill Deluce even spent a few days in Atlanta to learn about the low-fare model from the people at ValuJet. But he returned home persuaded that the smaller Canadian marketplace could not generate the traffic necessary to make a discount airline viable, according to Gilmore. A disappointed Gilmore shelved his plans, then watched from a distance as a group of Calgary entrepreneurs launched an extremely successful discount carrier in Western Canada. Gilmore hoped the success of WestJet would help revive CanJet's prospects.

In 1998 he dusted off the proposal and found that investors were more receptive this time around. He initiated discussions with John C. Munro Hamilton International Airport about basing the operation out of that underutilized airport. Then came a setback. "The merger buggered us up. We were actually making some fairly good progress towards raising the capital we needed when the Air Canada–Canadian merger came up," Gilmore recalled later. "The first instinct of a good Canadian investment person is not to look at the opportunity created by chaos but to sit back and say we'll see where all the dust settles on it – which left us with about half the money we felt we needed."

Investors knew that, if Air Canada wanted to, it could easily knock a start-up from the skies by slashing its fares or dangling promotional extras like frequent-flyer points. But Gilmore believed that if his fares were low enough – lower even than WestJet's – Air Canada would leave him alone. Low fares would expand the market, rather than steal market share from the dominant carrier. In his mind, the merger created the perfect environment for a new discount carrier. This conviction – and the fact that most of his investors had turned cool – led Gilmore to go cap in hand to Halifax businessman Ken Rowe, one of the richest men in Atlantic Canada.

Born in England, Rowe had trained as a ship's navigator and spent his late teens and early twenties travelling the world on large ships. He loved the sea, but moved into business to make some money. He became a chartered company secretary and worked in management at a British conglomerate until his bosses sent him to Halifax to run the company's fishing supply division. Rowe took to the port city and decided the region's prospects were sound enough to start his own business. Along with some partners, he bought two foundries and shifted them into marine equipment. He bought out the partners a few years later and renamed the operation Industrial Marine Products (IMP). As the company grew and diversified into aerospace, hotels, and medical supplies, Rowe shied away from taking on other partners or entering into joint ventures. "I am IMP and IMP is me," he once said.[7]

Although not well known outside of Atlantic Canada, IMP is the largest private corporation in Nova Scotia and one of the larger aerospace companies in Canada. IMP holds maintenance contracts for military and commercial aircraft and runs a fleet of business jets out of Montreal. Rowe had dabbled in passenger service too. In the early 1980s, IMP operated a small commuter plane between Halifax and Yarmouth, Nova Scotia, but withdrew when it could no longer compete with Air Canada's jet service on the same route. In 1996, Rowe bought Air Atlantic, a regional feeder for Canadian Airlines, but shut the carrier down two years later when he couldn't reach an agreement on terms with Canadian. The Atlantic routes were picked up by Inter-Canadian, a Montreal-based affiliate of Canadian Airlines. Inter-Canadian also hired most of Air Atlantic's workers, a point of pride for Rowe, who likes to brag that he has never laid off an employee.

When John Gilmore approached Rowe in 1999, his managers were working on their own plan for a new airline in Atlantic Canada. Despite Rowe's distaste for partnerships, they decided to try to mesh their radically different business plans. Rowe expected to base his airline in Halifax and to recycle the Air Atlantic name; Gilmore wanted it to operate from Hamilton as CanJet. Rowe proposed to start small and focus on Eastern Canada; Gilmore envisioned an operation that spanned the country. Rowe wanted fares to be lower than Air Canada's, but not necessarily as low as WestJet's; Gilmore said fares had to beat WestJet's. Rowe liked older, cheaper aircraft; Gilmore believed the savings were greater with newer, more fuel-efficient jets.

They tried to paper over their disagreements and pushed ahead. Rowe accepted the CanJet name and that the carrier should be based in Hamilton, but when Gilmore tried to sign a deal for facilities in the fall of 1999, he found that Air Canada had beaten him to the punch. The airline had locked up all the gates and landing slots on October 18, one day before Robert Milton announced his counter-bid to the Onex proposal and his own scheme for a discount airline. CanJet was grounded. "They want to snuff out the competition," Rowe told one reporter. "Their attitude is: 'If we can depress these small players for long enough, they will withdraw.'"[8]

After Air Canada emerged the winner in the takeover battle, however, Ottawa reined in Milton's plans to launch a discount airline out of Hamilton. As a condition of its approval for the merger, the federal government ruled that Air Canada would not be allowed to operate a no-frills subsidiary prior to September 2001, provided another new carrier launched its service in Eastern Canada during 2000. Rowe and Gilmore thought they saw their chance, but in February they halted plans for CanJet again, saying federal legislation did not go far enough in preventing Air Canada from targeting small competitors. Then in April, Rowe revived the airline one more time – without Gilmore. Rowe bought the CanJet name from Gilmore, and returned to his original notion of a Halifax-based airline under a single shareholder.

When Gilmore left, so too did Ed Wegel, an experienced U.S. airline operator, who had been slated to run CanJet. Rowe offered the job to

Mark Winders, a Canadian who was overseeing Cayman Airways in the Cayman Islands. Years before, Rowe had tried to recruit Winders for Air Atlantic when he was working as an executive at Air Canada. Back then, Winders had responded with an emphatic no; he was a loyal member of the Red Team. This time around, Winders felt differently. Balancing Cayman Airways' political needs with economic realities were frustrating, and he was ready for a change. "It was a once-in-a-lifetime opportunity to build something from scratch," Winders said. "I had watched WestJet with a lot of interest and very much admired what the WestJet team had put together, and I believed there was an opportunity in Eastern Canada for a clone of WestJet."

Like Gilmore before him, Winders impressed upon Rowe the importance of emulating the business plan that WestJet had unashamedly copied from Southwest Airlines. Keeping costs under control, turning planes quickly, and keeping staff happy and dedicated would make CanJet a success. Winders also believed that wooing the low-fare passenger – while staying away from the high-revenue business passenger Air Canada depended on – was the best insurance against an aggressive reaction from the big carrier. "My assessment was that it probably made more sense for Air Canada to see CanJet operating in the East than to see WestJet expand to the East," Winders said. "That was the strategic assessment. It turned out not to be the case."

Ted Shetzen likes to talk. His mind is in constant brainstorm, and the words flow fast and unfiltered. His ideas come so furiously that former co-workers at Wardair dubbed him Ted Jetson, after the space-age cartoon family. Some of his ideas are inspired, friends say; many are ridiculous. "The challenge is to figure out which are brilliant and which are not," says Roland Dorsay, a Wardair colleague, "because there's a never-ending stream of them."

Shetzen had made a career of being an ideas man for Canada's major airlines, for Air Canada, CP Air, and Wardair. His customary effusiveness was absent, however, from the voice-mail message he left for Leo Desrochiers in December 1999. He said simply, "It's time."

Those two words were enough to remind Desrochiers that Shetzen had always dreamed of starting a luxury airline for the Canadian business traveller. The imminent merger of Air Canada and Canadian Airlines would create an opening for this particular idea to take flight.

The two men had worked together years earlier at Air Canada. Now Shetzen was a self-employed airline consultant and Desrochiers was working for Skyservice Airlines, a Toronto aviation company. Shetzen invited Desrochiers to ditch Skyservice and work with him on a new airline concept. Desrochiers suggested instead that Shetzen bring his idea to Skyservice, where CEO Russ Payson was actively looking for a novel project, Payson had considered participating in John Gilmore's CanJet, but found it was too much of a WestJet clone to be exciting. But Desrochiers figured there were advantages to adding a new startup onto an existing airline already equipped with the necessary permits and infrastructure.

Shetzen wasn't sold on the idea. Skyservice had an excellent reputation for providing quality charter flights for tour operators, but what vacationers wanted on flights to Cancun was very different from what business travellers expected on flights to Vancouver. Shetzen was also concerned that the airline had no experience with marketing or branding or selling its flights to the public. Skyservice's customer was a middleman tour operator, who bought the seats and then sold them to travellers. Despite his initial reluctance, however, Shetzen pitched the idea to Russ Payson, who was immediately interested.

"Shetzen, I've got to say, is a very good salesman," Payson says. "He's also a very intelligent guy, and he seemed to have all the answers. He seemed to think there was a void in the marketplace for a good quality operator. And as soon as you start talking quality, you attract our attention."

Payson was another industry player who had wanted to be a pilot since boyhood. When poor eyesight denied him a career in the air force, he went to university for degrees in engineering and business and earned a private pilot's licence in his spare time. He bought floundering companies and combined them to form Skyservice, which provided a variety of aviation services, from operating air ambulances to maintaining corporate jets for people like Gerry Schwartz. In 1993, he was approached by Sunquest Vacations and asked to operate charter flights on their behalf. Payson was nervous about establishing an airline, but he struck a deal that minimized his risk. He didn't have to worry about selling the seats. Skyservice was paid a flat rate per flight no matter how many passengers were aboard. "We have always been risk-averse in our strategies," Payson says.

Shetzen and Desrochiers worked quietly for months in a Skyservice office at Toronto's Pearson International Airport. The concept was bold: a luxury airline, not unlike Virgin Atlantic, with gourmet food and exceptional service, more legroom, and a wide array of entertainment options. The airline's spanking new Airbus A320s and A330s would provide three classes of service – gold, silver, and bronze – instead of the two that Air Canada offered. Business travellers would surely flock to the airline for the extra frills. And if the business-class pricing was lower than Air Canada's – and Shetzen believed it could be – the new carrier would establish itself as a genuine alternative to the dominant carrier, which was being referred to more frequently as Air Monopoly. The airline would begin by serving the most popular long-distance routes in Canada, plus a route or two into the United States. Later, after making arrangements with other "customer-service focused" international carriers to swap passengers, the airline would be able to offer Canadian consumers dozens of destinations around the world. Although Shetzen and Desrochiers expected their airline to be hugely successful, they wouldn't allow it to become another Canadian Airlines. It would expand to perhaps eighteen aircraft in three years, but no more. "We're trying to be the small guy," Shetzen explained. "Small is good for us; less is more; but with a level of service that's never been seen before."

There were disagreements almost from the outset over issues like the name of the new airline. Shetzen, the branding expert, pressed for a fresh identity to differentiate it from Skyservice, whose association with "charter" connoted "down-market." Payson insisted that the Skyservice brand would serve just fine, and was insulted that Shetzen suggested otherwise. "I've spent all my life building the Skyservice name," he said indignantly. "Why the hell would I want to re-brand it?" But Shetzen talked and Payson relented.

Shetzen hired Michel Viau of Ove Design & Communications, a Toronto branding company, who came up with hundreds of possible names for the enterprise. Five of them were presented to Payson; none appealed. Viau then proposed another approach: co-branding with an existing label. Nothing you can do in terms of a new identity or a new name, he told them, will be as successful as finding a strategic partner with whom you can do a co-marketing deal. Viau had such a company in mind, one of the country's most valuable brands: Roots Canada Ltd. "They're stores, right?" Payson asked. He had seen Roots clothing before, but had never taken much of an interest. At home that night, he noticed a Roots shopping bag.

"Do you shop there?" he asked his wife.

"Yes, I shop there all the time."

Roots Canada, an athletic- and casual-wear retail chain built by two transplanted Americans, Michael Budman and Don Green, had, over twenty-five years, established a highly desirable profile. In 1998, Roots scored an enormous marketing coup when it was chosen to design the outfits worn by Canadian athletes at the Winter Olympics in Nagano, Japan. After controversial snowboarder Ross Rebagliati wore his Roots Olympic garb on the *Tonight Show* with Jay Leno (Rebagliati had lost his gold medal when traces of marijuana were found in his blood, but had later got it back), "Poor Boy" hats in particular became a sensation. Soon everyone from Rosie O'Donnell to Kevin Costner to Prince William was wearing them. "When people see celebrities, politicians, musicians, athletes wearing the product . . . that helps build demand for the product," Green once said. "It's the way you can impact the most people at once. It's more powerful than advertising."[9]

Russ Payson still wasn't convinced there was anything wrong with the Skyservice name, but if a new name was required, then Roots Air would do. He met with Budman and Green, who were wildly keen on the co-branding idea. Now it was Ted Shetzen's turn to express concerns. Shetzen could see that Roots was a strong brand that resonated with the young, urban, hip crowd, but he wondered how the airline's target market of conservative guys in suits would relate to it. Potential investors also questioned the connection: what did Roots Canada have to do with the airline business? In the end, Shetzen came around to Roots Air. He knew the Roots guys would help create a buzz with their celebrity friends, and it seemed Roots possessed the same sexy cachet as Branson's Virgin Atlantic Airways.

The Roots Air publicity launch in June 2000 generated all the buzz Shetzen could have hoped for. Michael Budman and Don Green were on hand, along with actor Dan Aykroyd. "In the twenty-first century, flying is a necessity," Aykroyd said at a glitzy ceremony in Toronto's Eaton Centre. "However, flying on only one Canadian-based airline does not have to be a necessity any longer." Aykroyd offered that he was considering an investment in the venture, but his involvement might have been seen by some as a bad omen. Four years earlier, in a CBC miniseries about the darkest chapter in Canadian aviation history, the actor had played the role of Crawford Gordon, chief of A.V. Roe, makers of the ill-fated Avro Arrow.

Green declared that the airline was "probably the most exciting thing that's happened to Roots." The deal would put the Roots brand everywhere, its name in giant letters on the side of every aircraft, its famous beaver logo on the back of every seat, a Roots catalog in every seat pocket. Naturally, the crew uniforms would be a Roots design – the pilots in black aviator jackets and the flight attendants in blue and purple. Roots Canada would invest $5 million for 20 per cent of the shares in the new company. The announcement went perfectly, with one notable exception. Shetzen was asked by a reporter whether he owned any Roots clothing. When he answered an honest no, some of his colleagues went ballistic. "Couldn't you have lied?" one asked.

Soon there were other, more serious, concerns. The capital markets, which had been so generous over the past couple of years to anyone with a reasonable business plan, were starting to dry up. "It was definitely becoming harder to raise money," Payson says. "I remember my wife nattering to me, saying if the money isn't there then there's a bigger message. But Ted was so enthusiastic with this thing – it was going to be a slam dunk – that we all just got pulled along." To ease his concerns, Payson toured travel agencies in Toronto and Vancouver. Everywhere he went, the agents spouted vitriol about Air Canada's poor service and corporate high-handedness. If there were another choice, they assured him, travel agents would support it, and so would business travellers. By September, Skyservice had raised $35 million through a private placement, just short of its goal of $40 million.

It wasn't just the capital markets that were shrinking, however. As the economy slowed, so did demand for business travel. How could an airline aimed at corporate Canada have any chance of success when corporate Canada wasn't flying? But according to Shetzen, it was all part of the plan. Roots Air had actually been counting on and hoping for an economic slowdown, he told a reporter in January 2001. "For the business guy who wants an alternative that isn't deep discount and no-frills," he said, "this is the ultimate value equation."[10]

Roots Air's promotional material asked, "What's different about the Roots Air cabin experience? A better question might be, what's not different." Prospective passengers were also advised, "With cuisine this delicious, you'll want to cancel the dinner reservations you made on land."

They started selling tickets in early February for a March 26 launch, and initial sales were highly encouraging to Payson. People really wanted to fly on Roots Air. But when he studied the bookings more carefully, he saw that almost all were for the cheap, bronze-class seats at the back of the plane. Few were buying the gold- and silver-class seats – the expensive seats that would make the difference between profit or massive financial failure. Shetzen told him not to worry, no one made business-class bookings more than ten days before a flight. Payson waited, but the business-class bookings still didn't materialize. There were other problems, too. One of the Airbus A320s was configured with just two classes of seats – like Air Canada's planes – instead of the three classes that were supposed to set Roots Air apart. Another aircraft wasn't delivered at all, resulting in the cancellation of flights.

Early reviews of the new airline were mixed. Jonathan Gatehouse, a *National Post* reporter, found that the airline largely lived up to its promise of frills and style, especially in the airline's first-class lounge. "Coffee tables are strewn with glossy picture books with titles such as *Yoga for You*, *The Story of Golf*, and *Bruce Mau's Lifestyle*. China dishes piled high with perfect pyramids of green apples were placed on the ledges of the floor-to-ceiling windows."[11] He said passengers appeared content with the experience, despite some "minor shortcomings," such as a breakfast entrée that was a little dry. But *Vancouver Sun* reporter Daphne Bramham was disturbed to learn that, because the plane hadn't been configured properly, her $808.62 one-way silver-class ticket didn't buy her anything more than could be had for a $323 round-trip economy ticket. "For five times the price, as the plane is configured, 40 business-class passengers sit in the same-sized seats and eat the same food as 66 people in economy class. They have none of the extras that luxury liners promise, such as computer connections or a choice in movies." Bramham complained that there was no coffee in the executive lounge and that it took far too long to be checked in by the smiley people in raspberry-and-grey uniforms.[12]

"You only have one opportunity in this business to make a first impression," Shetzen said later. "And boy, did we fuck that up."

If there was one thing that might have given the Roots Air founders solace, it was that they weren't the only ones providing disappointing customer service.

6

MILTON'S PARADISE LOST

An open letter to Robert Milton, Air Canada CEO: Dear Bob, Your freaking airline totally sucks. Sincerely, Everyone.[1]

— Scott Feschuk, *National Post*

Astrologers would have predicted a match made in heaven. Air Canada was born on April 10, 1937, when King George VI gave royal assent to the Trans-Canada Air Lines Act. The Blue Team's lineage can be traced back to the birth of Western Canada Airways on December 10, 1926, when James Richardson founded the carrier with a $200,000 investment. Those born under the signs of Aries and Sagittarius are highly compatible: always ready to take on the next adventure, never holding a grudge; quick to forgive and forget. Pairings of rams and centaurs are among the most favoured on the horoscope. But there are risks: Arians and Sagittarians are great at starting projects but not at following through; and both focus on the big picture to the detriment of the details. Theirs can be an accident-prone relationship.

Robert Milton also looked to the stars and forecast heavenly benefits for investors. Company spreadsheets promised that Air Canada would realize $700 million to $900 million in annual savings through its acquisition of Canadian Airlines. Rationalizing the schedules alone would reduce costs by $225 million annually, while another $358 million would be found when commissions paid to travel agents were lowered and the significant discounts Canadian Airlines gave to its corporate customers were slashed. Other economies would come from trimming food costs, consolidating airport operations, and carrying debt at lower interest rates than Canadian Airlines had been charged.

On May 17, 2000, Milton and his senior vice-presidents met with financial analysts in Montreal to brief them on the anticipated synergies. The analysts were already bullish on Air Canada stock, which was trading at about $18 a share, up from $8 in January. The next day, most analysts published glowing reports, recommending that their clients buy Air Canada shares. Kevin Murphy, an analyst with Morgan Stanley Dean Witter, noted that even with the recent run-up in Air Canada's share price, its stock still traded at a discount compared with other non-U.S. airlines, which tended to operate in less competitive environments than American carriers. James David, an analyst with UBS Bunting Warburg, predicted that Air Canada's management would surpass its goal of $900 million in savings, estimating gains in the $1-billion to $1.2-billion range. Yorkton Securities analyst Jacques Kavafian set a $35 target price for the shares, suggesting they would trade at that level within twelve months. The impact of the analysts' reports on the share price was immediate. Shares shot up $2.30 on May 18 to close at $19.90 in heavy volume on the Toronto Stock Exchange.[2]

At a meeting with the *Globe and Mail*'s editorial board on May 30, Milton outlined a bold and rosy vision for the Air Canada of the future. He mused about adding direct flights to ten new destinations on at least four continents, adding 15,000 new employees, and upgrading the airline's fleet with as many as 150 new aircraft. In addition to establishing a new discount airline, he was considering a dedicated fleet of cargo jets. "We are not going to be bashful at expanding anywhere in the world that we think we can provide an attractive return," Milton said.[3]

The stars seemed to be in perfect alignment. All signs suggested that Robert Milton's Air Canada was on a sure, quick track to success. But occasionally the stars can be terribly wrong. The marriage of Air Canada and Canadian Airlines was one of those times.

Four months earlier, in January, 2000, a numbered company affiliated with Air Canada took up the shares of Canadian Airlines. It was an unusual ownership structure, one designed to insulate Air Canada while it went to court to try to get off the hook for some of Canadian Airlines' debts. The Calgary-based carrier had been forced to pay a risk premium in order to borrow money, lease planes, and purchase supplies and services. Air Canada sought relief from these surcharges now that Canadian was under new ownership. Canadian had also granted generous discounts to keep its corporate accounts from jumping to the competition. Air Canada now disputed any obligation to honour such discounts.

Milton needed his own man at Canadian's Calgary offices to oversee the fiscal belt-tightening. In January, he sent Paul Brotto, who had held a variety of management jobs at Air Canada over a thirty-year career. Kevin Benson, who had worked tirelessly for the merger, stepped aside on February 29. "There is no room for two captains in the cockpit," Benson wrote to employees. "The past few years are ones that I would never have wanted to miss, but I sincerely hope I will never have to repeat. I leave with some very powerful memories, not of the sweaty days and nights when we tried to find the right answer."[4] With Benson's departure, Brotto became Canadian's last president and chief executive officer. His number-one priority was cost control, and expenses fell quickly as he and Milton applied pressure by threatening – once again – to let Canadian Airlines slide into bankruptcy.

In June 2000, after Air Canada executives had struck deals with most of the major stakeholders in Canadian Airlines, a Calgary judge approved a restructuring plan for the carrier under the Companies' Creditors Arrangement Act. In a press release, Robert Milton said he was "delighted" with the outcome, which would provide Canadian Airlines with the "stability" necessary to combine the two carriers. "Our focus," Milton said, "remains firmly fixed on a successful integration of the two carriers for our customers, employees, and all of Canada."

Politicians must have wondered what he meant by "integration." This was something new. The previous fall, he had assured members of parliament that, unlike Gerry Schwartz, he would not merge the airlines. Instead, he had insisted he wanted to keep Canadian alive as a separate brand with its own management team, board of directors, and Calgary headquarters. At the time, Milton believed he could squeeze most of the benefits from his acquisition without a full merger. The two carriers were flying half-empty planes against each other in many parts of the country. Simply integrating the schedules would allow him to eliminate those redundant flights and use the aircraft elsewhere. By serving a new city in the United States, for example, Milton could turn two half-empty planes into two nearly-full planes.

Milton had been loath to rush into a full merger, because he knew how difficult it would be to combine two enormous and cash-strapped carriers. He had seen hasty airline mergers in the United States create customer-service nightmares, and he hoped to avoid those mistakes. Besides, if the idea of maintaining two separate carriers created the illusion of competition and won him points from consumers and government, so much the better. With the takeover fight behind it, however, Air Canada began to reassess some of the commitments it had made in the heat of battle. Milton came to see that a complete merger of Air Canada and Canadian — perhaps two to three years down the road — might be inevitable and desirable after all.

The threat of allowing Canadian Airlines to go bankrupt had been a powerful negotiating tactic with suppliers and creditors, but these gains had come at a price. While Canadian's costs dropped, so too did revenues as nervous customers migrated en masse to Air Canada. Corporate clients likewise defected to Air Canada when they no longer enjoyed the deep discounts they had come to expect from Canadian. Paul Brotto tracked the airline's ticket sales and saw that the trend was only getting worse. In late January, he flew to Montreal to deliver an urgent message to his boss. "We can't wait two to three years," Brotto told Milton. "This thing is going to suck up billions. We've got to smash the two companies together by September. October at the latest."[5]

And smash they did. Milton had to set aside his qualms and move into full-blown merger mode. An operations plan designed to unfold over years was suddenly reduced to weeks. The integration of flight schedules, originally slated for late 2000 following the amalgamation of computer systems and workforces, was moved up to April. Air Canada touted the move as a great boon for customers, who would see a reduction in over-lapping flights and consequently more choice.

What customers saw instead was a reduction in every standard of the airline's service: confusion at check-in counters, an epidemic of lost baggage, insufferable wait times at call centres, and ever more delayed flights. Customer files were lost between the two airlines' independent reservations systems. There were mix-ups at some U.S. airports when Canadian had to switch terminals, because it was no longer an alliance partner of American Airlines. Patrons took out their frustrations on front-line workers, who sometimes retaliated in kind. "Airline Complaints Pour In – Air Canada Clerk Tells Passengers to 'Shut Up,'" tut-tutted a headline on the front page of the *Toronto Star*.

Several ill-timed factors contributed to the crisis. There was a higher-than-usual number of bad-weather days in the summer of 2000, as well as the threat of a strike during well-publicized contract negotiations with Air Canada's pilots. Passenger traffic soared, just at a time when the airline was shifting capacity out of its domestic market. And Air Canada chose the summer of 2000 to amalgamate its operations at Toronto's Pearson International Airport, the airline's busiest hub. The airport then comprised three distinct terminals, separated from each other by a five-minute drive. Canadian Airlines had operated its flights out of Terminal 3, while Air Canada had operated out of Terminal 2. With amalgamation, the flights of both were split between Terminals 1 and 2, often leaving customers and cab drivers unsure where they were supposed to be at the massive airport.

But the most serious problems arose from the fact that the workforces at the two airlines had not yet been integrated. Clauses in collective agreements prevented Air Canada workers from serving Canadian Airlines passengers. Despite the merged schedules, there remained sepa-rate queues at check-in counters. Passengers joined long lineups at the Air Canada counter, while Canadian Airlines employees twiddled their thumbs a few metres away. Two hours later, the Canadian desk might be a hundred passengers deep, while the Air Canada aisle was empty. Although less visible to the travellers, there were similar problems on the tarmac, where Air Canada workers were unable to load bags onto Canadian Airlines planes. Such anomalies did nothing to improve Air Canada's on-time performance, nor the public's perception of what life would be like under an Air Canada monopoly. "We knew that by rushing that quickly we were going to make some mistakes," Brotto recalls. "When I look at the summer of 2000, it was the summer from hell."

Things were bad in Canada's skies, but Canadians could take solace in the fact that they were not alone. The year 2000 is remembered as one of the toughest for American passengers as well. United Airlines cancelled hundreds of flights because of a contract dispute with its pilots. And, like Air Canada, all U.S. airlines struggled with weather delays and an unexpected surge in passenger traffic in the final days of a red-hot economy. Bookings were up so dramatically in the summer of 2000 that Robert Milton joked that what he really needed was a recession.

If the situation was disconcerting for Air Canada's customers, it was much worse for its employees. In strictly financial terms, most unionized employees benefited from the merger. Workers at Canadian Airlines got substantial raises to give them parity with their new colleagues, while most workers at Air Canada received "loyalty" bonuses for agreeing to concessions to hasten the marriage. But many felt the extra dollars didn't compensate for the emotional turmoil. Not only were they facing the wrath of patrons fed up with merger-related snafus, they also had to deal with the integration on a personal level. The merger brought together two workforces that had been locked in competitive combat for decades, and the struggle between Onex and Air Canada had only intensified that rivalry.

"Air Canada is the dragon," one Canadian Airlines worker had told the *National Post* when it appeared Onex would win the day. "We've slain the dragon. All we're waiting for now is to put its head in the guillotine and let Chrétien pull the cord." Air Canada pilot Raymond Hall had countered that the Onex proposal was "repugnant," because it would make "Air Canada employees pay for the mismanagement of Canadian Airlines."[6] Such sentiments did not augur well for a collegial working environment at ticket counters or in the cockpit.

Unionized personnel at both airlines were worried about the implications for their seniority and career prospects. Seniority is critically important to airline workers, because theirs is a twenty-four-hours-a-day, seven-days-a-week environment, with bases across the country. An abruptly lower position on the seniority list could trigger a forced relocation or an endless stream of weekend shifts. And in a business that peaks in the summer, at Christmas, and over March break, only a select few at the top of the list are allowed vacations when their kids have time off. The stakes are higher still for pilots, whose seniority determines the type of aircraft they can fly and whether they sit in the captain's seat or the first officer's chair. In the male-dominated world of commercial airline pilots, size matters. Status truly depends on the size of the equipment, and so does the pay.

Not surprisingly, the two airlines' employees held sharply divergent views about how their respective seniority lists should be combined. Air Canada workers argued that, since their employer had rescued Blue Team members from certain bankruptcy, the incoming employees should go to the bottom of the seniority list. Canadian Airlines wanted integration based solely on years of service, a formula the Blue Team had applied in the past when PWA acquired CP Air and Wardair. This approach favoured workers from Canadian Airlines, which had done little hiring during the late 1990s, while Air Canada had been growing.

Air Canada officials tried to stay out of the fray and leave the seniority debate to the unions to resolve. But most unions were equally reluctant to take a stand: CUPE, the CAW, and the IAM represented employees at both carriers. In the end, there was little consistency or harmony achieved. Air Canada's ticket agents fumed when their list was based on years of service, while Canadian Airlines pilots protested at Air Canada's annual general meeting after an arbitrator arrived at a list that seemed to favour Air Canada workers. There was even a whisper campaign suggesting that the seniority ruling had caused one Canadian Airlines pilot to commit suicide. The issue would simmer for years afterwards, leaving the airline with a sharply divided workforce and a vulnerability that would return to haunt it.

On May 4, 2000, the presidents of Air Canada and Canadian Airlines appeared together before the House of Commons transport committee in Ottawa. Paul Brotto spoke first, doing his best to assure the parliamentarians that he was in charge at Canadian. Yes, the Calgary-based carrier was coordinating scheduling and marketing with Air Canada, but he had his own mandate. The MPs wanted to know if Robert Milton was keeping his word that Canadian Airlines would be operated as a separate brand. Brotto answered vaguely, saying that Canadian would be run separately "for a period of time . . . but not in competition with Air Canada, in co-operation with Air Canada." He also acknowledged and apologized that "the most massive re-engineering we've ever had in this country" had resulted in a customer-service mess.

Milton began with a brief presentation designed to suggest a kinder, gentler airline, far from the smug former Crown corporation familiar to MPs. He did not refer to his earlier commitments concerning Canadian's independence, saying only that he intended to merge the two carriers as quickly as he could. But he would be sensitive. He was proud of his workers and proud of Canada, and he cared about getting the merger right. He even cared about "the important role of parliamentarians" in the process. "I care about every community we serve, and I care about the enormous legacy of trust that binds Air Canada to its proud history as one of Canada's flag-carriers. We are now charting a new course in this history and I want this legacy to reflect that we care."

The parliamentarians were in no mood for Milton's spin. For weeks their constituents had been complaining about big, bad Air Canada. So too had the citizens' and business groups who had appeared before the committee, organizations like the Association of Canadian Travel

Agents and the Canadian Association of Airline Passengers, a loose affiliation of left-leaning lobby groups. Members of parliament from all five political parties were itching to roast the airline and its public face, Robert Milton.

"As you gave your speech," Liberal MP Joe Fontana told him, "I was visualizing a white knight, violins in the background, the Canadian national anthem, and how you're not being appreciated for all of the darn good things you're doing." Fontana suggested Air Canada was delivering a product far different from that promised the previous year when it was under siege from Onex. "When we began the process, you said you were going to be considerate of Canadians, especially Canadian customers. From what we've been hearing from the customers, our mayors, our communities, and the competitors, Mr. Milton, I'm sorry, but the story is not as you see it or say it."

Dropping his conciliatory opening tone, Milton became defensive. "I think we're in a mode right now where we could do a relief flight to an earthquake zone and be ridiculed by people like those sitting around this table," he told Fontana. When another MP suggested Air Canada was rushing the merger process, Milton reminded the committee that Canadian Airlines had lost $2 million a day in the first quarter of the year. "Is the government going to give us half a billion dollars to take our time?" Milton asked.

Canadian Alliance MP Val Meredith took him to task for strong-armed attempts to squelch competitors. NDP member Bev Desjarlais charged bad-faith negotiating tactics with the unions. She wanted to know why Air Canada was signing contracts with union locals representing employees at Canadian Airlines, but not with those at Air Canada. Their exchange was typical of the hostile atmosphere.

Desjarlais: Have you made that agreement, where you signed with one side and not the other?
Milton: No. Essentially, that was all linked. So we go back to the drawing board and we talked to the CAW and the employees on how to make this thing work. That has been our focus. I want —

Desjarlais: So there are no deals being arranged with one side and not the other? Is there a deal being arranged with one side and not the other?
Milton: I can go [union] by union. It's not a straightforward answer. For example, the IAM –
Desjarlais: Mr. Milton, how can it not be a straightforward answer? Are you arranging a deal with one side and not the other?
Milton: Please let me finish. . . .

The politicians were frustrated by what they saw as Milton's arrogance in refusing to answer simple questions with simple answers. Milton regarded the politicians as grandstanders, more interested in press coverage than an understanding of the issues. Confronted by an emotional barrage from Liberal MP Lou Sekora, Milton simply declined to be engaged.

Sekora: You know, with everything you do you just hurt, hurt, hurt and destroy, destroy, destroy. Mr. Milton, this must come to a stop. I'll tell you, I'm willing to sit here for the next few months on this committee, and if I see for one minute that we're not moving ahead, that we're going backwards – destroying cities and communities, the businessmen, the travellers, the tourist bureaus – I'll be delighted to make a motion on this floor that we open up the skies in Canada. I'll be the first one to do it, my friend.
Milton: Obviously, I appreciate your view. Perhaps Calin [Rovinescu] can respond to that. I'm feeling a little hungry right now, so I'm not sure if I'm up to answering those questions.

Milton's reference to his appetite was probably a subtle gibe: Sekora had been quoted in that morning's *National Post* as saying he was looking forward to taking on Milton at the committee. "I'll be having him for a sandwich," Sekora vowed.

Milton's grilling at the Commons committee was only a prelude to the heat at Air Canada's annual general meeting two weeks later.

Shareholders – who usually favour low costs and high prices – went after Milton for excessive price-gouging and deplorable customer service. "You may be short of staff, but you're treating Canadian passengers with disdain and not dealing with them fairly and honestly," said one shareholder and frequent flyer. Milton apologized emphatically for disappointing his customers, and promised to fix the problem as soon as possible. But he was not humbled. "There are issues, and if people want to throw insult after insult or cream pies, whatever they want to throw at me, they can, because I believe in what I'm doing." Even if everyone else seemed to be telling him he was wrong.

The cream pies were coming from all directions. Peter C. Newman, one of Canada's best-known business journalists, urged Canadians to give Air Canada the finger, figuratively speaking, after recounting the tale of a Victoria cardiologist who had been thrown off an Air Canada flight for directing the gesture at a flight attendant.[7] The *Globe and Mail* published a story on its front page, detailing a litany of customer-service crimes, under the headline "Travellers Curse Airline Merger." The *National Post* responded a few days later with its own front-page story, quoting Prime Minister Jean Chrétien on the matter. "Now that we have only one carrier, this is causing some problems," Chrétien said. "Members in the caucus have mentioned that to me, the premiers have mentioned that to me, so we have to make sure that Air Canada provides proper services under the circumstances." Even Gerry Schwartz could not resist a bit of *schadenfreude*. At Onex's May 11 general meeting, a shareholder congratulated him for losing the bidding war. "When I think about it now, I bet Mr. Milton wishes we had [won]," Schwartz replied.

The media found anecdotes that allowed Canadians to feel justified in their dislike of Air Canada. They learned from the *National Post* that a travelling one-man band had been forced to cancel a show at an Ontario school after Air Canada lost $14,000 worth of music equipment. "Air Canada and its new monopoly," the story began, "were being blamed for the long faces on 350 disappointed children at a Toronto-area elementary school yesterday." The musician, Michael Mitchell, accused the airline of taking a cavalier attitude. "How unfortunate that a show that seeks to inspire confidence and patriotism through recognition of our national icons has been deflated by an organization like Air Canada, which holds itself to be one of our most prominent industrial icons," Mitchell lamented.

The *Toronto Star* noted that Air Canada had misplaced sports equipment belonging to touring Olympic athletes. "Reigning world whitewater kayaking champ David Ford of Edmonton is among those who have no faith in the airline, which lost teammate Jamie Cartwright's canoe on a recent trip to Europe," the story read. Ford explained that three World Cups leading up to the Sydney Olympics had been "completely destroyed" for Cartwright because Air Canada couldn't get his boat to Europe.

Then there was the story about a Bobcaygeon, Ontario, senior citizen who was left on hold for thirteen hours and fifteen minutes. *Globe and Mail* travel columnist Douglas McArthur reported that the trouble began for Diane Tilley when she made a tentative booking to Hawaii, which she needed to confirm within forty-eight hours. She called back the next morning at 8:30, but was asked to wait for a customer-service representative. She stayed on hold until 2:00 in the afternoon, when she hung up because of other commitments. She tried again that night at 10:30, but heard the same recorded voice asking her to stay on the line. "She did, falling into a fitful sleep with a pillow holding the phone to her ear. At 6:15 a.m., a reservations agent answered and completed the booking." When Tilley complained, she received a letter of apology and a $50 voucher good for a future flight.

During the first six months of 2000, the Canadian Transportation Agency, the federal airline regulator, received 257 written complaints about Canada's airlines, compared with 162 during all of 1999. While the agency didn't break down the complaints by airline, the majority were believed to be related to Air Canada. "Consumers shouldn't have to take this crappy service lying down, so I'm glad they're complaining," said Jennifer Hillard, vice-president of the Consumers' Association of Canada, in mid-July.[8]

Over the summer months, Air Canada appeared in five or six news stories a day, compared with one or two daily before the Onex bid, according to the airline's own media scanning service. And Milton himself had become the focal point for much of that coverage, according to Doug Port, then vice-president of corporate affairs. "Onex made Robert Milton a name that's known at every kitchen table across the country, which is great in one sense, but the legacy of that reputation and that profile carried through as Air Canada tried to come to grips with the reality of integrating these two companies."

Heroism, the cliché goes, is anathema to the Canadian psyche. Canadians view themselves as humble people, uncomfortable with too much success. For a nation fed up with the customer-service foibles at Air Monopoly, Milton was the perfect candidate for public vilification. But his fall from grace was remarkably quick, even by Canadian standards. Six months earlier, he had been hailed as a hero in Canadian business circles for scoring a victory over a seemingly unbeatable opponent, winning a legal and public-relations fight against formidable odds. Now he was being treated like a failure by the media and elected officials. The fact that Milton was American-born mattered again. The merger of Air Canada and Canadian was a shambles, and Robert Milton, the Yankee import, was to blame.

A few months before, in January, Milton and his wife, Lizanne, had become Canadian citizens. It wasn't a PR ploy, but a decision that was important to the couple, whose two children were Canadian nationals and knew no other home. Milton has joked that his wife will let him pursue any career opportunity in the world – as long as it's in Montreal. There was a certain pathos to Milton's plight. The plane-spotting boy wonder, who had grown up in a host of foreign locales, had chosen Canada as his home, only to be reviled by the Canadian people. It didn't help that Milton was brusquely dismissive of criticism, a response that struck his critics as presumptuous, aggressive, and just plain arrogant.

Milton was uncomfortable in the summer of 2000 and so was David Collenette. It was not lost on Canadians that the minister had opened the door to this chaotic merger with his decision to suspend the competition laws a year earlier. Under attack, Collenette resorted to a reliable method of coping with political crisis and deflecting blame: he appointed others to stand in the line of fire. Collenette named Debra Ward, the former president of the Tourism Industry Association of Canada, as an "independent observer" of the airline-restructuring process. Her job was to spend two years watching Canada's airlines and then prepare a report for the minister.

To placate irate consumers, Collenette looked for a complaints czar. Bob Kilger, a Liberal MP and former National Hockey League referee, recommended Bruce Hood, another former NHL ref, whose long career had made him as well known as many players. After hanging up his skates, Hood published a book on his officiating years, and he owned and operated a chain of travel agencies. This, and his quick, whistle-blowing justice, arguably qualified him to be the country's first air travel complaints commissioner. "I thought he was good, number one, because he would be seen as somebody of substance. The ordinary person could relate to hockey and a hockey referee," Collenette explained later. "And he was in the travel business." Hood also exhibited the kind of folksy charm that was regarded as a valuable asset in Ottawa.

Collenette announced Hood's appointment at a press conference in Ottawa on August 1. On the minister's advice, Hood produced a ref's whistle at the press conference and gave it a healthy blast. The photo ran in newspapers across the country the next day. "I've been a raging lunatic at the airport, let me tell you, with my luggage lost and the lights out and nobody around to tell you anything," Hood said. "I kind of look at it as an opportunity to blow the whistle on the airlines."

A few weeks earlier, Air Canada had appointed its own complaints ombudsman, Michelle Perreault-Ieraci, a twenty-five-year veteran of Air Canada who had held positions as director of social rights and director of employment equity and linguistic affairs. The role was created under duress. Milton had initially spoken against the idea, but relented under mounting criticism of Air Canada's service. Perreault-Ieraci's office was located outside Air Canada's headquarters to give the appearance of independence. However, she reported directly to Robert Milton. "She's a nice lady," Bruce Hood remarked, "but she's still got the Air Canada logo all over her body."

Milton expected Perreault-Ieraci to be Air Canada's liaison with Hood, but the commissioner insisted on a personal interview with him soon after his appointment. Hood attended the meeting alone, rejecting recommendations from colleagues that he take along officials from the Canadian Transportation Agency. When he asked how Air Canada was dealing with its customer-service crisis, Milton responded that there was no crisis. The airline provided terrific service to the vast majority of its customers, he said. When Hood interrupted to raise a specific customer complaint, the CEO became indignant. "He wasn't really there to listen to me. He was there to preach the gospel about Air Canada and its methodologies," Hood recalls.

Milton was equally blunt in his assessment of Hood and his office. In a 2002 interview, he referred to Hood as a "non-event" and his office as a "circus sideshow," adding that the appointment of an airline complaints commissioner was an example of wasted resources in a country that needed less government, not more. "If Air Canada doesn't deal with its customers properly, other airlines will grow and grow and grow and grow. It's that basic. You don't need some ombudsman."

At the time of Hood's appointment, Milton was preparing his own response to Air Canada's summer from hell. He knew the airline's service had suffered, but his team was working to resolve those problems. In his view, the real issue wasn't customer service, it was public relations. From where he sat in his corner office at Montreal's Dorval Airport, this merger was progressing quickly and painlessly, especially when compared to previous airline mergers in the United States and Europe. Air Canada's main problem was that the media had blown a few unfortunate incidents out of proportion. He had heard stories of reporters trolling airports for angry passengers, but ignoring those who had favourable comments. The airline was carrying record passenger loads during the summer of 2000, sometimes more than 120,000 passengers a day. If Air Canada bungled just 1 per cent of those passengers, there might be 1,200 complainers ready and willing to talk to the press. But Milton believed that the other 99 per cent of passengers had no problems with Air Canada's service. The media, Milton said, "created and fostered this view that flying on Air Canada was a difficult exercise, and it wasn't. The reality was not so."[9]

The perception needed correcting. In late June, Doug Port enlisted the help of Luc Lavoie, a former TV journalist turned public-relations consultant, who had won accolades for his efforts on behalf of former prime minister Brian Mulroney after he had been wrongly implicated in the RCMP's investigation of illegal commissions on the sale of Airbus jets to Air Canada. For this assignment, Lavoie studied Air Canada's customer surveys and found that satisfaction levels were dropping from bad to worse, as was the airline's image in media coverage. Lavoie was alarmed, but he found the Red Team in denial about the severity of the problem. Instead of owning up to their shortcomings, they blamed everybody else – the government, the press, the weather, the unions. But there was hope: Lavoie found Milton to be a man who was passionate about his company, and committed to fixing its shortcomings.

Lavoie told Air Canada's executives in no uncertain terms that they had a serious credibility problem. The public believed that the airline made serious mistakes, but was indifferent to the inconvenience and discomfort suffered by travellers as a result. He proposed an elaborate and expensive advertising campaign with a simple message: Air Canada is going through a tough time. Robert Milton and his team are doing everything they can to fix it. There's an end in sight.

"People want to hear you admit that you've got a problem," Lavoie told them. "They know you do. You know you do. But somehow you never say so."[10] Lavoie proposed a campaign built around a commitment to complete the merger and improve customer service in one hundred days. Air Canada would take responsibility for its foul-ups, explain how the damage was being repaired, and commit to a date by which the job would be done. Milton liked the idea, but his people couldn't guarantee solutions in one hundred days. The integration of computer systems for frequent-flyer programs, for example, was scheduled to take another six months. As a result, the hundred-day notion became a 180-day plan.

Lavoie envisioned Milton front and centre as the spokesman for the campaign, but insiders like Doug Port raised objections. Their feeling was that Milton had become well-known for all the wrong reasons in recent months; wouldn't it be better for Air Canada's image to have a spokesman who wasn't such a large target?

Lavoie intended to make Milton's controversial profile work to Air Canada's advantage. If Milton wasn't the front man, he argued, people would think the airline was hiding its general – or worse, that Milton himself didn't have confidence in Air Canada's ability to right its wrongs. He also believed that Milton's aggressive speaking style would work well on TV. He urged Milton to trust in his instincts over the advice of his own executives.

Although he had his doubts, Milton deferred to Lavoie, and agreed to put his personal reputation on the line in a series of television and print advertisements. He promised change and declared, "You've got my word on it." Lavoie not only produced the ads, but also the "180-day Bible," a detailed timeline that specified when each piece of the merger puzzle would be completed.

The 180-day scheme was made public on August 3, two days after Bruce Hood was named Air Travel Complaints Commissioner. If Robert Milton's wasn't quite a household name before the television ads aired, it certainly was one after. In the midst of the campaign, Milton was having some decorating done at his Westmount home. He asked the painters when they thought they would be done. "Before 180 days," they quipped.

The negotiations with Air Canada's pilots represented a potential stumbling block. Lavoie warned that, if a strike were called in the middle of the 180-day campaign, he and Milton would be laughingstocks. They were both relieved when Air Canada was able to settle the contract dispute without a strike on August 29.

Air Canada achieved two critical milestones midway through the 180-day schedule. On September 29, the airline reached an agreement with the Canadian Auto Workers, which allowed the integration of customer-service staff. This eliminated separate check-in lines for the two carriers. It was a significant breakthrough, but one that came at a price.

Buzz Hargrove insisted on, and Milton agreed to, iron-tight guarantees against layoffs. Then, on October 21, millions of computer-reservations files were merged without a hitch. "I don't want to sound arrogant, but, man, we are good," Milton told the *Globe and Mail*. "There is no doubt in my mind that this is going to work before the 180 days are over."[11]

Milton caught his public-relations department by surprise a few days later when he told reporters that the smooth operation of the reservations system would allow him to complete the 180-day plan two months early. "I'll up the ante on the whole thing. We'll have it done by the end of November," he bragged. "You hold me to it."

The sudden acceleration left PR officials scrambling to explain to reporters that not *every* element of the plan could be completed by the end of November. But at the 120-day mark, most industry observers acknowledged that Milton had delivered on his fast-tracked plan. Air Canada's customer-service surveys showed that public perception was shifting even more quickly. Lavoie had predicted that the 180-day campaign would stabilize customer-satisfaction numbers in short order, but that it would take six weeks for the downward trend to reverse itself. In fact, the numbers began to swing back within days. The media scrutinized the airline's performance, but could find little reason to quibble. Air Canada would continue to have its share of unhappy passengers, but it had overcome the worst of its merger-related crimes.

Lavoie regards the Air Canada campaign as one of the most successful he has ever been involved in. But Milton's aides still question the decision to trot their boss in front of the cameras. Doug Port says Milton was once again portrayed as the aggressive boss-man. "The word 'arrogant' was used," Port says. "Robert came out not unscathed, in my view."

The 180-day sprint was over at the end of January 2001. Milton could turn his attention from Air Canada's internal issues to the company's main external threat: WestJet Airlines. Two years earlier, Air Canada had seriously considered an unusual strategic alliance with WestJet, by which it would have retreated from a number of short-haul routes in Western

Canada. Milton had opposed that plan, championed by former CEO Lamar Durrett and CFO Rob Peterson. To Milton it made more sense to fight than to surrender. Now he intended to enter the lists.

In late January, Milton asked the Air Canada Pilots Association for some flexibility in his efforts to set up a discount carrier. The so-called "Low Cost Co." had been a sticking point in contract negotiations the previous summer. The union negotiators had agreed to allow their pilots to fly Air Canada's discount airline for reduced wages, but the carrier would be limited to just six aircraft, and it would be able to grow only the rest of the company grew along with it. Milton wanted the union to accept a larger discount operation. With signs that the economy was starting to slow and WestJet continuing to expand, the discount option was increasingly vital.

When the union balked at his request, Milton took his appeal directly to the membership. On February 22, he sent an ominous letter to the pilots, in which he painted a picture of an airline under siege. "In just four years, short haul routes in the west have become the most unprofitable in our system," Milton wrote. "This is not due to too few passengers, rather our customers are simply not willing to pay higher prices when they have a lower cost alternative." He pointed out that WestJet was on track to have fifty-five aircraft in its fleet before the end of 2004, which would make it as large as Canadian Airlines in its final days, "only with dramatically lower costs and a healthy balance sheet."

WestJet's remarkable growth curve was frightening to Milton, and he thought his pilots should be frightened too. The best way for them to protect their careers, he suggested, was to help him build Air Canada into a company that could compete with the threat from the West. "If we don't take action now," Milton wrote, "our prospects for success and growth in the future will be seriously curtailed."

7

THE THREAT FROM THE WEST

Does Air Canada think they can get rid of us? Probably not. But they probably think – in their typically arrogant fashion – that they can damage us, injure us, undermine us, or stop our growth.[1]

– Clive Beddoe, chairman and chief executive officer, WestJet

Mark Hill was stuck on the ground. The clouds and rain offered little hope that the novice pilot would be able to climb into the cockpit of his leased Cessna 172 for a recreational spin over Calgary. The plane did not carry the complex navigational equipment of larger commercial aircraft, so Hill was limited to visual flight rules, meaning he could fly only when he could clearly see the ground and other aircraft. As he waited for a break in the weather at a private terminal at Calgary International Airport, he chatted with Tim Morgan, a professional pilot who operated a small charter airline and flight school from the terminal. Their conversation turned to airfares. Hill told his friend how he saved money on his frequent business trips to Phoenix, where his boss had real-estate interests. Instead of flying Air Canada or Canadian Airlines, Hill would buy a cheap charter ticket to L.A., then connect to Phoenix on Southwest Airlines. He could fly from L.A. to Phoenix return for $80 U.S. – about $120 Canadian. Hill figured it would cost three times that amount to fly the same distance – roughly six hundred kilometres – on Air Canada or Canadian Airlines.[2]

"There's no reason for it," Morgan said matter-of-factly. "It's just that the Canadian industry is so inefficient. They charge it because they can."

It was June 1994, four years since Hill had taken his first flying lesson. The instruction had been a performance bonus from his millionaire boss, Clive Beddoe, a Calgary real-estate developer who was also an avid recreational pilot. As asset manager for Beddoe's Hanover Group, Hill's job was to oversee Beddoe's real-estate holdings, while his employer dabbled in other enterprises. With a sometimes ruthless, take-no-prisoners approach to life, Hill had done so well at boosting the occupancy rates in Beddoe's buildings that he had nearly put himself out of a job. His responsibilities also included finding new lines of business to invest in, but he was left with enough time to do what he loved best – flying.

Watching the skies with Morgan, Hill wondered aloud why no one had tried to start a discount carrier like Southwest Airlines in Canada. Hill and Morgan didn't know much about the economics of running a low-cost airline, but they knew that Southwest was bringing down airfares wherever it flew, and that it was extremely profitable – one of the few U.S. airlines to post consistent profits year after year. Other transplanted discount models like Wal-Mart and Costco were thriving in Canada. Why not an airline? They started theorizing about how one would structure a discount carrier in Canada. What routes would it fly? What kinds of planes would it use? It was just a game to pass the time until the clouds cleared but, as the two talked, the idea took on a life of its own. Maybe, just maybe, there was a business opportunity here. They decided on the areas that needed further research and agreed to meet again in Morgan's offices the following Saturday.

Morgan invited some other friends and acquaintances to the next get-together. One was Don Bell, also a pilot, who owned a computer company. They gave themselves a name – ABC Airlines Group – and brainstormed ideas, scribbling notes onto an erasable whiteboard. Hill presented a primitive spreadsheet based on the information he and Morgan had researched. He couldn't contain his excitement as he explained the numbers to the group. He estimated that, if an operator got decent utilization out of a used Boeing 737 aircraft, it would cost about $5,000 for each hour the plane was in the air. If all 120 seats on the plane were filled, the cost per passenger was just $42 an hour. Even if only half the seats were filled, the unit cost was less than $100 an hour. But Air Canada and Canadian Airlines were charging more than four times that amount for an economy-class ticket to Vancouver, barely an hour away. The numbers were so enticing. How could it not work?

Hill knew that the history of commercial aviation was littered with tales of entrepreneurs who had lost their shirts after being seduced by equally compelling spreadsheets. Investors are attracted to aviation not only by the machinery, but also by the allure of an economic model that can look irresistible on paper. More often than not, the spreadsheet's theoretical black ink bleeds red once the planes hit the skies. But Hill wasn't deterred. Another draw for investors is the naive notion that they will succeed where everyone else has failed. To a cowboy like Mark Hill, that notion must have been very appealing. It would be less so to his more conservative boss.

"Clive, I've got an idea to start an airline."

Hill was an excitable guy, but Beddoe had never seen him so enthused.

"Are you nuts? Why would you want to do that? Why would you ever want to do that?"

"I think it will work," Hill insisted. "Just look at these numbers."

In a city the size of Calgary, there were a dozen or so businessmen with serious stature in its power circles. Clive Beddoe was one of them, and one of the few not directly involved in the city's booming oil-and-gas industry. Despite Beddoe's warm British accent and gentle demeanour, people in the real-estate business knew him as something of a hard-ass. Clive didn't sell cheap or negotiate down for the sake of the deal. He was rich because he didn't take unnecessary risks; he could not be bulldozed by a blue-sky spreadsheet. Beddoe gave considerable leeway to employees he trusted, and he didn't want to dampen Hill's creativity, but he wasn't sure he wanted to encourage interest in a sector as precarious as the airline business – not with his hard-earned money.

"Give me a business plan. Show me it will work. Go prove it."

Hill left Beddoe's office with his bubble slightly deflated, but with renewed resolve to demonstrate that a low-cost airline could work in Canada. For the next two months he spoke very little about his work with ABC Airlines, all the while spending most of his time and a bit of the boss's money on a project Beddoe didn't yet believe in. The ABC Group met at least every second Saturday to share data and new information. As Hill's spreadsheets swelled to accommodate more variables, he twice went back to Beddoe to ask for more powerful computers. After two months of Saturday meetings and hundreds of hours sweating over the figures, Hill finally felt he had something to present to Beddoe. The document wasn't bound and it didn't look pretty, but the information was all there in a pile about 1½ inches thick. Hill was confident he had put together a plan so sound, even the risk-averse Beddoe wouldn't be able to put it down.

"I started to read it and I was amazed with what he had found," Beddoe recalled later. "In the first page and a half I was sold. What sold me was the Southwest model. I had never even heard of Southwest Airlines."

It may not be coincidence that WestJet Airlines was conceived in Alberta, while its business model and inspiration, Southwest Airlines, began in Texas. Canadians tend to think of Alberta as the Texas of the north, a likeness many Albertans are happy to embrace. Consider, for example, Clive Beddoe's reaction when he learned that Robert Milton is a vegetarian. "I like to kill what I eat," said Beddoe, an avid hunter.[3] Albertans, the stereotype goes, devour beef, sport cowboy boots, dislike gun control, and fatten their wallets on the oil-and-gas industry – just like Texans. The two also have a similar attitude to individual rights and freedoms and a general distrust of their respective federal governments.

Southwest Airlines was born out of this distrust of federal regulations in 1971, when the U.S. airline industry was still heavily controlled by the federal government. Washington told the airlines which routes they could fly and how much they could charge. Established U.S. carriers like United Airlines and American Airlines were run like quasi-utilities, members of a comfortable club. They didn't have to worry too much about costs, because they knew the government would allow them to charge enough to make a small profit on top of their expenses. And if flying was expensive, so what? It wasn't for everybody. People who couldn't afford air travel still had cars and trains and buses. Furthermore, government regulation protected the established players from any new-comer who might try to come into the market and do things differently.

The founders of Southwest Airlines – banker Rollin King and lawyer Herb Kelleher – found a loophole in the rules.[4] Washington had price and route jurisdiction only over airlines that flew between two or more states. The federal government couldn't stop them from setting up an airline that would confine its operations to the state of Texas. King and Kelleher expected to make a ton of money flying passengers between Dallas, Houston, and San Antonio. After a year in business, however, Southwest did not have enough traffic to sustain its four planes. The company's founders had no choice but to sell one aircraft, which would mean a 25-per-cent reduction in frequency and an even less attractive schedule compared to the big network carriers.

It might have been the beginning of the end, if not for a group of enterprising employees who proposed to operate the four-plane sched-ule with just three aircraft. It could be done by reducing the amount of time the planes spent on the ground between flights. Instead of turning around in, say, half an hour, the employees wanted to do it in ten minutes. It didn't seem possible, but with cash running out, Southwest had no other options. Pilots and managers pitched in by loading baggage. Flight attendants cleaned up the cabins as passengers were still leaving the airplane. Tickets were collected on board instead of at the gate. It was chaotic at first, but it worked. The low-cost airline model was born.

Southwest also shunned the hub-and-spoke system adopted by most other carriers in the 1950s and 1960s. Larger airlines discovered that they could connect more destinations with greater frequency by linking flights from smaller cities through major airports. In order to minimize connection times for passengers, dozens of flights were scheduled to arrive in a hub city at roughly the same time. But this clustering of flights meant that aircraft spent much more time on the ground. Southwest turned its planes as quickly as possible, keeping them productive, even if it meant some inconvenience for customers.

Southwest's lower cost structure allowed it to steal market share by undercutting its competition on off-peak, late-night flights. Braniff International Airways and Texas International charged $26 for an economy-class ticket between Houston and Dallas. Southwest charged the same during peak periods, but as little as $10 for a late-night flight – the equivalent of bus fare.

The veterans weren't about to roll over and let Southwest pinch their customers, however. Using the same loophole as Southwest, Braniff began advertising $13 fares on flights within the state – a 50-per-cent discount on Southwest's daytime fare. Southwest matched the fare and provided customers with another incentive. Customers who opted to pay the full $26 would receive a free bottle of booze or an ice bucket. Leisure-travel customers, who were paying for their own tickets, usually chose the cheaper fares. But business travellers flying on expense accounts tended to bill their companies for the full-priced tickets so they could take home a free bottle of Chivas Regal. This stroke of marketing genius – win the customer's loyalty with perks paid for by his boss – was the same principle that would lead American Airlines to invent the frequent-flyer program ten years later. It was a well-mannered and highly effective bribe. Southwest not only lured passengers away from established carriers like Braniff and Texas International, but the $13 fares attracted a whole new class of travellers to the skies. People who had previously driven their cars or taken the bus or stayed at home were flying. When Southwest introduced service on a route with fares at 40 per cent below its competitors, the average market grew by 140 per cent.[5] The big airlines attracted some of these new passengers when they matched the discount fares, but most went to Southwest.

The airline posted a small profit in 1973. Instead of handing over all the money to shareholders, or using it to buy airplanes, Southwest took a portion of its profits to buy shares for its employees. After all, they were the ones who were making the lower costs possible by achieving extra-ordinary turnaround times. Thereafter, the annual bonus of shares to employees paid off handsomely: workers' interests were aligned with the company's interests, and they were more willing to pull harder for the bottom line.

Some passengers chose Southwest simply because it continued to fly out of the slightly rundown Dallas Love Field Airport, after the established airlines had relocated to the new and gleaming Dallas–Fort Worth International Airport. Love Field was conveniently located on the perimeter of downtown Dallas; DFW was at least a forty-five minute drive from the city centre. A long drive to the airport didn't jibe with the idea of getting people out of their cars and into the skies.

The Love Field connection also contributed to Southwest's irreverent image, a profile that played well in 1970s Texas. The company's stock symbol was LUV and its in-flight almonds were called Love Bites. One television commercial promoted Southwest's frequent service with a sexy flight attendant asking, "How do we love you? Let us count the ways: eight thirty . . . eleven o'clock . . . one-thirty . . . four o'clock," as the image of an aircraft moved across the screen, its nose pointed provocatively towards her lap. The in-flight uniform for flight attendants – all women – comprised orange hot pants, a clingy top, and vinyl knee-high boots. Ads recruiting flight attendants called for "Raquel Welch look-alikes."

Southwest's anti-authoritarian reputation was mirrored by that of the airline's co-founder, Herb Kelleher, a hard-drinking, chain-smoking lawyer, who had moved to Texas to escape New Jersey winters. As the major carriers repeatedly tried to stymie Southwest's growth, Kelleher fought back and usually won. Texans could relate to this underdog airline, fighting the fat cats from Washington and New York. Albertans would show a similar allegiance to a Calgary-based upstart taking on the establishment from Eastern Canada.

Lower costs by turning planes as quickly as possible. Avoid the hub-and-spoke configuration. Use low fares to lure people out of their cars and into the skies. Fly out of secondary airports the big airlines have abandoned.

Get the interests of workers in line with those of the company. And do it all with renegade flair.

It made perfect sense to Clive Beddoe. These were the fundamentals that had made Southwest Airlines the most profitable airline in the world. It had taken years of trial and error for Southwest to perfect the formula that took it from a three-plane start-up in 1971 to an airline larger than Air Canada by the mid-1990s. ABC Airlines Group had an opportunity to benefit from Southwest's experience and get things right from the first flight off the runway. Beddoe couldn't be sure that the Southwest model would work in Canada, but he was prepared to bankroll the project – carefully – while they tested it. Beddoe had learned that, despite Herb Kelleher's fun-loving, hellraising attitude, Southwest's founder had been extremely conservative with his airline. Unlike other carriers, Southwest had avoided debt and took ten years to grow to just twenty-two aircraft. Beddoe would have no problem being just as conservative.

The son of a British civil servant, Clive John Beddoe was born on May 26, 1946, in Surrey, England. Beddoe didn't achieve high grades at his private school; he just couldn't see the point. But he liked sports – good English sports like rugby and shooting – and was skilled at them. And he had a passion for aircraft. He started flying in non-motorized glider planes, later learning to pilot small motorized planes, then float planes, then helicopters. Beddoe even mastered some aerobatic manoeuvres. After grammar school, he trained to become a chartered surveyor, hoping to go into business for himself. When he found the tax rates in Britain too high, he looked to Canada. There was just one problem: Canadian immigration policy, which had previously favoured Brits, now welcomed them only if they came with employment offers in hand. A year passed before he secured a job in his field in Calgary.

When Clive Beddoe stepped off the plane in Calgary on December 29, 1970, he was struck by how cold it was and by how wide and blue the skies were. He had surely come to the right place. His first job didn't work out, but there were others. With oil prices surging, Alberta's economy skyrocketed through the 1970s. Beddoe went to work for a local developer and in 1979 started his own real-estate business. He made his first fortune with one well-timed deal, leasing an entire building to Petro-Canada. But the price of oil peaked in 1980 and Canada fell into a brutal recession in 1982. Alberta was particularly hard hit: the province's unemployment rate jumped to 10 per cent from 4 per cent.

Beddoe looked for a recession-proof business and settled on the Career College, a Calgary vocational school. Running a profitable college was not unlike running a profitable airline. Since most of its costs were fixed, success depended on filling the seats.

From real estate and education, Beddoe expanded into other businesses. He bought a paper-recycling company that was nearly bankrupt, then purchased a plastics business, which required him to fly regularly between Calgary and Vancouver. Beddoe tired of paying $680 a ticket every time he or his colleagues travelled to the coast. So he bought a Cessna 421 and used his recreational pilot's licence to shuttle his associates around Western Canada. The eight-seat twin-engine airplane was well-suited to frequent flights over the Rocky Mountains, and it soon halved Beddoe's transportation costs. He supplemented the savings by making the plane available to other cost-conscious business travellers through Tim Morgan's aviation company. On occasion, he sold the empty seats on his own regular trips, charging $300 for a round-trip between Calgary and Vancouver.

This early dabbling in the airline business had been delightfully successful, but it paled beside the venture proposed by ABC Airlines. Beddoe liked Hill's plan as a concept, but he worried that the entrepreneurs in the Saturday-morning group didn't have the business skills to put it into practice. Although Beddoe and Hill were both pilots, and Tim Morgan ran a small charter aviation business, what did any of them really know about operating an airline? Beddoe was convinced they needed someone with a working knowledge of the industry, ideally an individual who had experience with Southwest or one of the other low-cost U.S. clones that had sprung up in its wake.

A colleague working with Beddoe on another project suggested that he talk to Morris Air, a Utah-based discounter that had been sold to

Southwest Airlines in 1993. The airline's CEO was June Morris, a sixty-three-year-old great-grandmother who was battling breast cancer. She wasn't about to leave Salt Lake City to run ABC Airlines Group. But what about the president, David Neeleman, who had been credited in the *Salt Lake City Tribune* as the "rambunctious ideas man" behind June Morris's business ventures?[6]

Like Clive Beddoe, Neeleman had never done well in school. Growing up in Utah, he had been labelled a slow learner by his teachers and held back in grade three. Neeleman now believes his early difficulties were related to undiagnosed attention deficit disorder, something he still struggles with today. After two years of Mormon missionary work in Brazil, Neeleman set up a travel business in Salt Lake City, packaging flights with time-shares. The business went bankrupt when he was just twenty-three. He was ready to give up on the tourism industry, until June Morris invited him to work for her travel agency. They made a good team: Morris gave Neeleman the creative freedom he relished, but could rein him in when necessary.

In 1984 they founded Morris Air, following the Southwest model meticulously, with a few distinctive Neeleman touches. Morris Air was the first airline to replace paper tickets with a reservation number – a practice that is now standard in the discount game and becoming the norm for full-service carriers. Morris Air grew to twenty-one aircraft in less than a decade, and eventually attracted the attention of its prototype. Southwest had typically shied away from mergers or acquisitions, which were viewed as an unwieldy way to grow, but it made an exception when it acquired Morris Air for about $125 million U.S. in stock in 1993. Herb Kelleher believed that the addition of Morris Air would allow Southwest to compete better against carriers like Continental and United, both of which were developing plans for their own discount brands.

Neeleman received $20 million in Southwest stock from the transaction and joined Southwest's executive planning committee. Five months later, he left. Industry observers speculated that Kelleher's reputation as a hard-living partyer with a penchant for Wild Turkey had clashed with Neeleman's Mormon values. The younger man doesn't even drink coffee. But the real mismatch was between Neeleman's bull-in-a-china-shop personality and Southwest's collegial culture. Behaviour that had been tolerated when he was running the show at Morris Air – barging into other people's offices unannounced or tactlessly blurting out whatever he was thinking at meetings – was frowned on at Southwest.[7] Neeleman left on cordial terms, agreeing not to work for another U.S. airline for at least five years.

Beddoe was relieved to learn that Canada was exempt from Neeleman's non-compete clause. He sent Mark Hill, Tim Morgan, and Don Bell to Salt Lake City to meet with him. An interview scheduled to last an hour stretched into six, as Neeleman regaled them with war stories about the airline biz, and Hill soon appreciated how little he himself knew about the industry, despite the hours he had dedicated to the ABC Airlines business plan. They convinced Neeleman to make the trip to Canada where, after visiting Vancouver and Calgary, Neeleman met with Beddoe and told him exactly what he wanted to hear: a Southwest clone would work in Canada.

Neeleman seemed like the perfect candidate to run ABC Airlines. He lived and breathed aviation and was excited by the prospects for a Canadian discounter. Best of all, he was out of work. But Neeleman had no interest in running another airline – or not at that moment. He would advise them and sit on their board of directors, perhaps make a small investment to show his support. But they'd have to find someone else to run the carrier.

Today, WestJet's executives play down Neeleman's role in the conceptual development of the airline. In the company's corporate mythology, there are just four founders: Clive Beddoe, Mark Hill, Tim Morgan, and Don Bell. Neeleman doesn't disagree. He provided them with their reservations system, Open Skies, and he introduced them to the idea of paperless tickets. Perhaps his most significant contribution was the value of his name and reputation when it came time to line up financing for the project. ABC approached twelve potential investors in Calgary and invited them to invest a minimum of $500,000 each in the carrier. Mark Hill says they had eleven bites and were able to raise $8 million in less than a month. This first round of financing allowed them to pay for everything the start-up needed, except airplanes.

The next priority was a name. Over Christmas dinner, Hill showed his mother a list of names the ABC founders had been considering. She didn't love any of them, but suggested one that wasn't on the list – WestJet. He brought the name back to the rest of the group and they pounced on it.

"But how can we fly into Eastern Canada with a name like WestJet?" one asked. Although they were content to start out as a Western-based regional carrier, they had long-term ambitions to expand east of Winnipeg into Air Canada's home turf.

"Simple," Beddoe answered. "If you're in Eastern Canada, everything is to the west."

Dick Huisman, president and CEO of Greyhound Lines of Canada, had been watching the trend for years, and he wasn't happy with the view. For half a century, value-conscious travellers had opted for the bus. It might take four days to get from Toronto to Vancouver, but as long as it was cheaper than flying, the extra time was acceptable to a healthy percentage of the travelling population. Not any more. By the mid-1990s, air travel had been transformed from a luxury for the wealthy into a commodity everyone could afford. Airlines like Southwest and Morris Air had pushed down fares throughout the United States. Even in Canada the fares had fallen, thanks to intense competition between Air Canada, Canadian Airlines, and charter carriers. The bus business in Canada could still make money on short trips, where airfares remained relatively high, but on long-distance travel, it was losing market share to the airlines at an alarming rate. And there was no way Calgary-based Greyhound, the industry's largest player, could lower its costs sufficiently to win back the price advantage it had enjoyed for five decades. If Greyhound couldn't beat the airlines, Huisman figured, it would have to join them.

A skeptic might say that Huisman – who had spent nearly a decade as senior vice president of marketing for CP Air before joining Greyhound – was just another bedazzled guy addicted to the intoxicating fumes of the airline industry. But Huisman envisioned Greyhound Air as more than a personal flight of fancy. And it was more than a way for Greyhound to recover the business it had lost to the airlines. Huisman was proposing a concept that was long overdue: a coordinated system of passenger transportation. Greyhound Air would serve just eight cities, but the airline would connect with Greyhound's bus lines to provide customers with service between 1,100 Canadian communities. As he saw it, a customer wanting to travel from London, Ontario, to Vancouver would take a Greyhound bus to the Hamilton Greyhound depot, catch a Greyhound shuttle bus to the airport, and board a Greyhound plane to Vancouver.

Three years earlier, Huisman had talked to Air Canada executives about creating an intermodal transportation network, but nothing came of it. By 1994 Greyhound was ready to do it alone. Huisman pitched the plan to his board and won the support of Phoenix-based Dial Corporation, which owned 68.5 per cent of Greyhound.

Federal law stipulated that foreign investors couldn't own more than 25 per cent of the shares in a Canadian airline; clearly the federal government wasn't about to give Greyhound a licence. But what if an existing licensed Canadian airline operated the planes on Greyhound's behalf? U.S. courier companies, prohibited from operating domestic flights within Canada, had similar arrangements with Canadian carriers. Why not a passenger airline? Greyhound struck a deal in February 1996 with Kelowna Flightcraft Air Charter, the B.C. firm that operated airplanes for Federal Express. It seemed a brilliant way to circumvent the ownership rules: Greyhound would be responsible for marketing and selling the ticket, everything up to the point at which the customer checked in for the flight. Kelowna Flightcraft would take over from there. With legal advice that the plan would work, Huisman told Kelowna Flightcraft to order six aircraft on Greyhound's behalf and prepare for a launch on May 1, 1996.

There was yet a third group working on plans for a Calgary-based discount airline in 1995. NewAir hoped to launch service in September of that year for five or six round-trip flights daily between Calgary,

Vancouver, and Edmonton. Its business plan was developed by Brian Campbell, a Virginia-based aviation consultant, who helped launch Midway Airlines in the 1970s, and Glenn Pickard of Calgary, a former executive with the Lethbridge regional carrier, Time Air. Their prospectus featured many of the same elements as Mark Hill's blueprint for WestJet. "NewAir plans to emulate Southwest and to adopt many of its ingredients of success," said a draft dated January 1995. The document pointed out that Canada's lower population would be a challenge, but its authors believed that "whole new markets" could be created "by virtue of an unrestricted fare structure."

If the Canadian market was risky for one discount start-up, there certainly wasn't room for three. "We tried to intimidate each other through the press about who was furthest along," Mark Hill recalled later. "We were all trying to piss in each other's cornflakes to scare the other guy off." Greyhound was clearly the early leader. It enjoyed the familiar name and reputation of a sixty-five-year-old transportation institution, and its U.S. parent, Dial, had deep pockets. WestJet and NewAir were wooing investors, but Greyhound didn't need any. The WestJet group estimated they were a little ahead of NewAir, if only because they had David Neeleman on their side.

But NewAir had one advantage over WestJet – an experienced, respected operations man who would run the airline, in the person of Glenn Pickard. Hill and company went after Pickard and convinced him to switch allegiance and become WestJet's first chief operating officer. But the fickle Pickard would defect again before WestJet took its first flight, accepting a job from Air Bahamas. Eventually, the WestJet founders decided to run the airline themselves, with Beddoe as CEO and Morgan and Bell sharing the job of chief operating officer. Mark Hill became vice-president of strategic planning. Pickard's departure from NewAir effectively ended that company's chances of getting off the ground. So now there were two.

Ian Griffin, chairman of Research Capital, set up a meeting between WestJet and Greyhound in November 1994. WestJet had retained Research Capital to help raise start-up financing, and Griffin wanted to find some common ground between the two so they could focus their firepower on Air Canada and Canadian Airlines instead of each other. In his mind, their business plans didn't seem to be in conflict. WestJet sent its big guns to the meeting – Clive Beddoe, Mark Hill, and David Neeleman – while Dick Huisman was the lone Greyhound representative. Huisman's goal was simple: to scare off the other side. The two airlines might not be direct competitors, with WestJet specializing in short-haul routes and Greyhound offering transcontinental service, but he saw the WestJet plan as a serious threat to his own short-haul bus business.

"We've done the research," a blustery Huisman told them. "We know all about Southwest Airlines and Morris Air. And we know that a low-cost regional airline can't work in Canada." Huisman suggested that they abandon their scheme before they all lost their shirts. Huisman was talking out of fear, but it came across as patronizing condescension.

Greyhound wouldn't be a competitor to WestJet, but it had made itself a rival. "From that point on, there was no love lost between us and Huisman," Hill said. "He tried to steamroll us and it didn't work." The rivalry intensified a few days later when the WestJet group was in Toronto for a series of meetings with potential investors. That morning the newspapers simultaneously broke the story about Greyhound's plans on their front pages. "Greyhound Canada set to take flight," announced the headline on the *Financial Post*. The *Globe and Mail*'s *Report on Business* quoted a Greyhound executive explaining that the airline would provide "a low-cost, low-frill, long-haul service across Canada." Investors who had been keen to meet with the WestJet crew were suddenly calling to cancel. Yet the company managed to do well in its second round of financing, raising a total of $28.5 million. It was enough to take flight with virtually no debt, a rarity in the airline business.

The timing of Greyhound's announcement rankled, however, and Mark Hill's competitive instincts kicked in. He suspected that Huisman had deliberately timed its release to damage WestJet's efforts. He could play that game too. He sat down at his laptop computer and drafted a letter to the National Transportation Agency, the government office that regulated airlines. "I am writing you to express our extreme concern for the apparent way in which Greyhound Lines of Canada is intending to circumvent the National Transportation Act," began the letter, dated February 22, 1996, and signed by Clive Beddoe. The letter reminded the government that a U.S. conglomerate owned more than two-thirds of Greyhound's shares.

> We are of the belief that it is the intent of Dial Corporation to use its financial strength to undercut the domestic Canadian transportation industry to the benefit of their U.S. shareholders and Dial's Canadian subsidiary, Greyhound Lines of Canada. Having recently met the strict criteria stipulated by the NTA to ensure the ownership and control of the airline industry remains in the hands of Canadians, we find this backdoor approach to be highly offensive.

WestJet took to the skies on February 29, 1996 – a date chosen because it occurs only once every four years – with flights serving Winnipeg, Edmonton, Calgary, Vancouver, Victoria, and Kelowna, B.C. Some carried just a handful of passengers, but that didn't matter. The WestJet founders had demonstrated that they could turn a business plan into an airline. They had outlasted NewAir and they had beaten Greyhound to the gate. Now the real fun would begin.

One month after WestJet's launch, Greyhound Air opened its reservations centre for an anticipated May 22 takeoff. Four days later, the National Transportation Agency ordered the airline to stop selling tickets. In a ruling dated April 12, the government agency said that, despite its arrangement with Kelowna Flightcraft, Greyhound was subject to the foreign-ownership regulations. As long as Greyhound was majority-owned by Dial, Dick Huisman wasn't going to get an operating licence. The WestJet letter and a similar complaint filed by Canadian Airlines had stirred the government to action. Huisman was livid, as were the people at Kelowna Flightcraft. "I'm shocked as hell," Kelowna president Barry Lapointe said. "Who are they protecting? Are they protecting Canadian and Air Canada? Because they sure aren't protecting the traveling public that wants cheap fares."[8]

Huisman appeared to have the public and the press on his side. One columnist called Greyhound's proposal "a simple but brilliant combination of two existing industries into a new product that would benefit consumers."[9] Huisman was convinced he had the law on his side too. Wasn't Greyhound doing the same thing that Federal Express had done with Kelowna Flightcraft? Greyhound continued to take bookings – without payment – for a May 22 start-up, while it filed an appeal and pushed for a ruling by the end of April.

In the meantime, Greyhound enacted a restructuring plan to put the company squarely in Canadian hands. Greyhound's intercity bus business and would-be airline was spun off to Canadian investors, while Dial Corporation became the sole owner of Greyhound's hotel, sightseeing, and tourism business, known as Brewster Transport. The move persuaded then–transport minister David Anderson and his Cabinet colleagues to overturn the NTA decision and allow Greyhound Airlines to take flight. "The decision was made on the basis of the consumer interest, the wider Canadian interest," Anderson said. "We need a transportation system that gets people to where they want to go at low cost."[10] For Dick Huisman, the Cabinet decision was the end of an eight-week nightmare. But he had learned a valuable lesson. Despite WestJet's folksy corporate image, its top executives were aggressive combatants who wouldn't allow anyone to get in their way.

Greyhound Air operated its first flights on July 8, 1996, but Dick Huisman's dream didn't last long. On September 2, 1997, Burlington-based Laidlaw Inc. announced that it had acquired Greyhound Lines for $100 million. The conglomerate saw great potential in the bus business, but had no enthusiasm for the airline, which had lost approximately $24 million in its first year. Huisman worked hard to convince Laidlaw president and CEO James Bullock that his baby was turning the corner: it had posted profits of more than $5 million through July and August. But the

Laidlaw executives knew that almost any airline could make money in the summer. The airline was grounded on September 21 after less than fifteen months in the air.

NewAir had never sent a single plane into the skies and Greyhound had fizzled; WestJet was the sole survivor.

As the plane neared eleven thousand feet, Captain Candalyn Kubeck heard a loud pop.

She couldn't identify it, but it was likely the sound of a tire exploding on her DC-9, the result of a fire that had broken out in the plane's cargo hold. ValuJet Flight 592 had departed from Miami International Airport a few minutes earlier for a 110-minute flight to Atlanta. Above Kubeck's head, a cluster of meters showed that most of the plane's electrical systems were shutting down. "We're losing everything," she said to First Officer Richard Hazen. As cries of "Fire!" erupted in the cabin, Hazen told air-traffic controllers that 592 needed clearance for an immediate return to Miami. There was smoke in the cabin and cockpit. Moments later, the plane crashed nose first into the Everglades west of Miami, killing all five crew members and 105 passengers.[11]

In the previous three years, ValuJet had grown into a model discount airline with fifty-one planes serving thirty-one cities. But the fortunes of all low-cost carriers changed overnight when Flight 592 sank into the Florida swamp on May 11, 1996. Bookings on U.S. discounters plunged as consumers worried that "discount" meant "unsafe." When the National Transportation Safety Board released its final report, it blamed the airline and its maintenance contractor, as well as the U.S. Federal Aviation Administration (FAA), which was responsible for setting safety rules and inspecting maintenance facilities. In one citation, for example, the safety board concluded that smoke detectors might have helped prevent the crash, but ValuJet's aircraft did not carry them because the FAA did not require them. Government inspectors on both sides of the border appeared determined to pay closer attention to discount airlines.

Five months later, in September 1996, Beddoe arrived at Transport Canada's Calgary offices to discuss the airline's first safety audit. He was stopped in the parking lot by a stranger.

"You're Clive Beddoe, aren't you?"

"Yes . . ."

"I just wanted to let you know that you should run as fast as you can and get a lawyer involved in this audit, because Transport Canada is out to kill you."

"What do you mean?"

"They want you dead."[12]

The man wouldn't give his name, but said he worked in avionics at Transport Canada. The warning would have been dismissed as nonsense if there hadn't been a string of unusual events around the same time. Sensitive files had disappeared from WestJet's head office. Holes had been knocked in some airplanes, either by accident or sabotage. And in Salt Lake City, the building that housed Open Skies, the reservations-software provider used by WestJet and founded by David Neeleman, had burned to the ground. The FBI were investigating the fire as an arson. The events were almost certainly unrelated, but it all seemed suspicious.[13]

All new Canadian airlines undergo thorough safety inspections after their first six months in the air. As WestJet's safety audit progressed, Beddoe came to believe that, indeed, Transport Canada wanted his airline dead. A dispute arose over aircraft-maintenance procedures. WestJet was following the maintenance manuals that had come with its first two airplanes, procedures that had been approved by Transport Canada for use by Astoria Airlines, a small luxury carrier that had suspended service after just five months in operation. Beddoe thought Transport Canada had given the okay for WestJet to use those same operating procedures before its launch. But now that the audit was under way, Transport inspectors said WestJet should have been following a different maintenance manual. Beddoe grudgingly agreed to have the airline's maintenance experts rewrite the manuals over the next few months to conform with Transport Canada requirements. That wasn't good enough. Transport Canada claimed it had no choice but to audit WestJet as if it had already been following the correct set of procedures – a standard the airline was certain to fail.

In late September, Transport Canada issued a formal notice of suspension, giving WestJet fifteen days to rewrite its operations manual or lose its operating certificate. Beddoe decided that the only way to win was to concede. He suspended the airline himself, rather than wait for the government to do it. He wanted to eliminate any perception that WestJet's planes were suspect, especially so soon after the ValuJet crash.

"We will not compromise the safety of our passengers," Beddoe said. "If there are rumours out there, if there are any doubts about our safety, then we have to stop flying."[14] He put on a brave face, threatening to sue the federal government for irregularities in the audit and promising customers that the airline would rise again in seven to thirty days, after it had revised its operating procedures. Deep down, Beddoe wondered if WestJet would ever fly again, given Transport Canada's apparent antipathy.

If there was a silver lining, it was that the airline shut down in September, one of the slowest times of the year for the industry. After a strong summer season, WestJet had $10 million in cash in the bank and no debt. But in another sense, the timing couldn't have been worse. At 10:00 on the morning after Beddoe grounded the fleet, WestJet was scheduled to convene its first annual general meeting. Investors flew to Calgary expecting to celebrate the fledgling airline's achievements and the 380,000 passengers it had carried in just six months. Instead, it seemed they might be gathering for a wake.

In an effort to protect employees, WestJet told its airport staff not to come in to work, a move that angered and confused those passengers who showed up for flights without knowing the airline had been grounded. But as the details emerged, customers rallied round their airline, especially in Calgary. To Westerners, the government's actions reeked of the worst kind of central-Canadian bureaucracy, designed, no doubt, to protect Air Canada. Callers to a Calgary radio station were almost unanimous in their support of WestJet. Demonstrations were organized by employees and customers outside the WestJet offices. The community response reassured Beddoe that WestJet would thrive if Transport Canada allowed the planes back into the air.

After three weeks of long days and nights, WestJet's operations crew produced an operating manual that satisfied Transport Canada. When the airline resumed flying on October 4, WestJet offered any seat in its network for just $45. Air Canada immediately matched the seat sale on its corresponding flights. Mark Hill says it was the worst thing the Montreal-based carrier could have done. "The public weren't sure these guys were after us. When that happened, they knew they were after us."

Hill would exact a small revenge a year later. He claims Robert Milton tried to hire him away from WestJet for a job with Air Canada. Hill says he accepted the invitation to meet with Milton only to find out what Air Canada was up to. The airline put him up in an airport hotel. After the interview, Hill says he went to the hotel bar and bought drinks for total strangers on Milton's tab. "He's probably still pissed at me about that," Hill says. Air Canada's CEO says he has no recollection of the meeting or the job offer.

Many airlines have tried to copy Southwest's business model but most have not succeeded, because they failed to grasp the importance of its unconventional corporate culture and labour-relations strategy. WestJet did not make that mistake.

Outsiders who have attended get-togethers for WestJet employees or the company's annual general meetings have observed that workers seem to be fully indoctrinated into the WestJet way of thinking. They possess an unquestioning devotion to the company and its founders, and an unshakeable faith that the WestJet way is the right way. Similarly, working at Southwest is "not a job, it's a crusade," according to Kevin and Jackie Freiberg in their flattering corporate history, *Nuts! Southwest Airlines' Crazy Recipe for Business and Personal Success.* "The people of Southwest Airlines are crusaders with an egalitarian spirit who truly believe they are in the business of freedom. Their mission is to open up the skies, to give

ordinary people the chance to see and do things they never dreamed of."
Employees, they write, are "impassioned about treating each other like
family. They hug, kiss, cry and say 'I love you' on the job."[15]

David Arnott, a Dallas-based management professor, compares
Southwest to a religious cult in his book *Corporate Cults: The Insidious Lure
of the All-Consuming Organization.* "It's a paradox that Southwest Airlines
screens so carefully for 'spirited' employees, then claims to allow people to
be themselves," Arnott writes. "In corporate cult terms, the rules are, 'You
will be funny, and you *will* conform to the culture of this organization.
You are allowed to 'be yourself' as long as yourself fits in with the narrowly defined culture of the organization.'"[16] Remarkably, Southwest is
heavily unionized, with some 85 per cent of its workers belonging to a
union. However, the Southwest Airlines Pilots' Association, formed in
1978, is considered more pragmatic than the much larger Air Line Pilots
Association, which represents pilots at most other airlines.

At the core of the WestJet philosophy is the belief that the customer
comes second. Take care of your employees, WestJet managers are told,
and they will take care of your guests. WestJet gives its employees a generous degree of latitude to do just that. While Air Canada has policies
governing when, where, and in what circumstances its employees can
dispense free travel vouchers, WestJet has only loose guidelines. Employees are instructed to do whatever they think is appropriate to fix the
problem. It's all part of a grassroots, bottom-up management style that
begins with hiring. With the exception of pilots, airline experience isn't
considered an asset for a job at WestJet. Instead, managers look for people
who are optimistic, outgoing, fun-loving, and entrepreneurial. It's possible such individuals are more likely to be trusting of management and
suspicious of unions.

If the company does well, employees reap the rewards. WestJet aims
to pay a base salary of 95 per cent of the industry-standard wage, but it
tops up salaries through profit-sharing and a share-purchase plan. Pilots
get stock options as well. Close to 90 per cent of WestJet employees own
shares in the company, reinforcing the notion that what is good for the
airline is good for its workers. Beddoe remembers an occasion when a

worker came into his office demanding to know why he had squandered the company's money on a catered barbecue for middle and senior managers. Beddoe told the man he had paid for the party out of his own pocket. "He was a little humbled, but I congratulated him on his attitude," Beddoe said. "He's like a watchdog and he hates inequities. That's the spirit of WestJet."[17]

In early 1998, however, there was trouble in paradise. The company's flight attendants were upset about a number of issues, including the way overtime was accounted for and the fact that they weren't allowed to swap shifts. Some were talking to the Canadian Union of Public Employees, which represented flight attendants at Air Canada, Canadian Airlines, and Canada 3000. Nearly half of the company's sixty-five attendants were in favour of forming a union bargaining unit. Many others were strongly opposed, believing that unions posed a threat to the friendly WestJet culture. Management called in Rob Winter, a labour consultant. Winter had been an active union member as an Air Canada employee, before switching sides (and colours) to become manager of labour relations for PWA. At WestJet, Winter was able to resolve the flight attendants' concerns and douse their interest in unionizing by acting as a mediator. "I didn't even talk about unions. I wasn't called in to get rid of a union drive; I was called in to solve problems," Winter explained later.

Impressed by Winter's success with the flight attendants, Beddoe asked him to "solve problems" on a wider scale. As the company grew, workers would have less opportunity to address issues one-on-one with senior managers. It seemed inevitable that staff would want to formalize their representation within the company. "If people want to do something," Beddoe told Winter, "if they want to unionize or whatever, I'd just like to get it over with." Beddoe asked Winter to work with the company's non-managerial staff to help them form an employee group. His only request was that Winter aim for a company-wide association, rather than separate units for different employee groups.

Winter met with workers at WestJet's bases across Western Canada and presented them with three options: they could join an existing union, form their own union, or come up with an alternative, made-for-WestJet, solution. Winter says Beddoe never asked him to steer sentiment away from unions. "Clive's a pretty smart guy," Winter says. "He probably realized that the people who were hired would be interested in doing a WestJet-type thing." In May of 1999, 92 per cent of WestJet's employees voted to be represented by the non-union Pro-Active Communication Team (PACT). WestJet workers don't have the right to strike. But Winter says PACT is better than a union, because workers contribute directly to the solution instead of being caught up in an adversarial relationship.

Outsiders wondered if unions might eventually move on WestJet, perhaps when reduced profits undermined the company's profit-sharing plan. Southwest Airlines, it is often pointed out, is one of the most heavily unionized airlines in the world. But unions wouldn't have an easy time breaking into WestJet. The PACT constitution requires that 75 per cent of the employee group must vote to leave PACT before it can form another association.

"If anybody here is wanting to get a union card signed, they're sure not talking about it," said PACT administrator Louise Feroze. "There's so much information to the contrary, saying the reason we can do all the things we are doing, and doing it with the amount of flexibility and latitude, is that we're not hemmed in by a union."

On June 16, 1998, the Detroit Red Wings were up 3−0 in the Stanley Cup final and were poised to sweep the series with the Washington Capitals. Executives from Air Canada and WestJet were watching the game in the same downtown Toronto bar after a long day of presentations at an airline investment conference. Air Canada CFO Rob Peterson had spoken at the conference, as had Canadian Airlines CEO Kevin Benson. Clive Beddoe was there because WestJet was attempting to raise money in the stock market with an initial public offering.

In just two years, the Calgary-based carrier had lowered airfares dramatically on short-haul routes in Western Canada − below the point at which Air Canada or Canadian Airlines could operate them profitably. The sensible solution for Air Canada was to abandon the money-losing routes, but that was not an option. The carrier needed them to feed passengers onto its longer, profitable flights across the continent and overseas. Rob Peterson knew that, if Air Canada gave up the routes, passengers would turn to Canadian Airlines for their entire trip.

Beddoe couldn't resist a jab when he saw Peterson at the back of the bar.

"You guys should just get out of the short-haul business," Beddoe teased. "We'll feed you short-haul and you can focus on long-haul, which is where you make the money."

"In your dreams," Peterson snapped back, before turning his attention to the television and Detroit's 4–1 Stanley Cup victory.

Beddoe didn't think any more about the exchange until Peterson called him a few months later. Peterson had taken Beddoe's lighthearted proposal to Lamar Durrett, then Air Canada's CEO. Durrett was interested. By entering into an agreement with WestJet, Air Canada could get the short-haul feed it needed without losing money on the routes. The deal would allow WestJet to accelerate its growth, since it would pick up Air Canada's former passengers in the West. And it could increase its profitability in the absence of Air Canada's price competition. At Air Canada's Montreal headquarters, the proposed partnership became known as the Visions Project.

In a report dated December 4, 1998, Air Canada briefed its board of directors on the talks under way with WestJet. In the course of outlining the history of North America's discount airlines, the document offered a rare glimpse of Air Canada's approach to its competition. The "Visions" report began by explaining the low-cost formula, noting that discounters like Southwest Airlines were "very hard to dislodge," because they stimulate traffic to create their own market. The major U.S. carriers had had limited success in containing the growth of the discounters. "The more the major lowered the price, the more the market grew and filled the start-up's capacity," the report said. "Only when the majors took instant, brutal action below the break-even fare of the start-up did [the start-up] go under." The report suggested that WestJet was successful because Canadian Airlines International Ltd., the dominant Western carrier, did not respond aggressively enough. "As market leader, only CAIL was in a position to take the brutal action required to halt WestJet's development. However, whilst CAIL more or less matched WestJet's price and conditions, it failed to add enough capacity to soak up the demand."

Air Canada's response to WestJet, the directors were told, had been to scale back its Western service to reduce its losses. It hadn't worked: "Profitability is still inadequate (annualized losses in the region of \$50-million) and returns are substantially below the weighted average cost of capital and drag down Air Canada's overall margins significantly."

In a follow-up brief prepared in mid-January, the directors were told in blunt terms that WestJet posed a serious threat. "If no action is taken," the report warned, "we must assume continued growth by WestJet or similar airlines, both in Western Canada and in other Air Canada markets, virtually eliminating net profit even for a normalized year."[18]

This second report laid out several alternatives for the directors' consideration:

We have four primary response options to address the current low cost threat in Western Canada and the potential threat for the rest of the network.

1. Abandon Western Canada – cease operations of all routes in Canada except the transcons
2. Dilution – respond aggressively to low cost competition by reducing price to below competitor's break-even and adding enough capacity to capture most of the stimulated demand
3. Create an airline within an airline – build or buy a separate low cost airline to feed traffic and compete with other low cost carriers on short haul routes
4. Develop a strategic alliance with a low cost partner – team with a carrier with a low cost business design to offer the appropriate value proposition and economics to each market

The section on "dilution" paints a picture of an airline eager to eliminate its competitors. The report said Air Canada was able to "drive out" several low-cost rivals through the 1990s, including Nationair, Astoria Airlines, and Vistajet. Dick Huisman's Greyhound Air was also on the list. The report revealed the cost of "defending against" Nationair was $16 million. While Air Canada was able to rid itself of a number of such competitors in Eastern Canada, the report said, the strategy did not work in Western Canada, because Air Canada was not the market leader and because WestJet had a "successful business design."

The report argued in favour of the fourth alternative. It stated that the financial implications of the first option, abandoning the West, would be "prohibitive," since Air Canada needed the feed for its transcontinental and international flights. It declared the third alternative – creating an airline within an airline – "very difficult to implement, particularly within the current labour environment." Developing a strategic alliance with a low-cost carrier, however, "is almost as attractive as creating an airline within an airline, but with much less risk."

Most of Air Canada's top executives, including Durrett and Peterson, thought a deal with WestJet made great sense. But there was one dissenting view. Chief Operating Officer Robert Milton thought an alliance with WestJet would be a mistake.[19] He doubted Air Canada's pilots would agree to surrender their routes, and their livelihood, to a non-unionized workforce. More importantly, he feared WestJet would gain much more than Air Canada from the arrangement. By retreating from these key markets, Air Canada would give WestJet a green light for growth that would someday allow the discount carrier to challenge Air Canada in markets elsewhere in the country. Lamar Durrett, the gentleman CEO, was prepared to retreat on the Western front if it would help Air Canada win the war. But Milton knew that one of the fundamental rules of the airline business was that, all other things being equal, profitability depended on market share. Retreating from a few routes in Western Canada might help Air Canada with a short-term problem, but it did nothing to address the real issue: Air Canada's costs were too high. Milton expressed his concerns, but didn't object too strenuously. The day would soon come when he would be directing Air Canada's strategy with respect to the discounters.

In January 1999, an alliance between Air Canada and WestJet appeared inevitable, but the situation changed dramatically on February 4 when Kevin Benson proposed an Air Canada–Canadian Airlines merger. The WestJet discussions were eclipsed by merger talks with Canadian, followed by the hostile takeover bid from Onex Corporation. But the essential issue remained: Air Canada's costs made it impossible to compete in an industry that was undergoing a low-cost revolution. It was clear that Air Canada had to make some fundamental changes if it were to survive the WestJet challenge. Robert Milton's answer was to tackle WestJet on its own terms, by starting up Air Canada's own discount airline, without meals or business-class frills – or expensive union contracts.

Steve Smith was growing restless. The president of Air Ontario had overseen a period of healthy revenue and profit growth at the regional carrier through the mid-1990s, but the Air Canada subsidiary seemed stalled by 1998. Air Canada's labour contracts prevented Smith from expanding Air Ontario the way he would have liked. He told his bosses he was ready to try something new, but got the impression they weren't in a hurry to move him out of Air Ontario. Smith rarely stayed in a job for more than two years and he wanted a change, even if it meant leaving the Red Team. When the call came from WestJet late in 1998, it seemed like providence.

Clive Beddoe had decided it was time to step back from the day-to-day management of WestJet. He was an entrepreneur at heart; his strengths lay in starting businesses, not running them. He was happy to remain chairman, but he was looking for a successor, someone with a fresh perspective, to take over the role of president and CEO. "I didn't really want somebody from the airline business," Beddoe recalls. "But when I met Steve the first time, he was very energetic and enthusiastic. He seemed to aspire to the same values and culture that we talk about." Beddoe offered him the job, and Smith readily accepted. WestJet was engaged in the "Vision" project alliance negotiations with Air Canada at the time; consequently his bosses were extremely accommodating, letting him work at Air Ontario until the day he officially took over from Beddoe.

Smith was instantly struck by the WestJet environment, which was very different from that of Air Ontario, where enthusiasm levels had flattened. "At WestJet it was sky-high," Smith recalls. "It was contagious; it was energizing; it was exciting; it was dynamic. It made you want to get to work in the morning." Before he was officially gone from Air Ontario, Smith flew to Calgary to deliver a speech at WestJet's "Wheels Up" party, a huge birthday celebration held each year. Smith was amazed to hear the crowd cheer his every line. The cheering wasn't for him, he understood, but simply an expression of the love these people had for their company. It was seductive, and Smith felt like he was finally home.

Smith arrived at the event wearing a jacket and tie, attire deemed too formal for WestJet's relaxed atmosphere. Smith had flown to Calgary on Air Canada, which required employees to dress up when they occupied business-class seats. But Smith's wardrobe telegraphed an unfortunate signal. Ties were contrary to WestJet's culture; they separated managers from workers. WestJet's egalitarian philosophy had helped make the founders millionaires many times over, and wasn't to be ignored. Beddoe welcomed Smith to the fold by loosening his tie and joking about his Air Canada costume.

That wasn't the only rookie misstep. Parts of Smith's speech didn't sit well with Don Bell, another of the original WestJet veterans. Smith conjured a pretty future for WestJet, with better returns for investors, satisfied "guests" (WestJetters never used the word "passengers"), and happy employees. It was the right list of stakeholders, Bell thought, but the order was backwards. At WestJet, employees came first, even before guests.

From the outside, Steve Smith and WestJet seemed a perfect fit. He became the charismatic promoter the airline needed as it expanded from an Alberta regional carrier to a national discount airline. He was a tireless salesman for the company when WestJet turned to the stock market to raise capital for its expansion plans. He was the convert who could explain to analysts and potential investors why WestJet's corporate culture was so critical. Smith soon indulged in the Air Canada–bashing that helped define that culture. The anti–Air Canada sentiments were as thick as ever now that the Montreal carrier had abandoned alliance talks with

WestJet. When Milton announced plans to launch a discount carrier out of Hamilton, Smith commented that one airline "should not dominate all facets of the industry." Air Canada, he said, should "stick to long-haul business flights."[20]

Inside the company, however, tensions between Smith and the four founders were intensifying. There were disagreements about how quickly WestJet should expand to the East, and about the seating capacity of new jets that were about to be ordered by the dozens. It got to the point where the founders didn't pay any attention to Smith at the weekly executive meetings. "He'd kind of pretend like he was CEO, but we'd go out afterwards and say, 'Okay. We know he said this – but let's just do that,'" said Mark Hill.[21] It was an open mutiny. There was more conflict when Smith proposed cutting the commissions that WestJet paid to travel agents. Other airlines were reducing commissions, and Smith thought WestJet could boost its margins by following suit. Smith believed it was a decision to be made by management, but his call was overruled by the chairman of the board, Clive Beddoe. "He said in his gut he didn't think it was the right decision. He made us reverse it," Smith said. "It called into question the role of the board versus the role of management."[22] Beddoe counters that, as executive chairman, he was well within his rights to veto a decision he didn't agree with.

By the summer of 2000, Hill and Morgan felt their power was being usurped by a know-it-all from Toronto. Hill told Beddoe he couldn't work with Steve Smith any more, that he was leaving the company he had helped found, but would be back when Smith was gone. It didn't take long. On September 11 of that year, WestJet announced that Steve Smith had left the company. In a remarkably candid conference call with analysts, Beddoe said Smith had micromanaged managers and had practised a "top-down" style that didn't fit at WestJet. "Our style and his style were like chalk and cheese," Beddoe said. "He wants to interfere . . . and second-guess people and change the decisions they've made. And that makes them throw up their hands and say, 'What's the point?'"

CEOs are pushed out of companies all the time, but rarely if ever had a board chairman been so voluble about the alleged shortcomings of an ousted executive. More common was the one-line announcement that an executive had departed "to pursue other interests." Beddoe refused to whitewash executive-suite turmoil. He felt he had a responsibility to WestJet's employees to be blunt about his reasons for jettisoning Smith. "They have to have confidence that they are not going to be fired for no reason at all," Beddoe explained later.

Smith had his own version of events. On the day of his ouster, he telephoned reporters to say Beddoe's public flogging reaffirmed that he had made the right choice in leaving WestJet. He called Beddoe's comments "unfortunate," and disagreed that he had a top-down management style. Smith later said he had tried to make the best of a bad situation, but it proved impossible. "It's a very difficult situation where you've got three founders reporting to you and one founder that's the chairman of the board," he said. "We ended up not being a good match. It was easier for Steve Smith to leave than for the four founders to leave."

The circumstances surrounding Smith's departure led to a number of conspiracy theories. Some WestJet employees wondered if Smith had been "on assignment" from Air Canada during his eighteen months in Calgary. Smith's allies at Air Canada suspected the WestJet founders had simply used him when they needed a good talker to help raise investment money, only to cast him aside when the job was done.

In order to qualify for a resignation payment of $704,400, Smith agreed not to work at another airline for at least a year. But the day would come when Smith would attempt to beat his former WestJet colleagues at their own game.

WestJet had faced tough competition from Air Canada since the day it started selling tickets in 1996. But the acquisition of Canadian Airlines in 2000 gave the larger carrier unprecedented and dangerous monopoly power. If it wanted to, Air Canada could easily put its smaller competitors out of business. The federal government responded to these concerns by granting significant enforcement authority to Konrad von Finckenstein, the federal commissioner of competition. WestJet officials were eager to test the new regulations, so they waited and watched for the first clear example of possible abuse of dominance. They didn't have a long wait. On WestJet's "first" birthday, February 29, 2000, the airline announced that it would launch service between Hamilton and Moncton as part of its expansion into Eastern Canada. The timing seemed right. After the merger, Air Canada had cut back on domestic capacity by about 15 per cent, leaving some room for new service. And perhaps consumers would be looking for an alternative to Air Monopoly.

WestJet selected the John C. Munro Hamilton International Airport as its eastern hub. The airport was cheap, underutilized, and could handle large aircraft. For people living in Hamilton, London, Kitchener-Waterloo, and St. Catharines–Niagara, it was much more convenient than Toronto's bustling Pearson International. These were four of Canada's twelve largest cities, with a combined population of some 1.8 million, roughly the same size as Vancouver. WestJet had a huge catchment area to draw from, in addition to the four million residents of the Greater Toronto Area, who might be tempted to drive the extra forty minutes to Hamilton airport for WestJet's lower prices.

Before WestJet's entry into the Eastern Canadian market, Air Canada sold one-way fares between Toronto and Moncton for as much as $605. WestJet offered Hamilton–Moncton fares for $129 to $339, in keeping with its strategy of stimulating traffic with lower fares. Nine days before WestJet was scheduled to commence service, Air Canada slashed its Toronto–Moncton fares and boosted capacity by 55 per cent, shifting from three F-28 aircraft to two DC-9s and one Bombardier regional jet. The dominant carrier matched WestJet's lowest Hamilton–Moncton fare, and undercut its walk-up fare – the price customers would pay if they bought a ticket at the airport right before a flight – by 27 per cent. Air Canada's most expensive one-way fare had fallen to $249, an overnight drop of 59 per cent. At the same time, Air Canada added an extra flight a day between Toronto and Moncton, making it more difficult for WestJet to fill the seats on its planes. Slashing fares and adding capacity – was this the "dilution" strategy that had been described a year earlier in the report to Air Canada's board of directors? If so, it worked.

WestJet lost $182,585 during the first ten months of service on the Hamilton–Moncton route.

WestJet filed a complaint with von Finckenstein, who investigated and agreed that Air Canada appeared to have broken competition laws. In March 2001, the commissioner announced that he would take a case against Air Canada to the federal Competition Tribunal, the quasi-judicial body charged with enforcing competition law. In an affidavit submitted before the tribunal, Mark Hill said Air Canada had cut fares and dumped capacity "with the foreseeable effect of rendering WestJet's operations on the route unprofitable for the purpose of curtailing WestJet's plans to expand operations to points in Atlantic Canada." Air Canada objected strenuously to the allegations. The dominant carrier did not dispute that it had targeted WestJet, but insisted it had done so within the law.

It was not the first time Air Canada had been accused of predatory behaviour, and it would not be the last. WestJet wasn't the only carrier trying to establish a toehold in Eastern Canada. Canada 3000, Royal Airlines, and CanJet were all scrambling for a piece of Air Canada's pie. And Robert Milton was adamant that Air Canada had every right to defend its territory by strategically – some would say ruthlessly – matching fares.

8

THE FIGHT FOR THE EAST

It appears that Air Canada wants to put us out of business and we are determined to prevent this from happening.[1]
– Ken Rowe, owner, CanJet Airlines

It would seem apparent to us that, if CanJet is seriously under threat of being eliminated as a competitor after a little over a month of operations, it is more as a direct result of their business plan and other carrier activity than our fare initiative.[2]
– Calin Rovinescu, executive vice-president, Air Canada

*A*irfares, *Miami Herald* columnist Dave Barry once explained, are determined by Rudy the Fare Chicken, who decides the price of each ticket "by pecking on a computer keyboard sprinkled with corn." If the airline tells you it's having computer problems, Barry wrote, "this means that Rudy is sick, and technicians are trying to activate the backup system, Conrad the Fare Hamster."[3]

This whimsy rings all too true: airfares appear to be entirely inconsistent and arbitrary. In fact, the opposite is true. Airlines use complex computer programs designed to maximize the revenue on every seat, based on a variety of factors including class of service, time of year, day of the week, how far in advance the ticket is purchased, and whether the stay at the destination includes a Saturday night. A full-service airline like Air Canada can have more than fifty different published fares on any given route.[4] It is not uncommon for the passenger in 12A to have paid more than twice the price as his seatmate in 12C for exactly the same level of in-flight service. Since altering a fare requires only a few key-strokes on a computer, airlines can respond to a rivals's pricing – or to the arrival of a new competitor – in an instant.

On September 1, 2000, Air Canada introduced a new fare on a handful of routes in Eastern Canada and loaded it into the computer-reservations systems. The so-called L14EAST fares carried more restrictions than Air Canada's existing one-way fares – they had to be booked fourteen days in advance – but they were far less expensive. Between Halifax and Ottawa, for example, Air Canada's lowest one-way fare was slashed to $109 from $605. Previously, Air Canada had sold cheap seats on the route – at $390 – only as round-trip tickets.

The previous day, CanJet Airlines had received its operating certi-ficate from the federal government, and with it, approval to launch passenger service on Eastern Canadian routes stretching from Winnipeg to St. John's. CanJet was offering low fares and it sold them on a one-way basis. Air Canada's L14EAST fares were offered on the routes flown by CanJet: Halifax–Toronto, Halifax–Montreal, Halifax–Ottawa, Halifax–St. John's, Toronto–Winnipeg, Toronto–Windsor, and Ottawa–Windsor. At first glance, Air Canada's actions seemed gratifying evidence of the benefits of competition. Now consumers would enjoy reduced fares – not just from an unproven start-up, but from an established network carrier that awarded frequent-flyer points and offered connections around the world. But Air Canada's response to CanJet's arrival raised questions: why was the dominant carrier charging so much in the first place, and what would happen to Air Canada's fares if CanJet disappeared?

Ken Rowe, CanJet's owner, was not amused. Air Canada's move to slash fares seemed like bullying. There could be little doubt that the L14EAST fares were aimed squarely at the Halifax-based start-up. Not only were the special fares confined to those routes where CanJet was competing, at first they were offered exclusively on flights that departed at around the same times as CanJet flights.

Rowe had launched his carrier with the expectation that the new competition laws would prevent Air Canada from savaging its competi-tors. It was time to put those laws to the test. On September 7, two days after CanJet took to the skies, Rowe filed a complaint with the federal Competition Bureau, alleging that Air Canada's "massive selective fare reductions" constituted predatory pricing and an abuse of Air Canada's dominant market position. "It certainly is clearly activity aimed at CanJet and trying to minimize our impact in the marketplace, which ultimately is aimed at trying to make sure we don't get established," CanJet's chief operating officer Mark Winders told the *Globe and Mail*.

There are times when it makes good business sense for a dominant firm to engage in predatory pricing – that is, to be willing to sustain losses on a product – in an attempt to drive out a competitor. It might suffer severe losses for a time, but it will reap the benefits through higher prices once the target firm has been eliminated from the marketplace.

Competition law is based on the assumption that, in rare cases, government intervention in the market can improve economic efficiency and consumer welfare. Buyers usually benefit when suppliers compete to provide the lowest possible price for a good or service – but not always. Exceptions arise when one firm has enough clout to put a weaker competitor out of business through predatory pricing. Bankruptcies are a fact of life in a healthy market-based economy. In industries where there are lots of competitors, a single bankruptcy is not likely to affect the price that the consumer pays. But in a consolidated industry, a bankruptcy gives the surviving firms an increased ability to raise prices. As a result, there is a generally accepted view that governments must sometimes put limits on free-market competition.

Michael Trethaway, a British Columbia economist specializing in the airline industry, has pointed out that airlines are particularly susceptible to predatory behaviour. In research prepared for the Competition Bureau, Trethaway explained that a targeted airline is vulnerable because it has high fixed costs and no ability to store inventory.[5] Unlike other businesses that have flexibility to adjust manufacturing levels based on demand, an airline must commit to a flying schedule before any seats are sold. It has no ability to store inventory, since every empty seat is "spoiled" as soon as the aircraft pushes back from the gate. A manufacturing company that is subjected to predation might be able to store its inventory and wait for the threat to pass, or even borrow operating funds against its inventory. An airline that is so targeted can do neither.

In addition, dominant airlines have powerful tools in their arsenal to facilitate predatory behaviour, Trethaway suggested. Because tickets are sold over the Internet or through computer-reservations systems, prices are transparent to other competitors and can be matched or bettered almost immediately. And through the use of advance-booking requirements, a dominant airline can lock up passengers for weeks with a seat sale that lasts just a few days. "Thus in a matter of hours, or at best days, a predatory action could remove revenue from a small or new target carrier, not only for the period when the low ticket prices are available for sale from the dominant carrier, but for future travel beyond the sale period as well. My main observation is that, in the airline industry, a small carrier subject to predation by a dominant carrier can fully expend its working capital in a short period, one measured in weeks," Trethaway wrote.

Air Canada never denied that its L14EAST fares were aimed at CanJet, but the airline vigorously contested Rowe's claim that the move broke the law. "A fare reduction 'targeting' CanJet or otherwise is not an anti-competitive act," Air Canada senior vice-president and general counsel John Baker wrote in an affidavit. "Indeed the state of the law in Canada is that reducing prices to meet or match competition cannot be anti-competitive."

Robert Milton believed that, as a dominant airline, Air Canada would be in the wrong if it undercut a competitor's lowest prices. He maintained Air Canada had been careful never to do so. But he was emphatic that Air Canada should always have the right to match a competitor's price. "Otherwise, how do you stay in business?" he asked in a 2002 interview. Milton illustrated with the example of an intersection with a gas station on each corner. Three of the gas stations are charging 70 cents a litre, but the fourth is being told by the government that it must charge 84 cents. "Nobody's going to [pay] 84 cents a litre, so how can you not be able to match a competitor's prices?"

Whether Air Canada has ever undercut a competitor's fares is a matter for debate. After WestJet launched flights into Moncton, Air Canada matched the discounter's lowest fares, and undercut its top prices. Furthermore, some observers argue that Air Canada undercuts its competitors every time it matches prices, since its tickets include extras like frequent-flyer points and network connections to hundreds of destinations. Economists will sometimes establish a relative, or "hedonic," price to compare products with different qualities. The concept of hedonic pricing was invented in 1938 by an economist working for General Motors to show that cars were becoming less expensive every year – despite price increases – since every new model carried more features than that of the year before. Applying the idea to airfares, a $99 ticket on Air Canada could theoretically have a lower hedonic price than an $89 ticket on CanJet, since customers earn frequent-flyer points, enjoy the ease of network connections, and sometimes are served meals.

On October 12, Konrad von Finckenstein gave Ken Rowe what he wanted. After a quick investigation of Air Canada's pricing practices, the commissioner of competition used his new powers for the first time, ordering Air Canada to "cease and desist" from selling L14EAST fares on five routes. He was of the opinion that Air Canada had "engaged in conduct which could constitute anti-competitive acts." The commissioner said that, without the temporary order, CanJet was "likely to be eliminated as a competitor on specific routes." CanJet's bookings and revenue increased substantially in the days following the order.

Air Canada challenged the decision, arguing von Finckenstein had no constitutional authority to issue a cease-and-desist order on his own. The airline said it was committed to respecting the government's abuse-of-dominance provisions, but claimed that the cease-and-desist order itself was "contrary to the spirit and letter" of the law. "Air Canada's fare initiative on the five routes in question is entirely consistent with our long-standing policy of offering competitive pricing in all markets we serve," said Calin Rovinescu, the former Stikeman Elliott lawyer who had advised Air Canada on the takeover battle with Onex. Milton had recruited him away from the law firm only a few months earlier, offering a lower salary but an impressive title: executive vice-president, corporate development and strategy.

Unlike so many others at Air Canada, Rovinescu did not grow up with a love of airplanes. The son of a Romanian surgeon, Rovinescu and his family moved to Canada when he was an infant. His father stressed the importance of having a profession – not a business career – and law was a suitable second to medicine. Rovinescu wanted to do criminal law but his future was cast as a business lawyer when he was hired by Stikeman Elliott in 1978. On his first day on the job, Rovinescu was sent to pick through an estate – a man's life in dozens of garbage bags crammed inside a garage – to find an expensive stamp collection. It was a favour by the firm for the Consul General. The stamp collection was nowhere to be found, and by mid-afternoon, Rovinescu was ready to quit. But the next day, he was working on a $250-million financing transaction. Such diversity was good training for a career in law, where every day brought something new. In his early years, Rovinescu made a name for himself specializing in film financings. But he also worked on more conventional jobs, including raising money for Air Canada when it was still a Crown corporation. He spent a few years at the Stikeman office in England before returning to Canada to become the firm's managing partner in 1992. In 1999, working on the Onex defence, Rovinescu was attracted to the airline business – for all the wrong reasons. "I'm not really in love with the industry; in fact, I see it as an industry that's broken," Rovinescu said. "I'm not somebody who takes out his binoculars and studies the movement of aircraft. . . . It is a business that is highly stimulating because of the number of complexities."[6]

In late November, the federal Competition Tribunal, a quasi-judicial body with jurisdiction over competition law, rejected Air Canada's effort to overturn the cease-and-desist order. In the ruling, Justice Sandra Simpson pointed to the fact that CanJet's bookings had increased in the two weeks following the commissioner's intervention. She said the carrier would "likely suffer a significant loss of revenue" in the absence of the order, and she extended it to the end of the year to give the Competition Bureau time to determine whether it would bring formal charges of predatory behaviour against Air Canada.

That was not the only trouble Air Canada was experiencing with regulatory agencies.

On Thursday, October 5, 2000, Air Canada's director of investor relations, Valerie Peck, placed after-hours calls to thirteen financial analysts, warning them that Air Canada's third-quarter profit would come in at around $80 million, about half of its original published projection. The bad news didn't end there. In the fourth-quarter, Peck revealed, Air Canada was facing a $50-million loss, instead of the $7-million profit the airline had forecast. The early warning allowed brokerage firms to advise their best clients to program in their "sell" orders before the opening bell the next morning. On October 6, Air Canada's shares opened the day at $14 on the Toronto Stock Exchange (TSX), 7 per cent below their closing the previous afternoon. The shares continued to fall, dropping as much as 14 per cent, before recovering slightly at the end of the day.

The message Peck had left on the analysts' voice-mail machines named and quantified Air Canada's unanticipated liabilities. Higher fuel prices would cost the airline an extra $65 million; the new contract with pilots would push up wages and benefits an additional $30 million; efforts to improve customer service as part of the whirlwind 180-day campaign would total $15 million. Lastly, the threat of a strike at Air Canada and its partner, United Airlines, had discouraged business to such an extent that the bottom line would be short another $30 million. Taken individually, any one of these factors would be understandable, even forgivable, since they were generally beyond Air Canada's control. Taken together, they totalled a whopping $140 million, and turned an anticipated second-half profit of $170 million into a lacklustre $30 million.

The warning itself was alarming, but the way it was delivered raised more serious questions. Companies like Air Canada, with shares trading on a stock exchange, are known as "public" companies because members of the public have the opportunity to own part of the business by buying or selling fractional shares on the exchange. In theory, the market is constantly attributing a real-time value to the company, using all the information that has been disclosed to gauge a firm's earning potential. The concept works well when companies are transparent, disclosing material information to every potential investor at the same time. Usually this is done through news releases posted on the company's Web site and other related sites, or immediately sent by e-mail to subscribing investors. When Air Canada disclosed information about its earning potential to a select group of analysts at brokerage firms, however, investors associated with those firms received the information ahead of others. Some had enough information to sell at $14 a share at the opening bell, while others sold at the day's low of $12.85. For an investor with 1,000 shares, the delay in selling meant a loss of $1,150.

TSX officials noticed that Air Canada's shares were down significantly first thing in the morning. At 9:41, they put in a call to the company to ask about a vague wire story reporting that an Air Canada official had guided analysts' expectations downward. The exchange's immediate concern was that Air Canada right its wrong. If the company had selectively disclosed any information, it should make sure the same details were released to all potential investors as quickly as possible. Minutes before the closing bell, however, Air Canada had yet to comment on Peck's calls the previous night. The analysts, meanwhile, were talking. Jacques Kavafian of Yorkton Securities defended the company's actions, saying there would have been a "panic in the stock" if Air Canada had issued a news release. "Everybody wants to have this news before everybody else so they could sell the stock before the stock went down," he said.[7]

Finally, at 3:57 p.m., Air Canada issued a news release. Instead of broadly disclosing the information that had been relayed to analysts the night before, the airline sought to cover its corporate butt. The company expressed "disappointment" in the share drop, but said it had simply reviewed information with analysts that was "already in the public domain." It was a critical point. If the facts and figures had already been made public, then how could Air Canada be accused of selectively disclosing it in voice-mail messages to the thirteen analysts?

Officials at Air Canada would cling to this argument, even after agreeing in July 2001 to pay $1 million in fines to regulators in Ontario and Quebec for violating securities laws. In a legal document related to the settlement, Air Canada acknowledged that the information in the messages had not been "generally disclosed by Air Canada" before it was shared with the analysts. It recognized that it had broken the Ontario Securities Act, the TSX regulations, and its own internal guidelines. But in a classic display of institutional arrogance, the company thumbed its nose at the regulators in a news release issued hours after the settlement was finalized. Air Canada claimed that the settlement did not include "any finding or admission of illegal conduct or breach of securities laws." A spokesman for the Ontario Securities Commission could only sputter that Air Canada's press release was "not in the spirit" of the settlement agreement.

The executive who coordinated the calls to the analysts now says the intent was to make sure the recipients wouldn't misunderstand Air Canada's third-quarter numbers when the results were released four weeks later. Chief financial officer Rob Peterson still maintains that the information had been disclosed earlier, but says no analyst had been able to pull together all the data to properly forecast the bottom line. As a result, most were expecting higher profits than Peterson could deliver. He says he worried that, if the analysts were surprised by the actual results, they would jump to conclusions about Air Canada's future profitability. Peterson claims he simply wanted to remind the analysts that most of the charges wouldn't represent recurring items. "That's what we were trying to do," Peterson said. "Now clearly history has said that was not the right thing to do."

There were two postscripts to the story of Air Canada's tangle with securities regulators. The first came on October 26, when Air Canada's third-quarter profit came in at $107 million, easily beating the results that the airline had told the thirteen analysts to expect. The second occurred a year later when Valerie Peck left Air Canada. Her departure prompted suspicions that she had become an easy scapegoat, when in fact she had simply followed orders. But Peterson said Peck's departure was unrelated to the incident. In fact, he said, Peck had stayed with the company longer than planned, because of the investigation by securities officials.[8]

Just before Christmas 2000, Canada 3000 president Angus Kinnear predicted that the turmoil in the Canadian airline industry would continue through 2001 and result in at least one bankruptcy before the end of the new year. He declared the discount market was already overcrowded with Canada 3000, Royal Airlines, CanJet, and WestJet fighting for a finite number of passengers. Things would only get worse, he said, if Air Canada followed through on its plans to launch a discount carrier. "There will be some winners and some losers, as always," Kinnear told a reporter from his office near Toronto's Pearson International Airport. He wouldn't speculate about the losers, but he was adamant that Canada 3000 would be one of the winners. Though he didn't mention it at the time, Kinnear was preparing to merge with one of his low-cost rivals.

The moody Brit – once described by *National Post* reporter Peter Fitzpatrick as a "charismatic curmudgeon" – had been with Canada 3000 since its creation in 1988. Born in 1943, Kinnear grew up in London with a passion not for the skies, but for the seas. He never doubted that he would follow his father, a steamship engineer, into the business of ships. But ocean travel was undergoing a revolution by the time Kinnear went to work for the cruise-ship company Cunard Lines in his late teens. In 1958, Pan American World Airways had introduced the Boeing 707 jetliner, the safest, fastest plane to date. The jet brought down the cost of air travel, making it accessible to many more people as a means of travel between Europe and North America. Realizing that its traditional business was on the verge of extinction, Cunard bought a controlling interest in Eagle Airways in 1960 and acquired a couple of Boeing 707s of its own. Kinnear says that, when he was twenty years old, his bosses advised him to work for the airline to find out what "this flying thing" was all about.

He found the business exhilarating. After a couple of years he went to work for Donaldson International Airways, a Scottish carrier, which sent him across the Atlantic to run their Canadian operations. After four years, he returned to England, but he never stayed in one place very long. With no wife or children to tie him down, Kinnear soon established himself as the guy who could be sent into the world's hot spots on a moment's notice, places like Iraq, Nigeria, and Afghanistan. When Bangladesh declared its independence from Pakistan in 1971, Kinnear was sent to Karachi to shuttle Bengalis into Bangladesh. When Idi Amin ordered Asians out of Uganda in 1972, Kinnear ran the airplanes that evacuated the exiles. He frequently feared for his life, but he loved the thrill of a vocation in which every day was different.

"When somebody said we have a job to do, you got on an airplane and did the job," Kinnear says. "Wherever there was a problem in the world during that period, I tended to end up there."

One night as he was getting ready to meet his boss for dinner, Kinnear called to say he would be late, because he wanted to watch the news before he ate.

"Angus," his boss replied, "we make the news, not watch it."9

In 1986, Kinnear moved to Manchester to help found a new airline for Owners Abroad, a large British tour operator. Air 2000 would be a Manchester-based leisure airline, inspired by an unconventional model. The accepted rule for charter airlines was that the guy with the cheapest planes won. Charter airlines usually flew the stuffing out of their planes on weekends, when people wanted to fly, then allowed them to sit idle during the week. If they were parking their planes, they wanted the oldest, cheapest jets they could find. The founders of Air 2000 intended to try something different, emulating an approach being pioneered at the time by Air Europe. Instead of flying old warhorses, Air 2000 leased two brand-new Boeing 757 aircraft. The aircraft leases were expensive, but the fuel and maintenance costs were low. If Air 2000 got enough hours out of the planes, unit costs would fall below those of older jets. But in order to cover the cost of the leases, the airline had to fly the aircraft for long days, 365 days a year. This represented a challenge during the winter, when the traditional European charter market slowed down.

Kinnear was told to find a place for the aircraft during the winter months. He struck a deal with Paul Gervais and Colin Hunter, the owners of Adventure Tours, to launch a Canadian wing of Air 2000. Since federal legislation limited the British company to a 25-per-cent stake, Hunter and Gervais would own most of the enterprise, along with John Lecky, a Calgary investor. The grandson of H.R. MacMillan, one of the founders of forestry giant MacMillan Bloedel Ltd., Lecky was born into money. He was active in the Olympic movement and had been a member of the Canadian team that won a silver medal in eight-man rowing at the 1960 Rome Olympics. Following seven years at Greenshields Inc. as an invest- ment banker, he set up his own investment company, Resource Funding Ltd., which dabbled in various industries, from oil and gas to helicopters and airlines.

Kinnear owned a home close to London's Gatwick Airport, but spent little time there. Constantly travelling, he felt most comfortable in hotels. He lived at a Hilton hotel for his first eight months in Manchester, before finally buying a townhouse near the Manchester United football pitch. The day the curtains were hung, his bosses informed him that he was being relocated to Canada. Brian Walker, the Canadian who had been hired to run the Canadian operation, had left to set up Odyssey Inter- national, a new charter airline, leaving Air 2000 with no president. Kinnear decided never to buy another house.

Once in Toronto, he took a room at the Hilton near Pearson Inter- national Airport and made it his home for the next thirteen years. Air 2000 received its licence on August 11, 1988, and took office space on Fasken Drive, a short walk from the Hilton, a few weeks later. Kinnear hired staff and began training pilots and flight attendants in anticipation of a November 9 launch. A crew was sent to London to pick up the first plane on November 4. Four hours before the plane was scheduled to leave England, the company received a call from the National Transportation Agency, saying the airline's licence had been revoked. Although Canadians owned the required 75 per cent of the company, regulators believed it was effectively controlled by a foreign firm. The airline had the same name as its British affiliate, it used the same planes, and it was managed by the same executives. Even the motto was the same: "Tomorrow, Today."

The carrier was launched nearly a month late, on December 2, after meeting the transportation agency's requirements. The British company agreed to sell its shares to Canadian investors — the Deluce family, who were part owners of Air Ontario and other regional carriers. Bob Deluce took the president's title from Angus Kinnear, but Kinnear continued to perform the office's duties as "assistant to the president." Years later, after Kinnear reclaimed the presidency, his business cards still did not include a job title. On the issue of what the airline would be called, Kinnear offered to change the name to Air 3000, but regulators deemed it too similar to Air 2000. In the end, they settled on Canada 3000, a brand name designed to appeal not to consumers but to regulators.

Canada 3000 took off into increasingly crowded skies. Air Canada, Canadian Airlines, and Wardair were competing for scheduled passengers, while Nationair, Worldways, and Odyssey were vying for charter business from the tour operators. Canada 3000 would outlive almost all of its early rivals, and Angus Kinnear would prove to the doubters that new, fuel-efficient jets can be cheaper than old clunkers. Or, as Kinnear liked to say, technology rules.

There were, however, two sturdy survivors on the charter side of the business: Royal Airlines and Air Transat. For years, the three carriers engaged in on-again, off-again merger talks. Canada 3000 executives would try to do a deal with Royal Chairman Michel Leblanc. When those talks grew stale, they'd explore the possibilities with Transat. Soon after, they'd be meeting again with Leblanc. An amalgamation of some kind seemed inevitable; the question was when.

Like so many of his contemporaries in the aviation industry, Michel Leblanc was hooked on jet fuel from a young age. He was born in Montreal in 1946, the son of a wheeler-dealer. His father was a used-car salesman with a love for planes and a knack for trading up. He sold the used-car lot for a General Motors dealership, traded up again for a Cessna dealership, then opened a flight-training school.

When Michel was seven years old, his father took him on his first plane ride in a Piper J3 seaplane. Leblanc was terrified — and smitten. As a teenager, he worked at the airport washing and fuelling planes and got his student pilot's licence on his sixteenth birthday – the earliest possible date – through his father's flight-training school. He earned a private licence exactly one year later and a commercial licence exactly one year after that. Leblanc studied economics at the Université de Montréal, then took an M.B.A. at the University of Buffalo, before returning home to the family business. He once sold seventy-eight airplanes in a single year, a wheeler-dealer just like his dad.

One of Leblanc's customers was Guy Bernier, an acquaintance who operated a crop-spraying business. The business was doing well, but Leblanc thought it could do better. In 1979, he went into business with Bernier, leasing bigger planes to do tree-spraying for the provincial government under the punning moniker Conifair Aviation.

In 1986, he took on new partners and purchased Québecair, a money-losing regional carrier, from the provincial government. Renamed Inter-Canadian, the carrier grew quickly and profitably until the partners decided to try their luck against Air Canada and Canadian. In 1989, they re-branded the airline as Intair and launched service on the Toronto–Ottawa–Montreal triangle. In February 1990, Leblanc boasted that Intair was already profitable on its share of the highly competitive Toronto–Montreal route.[10] A very different picture emerged by November when the airline sought protection from its creditors under the Companies' Creditors Arrangement Act. Leblanc sold out to his partners a few months later.[11]

"I basically lost my investment," Leblanc says. "Financially it was not a good operation for me, but it was certainly good as experience."

Leblanc drew on that experience a year later when he established Royal, a charter airline division of the Conifair tree-spraying business. The airline's maiden flight took place on April 29, 1992, between Toronto and Vancouver, with just a few passengers, but Royal soon established a foothold, operating flights to the Caribbean, Mexico, and Europe on behalf of tour operators. Its fortunes rose in 1998 when it won the contract to operate flights for Signature Vacations, Canada 3000's main client for years. By mid-2000, Royal had eight aircraft in its fleet and Leblanc wanted more. He was encouraged by transport minister David Collenette's publicly expressed desire for domestic competition for Air Monopoly.

"He was sending signals through the media that there was still some need for competition out there and some buoyancy in the market, and we listened to those signals," Leblanc said.

In August 2000, Leblanc hosted a lavish press conference in Toronto to announce that he was transforming Royal Airlines into a full-fledged scheduled carrier. He would acquire four new Boeing 737 aircraft, add flights on key routes, and offer new destinations, such as Calgary, Edmonton, and Thunder Bay. He would also introduce a premium service, with more legroom for passengers willing to pay for it. Leblanc and his PR advisors knew exactly how to ensure the expansion was well covered by the media. They played up the competition angle and reminded the press that Air Canada was going through its worst summer in memory. "I think the market is looking for alternatives. It's all about competition," Leblanc said.

Canada 3000 had likewise risen to Collenette's challenge. In May 2000, the airline decided the time was right to take the company public on the Toronto Stock Exchange. WestJet's initial public offering the previous June had been extremely successful, and Lecky and Kinnear hoped to raise $25 million. With that war chest, Canada 3000 would be able to turn itself from a niche charter carrier into a full-service scheduled airline. It announced that it was leasing four new Airbus A319 aircraft – all for use in the domestic market – that would boost its domestic capacity to forty thousand seats a week from twenty-four thousand. The executives at Canada 3000 and Royal saw the Air Canada–Canadian merger as a huge opportunity for whichever airline could grow quickly enough to establish itself as the main competitor to Air Canada.

It was not an opportunity that attracted Transat A.T. Inc. Transat was founded as a package-tour operator in 1983 by Jean-Marc Eustache, a one-time student radical from Quebec, and his partner, Philippe Sureau. They launched Air Transat in 1988 to provide "lift" for their package tours, but regarded airlines as chronically unprofitable. Their planes flew south in the winter and to Europe in the summer, with limited exposure to the domestic Canadian market. If Air Transat had an aircraft in Vancouver that was needed in Toronto for a charter flight, it might sell a few cheap seats to help cover its costs, but it had no interest whatever in running regularly scheduled flights in Canada.

Every other airline seemed eager to jostle for the number-two spot behind Air Canada. WestJet, Royal, and Canada 3000 had announced major expansions, while new start-ups like CanJet and Roots Air were also lining up for a chance to occupy second place. Air Canada appeared to have a stranglehold on the domestic market, flying more than three-quarters of the country's passenger miles, but there was extraordinary competition for the remaining 25 per cent. These small discounters were putting pressure on Air Canada of a kind that Canadian Airlines never could: with lower operating costs they could lead on pricing, especially since they were willing to sustain losses while they jockeyed for position.

"Competition is alive and well. For about the price of a tank of gas and lunch at Tim Hortons, you can now fly to Montreal," Robert Milton told the Canadian Club of Toronto in February 2001. "The fact is there are more choices for Canadian consumers than ever before, and Air Canada is now being challenged by a new generation of airlines which didn't even exist a few years ago." David Collenette was pleased too. He gloated to reporters that, despite fears that the merger would leave the airline industry with little real competition, the opposite had occurred.

In January 2001, Canada 3000 executives finally accomplished a merger deal. The chairmen of Canada 3000 and Royal met in Suite 1742 at Montreal's Queen Elizabeth Hotel to finalize the details. It was the same suite where John Lennon and Yoko Ono recorded "Give Peace a Chance" during their famous bed-in during the summer of '69. Angus Kinnear and Michel Leblanc agreed to combine their companies to form an airline with the critical mass necessary to take on Air Canada. LeBlanc was coming with his company; he would be named vice-chairman of Canada 3000.

When the merger was formally announced in Toronto on January 29, Kinnear was nowhere to be seen. He was in India, laying the groundwork for the airline's latest exotic destination. Chief financial officer Don Kennedy announced the agreement in his place, stirring speculation that Kinnear was unhappy with the arrangements. In fact, while the company's executives had been divided on the merits of the merger, it was Kennedy who had opposed it. Kennedy agreed that a merger could help Canada 3000 to grow quickly, but he was not convinced that Royal was the right vehicle. Despite his concerns, Kennedy did his best to put a positive face on the result. "We believe this is in the Canadian public's interest, as it does provide a viable national alternative," Kennedy told reporters.

Reaction was mixed. Transport minister Collenette said the merger was a sign that competition was developing as it should. Yes, the acquisition would take one player out of the game, but it would allow Canada 3000 and Royal to put together a schedule that might provide some serious competition to Air Canada in the domestic market, with a wide enough range of flights to satisfy even business travellers. But some airline analysts suggested the merger could lead to disappointing results for Canada 3000 shareholders. Ben Cherniavsky, an analyst with Raymond James, said it looked as if Canada 3000 was pulling a bait-and-switch on its investors. In a prospectus, issued in May 2000 to interest investors in its initial public offering, the airline spelled out the key components of its business plan: maximize utilization on modern aircraft; don't offer a business class; and vary the schedule to avoid direct competition with Air Canada. With the Royal merger, Canada 3000 was obtaining a mixed fleet of older, less-fuel-efficient jets, contemplating a business-class service, and competing directly with Air Canada on the Toronto–Montreal–Ottawa triangle.

"It doesn't make any sense to me," Mr. Cherniavsky said. "Everything goes out the window, basically, and I'm left with no landmarks for confidence except blind faith in management."[12]

Before the Canada 3000–Royal deal closed, the two carriers continued to discount heavily. And, despite the Competition Bureau's cease-and-desist order, Air Canada remained aggressive in its pricing. In the midst of this intense competition, CanJet Airlines was in talks with US Airways to add three new jets to its fleet – an increase of 50 per cent. It was hard to believe CanJet would be able to fill more planes.

Then, on Valentine's Day, 2001, CanJet withdrew, announcing that it had been unable to strike a deal with US Airways. CanJet had insisted on an "out clause" that would have allowed it to return the jets without penalty if its expansion plans soured. But the aircraft leasing unit of US Airways had refused to grant anything less than a fixed lease. "It would be fair to say we have not achieved our expectations, there's no question," Mark Winders said. "We're in a major competitive battle with Royal Airlines and we are under attack and have been constantly from Air Canada."[13]

Winders's comments violated a cardinal rule in the aviation business: Never admit that things are going badly. Since consumers pay in advance for a product that won't be delivered until the flight departs, they want to be sure their investment is sound. All else being equal, customers will choose the airline with the best chance of delivering them to their destination and bringing them home. A carrier that suggests it can't fill its planes will have as much chance of survival as a bank that reveals it doesn't have enough cash to cover its deposits. Ironically, the Competition Bureau process contributed to CanJet's difficulties. An airline had recourse to protection from the bureau only if it admitted it was in trouble.

And CanJet was once again in trouble. On February 13, Air Canada had introduced another class of fares that targeted CanJet. The so-called LAC fares were available on flights between Halifax and Toronto, Ottawa, Montreal, and St. John's, as well as on the Toronto–Winnipeg route. They were offered on a one-way basis as before, but this time no four-teen-day advance booking was required. These fares – as low as $89 between Halifax and Montreal – matched the lowest fares CanJet offered at the time. CanJet responded with even lower fares, offering Toronto–Winnipeg from $99, Toronto–Halifax from $79, and Halifax–Montreal from $69. When the Competition Bureau threatened to issue another cease-and-desist order, Air Canada grudgingly withdrew the LAC fares on three routes: Halifax–Montreal, Halifax–Ottawa, and Halifax–St. John's.

In a conference call with analysts, Milton said it was "baffling" that Air Canada was being prevented from selling seats at a discount. "I think the pressure will mount on [regulators] when it's recognized that what's happening here is that Canadians are not being allowed to be offered low fares by Air Canada," he said. Milton was especially perturbed that the competition commissioner was able to issue cease-and-desist orders without even having to prove that Air Canada was behaving inappropriately.

In March 2001, Konrad von Finckenstein thought he had found his proof. He asked the Competition Tribunal for a formal order preventing Air Canada from engaging in anti-competitive practices against WestJet and CanJet. The Competition Bureau said it believed Air Canada's "pricing and capacity management" would result in the discounters abandoning their routes and consequently in "higher prices in the long term." True to form, Air Canada challenged the allegations. "We have to be capable of meeting our competitors' pricing initiatives on our key routes in Canada," said Calin Rovinescu. "All competitors regardless of size should have that right. We are aware of no precedent in the airline industry of a regulator disallowing price matching."

Air Canada and the Competition Bureau both expressed an interest in a quick resolution to the dispute, but it dragged on for years. In some respects, it would be Canada's version of the U.S. Department of Justice case against Microsoft, in which the computer giant was accused of using predatory practices to protect its monopoly in personal-computer operating systems. But the Air Canada case lacked the resonance of the Microsoft case, since most consumers didn't mind that Air Canada offered low fares. To the contrary, consumers wanted them.

Predatory pricing often goes unprosecuted because it is notoriously difficult to prove according to Pat Hanlon, an airline economist at the University of Birmingham, England. In his 1999 book, *Global Airlines*, Hanlon writes that it can be almost impossible to distinguish between a reduction in price designed to eliminate a competitor and one that represents healthy competition, made possible when the dominant firm cuts costs.[14] It is rare to find a smoking gun, such as an e-mail confirming a scheme to get rid of a competitor. (The case against Air Canada would include the January 1999 report to its board, in which it was noted that Air Canada had been able to "drive out" its rivals in Eastern Canada. But in testimony at the hearing, Air Canada executives distanced themselves from the document, saying it had been prepared by an outside consultant and claiming that its account differed from the actions actually taken by Air Canada.)

Even when such documents exist, judges are likely to minimize their significance, seeing them as healthy corporate bravado, rather than as evidence of illegal activity. Consider a U.S. case involving a pricing battle between egg producers (*A.A. Poultry Farms, Inc. v. Rose Acre Farms, Inc.*), in which the dry financial testimony was enlivened by colourful quotes suggesting intent, such as, "We are going to run you out of . . . business. Your days are numbered." In a 1989 ruling, Justice Frank Easterbrook concluded that intent was irrelevant. Most businesses, he wrote, "intend to do all the business they can, to crush their rivals if they can. . . . Firms need not like their competitors; they need not cheer them on to success; a desire to extinguish one's rivals is entirely consistent with, often is the motive behind, competition."

Instead, the burden of proof in predatory-pricing hearings rests on economics. Traditionally, courts have relied on a test developed in 1975 by two Harvard Law School professors, Philip Areeda and Donald Turner. They theorized that a dominant firm selling below its average "variable costs" is very likely engaging in predatory behaviour. Unlike fixed costs, variable costs are those that increase with each unit produced. As long as a firm prices its product so revenues exceed variable costs, even if they don't cover total costs, it is earning a contribution towards overhead – a rational short-term business strategy. But if pricing is such that revenues don't cover variable costs, the firm is losing more money with each unit it produces. There can be little economic justification for doing so other than to eliminate a competitor in anticipation of recouping losses through higher prices in a less competitive market.

The problem with applying the Areeda–Turner test to airlines is that the variable costs associated with selling a single seat or operating a flight are minimal. Once an airline has committed to offering a flight, most of its

Father of Aviation: James Richardson's Western Canada Airways was one of the forerunners to Canadian Airlines. By 1930, it was world's largest air-cargo company, but Richardson wanted more.

Howe's Airline: C.D. Howe (left) known as the minister of everything, on the steps of an early Trans-Canada Air Lines plane with TCA president Herb Symington (right). Howe once said of TCA: "That's not public enterprise, that's my enterprise."

Up and Away: Canadian Pacific Airlines president Grant McConachie fought to smash TCA's transcontinental monopoly. The flamboyant pilot and entrepreneur secured rights to Australia and Asia, which would become the Blue Team's chief asset.

Slow and Steady: Despite winning the Distinguished Flying Cross in the war, Trans-Canada Air Lines president Gordon McGregor was cautious and conservative. Successors would rue his reluctance to take risks.

Succession Planning: Air Canada's board of directors did the unthinkable in 1992, hiring an American to run Canada's flag-carrier. Hollis Harris brought along two American protégés: Lamar Durrett and Robert Milton. The trio would run Air Canada for more than a decade.

Plane-Spotter: Friends saw Robert Milton as blunt but considerate; critics called him arrogant and self-important. Shortly after arriving at Air Canada, Milton hatched a plan to boost productivity by distributing phony flight schedules to the operations staff.

Project Peacock: When Air Canada resisted a friendly merger, Canadian Airlines president Kevin Benson crafted a plan to take over the larger carrier. He found Onex Corp. more than willing to assist.

From Fizz to Flight: After losing out on John Labatt Ltd. in 1995, Gerry Schwartz desperately wanted to own a well-known Canadian brand. He became the public face for the controversial plan to merge Canada's airlines.

O Air Canada! During the takeover battle, all sides embraced the maple leaf in an effort to convince the public that their position was the best for Canada. The battle pitted Don Carty (above), the Canadian-born CEO of American Airlines, against Robert Milton, the American-born CEO of Air Canada.

Strange Bedfellows: Under fire for his Liberal connections and his involvement with American Airlines, Gerry Schwartz (right) was desperate for an ally in his fight against Air Canada. He secured an endorsement from CAW president Buzz Hargrove (left).

Brush-Off: David Collenette (right) suspended the Competition Act, neutering competition commissioner Konrad von Finckenstein (left). Later, the pair worked together to impose conditions on the proposed merger.

WestJet Too: Mark Winders (right) impressed upon CanJet founder Ken Rowe (left) the importance of emulating the low-cost model WestJet had copied from Southwest Airlines.

Brand New: Roots Air was all about marketing. "I've branded more things than I know what to do with," said executive vice-president Ted Shetzen (far right). Also shown here (left to right) are Roots founder Michael Budman, actor Dan Aykroyd, Roots founder Don Green, and Skyservice Airlines CEO Russell Payson.

Canadian Transportation Agency

Tibor Kolley/ Globe and Mail

Whistle-Blower: David Collenette appointed former NHL referee Bruce Hood as the country's first air travel complaints commissioner. Hood and Robert Milton disliked one another vehemently.

Charismatic Curmudgeon: Angus Kinnear ran Canada 3000 from its inception in 1988 until its spectacular failure thirteen years later. He lived alone in a hotel near the Toronto airport.

WestJet Airlines Ltd.

The Little Airline That Could: WestJet Airlines has grown remarkably fast since its 1996 launch. In 2001, the airline's four founders were named Ernst & Young's entrepreneurs of the year. Shown (left to right) are Mark Hill, Don Bell, Tim Morgan, and Clive Beddoe.

Tibor Kolley/ *Globe and Mail*

Routs Air: Robert Milton (left) and Skyservice CEO Russ Payson (right) announce in 2001 that they will ground Roots Air and re-brand it as Air Canada's discount affiliate.

Deborah Baic

If at First You Don't Succeed: Michel Leblanc is a perennial figure in Canada's airline industry. After Inter-Canadian and Royal Airlines failed to prosper, Leblanc founded Jetsgo in 2002.

Chalk and Cheese: Steve Smith was happy to return to Air Canada to run Zip Air Inc. after an unhappy stint at WestJet Airlines, where he locked horns with the airline's founders.

Spoils of War: When Hong Kong investor Victor Li struck a deal to buy nearly one-third of Air Canada in late 2003, he insisted on the continued employment of Robert Milton (left) and Calin Rovinescu (right). Each would receive valuable stock grants as retention bonuses.

costs are already fixed. The expense of "producing" the last seat might be the cost of a soft drink, some pretzels, and a negligible increase in fuel costs due to the weight of the passenger. Since airline seats can't be put into inventory, an airline is smart to sell off empty seats for whatever it can get.

Instead, regulators looking at airlines use a variation on the Areeda–Turner test known as the "avoidable cost" test, which includes not just variable costs, but fixed costs that could have been avoided – for example, by shifting aircraft to other routes.[15] For an airline, the test can be applied to a single flight, multiple flights, or all flights on a route. If a carrier has avoidable costs of sixteen cents per passenger mile, but revenue of just thirteen cents, this would raise suspicions of predatory pricing.

Simple, right? It's not – because Air Canada and the Competition Bureau have quite different views on what costs are avoidable and how to quantify revenue. Konrad von Finckenstein pushed for a broad definition of cost and a narrower definition of revenue, while Robert Milton argued the opposite. For example, Air Canada said its labour costs were not avoidable because pilots had to be paid whether they were flying or not. If most of Air Canada's costs were not avoidable, the airline had sound economic justification for offering cut-rate fares. The bureau argued that labour costs were avoidable on any specific flight, because they could be redeployed to other routes. If the bureau could prove most costs were avoidable, then it could prove the airline had engaged in predatory behaviour. Similarly, Air Canada maintained that "revenue" calculated in the avoidable-cost test should include a segment of income earned from passengers connecting to other flights in its network, an argument with which the bureau disagreed.

Air Canada and the Competition Bureau were generally in agreement about the facts, but they differed on the interpretation. As Dave McAllister, a senior competition-law officer at the bureau, put it: "If a police officer finds a dead body with a bullet hole, it's clear there's been a murder. The question is who did it. In our line of work, we know who did it. The debate is whether what they did is a crime."[16]

The flip side of predatory pricing to eliminate competition is price gouging where none exists. While the Competition Bureau investigated allegations of illegally low prices in early 2001, the Canadian Transportation Agency (CTA) was pursuing complaints that Air Canada was exploiting customers on routes where there were few or no alternatives. Federal law allowed the CTA to regulate "unreasonable" fares, but only on monopoly routes.

On March 7, two days after von Finckenstein announced that he would seek a formal order at the Competition Tribunal, the CTA ruled that Air Canada's $398 fare between Vancouver and Prince Rupert was unreasonable. The CTA found that, on the Winnipeg–Saskatoon route, where Air Canada faced competition from WestJet and Athabasca Airways, the equivalent fare was just $200. The routes were comparable, according to the agency, because they were roughly the same distance apart (755 km for Vancouver–Prince Rupert versus 704 km for Winnipeg–Saskatoon) and they were travelled by about the same number of passengers annually (41,200 passengers versus 57,800).

However, the CTA decision was confounded by the fact that a new competitor, Hawkair Aviation Services Ltd. of Terrace, B.C., had entered the Vancouver–Prince Rupert market a few weeks before. And if things weren't complicated enough, Air Canada faced a predatory-pricing complaint from Hawkair related to another route. "This is starting to look like a Marx Brothers movie," said Andrew Reddick, a spokesman for the Canadian Association of Airline Passengers.[17]

Air Canada played its PR hand brilliantly. "Should Air Canada comply with the pricing directive sought by the agency as a remedy to this complaint, we would be significantly undercutting the fares offered by a competing airline that recently introduced service on this route," said Calin Rovinescu. "The decision rendered by the agency highlights the challenge currently faced by Air Canada in complying with the conflicting mandates of the Canadian Transportation Agency and the Competition Bureau."

Analysts were concerned that Canada 3000 had bitten off more than it could chew with the Royal merger in January 2001. But by mid-March, there was speculation that the happy couple would become a threesome. Ken Rowe had been sending signals that CanJet was for sale. He had stopped in Calgary on a trip back from Australia to discuss the possibility of a WestJet–CanJet merger, but Clive Beddoe said he wasn't interested. What about Angus Kinnear then? When a reporter asked about rumours that Canada 3000 would add CanJet to its collection of airlines, Kinnear said he was too busy managing the integration of Royal to think of anything else. "It's a little early to consider dessert," Kinnear said.[18]

One week later, Kinnear developed a sudden appetite, announcing that Canada 3000 would buy CanJet's assets for $7 million in stock.

Kinnear had been around the airline business long enough to know that size counts. Passengers are willing to pay a premium to travel on the airline that gives them the most destinations and the highest frequency. The Eastern Canada discount market was in chaos, with three airlines engaged in a costly battle for market share. None could put together anything resembling a network on its own. "If we all sit and squabble on the sidelines and fight amongst ourselves, Air Canada's going to roll right over us," Kinnear had told Rowe and Michel Leblanc. "If we're going to make some impression here, we've got to combine our capacity."[19] With the three-part merger under way, Canada 3000 was poised to become the country's second-largest carrier and a true alternative to Air Canada's near monopoly.

9

A BROKEN INDUSTRY

A recession is when you have to tighten your belt; depression is when you have no belt to tighten. When you've lost your trousers – you're in the airline business.[1]
— Sir Adam Thomson, founder, British Caledonian Airways

*I*t was another snowy day in Toronto. On December 21, 2000, Air Canada issued its eighth storm warning of the young winter season, advising customers of delays and cancellations at Pearson International Airport. Hours later, the airline unleashed a storm of a different sort, with a statement that angered investors, employees, customers, and government; in short, all the constituency groups that mattered to Air Canada. It warned investors that it would not achieve its profit forecasts for the quarter. It told employees it would slash 3,500 jobs. And for customers? A 6-per-cent increase in domestic airfares.

"Year 2000 has been a year of tremendous challenge, success, and setback for Air Canada," Robert Milton said in the press announcement. He clearly had mixed feelings about his first full year in the captain's chair. Rising fuel prices were eating into profits, and the company would post a loss for 2000. But Milton was hopeful about 2001. The company's internal numbers suggested that it was beginning to achieve some of the projected $700 million in cost synergies as a result of the merger with Canadian Airlines. Economists were forecasting lower fuel prices and Air Canada's 2001 income statement wouldn't be littered with one-time integration costs.

Milton's customers were less optimistic about the prospects for customer service. Passengers stranded in Toronto by weather delays grew testier when news of the fare hikes and job cuts was spread by reporters who had descended on the airport. "Well, that will improve service!" dentist Mark Panzer quipped caustically to one journalist. While he waited for a flight that was already an hour and a half late, Panzer expressed dismay that Milton would cut jobs and raise fares on the heels of the 180-day campaign to improve service and mend customer relations. His skepticism reflected a lingering view that Air Canada didn't care about its customers. "The bottom line is the bottom line," Dr. Pazner said, "but he made a commitment and as far as I can see, the commitment isn't being met."[2]

When Air Canada reported its year-end financial results a few weeks later, Milton was less bullish about 2001. He had hoped Air Canada would increase capacity by 8 per cent. Now he was forced to concede that there would be no growth in 2001, forestalling his ambitious plans for new foreign destinations. Milton said that, despite his "enthusiasm for international growth," he wouldn't proceed unless it made sense for shareholders. "Obviously, the slowing economy dampens the interest in doing it right now because it becomes more difficult and increases the risk," he said.

Air Canada's pre-Christmas announcement did nothing to improve relations between the airline and air travel complaints commissioner Bruce Hood. Asked by a reporter what he thought about the fare increases and job cuts, Hood unleashed a windy tirade. "They've got this whole image problem that is so prominently important to them and yet they go shoot themselves in the foot by doing what they just did. I get a little bit frustrated when I've gone to great lengths to tell them how I think they could do better."[3] Some of his frustration arose from the unsatisfactory level of co-operation he felt he had received from the airline. He was especially perturbed that Air Canada seemed unwilling to apologize for its service glitches.

The mild-mannered career civil servants at the Canadian Transportation Agency couldn't understand Hood's rabble-rousing. "Why are you so hard on Air Canada? We have a lot of relationships there," one official asked him.

"Maybe that's the problem," Hood shot back.[4]

Throughout his mandate, Hood was an outsider, neither respected by the airlines nor accepted by his colleagues at the CTA. Early on he had considered resigning the post, but persevered out of a healthy sense of self-righteousness. Among the hockey and travel memorabilia that adorned his office was a framed piece of embroidery that read: "Rule #1: The referee is always right. Rule #2: In case of misunderstanding, refer to Rule #1."

It didn't take Hood long to discover that Air Canada played by its own rules. The airline fired back at the commissioner in March, with a charge of conflict of interest. Hood had intervened on behalf of a couple from Milton, Ontario, who blamed Air Canada for problems during their Hawaiian vacation. Some of their travel arrangements had been made by Bruce Hood Travel. Although Hood had sold his 25-per-cent interest in the agency, the complaint against Air Canada dated back to the period when he was still part-owner. After consulting with federal ethics counsellor Howard Wilson, Hood agreed that there was an appearance of conflict. But Wilson told the *National Post* that Hood had done nothing wrong. "In my view it was done not with an intent of assisting at all his former travel agency . . . but out of enthusiasm for his job. It was innocent and well-meaning."[5]

Only days later, in late March, Hood released his first semi-annual report on passenger complaints. On the surface, the statistics were astonishing, suggesting that customer service had taken a sharp turn for the worse, despite the 180-day blitz. Hood said his office had received complaints from 1,248 passengers in the final six months of 2000 – almost five times the number the CTA had received in the first six months of the year. While the increase was related, in part, to problems with Air Canada's merger with Canadian Airlines, it was also a predictable response to the creation of a formalized federal office to receive passenger complaints. Hood said his greatest concern was not with the service problems themselves, but with the inability of the airlines to respond to them. Far too often, the companies replied with form letters, extolling their virtues without really addressing the specific concern. "If you have a complaint, you want to feel like your complaint was looked after. The carriers need to accept the responsibility for it, acknowledge it and deal with it," Hood said.[6]

On March 17, 2001, Canada 3000 chairman John Lecky wrote an anxious letter to president Angus Kinnear outlining the long list of tasks before them. It included completion of the merger with CanJet and Royal Airlines, the creation of business-class service, and the introduction of flights to India. "*Our priority*," Lecky underlined in a handwritten fax, "is to get the best advantages possible out of the Royal deal. Everything else is *secondary*, and should *be postponed* until you are confident of a profitable/non-crisis introduction."[7]

Subsequent letters made plain Lecky's reservations about the India program and the new business-class service. Kinnear had announced service to India through a *Globe and Mail* article in late January. He said Canada 3000 would offer the first commercial non-stop flights between Toronto and New Delhi, using the polar route to fly over the top of the world instead of around it. But Canada 3000's board of directors had not yet approved the India plan. In a fax dated April 3, Lecky accused Kinnear of treating the directors like employees.

"Major initiatives, i.e., Polar flights, should *not* be announced publicly, until you have had an opportunity to bring the Board on side. . . . If the Board were shown to be irrelevant in this procedure, one of two things would happen: either the Board composition would change over, or the president would be asked to. Obviously with things going so well, we don't want to be roasted on these coals of procedure."

There were also top-level tensions between Lecky and vice-chairman Michel Leblanc. On Saturday, June 16, Leblanc boarded a plane for the Paris Air Show, a biannual event at which airline executives check out the latest offerings from aircraft manufacturers. Leblanc was there to shop for possible replacements for Canada 3000's aging Boeing 737s. On

Sunday night, Leblanc returned to his hotel room to find an urgent message to call John Lecky.

"He basically told me our paths were parting and he didn't see any reason to keep working together," Leblanc said. "He told me there would be a letter forthcoming." Lecky advised him that Canada 3000 was terminating three other employees who had come to the company with Leblanc: his wife, her brother, and Roland Blais, Royal's former chief financial officer.

At first, Canada 3000 didn't have a lot to say about Leblanc's sudden departure. On June 20, in announcing a healthy profit of $18 million for the year ended April 30, Angus Kinnear cited an unspecified "basic disagreement." More details emerged in mid-August when Canada 3000 filed a $45-million lawsuit against Leblanc, Blais, and Groupe Royal Aviation Inc., an investment company controlled by Leblanc. Canada 3000 alleged that the three defendants had conspired to overstate Royal's pre-tax profit and profit projections by $20.2 million for the third and fourth quarters of fiscal 2001. The airline sought $40 million in damages for "fraud, negligence, breach of contract, conspiracy," and fraudulent or negligent misrepresentation of Royal's financial statements and records. The company also sought $5 million in punitive damages. "Leblanc, Blais and Groupe Royal engaged in the aforesaid conspiracy in order to induce Canada 3000 to make its offer and complete its acquisition of Royal and to ensure that Canada 3000 offered the highest price possible for the common shares of Royal," the claim alleged. At the same time Canada 3000 warned its shareholders that the Royal problems would affect short-term earnings.

Leblanc and Blais countered with their own $30-million suit against Canada 3000, claiming that the airline had sullied their reputations and breached contractual obligations. Leblanc said it appeared that Canada 3000 simply wanted to get rid of him once the merger deal was done. "This was a hostile takeover camouflaged as a friendly merger," he told the *Globe and Mail*.[8]

Ben Cherniavsky at Raymond James recommended that his clients sell Canada 3000 shares, saying the lawsuit raised questions about whether the airline had done enough research into the financial state of the company it was buying. "Irrespective of whether or not Royal's statements were actually misrepresented, the fact that they were not what they appear to be suggests, in our view, that management's due diligence process was weak," Cherniavsky wrote. Canada 3000 had not hired truly independent financial advisors on the deal. Instead, they relied on counsel from Capital Canada, which received $800,000 for its role in the negotiations. Robert Foster, the president and CEO of Capital Canada, was a member of Canada 3000's board of directors. Cherniavsky said the Royal imbroglio raised concerns that there might also be problems with the subsequent acquisition of CanJet.[9]

By midsummer, John Lecky was preoccupied with Canada 3000's liquidity. On July 31, the airline had just $82 million in cash available, but faced $106 million in liabilities for prepaid flights. In other words, the airline had taken in revenue for roughly twenty-six days worth of tickets, but had funds available for only twenty days of operation. Every week, Lecky studied the cash-flow projections from the airline's finance department, paying special attention to October 28, which was expected to be the low point of the cash supply. On June 13, it looked as if there would be enough cash to get the company through the fall, with a projected balance of $7.3 million on October 28. A month later, that figure had become a $7.3-million deficit. When the projected shortfall ballooned to $31.6 million in early August, Lecky called an emergency meeting in Vancouver with Angus Kinnear and David Hardouin, the president of Canada 3000 Holidays. Lecky urged them to take action to avoid running out of cash, perhaps by cancelling flights and postponing the airline's planned entry to India.[10]

Eddie Rickenbacker, the legendary president of Eastern Airlines, once described airline economics as "the business of putting bums in seats." Ryanair CEO Michael O'Leary has said air transport is "just a glorified bus operation." And Mike Batt, the marketing director of British Airways, says that, despite the "mystique and romance" surrounding aviation, "there's no difference between selling airline seats and chocolate bars" when it comes to the principles involved in satisfying customers.[11]

But most people who have spent time running airlines will say that it is a business unlike any other. Airline executives are called upon simultaneously to act like theatre directors, greengrocers, landlords, and merchants in a bazaar. Air travel is manufactured at exactly the same time it is consumed – as is live theatre. Like a grocer selling produce, airlines sell products with a fixed expiry date. A head of lettuce that hasn't been sold before it turns brown is worthless; it's the same for an airline seat that hasn't been sold by the time a flight takes off. It's also a business with a high percentage of fixed costs and a low number of variable costs – much like an apartment building. When the occupancy rate is high enough to cover those fixed costs, everything else is pure profit. An airline that breaks even selling 65 per cent of its seats can make healthy profits at 66 per cent – or go out of business at 64 per cent. As a result, airlines fight ruthlessly for every point of market share. They might lose a fortune selling seats below cost, but they'd lose considerably more if they didn't sell them at all. Hence the airline executive, like the overeager merchant, will haggle to sell his product for whatever he can get.

In economic parlance this haggling is known as prejudicial pricing: selling essentially the same product to different customers for very different prices. Leisure air travellers, who generally look for the cheapest seats, are said to be price inelastic and service elastic. Business travellers, who want frills and an ability to change and cancel flights without hassle, are said to be price elastic and service inelastic. A businesswoman who needs to get to Vancouver from Toronto to close a deal might be willing to pay $2,500 for her return ticket, while a senior citizen wanting to visit his grandchildren might refuse to pay more than $600 for the same seat. Both will be accommodated – to the airline's advantage – by computerized yield-management programs.

Yield management is, first and foremost, an attempt to make business people pay as much as possible, then to fill the remaining seats with leisure passengers. On major international airlines like Air Canada, high-fare passengers have traditionally accounted for 30 per cent of the passengers, but 70 per cent of the revenue.[12] Airlines erect what they call "fences" to differentiate between business and leisure passengers and to discourage high-yielding passengers from buying cheap tickets:

- Business travellers like to travel between Monday and Friday, so passengers who want cheap seats usually have to stay at their destinations over a Saturday night.
- Business travellers tend to cram several destinations into their trips instead of buying multiple return tickets, so airlines tend to charge more for one-way trips than for return bookings.
- Business travellers are eager to spend more of their employers' money to earn perks for themselves, so airlines will coax them into higher-fare classes with frequent-flyer points.
- Business travellers often need to travel at the last minute, so cheap tickets need to be booked days in advance.
- Business travellers want the ability to cancel bookings or change flights at the last minute, so low-end fares are usually non-refundable.

Yield-management programs are incredibly sophisticated. If a customer calls at 2:00 on a Thursday afternoon to book a Toronto–Vancouver flight departing the following Wednesday morning at 8:00, the yield-management program will analyze historical booking data to see how many people customarily book during the final five days. It will then predict the current trend based on seasonal and schedule variables, competitors' fares, the health of the economy, and the number of seats available on other Wednesday-morning flights. At the end of the process, it spits out a choice of fares. A business traveller will likely choose a high fare with few fences and lots of flexibility, while the leisure traveller will usually pick a low fare with many fences and few frills.

These programs are also responsible for the most serious exasperation air travellers face – overbooking. The problem isn't that airlines can't count the number of seats they sell; it's that they intentionally sell more tickets than there are seats, on the assumption some business travellers won't show up for their flights. Since high-fare customers are allowed refunds for missed flights – even if they don't call to cancel – lots of them don't show up. If more check in than the airline is expecting, it can bribe some of its low-fare passengers to wait for the next flight – and still come out ahead.

But by early 2001, discount carriers had fundamentally altered the rules of the airline industry to the point at which yield-management programs had become irrelevant. With the economy slowing, businesses across North America slashed their travel budgets. Companies directed their employees to make fewer trips and buy cheaper seats. Some tried the discount alternatives and found they weren't so bad. The Southwest clones, which were supposed to appeal to low-fare leisure passengers, began to win business travellers from the full-service carriers. WestJet, for one, did away with complex price discrimination, offering low fares on a first-come, first-serve basis, regardless of whether passengers were staying over a Saturday night, buying one-way tickets, or might have to cancel.

Some airline executives hoped that the business traveller would return with a stronger economy. But Robert Milton wasn't holding his breath. As he acknowledged in his letter to Air Canada's pilots in February 2001, customers of all kinds were less willing to pay higher prices when they had a low-cost alternative. The traditional airline business model had cracked; airlines that didn't adapt would disappear.

Russ Payson wasn't sleeping and he could barely eat. April 2001 was, without a doubt, the worst period of his career. Day after day, the CEO of Skyservice Airlines sat alone in his office running spreadsheets on a simple Lotus program. After just four weeks in operation, Roots Air was failing so badly that it threatened to destroy Payson's life's work.

He stared hopefully at his computer screen, juggling numbers, modifying assumptions, raising this figure and lowering that. What if fuel prices fell back to normal levels? What if bookings increased by a third? The most optimistic estimates suggested that Roots Air could survive the seasonably slower months and get through to the following spring. But the more realistic spreadsheets all forecast that Roots Air would run out of cash by November, pulling all of Skyservice into bankruptcy.

So many things had gone wrong. Passengers continued to buy the least-expensive bronze-class seats, not the gold and silver seats that were supposed to set Roots Air apart from the competition and pay the bills. Air Canada had bowed to federal-government pressure to make its Aeroplan frequent-flyer points available to competitors for a fee, but it soon became clear that the program would not be in place in time for Roots Air's launch. "So much for their promises," Payson said in a speech in Vancouver. "These tactics are for one purpose only – to discourage you from choosing Roots Air and to try to financially injure Roots Air." Air Canada countered that it had every intention of fulfilling its obligations, but needed time to work out the details of a frequent-flyer agreement with Skyservice. In the end, Roots Air joined forces with Alaska Airlines to set up its own frequent-flyer program.

In January, Air Canada had added to the injury with a new class of fares designed to appeal to the "price sensitive business traveler." The ACFlex fare required passengers to book ten days in advance, while eliminating the Saturday-night-stay requirement, a direct challenge to Roots Air's efforts to establish itself as the affordable business-class alternative to Air Canada. Then, just weeks before Roots Air's March launch, Air Canada introduced yet another class of low fares. These were available only on Toronto–Vancouver and Toronto–Calgary flights – the same markets that Roots Air was serving. A three-day advance-purchase fare between Toronto and Calgary started at $909. The Toronto–Edmonton fare – where Roots Air didn't fly – remained at $1,903.[13] At these levels, Air Canada's fares were still higher than Roots Air's, but the timing was suspicious to Ted Shetzen, the ideas man behind Roots Air. "They're very selective about what they do," Shetzen said. "If there's a new entrant that could be labelled troublesome to their market dominance, they go in and do a surgical strike."[14] Air Canada insisted that the new fares were unrelated to Roots Air's inauguration. The two routes were chosen as test markets for the new fares because they both carried high volumes of passengers, the airline said. It was simply a coincidence that Roots Air would be providing competition in precisely the same markets.

Yet Air Canada was a mere distraction compared to Canada 3000. On day seventeen of Roots Air's existence, Canada 3000 announced that it, too, would offer business-class seats starting in May. With greater frequency and prices that Roots Air couldn't match, Canada 3000 would capture the niche that Payson and Shetzen had expected to fill. Michel Leblanc later acknowledged that Canada 3000's "Big Seat" program had just one motive: to eliminate Roots Air. And in a letter to his board of directors dated October 23, 2001, John Lecky noted that the company philosophy was, "we needed Big Seats to kill Roots."

For Russ Payson, the situation was desperate. He took a much-needed break from the pressure in April and went to Mont Tremblant for a few days of skiing. Halfway down his first run, Payson stopped on the hill and stared at the tips of his skis, the sun glinting off the sparkling snow. "This is crazy," he said to himself. He skied to the bottom and told his wife that he had made up his mind; it was time to pull the plug on Roots Air. They drove back to Montreal and took the next flight home to Toronto.

The next morning, Payson informed Shetzen and the rest of the management team of his decision. "We nearly got into a fist fight. They thought I'd fallen off my rocker," Payson recalled later. "It was not a pleasant meeting." Ultimately, everyone accepted the inevitable and agreed to work together for an orderly shutdown, ensuring that customers who had bought tickets were protected on another carrier.

Someone might even be willing to buy Roots Air, they thought, and a list of possible buyers was compiled. There was Canada 3000, which had recently bought Royal Aviation and CanJet Airlines; maybe it would be interested in one more carrier. Or perhaps Virgin Atlantic, since Richard Branson had mused about the possibility of starting a domestic airline in Canada. Roots Air initiated some preliminary discussions with Virgin, but quickly discovered that the British carrier was interested in little more than access to Roots Air's handsomely appointed executive lounge at Pearson International Airport.

Ted Shetzen had a different buyer in mind. Robert Milton had repeatedly talked about Air Canada's need to get into the low-cost airline business to compete with aggressive upstarts like WestJet. His greatest stumbling blocks were the unions, who maintained that Milton had no right to hire low-cost labour for the operation without their consent. Shetzen made a trip to Montreal to visit Rupert Duchesne, the president of Aeroplan, Air Canada's frequent-flyer division. Since Duchesne was one of the few executives hired directly by Milton, Shetzen thought he might be a good ambassador for the proposal. Shetzen's idea was that Milton could get around the unions by striking a partnership with an existing carrier. "My strategy all along was to let Air Canada take its problems with its pilots . . . and its flight attendants, and use Skyservice as an opportunity," Shetzen said.

The meeting left Shetzen hopeful, and he returned to Skyservice's Toronto offices expecting to be greeted like a hero. He told Payson that Air Canada appeared genuinely interested in the idea of turning Roots Air into its own discount airline. Payson, however, was anything but enthusiastic about a deal with his adversaries. Hadn't they stymied Roots Air's efforts to offer Aeroplan points? Hadn't they cut their fares in the markets Roots Air would be serving? But with Roots Air burning cash, Payson couldn't afford to be picky. He too flew to Montreal, meeting there with Calin Rovinescu.

"We're not coming in here posturing. We're going to shut this thing down," Payson told Rovinescu. "But is there anything you could use?"[15] They talked through the weekend, arriving at an agreement through which Air Canada would not only acquire the assets of Roots Air, but take a controlling interest in Skyservice Airlines.

The day before the deal was announced, Air Canada quietly eliminated its ACFlex fare. Once again, travellers wanting discounted fares were required to stay over a Saturday night at their destination. Those unable to do so were faced with a $1,537 bill for a one-way trip between Toronto and Vancouver, more than double the ACFlex fare offered when Roots Air was a competitor. Of course, Air Canada insisted, the elimination of the cheaper fares had nothing to do with the demise of Roots Air.

The Air Canada–Skyservice arrangement was made public on May 3, 2001, Russ Payson's fifty-seventh birthday. (The same day, Air Canada announced a $168-million loss for the first quarter of 2001.) Roots Air would make its final flight the next day after less than six weeks in the air, and Air Canada would buy an 85-per-cent stake in Skyservice for about $15 million. It would distribute a 35-per-cent stake to its shareholders the following year, and retain a 50-per-cent voting block for itself. Payson would stay on as president and CEO of Skyservice.

It was the sort of day the spin doctors love. The Roots Canada founders did their best to put the failure of Roots Air in a positive light, saying they were "delighted" with developments. Michael Budman said it was a "totally positive" experience for the Roots brand. Russ Payson claimed that, while Roots Air was "winning a number of battles on a number of fronts," the war had become too costly. Robert Milton played down Air Canada's role, making sure everyone understood that it was Skyservice that had approached Air Canada and not the other way around. He called the deal a "strategic partnership" – unusual terminology, given that Air Canada would hold an overwhelming majority stake. Milton insisted that, while Air Canada would become the controlling shareholder, it would not control Skyservice's operations. This, he emphasized, was neither an acquisition nor a merger. The argument was critical to Air Canada's ability to complete the transaction, since the federal Competition Bureau might hesitate to approve a new acquisition by an airline that already controlled three-quarters of the domestic market.

Konrad von Finckenstein was quick to point out that the arrangement looked to him like a merger, and he used the opportunity to recommend again that the government open Canada's skies to foreign competition. Transport minister David Collenette shrugged off the suggestion, saying that international carriers would just "cream off" the best routes and leave Canadian carriers to serve the smaller, less profitable ones. "Once we allow any of those foreign carriers in, do you know what they will do? They'll run on the main trunk routes where the money is to be made: Toronto to Vancouver, Toronto to Calgary," Collenette said.

"And who is going to suffer? It will be WestJet, it will be Canada 3000, and it will be Air Canada."[16]

WestJet Airlines chairman Clive Beddoe called on the government to block the Air Canada–Skyservice deal, saying there was obviously something wrong with the government's airline policy when six airlines – Greyhound, Vistajet, Canadian Airlines, Royal Aviation, CanJet, and Roots Air – had disappeared in five years. Even Air France warned Ottawa that it would be bad for Canadian consumers and other small carriers – not to mention Air France. The French national airline had been on the verge of announcing an agreement to exchange passengers with Roots Air.

The most serious objection came from Air Canada's pilots, who had signed a new contract with the airline a few weeks earlier. The bargaining had been long and bitter, nearly resulting in a strike during the terrible summer of 2000. The airline's plan to launch a discount carrier, known internally as Low Cost Co., had been one of the sticking points during the negotiations. The Air Canada Pilots Association had settled for relatively small wage increases in order to obtain protection for its members' jobs. Air Canada had agreed to the union's demand that the discount carrier's flights be flown by ACPA pilots, that it be limited to just six aircraft, and that it could grow only if the mainline carrier grew as well. The Skyservice deal appeared to nullify these hard-won concessions. "We find it repugnant that Air Canada is trying to circumvent the provisions of a contract that we worked out together in a collective bargaining process," said ACPA chairman Raymond Hall. The union filed a formal grievance, complaining that the company had violated its collective bargaining agreement.

At first, Air Canada insisted that nothing in the pilots' contract prevented it from investing in another carrier. At the company's annual general meeting in May, Milton vowed that the deal would go ahead despite the concerns of the Competition Bureau and the pilots. Behind the scenes, things were not going so smoothly. In early July, Payson acknowledged that the July start-up date had been pushed to October because of the pilots' challenge.[17] He confessed that the Air Canada–Skyservice agreement was still nothing more than a letter of intent.

Then, in late July, Air Canada abandoned the Skyservice "partnership." Instead, Air Canada announced it would establish its own discount airline, to be flown by unionized Air Canada pilots. The pilots allowed Air Canada to shift twenty aircraft to Low Cost Co., rather than the six it had agreed to in previous contract talks, and they accepted a lower wage scale for Low Cost. But even with the pay cut, their base salaries would be almost twice those of WestJet pilots with comparable experience.[18] Milton conceded that his discount airline would be more expensive to operate without Skyservice's non-unionized staff, but he said the savings weren't worth the cost of a disgruntled workforce.

After the demise of Roots Air, the collapse of the Air Canada agreement was crushing for Russ Payson. "Obviously we're disappointed, but there's no point in doing a bad deal," he said philosophically. "It was becoming apparent that we could not achieve a good deal that involved Skyservice."

So who would run Air Canada's new discount carrier now that Russ Payson was out of the picture? Robert Milton answered that question at the end of the summer when he named former WestJet president Steve Smith to the job. Smith had been lobbying Milton to hire him back ever since his falling out with the WestJet founders. Milton announced that Smith would rejoin Air Canada on September 10, 2001, exactly one year after his acrimonious exit from the Calgary discounter. Milton said Smith's appointment reflected his commitment to make the low-cost carrier a success. "Simply put, we went out and landed the top individual in the field for the job." WestJet executives were likewise cheered when they learned that their former president was going to work for Air Canada, but for different reasons. "That's the best news I've heard today," one said.[19]

Air Canada wasn't the first full-service airline to try to beat a discount rival with an airline within an airline. Several carriers in the United States and Europe had tried it, with little success. Continental Airlines was the first, setting up Continental Lite in 1993, shortly after Hollis Harris's departure. Dreaming of Southwest-like profits, executives at Continental took a third of their planes and re-branded them as Continental Lite. They removed the twelve first-class seats on each jet and replaced them with eighteen coach seats, which immediately brought down the unit cost. With lower fares, revenue would fall too, but competing with Southwest was about expenses, not income. They turned the planes more quickly and took away the meals, sacrificing cleanliness and customer service in the quest for reduced costs.

It seemed like a fine idea. But Continental Lite was a "dismal failure," according to the airline's chairman, Gordon Bethune, who wrote about the "costly experiment" in his book *From Worst to First*. "Continental Lite," he observed, "is the kind of product you get when you use backward thinking, when you define your products by what would be really nice to sell. It would have solved a great problem for Continental Airlines if we could have run those 100 airplanes with their coach seats and no food and 2-hour flights. It would have given us a nice revenue stream and a chance to compete in a market we were having trouble competing in. The problem was . . . it still wasn't a product people wanted to buy." Continental Lite not only failed to attract new customers, it cannibalized passengers from the mainline carrier. "Although we have two separate products – full service and bare bones – the passenger only remembers that when he flew Continental he didn't feel good about it."[20] Continental dismantled its airline-within-an-airline less than two years after launching it.

Most other U.S. airlines that had set up discount subsidiaries were still trying to figure out how to make them work. United Airlines had launched Shuttle by United in 1994 to counter Southwest. By 2001, Shuttle had pulled out of most Southwest routes to become little more than a regional feeder for the Los Angeles and San Francisco airports. US Airways, meanwhile, had slowed its ambitious growth plans for its discounter, MetroJet.

European carriers hadn't done much better. British Airways executives learned the hard way that discount subsidiaries don't make sense within business-class airlines, and sold their discounter, Go, to a management-led buyout team in June 2001. It was impractical, they said, for one company to run two parallel carriers. KLM Royal Dutch Airlines had considered buying Go, but after the deal fell through, KLM said it would review whether or not to sell all or part of Buzz, its own discount airline.

In late 2001, many observers saw Milton's plan to save Air Canada with a low-cost subsidiary as a desperate move that was doomed to failure. "At the end of the day," Merrill Lynch analyst Michael Linenberg said in August 2001, "most big carriers that try to do an airline-within-an-airline, from a profit-and-loss perspective, they're never all that successful." But Linenberg suggested that the enterprise could lose money and still be deemed a success if it helped Air Canada protect its turf from competitors like WestJet and Canada 3000.

In early September 2001, the chief financial officers at Canada's two largest airlines were keeping a close eye on their companies' respective bank balances. Canada 3000's cash-flow projections now showed the airline would have a shortfall of $30.6 million for October 28, the bottom of the slow fall season. CFO Don Kennedy approached the aircraft-financing arm of General Electric for a loan to help get through to the new year. GE Capital Aviation Services (GECAS) appeared willing to help. The financing company made good money leasing planes to Canada 3000, and it was in its interest to make sure Canada 3000 survived.

"It was going to be tight for us if we didn't arrange financing," Kennedy said. "We had just put together three airlines, and we were going into the fall, which is a very tough travel season. November is the worst time of the year; we usually go through large sums of money in November. I was warning everybody that we were going to have an even bigger problem that year, because we had a bigger organization to channel it through."[21]

Weathering the slow fall period would be difficult, but not impossible: bookings were strong. On September 10, 2001, Canada 3000 sold about 25,000 tickets – the best day in the company's history.

On August 1, 2001, Robert Milton announced that Air Canada had lost $108 million in the second quarter of 2001, due to the significant drop in business travel. Revenue from Nortel Networks Corporation, Air Canada's largest corporate customer, had fallen to roughly $40 million from $100 million. Milton intended to eliminate some business seats on the aircraft so he could cram in more coach passengers. Further, he cut another 4,000 jobs in addition to the 3,500 that had been slashed at the end of 2000. "We have announced today a fundamental plan to alter some of our business processes," Milton said in a conference call. "The most difficult of these measures are the layoffs." The timing of these job cuts would be especially onerous because of the airline's commitment, made as part of the Canadian Airlines acquisition, to avoid involuntary layoffs until March 2002. On a personal level, the announcement itself was also painful. The CEO who had dreamed of creating a major global carrier, who wanted to add new destinations, purchase dozens of new aircraft, and create thousands of jobs – who had once boldly declared, "My aspirations in life are not to stay small" – was slowly shrinking the national flag-carrier.[22]

Milton and CFO Rob Peterson were seriously concerned about Air Canada's cash position. They liked to have $1 billion to $1.5 billion in cash on hand, in case of unexpected financial or operational crises. But by June 30, the airline's cash reserves had fallen to $535 million. "I was always trying to raise funds," Peterson said later. "Every time I raised a couple hundred million dollars, there was some reason it was being spent. I was always trying to keep up."[23]

Peterson had been in talks with a number of banks and aircraft-leasing companies in an effort to bring in cash by selling aircraft or engines, then leasing back the equipment. These transactions weren't ideal, since they drove up future operating costs. But for now, Air Canada officials were grateful that there were still banks willing to finance aircraft. On

September 10, Robert Milton boarded a plane for London, England, to see bankers from a subsidiary of the Royal Bank of Scotland. Milton was close to finalizing the mortgaging of some Airbus A321s. Rob Peterson was scheduled to join him the next day. So far, the discussions had progressed nicely and these meetings in London would allow the British bank to do its due diligence. Milton desperately needed everything to go right on September 11.

10

The Day the World Changed

I could not allow myself to deal with the human side of it. The tragedy. The loss of life. The emotions. I had to compartmentalize. I had a job to do. My deputy had a job to do. The time for grief and sadness came much later.[1]
— David Collenette, federal transportation minister

It was nauseating. It was depressing. I was half the world away from my family. . . . I thought of my family first and then the airline, making sure it was safe and buttoned down.[2]
— Robert Milton, chief executive officer, Air Canada

Rob Reid rolled out of bed and stumbled towards the computer. It was 5:30 on the morning of Tuesday, September 11, 2001. Reid never used an alarm clock; he woke at the same ungodly hour every morning, whether it was a work day or not. This was a work day, and Reid would start it as he had finished the night before, logging on to the Internet to check the weather forecasts across the Air Canada route network. It drove his wife crazy, this constant monitoring of the weather, but it was his job. He was responsible for the safe and efficient operation of Air Canada's day-of-flight operations, an assignment he took extremely seriously. Never knowing what to expect day to day – be they blizzards or bomb threats or aircraft failures – was exhilarating. Working with his team to resolve every crisis, large or small, was immensely rewarding. It was equally satisfying when, at the end of the month, he would pore over the airline's operating statistics and find improvements in on-time performance or a reduction in the amount of lost luggage.

Reid had been enchanted with airplanes for as long as he could remember. His grandfather, a fighter pilot who had been shot down in the First World War, spun stories of his flying days and shared his logbook with his young grandson. The child pestered his parents incessantly until he was taken to Toronto's Island Airport for a short aerial tour of the city on his sixth birthday. By the age of seventeen, Reid had earned his private licence; by eighteen, his commercial licence. In his last year of high school, he took a job flying his own sightseeing tours out of the Island Airport. When Reid was hired as an Air Canada pilot in 1976, his parents presented him with a framed drawing of an airplane that he produced in kindergarten; it carried the caption, "I want to be a pilot." Through his years at Air Canada, Reid moved comfortably from the cockpit to management. He loved both sides of the business, and continued to fly the occasional shift long after being named vice-president of the airline's systems operations control centre. His office at the centre, adjacent to Pearson International Airport, was atop the operating heart of the airline.

Against the uncertainty of the job's demands, Reid imposed a sense of order by controlling those events he could, living as much as possible by routine: open the eyes at 5:30 a.m.; check the weather forecasts on the Internet; skim the newspaper headlines; leave home in Oakville at 6:30; stop for breakfast at Tim Hortons (always the same: two chocolate-chip cookies, medium coffee in a large cup with cream); arrive at the office shortly after 7:00; check the weather again; survey the fleet to identify any mechanical problems; put in calls to the various airports to see how things are shaping up across the country; deal with unforeseen developments; drive home around 5:30 p.m.; plan for the next day's operations during the 8:30 p.m. conference call; go to sleep; wake up and do it all again.

At 5:30 that morning, the forecast was for beautiful weather across the network. Overnight, Hurricane Edna had been downgraded to a Category 2 storm and had blown away from North America. Passenger loads were expected to be light, which was typical for a Tuesday in

September. Light passenger loads weren't great for the bottom line, but they usually meant an easy day operationally. The only concern that had been discussed the previous evening during the conference call was the possibility – just a rumour, really – that the Public Service Alliance of Canada would set up a picket this morning in front of the air-traffic-control tower at Pearson. It was probably an idle threat, but Reid had heard these rumours from three or four different sources. A picket at the control tower could have a serious impact on the airline's operations. Reid decided he would drive over to the control tower later that morning to check out the situation for himself.

David Collenette wasn't sure what to make of the chatter that rippled through the conference hall of the Montreal Convention Centre. His speech wasn't earth-shattering – he knew that – but his audience didn't look bored so much as otherwise occupied. A career in politics had taught the transport minister how to read a crowd, and he knew he had to either change focus or wrap up. Collenette was speaking at the opening of a major conference of airport executives from around the world. Its organizers had asked the minister to stretch out his remarks, because another scheduled speaker had cancelled at the last minute. The delegates seemed interested enough when Collenette first stepped up to the podium at 8:35, but a few minutes before 9:00, he noticed that people were milling in small groups at the side of the room. Some were speaking on their cellphones or staring at their pagers. Debra Ward, the government's independent airline observer was disturbed by the lack of respect. It was unusual, almost insulting, behaviour before a minister of the Crown. Even Louis Ranger, his associate deputy minister, had jumped up from his front-row seat and left the room.

Paul Benoit, the chief executive of the Ottawa airport and one of the conference organizers, passed the minister a slip of paper. Collenette set the note aside and continued talking, determined to win back the crowd. Then Ranger reappeared, signalling for him to read the note. Collenette unfolded the paper and saw Ranger's distinctive handwriting. "Wind up the speech. There has been a tragedy. Don't talk to the media until you have been briefed." Collenette took just ninety seconds to finish, then left the podium. He was immediately surrounded by aides, who told him that a plane had hit the World Trade Center in New York. They speculated that it was a terrible accident, but Collenette knew at once that it had been a deliberate act. "I've been around Transport long enough to know that large passenger planes just don't crash into tall buildings," the minister recalled later. "Even in hopeless emergencies, every pilot's instinct is to save lives."[3]

Rob Reid was driving from his office to the air-traffic-control tower at Pearson to see if picket lines had been set up, when at 8:53 his car radio suddenly fell silent. Instead of the song that had been introduced – "Time of the Season" by the Nylons – there was more than a minute of dead air. The producers and deejays at CHFI were so consumed by the images being broadcast over CNN that they hadn't realized a technical glitch had cost them eighty seconds of air time. Morning hosts Bob Magee and Erin Davis broke in at 8:54 to tell listeners that the north tower of the World Trade Center was on fire, and that CNN was reporting that it had been hit by a Cessna 172.

Instinctively, Reid turned his car around, went back to the systems operations control building, and made his way inside to the emergency-response centre. He knew that, at the very least, the incident would affect the flow of Air Canada flights in and out of New York. As he drove, he spoke briefly by cellphone with his boss, Rob Giguere, Air Canada's vice-president of operations. They agreed that the clear skies over Manhattan made the apparent accident all the more extraordinary. When Reid arrived at the emergency-response centre, a handful of staff had already gathered to watch the live coverage on CNN. Moments after he joined them, they watched in horror as a United Airlines plane crashed into the second tower. It hit Reid like a punch in the stomach. Something was radically wrong, and the implications for his airline's day-of-flight operations were chilling.

Reid made his way from the emergency-response centre to the floor of systems operations control. This was the nerve centre of Air Canada's day-of-flight operations, a large room constantly humming with activity and illuminated by bright computer monitors, where workers coordinated the activities of pilots, airport workers, managers, and mechanics to keep the airline secure and on schedule. The men and women who sat before the computers were trained to deal with crises like hostage-takings or plane crashes, training they hoped they would never have to use. Information was pouring into the emergency-response centre from a variety of sources. The first indication of trouble had come when U.S. air-traffic controllers began restricting traffic over New York City minutes before news of the first plane crash was broadcast to the world. Air Canada's internal security team, made up of retired Mounties and Canadian Security Intelligence Service agents, were contacting their sources to try to find out what was going on.

Reid interrupted their efforts to deliver a brief and unprecedented directive. He wanted all of Air Canada's planes out of U.S. airspace as soon as possible. "If somebody's bound for the U.S., I want them turned back. If somebody's in the U.S. coming north, I want them grounded. If somebody's in New York taxiing out, I want them stopped." At about the same time, Rob Giguere sent out a data message to every aircraft in the skies. "There's been a security breach with the loss of aircraft through on-board interventions. Lock and secure cockpit doors."[4]

Shortly thereafter came reports of two other hijacked-plane crashes, one at the Pentagon in Washington and another in a field in rural Pennsylvania. Giguere and Reid decided they had no choice but to ground the airline's entire fleet. Aircraft that were close to their destinations were allowed to complete their journeys; others were directed to landing sites by officials in operations control. If it was the right call, lives might be saved; if not, the cost of their misjudgement would be enormous.

At first, nobody knew whose planes were involved in the attacks, but Reid's staff were able to determine quickly that all of Air Canada's planes were safe, at least for the time being. There was, however, an Air Canada connection on United Airlines Flight 93 heading to San Francisco from

Newark, New Jersey, the plane that went down in Pennsylvania. Because of Air Canada's marketing agreements with United, Flight 93 had also been advertised as Air Canada Flight 4085. The airline's records showed that none of its customers were aboard the flight, the one fated to become a symbol of American defiance when it was learned that its passengers had likely prevented the hijackers from reaching one of their targets.

The initial reports were that thousands – perhaps tens of thousands – of people had died on the ill-fated aircraft and at the World Trade Center and the Pentagon. (The final tally would be 3,030 dead and 2,337 injured.) A very public tragedy was unfolding live on television, a horror story that touched millions in a way that nothing had before. But Rob Reid and his colleagues had no time to think about the loss of life. "I was working on trying to piece together a puzzle," Reid recalled later, "shutting the airline down and shutting it down quickly."

Afterwards, Reid remembered that rumours of pickets at the air-traffic-control tower had been his sole concern on rising that morning. There had been no strikers at Pearson that day, but in Ottawa it was a different story. Early that morning, PSA union members had circled Tower C of Place de Ville, the headquarters of Transport Canada and the tallest office building in Ottawa. Anticipating a strike, some officials had arrived at their desks well before 8:00 a.m. Others had trouble crossing the picket line. When news reached the picketers that two hijacked aircraft had struck the World Trade Center, however, they set down their signs and went to their work stations. It was going to be a long day.

Robert Milton had not been asleep long when the ringing telephone roused him from his slumber. The clock in the airport hotel showed 2:00 p.m. local time, a little early for the wake-up call he had requested. He had flown to London from Canada that morning and was catching a quick nap before a meeting with bankers. Milton was still groggy when he answered the phone, but the urgency in his secretary's familiar voice snapped him awake. "I thought you should know," Pauline Boisvert said. "An airplane has hit the World Trade Center in New York." Milton's first image was of a small plane accidentally striking one of the towers. Big planes had too many safety features to allow such an accident. Milton flipped on the television. The instant he found live pictures from New York, he saw the second plane slice into the south tower. It took newscasters a few moments to identify the aircraft type, but Milton, the life-long plane-spotter, could read its shape in the split second before impact. The plane was unmistakably a Boeing 767, and this was no accident.

Milton asked Boisvert to connect him with Rob Giguere, who informed him that they had already ordered the grounding of the airline's fleet and cautioned pilots in the air to close and lock cockpit doors. Air Canada had good visibility on its aircraft at that time, Giguere said, but there was no way of knowing what might yet happen.

For the rest of the day, Milton remained in his hotel room, trying his best to keep in touch with what was going on across the Atlantic. He participated in some of the operations calls, but said little. The immediate crisis could best be dealt with by Reid and Giguere. Throughout much of the day, he was unable to participate in the conference calls, because it was almost impossible to secure an open phone line. Montreal had never seemed so far away, and no one knew how long it would be before aviation authorities allowed flights to resume to North America.

Milton put in a call to Bombardier president Robert Brown. As the world's largest supplier of regional jets, Bombardier executives were always eager to accept a call from an airline president. Milton needed a favour.

David Collenette was supposed to fly to Toronto after his Montreal speech; instead, he made for Ottawa as quickly as possible. The minister had not yet closed Canadian airspace, but he had no intention of getting on an airplane. The fastest transport between Montreal and Ottawa on this day would be by car. Collenette climbed inside a government sport utility vehicle with associate deputy minister Louis Ranger and aide Marie Hélène Lévesque. They had not seen the television images that were riveting viewers around the world, but they listened to continuous

coverage over the radio. Each time the CBC broadcast another uncon-
firmed report of a terrorist attack, the driver leaned a little more heavily
on the gas pedal as they sped along Highway 417.

The minister spent most of the journey on his mobile phone,
speaking with Margaret Bloodworth, Transport's deputy minister, and
Sue Ronald, his executive assistant. Bloodworth explained that the U.S.
Federal Aviation Administration was closing U.S. airspace, and she
suggested that the government of Canada do the same. She needed a
formal order from the minister to halt air traffic, which he gave at about
10:00. Within seconds, the order was relayed to Nav Canada, the not-
for-profit company that runs Canada's air-traffic-control system.

Next, Bloodworth told Collenette that Washington was requesting
that Canadian airports accommodate overseas flights destined for the
United States. Collenette and Bloodworth quickly made the decision to
turn back any planes with enough fuel to return to Europe or Asia, and
to accept the rest. Bloodworth recommended that these two hundred or
more flights be kept away from Toronto and Montreal, and be diverted
to smaller airports in places like Gander, Newfoundland. Collenette
agreed. He wasn't too worried about attacks on major Canadian cities –
he allowed flights to land in Vancouver and Halifax – but he wanted to
keep incoming Atlantic flights away from possible targets in Washington
or New York. He made an exception for the plane carrying foreign affairs
minister John Manley. Collenette allowed Manley's Air Canada flight
from Frankfurt to land in Toronto, where it was met by a government
jet, which shuttled him to Ottawa. At 10:43, Transport Canada issued a
notice to all pilots – the first such notice in Canadian history: "Due to
extraordinary circumstances and for reasons of safety, all departure
services from Nav Canada–served aerodromes are ceased, effective
immediately. Due to closures of U.S. airports and airspace, all National
Traffic will be recovered in Canada."

At Nav Canada centres across the country, controllers scrambled to
implement the minister's simple yet daunting orders. They had never
done anything like this before, even in training. Elaborate procedures
existed for closing particular sectors of airspace: officials had envisioned

worst-case scenarios in which planes would have to be "sanitized" from certain parts of the sky – if a fire had caused evacuation of one air-traffic-control centre, for example. But no one had imagined a situation in which it would be necessary to sanitize every bit of Canadian airspace. By 10:00, Nav Canada officials had fashioned an emergency command centre in a couple of boardrooms on the twelfth floor of their Ottawa headquarters at 77 Metcalfe Street. Controllers were told to lock their doors at towers and air-traffic centres across the country and to try to establish contact with each and every plane in their immediate airspace. "I had confidence that we would be able to get all the airplanes down," said John Creighton, the CEO of Nav Canada. "I was more concerned about, who's out there, and is somebody else going to use an airplane and turn it into a missile here?"[5]

A few aircraft raised alarms when they failed to respond properly, including an Air Canada flight destined for San Francisco. Communication was soon established with most of the errant aircraft but, just in case, Canadian Air Force pilots readied their CF-18 Hornets to intercept any hijacked planes.

Landing the domestic flights was relatively easy: Air Canada had begun grounding planes on its own before the official order came down from Transport. But there were about four hundred flights from Europe and another ninety flights from Asia en route to North America, coming at a rate of two per minute. Planes with sufficient fuel were turned back in a series of giant U-turns in the sky; the others needed prompt instructions on where to land. Those too heavy with fuel to touch down safely circled back out over the ocean to dump fuel.

By the time the minister's SUV reached Casselman, Ontario, some thirty minutes east of Ottawa, every cellphone in the vehicle was out of power. Arriving at Tower C in Ottawa, Collenette and his officials went straight to the SitCen, Transport Canada's emergency-situation centre. On most days, the room was dead quiet, with just a skeleton crew in place to open the facility in the event of a train derailment or plane accident. The SitCen had been activated for crises such as the 1998 ice storm in Ontario and Quebec and the crash of Swissair Flight 111 off Nova Scotia that same year. Occasionally, Transport officials would gather to watch a space shuttle launch on one of the SitCen's two giant projection screens, which lowered from the ceiling to block the room's windows.

When Collenette arrived at about 11:30, the room was very much alive, buzzing with Transport Canada workers and representatives from the military, the RCMP, and the Canadian Security Intelligence Service. A member of the U.S. embassy's staff was present to help facilitate the exchange of information. That day, the SitCen functioned as the focal point for the government's response to the terrorist attacks, coordinating communication between airports, airlines, and the air-traffic controllers at Nav Canada, who had the responsibility of guiding some 1,500 aircraft to safe landings.

Collenette stood before the group and gave a short pep talk. "This is an unprecedented situation," the minister said. "You're going to be called on to work in a way you've never worked before. I know some of you were out on the picket lines and immediately came in and went back to work. All I can say is we need your help. Just do the best you can."[6]

Then the minister got out of the way and allowed the experts do their jobs. The way he saw it, his role was to give the final yes or no to the big decisions, not to micromanage. When he returned to his office, Collenette watched, for the first time, the terrible images of that morning's events. It was too much for the minister, who felt he couldn't yet indulge in reflection or mourning. The time for grief and sadness would come later. "In my case it didn't come until Christmas, when I started to get some sleep," Collenette said.

Officials at ARINC, a Maryland aviation company that transmits communications to and from jets, were hurriedly searching for evidence of other hijackings. As they examined dozens of messages sent on September 11, one frightening transmission jumped out. At 11:08 Eastern, a Korean Airlines Boeing 747 bound for New York had transmitted a message to its Seoul head office that included the letters "HJK" – an abbreviation of "hijacked."[7] Fearing the transmission was a coded distress signal, ARINC passed the information to the U.S. Federal Aviation Administration, which alerted the North American Aerospace Defense Command (NORAD). As the jet soared over the Pacific towards North America along a route that passed important oil facilities in Alaska, NORAD sent fighter jets to trail Korean Airlines Flight 85.

Air-traffic controllers radioed coded questions to the pilots in an effort to determine if this was another plane under the control of terrorists. The pilots signalled an alarming reply by setting their transponder to 7500, the universal code for hijacked. Within minutes, evacuations were underway at hotels and government buildings in Anchorage, Alaska, and the U.S. coast guard ordered oil tankers away from the coast at Valdez. Fearing the worst, NORAD officials ordered the airliner away from Anchorage and Valdez, even though they were aware that its fuel reserves were running low. Officials at the remote airstrip at Yakutat, Alaska, wouldn't accept the plane, because their instrument-landing system wasn't working. U.S. air force authorities then contacted their Canadian counterparts with a difficult question: Would Canada allow a possibly hijacked passenger jet – and the U.S. air force jets trailing it – into Canadian airspace?

Virgin Atlantic Flight 21 was precisely halfway between London's Heathrow Airport and Washington, D.C., when Captain Robert Burgess overheard an extraordinary conversation on the aircraft's high-frequency radio. Two American Airlines pilots were talking about a dreadful accident: one of their planes had crashed into the World Trade Center. Burgess and his co-pilot listened, stunned, wondering how such a tragedy could have occurred. A few minutes later, a third voice joined the exchange to report that a second aircraft had hit the other tower. Burgess and his first officer made a quick decision to secure the door to their cockpit.

Burgess suspected that landing in Washington would be out of the question. He got on the intercom and made a vague announcement to the aircraft's three hundred passengers. "Look, folks, there's nothing wrong with the aircraft," he started, "so please don't worry. But for operational reasons, we're going to have to divert. The moment we get on the ground, I'll explain more fully, but please don't worry, there's nothing wrong with the airplane."[8]

Although he was already in Canadian airspace, Burgess hoped to return directly to London, but Canadian air-traffic control denied the request. They were turning back dozens of flights behind him, but his was past the point of safe return. Aircraft cross the North Atlantic on a timed aerial highway; planes may break out of the track system only in case of an emergency. Burgess made some quick calculations to see if he had enough fuel to reach Ireland at least, once he got out of the track system. Officials at Virgin Atlantic's offices in Britain crunched the same numbers. They agreed there wasn't quite enough fuel; Flight 21 would have to touch down at one of the remote airports along Canada's eastern shore for refuelling before heading back to Europe. When Burgess learned that all U.S.-bound aircraft were being rerouted to Canada – most along the east coast – he realized that the stop would not be as short as he had hoped.

The plane touched down at Gander International Airport at 2:02 p.m., local time. It was the sixteenth of thirty-eight aircraft that would arrive that day before local authorities declared the airport full. Canadian officials suggested it would be hours before the passengers could be allowed off the aircraft, since every new arrival was being thoroughly questioned. Burgess implemented a rationing system for the remaining food and water.

He made another announcement to his passengers, giving them as many details as he knew about the morning's events, including the fact that a third aircraft had crashed into the Pentagon. Burgess later regretted telling his passengers so much about the attacks. Because the flight was bound for Washington, there were passengers aboard who had close connections to Pentagon workers. When Burgess was informed that a fourth aircraft had crashed in Pennsylvania, he decided it was better to say nothing.

It was the kind of conversation that should take place only in Hollywood thrillers. Nav Canada CEO John Creighton was on the phone with American military officials, urging them to think twice before blasting Korean Airlines Flight 85 and its 215 passengers from the skies. The plane's transponder was still set to 7500, but other evidence suggested the pilots remained in command. Perhaps when the pilots were asked if they had been hijacked, the captain misunderstood, and thought he was being ordered to punch in the code for a hijacking. "I indicated that if it was me making the decision, I wouldn't be too quick on the trigger," Creighton recalled.[9]

Prime Minister Jean Chrétien had allowed U.S. fighter jets to trail Flight 85, because Canadian CF-18s could not catch up to it. The plane was headed for Whitehorse, one of three aircraft directed there on September 11. Chrétien authorized U.S. pilots to shoot down the plane if it displayed any hostile behaviour, but stipulated that he would make the final decision. In an interview aired on CBC television on the first anniversary of the attacks, Chrétien said he faced a decision he might regret for the rest of his life. "They could not communicate with this plane and they didn't know where it was going," Chrétien said. "So I authorized it in principle, yes. It's kind of scary . . . this plane, with hundreds of people, and you have to call a decision like that."

Whitehorse residents scrambled to prepare for the wayward aircraft. The city's downtown was evacuated and schools were closed. While the fighter jets circled overhead, Flight 85 barrelled onto the runway at Whitehorse airport. Following the RCMP's directions, the aircraft taxied to a spot as far from the terminal as possible. The co-pilot emerged from the plane without his tie, jacket, or hat, lifting his shirt to show he was unarmed. RCMP officers whisked him away for questioning, while the rest of the crew and passengers remained on board. The RCMP soon established that it had all been a misunderstanding, fuelled by a language barrier and the day's heightened sense of danger.

Airlines keep meticulous lists detailing the correct procedures for any kind of emergency. If an Airbus A340 loses two of its engines over the

Pacific Ocean, the crew and the operations people on the ground know exactly what to do. If a fuel truck collides with a Boeing 737 at Victoria airport, there's a ready list of steps to follow. Canadian airlines keep these emergency procedure manuals for their own safety and because Transport Canada requires it. But there were no procedure manuals for the terrorist attacks of September 11. Air Canada had shut down its operations in the past, most recently in September 1998 when the airline's pilots went on strike for nearly two weeks. But previous shutdowns had been anticipated and prepared for, allowing the airline to decide in advance where to park each plane and how to ensure the safety and comfort of its passengers and crews.

No one had foreseen or planned for a situation in which all airlines had to ground their fleets simultaneously and as quickly as possible. In Air Canada's emergency-response centre, someone used an erasable marker to list the flight numbers of every aircraft Air Canada had in the air, more than a hundred in total. Each time a flight landed safely, its number was wiped from the board. The operations staff tried to find the best place for each aircraft, searching for the ideal combination of maintenance facilities and adequate accommodation for passengers and crew. They also considered which airports would enable a quick restart when the time came to get the planes back in the air. But in many cases, they didn't have an option. U.S. authorities decided where to land planes in American airspace, parking Air Canada jets in places like North Dakota, where they had no support resources. In a few cases, pilots assumed the roles of custodians of their passengers, taking personal responsibility for their comfort and well-being.

The final flight number – AC3091 – was erased from the whiteboard at 6:08 p.m. Eastern time, when a Boeing 747-400 touched down in Vancouver. The operations people knew that their passengers and crews were safe at last. But it was no time for celebration; idle planes cost money. Air Canada's personnel were already working on the logistics of getting their planes airborne again.

Mid-afternoon, Louis Ranger walked through the empty halls of Place de Ville Tower C and into the office of David Collenette. Most non-essential workers had left the building to be with their loved ones. The televised coverage of the airplanes crashing into the towers of the World Trade Center struck too close to home. Tower C was just twenty-eight storeys, but at 112 metres it was the tallest building in Ottawa – twenty metres higher than the Peace Tower. That was enough to make it a potential target in the minds of many workers.

"Minister, we're almost alone here," Ranger said.

"This place has never been as safe as it is now," Collenette retorted. "Nothing's flying."

If Collenette seemed grumpy, he had reason to be. The minister had spent much of his day fielding calls from people with Liberal Party connections, asking for special permission to travel on corporate or charter jets, despite the closure of Canada's airspace.[10] Collenette bluntly reminded them that an international tragedy was no time to ask for special treatment. However, Collenette did grant two exceptions. The first was for Pat Ryan, the chief executive of Aon Corporation, an insurance company believed to have lost many employees in the World Trade Center. Ryan was stranded at Deer Lake, Newfoundland, and Collenette arranged to get him to Sarnia, the closest Canadian airport to the company's Chicago headquarters. The second was for Air Canada president Robert Milton, who had arranged to cross the Atlantic to return to his incapacitated airline on a Bombardier Challenger jet.

Fifteen floors below, the SitCen remained crowded. The job of looking after 239 diverted planes and 33,000 displaced passengers became known as Operation Yellow Ribbon. Transport personnel coordinated the effort with airport staff and relief organizations. Many of the planes landed in Halifax (47 aircraft) and Vancouver (34), the largest airports on the east and west coasts. But many others were directed into tiny communities in Newfoundland, places like Gander (38), Stephenville (8), and Goose Bay (7). Before the last plane touched down, another team of government officials was at work on plans to reopen the country's skies.

This, too, was a formidable task. They reviewed every security regulation to make sure it made sense in a post-9/11 environment. Normally the government would take two years to process a set of security regulations. In the fourteen days following September 11, Transport Canada processed ten sets of new security regulations at an average rate of one regulation every six hours.[11] They debated issues such as what kind of identification would be required before someone could board a flight, and what additional items should be banned from aircraft. "We had a discussion about the definition of a steak knife. Then another discussion about the definition of a plastic steak knife, but not a plastic butter knife," recalled Jean LeCours, Transport Canada's director of preventative security.[12]

The government established a hotline to answer questions about the new security rules. The number was intended to be used by airlines only, but it was inadvertently broadcast on national television, resulting in as many as five thousand calls a day from members of the media and the general public. People called to ask when the planes would be flying again or to check on the location and condition of grounded friends and family members. There were about twenty calls from dog owners, fuming that the initial ban on animals in air cargo would prevent them from showing their pooches at a dog show in London, Ontario. One elderly woman even called to suggest, in all earnestness, that passengers show up for their flights naked, so they would not be able to conceal weapons.

On the night of September 11, a group of executives in charge of flight operations for North America's largest airlines gathered for a surreal dinner at the Keg Steakhouse & Bar near Toronto's Pearson International Airport. These were the very men responsible for overseeing major operational crises like the one that gripped the industry that night. Instead, they were stuck in Toronto, just as the world's top airport executives were stuck in Montreal. The various vice-presidents had been meeting at a fishing resort near North Bay, Ontario, to talk about their businesses and to have some relaxation time. They had left the resort early that morning to connect with flights back to their headquarters in Chicago and Fort Worth and Atlanta. Some were in airport lounges about to board when the terrorist attacks caused their flights to be cancelled. The group included Rob Giguere, whose home base was Montreal, and his good friend Steve Forte, the vice-president of flight operations at United Airlines. Things were tough for Giguere, but he couldn't imagine what it was like to be in Forte's shoes that night. Forte had lost two aircraft, ninety-four passengers, and sixteen colleagues in the attacks. "Everybody ate a little bit, but it wasn't an enjoyable meal; it was for sustenance," Giguere recalls.

The executives generally kept their emotions to themselves and talked the way operations people talk, pragmatically, technically, speaking in checklists. *How did this happen? Will there be more attacks? How do we restart our operations?* Any sense of rivalry that might have existed between them disappeared as they wrestled with this common challenge. They saw the shutdown and start-up almost as mysteries to be solved, and they were quick to share hints and clues with their competitors.

Rob Giguere was the son of one of Air Canada's first pilots. He and his father had six decades of history at the airline between them, but neither had ever dealt with a task of this magnitude. Giguere believed Air Canada would have a limited schedule back in the air the next morning. In fact, it wasn't until Thursday, September 13, that Air Canada sent its first flights down the runways. The airline operated just one-fifth of its usual schedule that day; the following Monday it was still at 80 per cent of its normal volume.

It was early on the morning of September 12, at 2:00 Gander time, that the passengers of Virgin Atlantic Flight 21 were finally allowed off the aircraft. Yellow school buses transported them to the terminal building, where they went through customs. In the middle of the night they wound up in the hands of the Salvation Army and the Canadian Red Cross, where volunteers – many of them senior citizens – met the passengers and offered them food and drink and the use of a telephone. The 300 men, women, and children were then transported to Gander Academy, where they were accommodated in gymnasiums, cafeterias, classrooms, and office space, along with another 450 passengers from Sabena Flight 439 and Lufthansa Flight 416. Captain Burgess and his crew, meanwhile, were put up at Sinbad's Hotel and Suites. Gander authorities had insisted that the town's 550 hotel rooms be reserved for flight crews, so they could be well rested and ready to take off when the call came.

Regular life stopped for Gander's 10,000 residents as they worked tirelessly to care for their 5,579 visitors. Newfoundlanders made casseroles and sandwiches and squares; striking bus drivers came off the picket line to shuttle people to temporary residences in schools, meeting halls, and churches; a military transport brought five thousand cots for them to sleep on; stores donated blankets and coffee pots; truckers drove for hours to bring in additional food so the residents of Gander could feed their guests with grilled steaks and roast beef and mashed potatoes; townspeople invited the refugees into their homes for showers and took them out on their boats for sightseeing tours.

Burgess visited the gymnasium every day to brief his passengers on the situation. There wasn't much to say. He told them that he didn't know when they would be able to leave or even where they would be going – on to Washington, back to London, or to Toronto, which Virgin Atlantic served on a regular basis. And he persuaded those wanting to find their own way to reconsider. It was a six-hour drive to the ferry, followed by a four-hour ferry ride to the mainland. From there it was an eight-to-ten-hour drive to the U.S. border, where there were lengthy delays.

A large rainbow emerged over Gander on September 15, the day Virgin Atlantic got clearance to leave Newfoundland. As the plane reached its cruising altitude, Burgess switched on the intercom for one more announcement. "We owe these people of Newfoundland a tremendous debt," he said. "We spent that school's telephone budget for the next three years. We've taken every piece of hospitality they could offer us and we just said cheerio and thank you."[13] Burgess said he was going to pass around a hat and encouraged people to donate whatever they could. The passengers of Flight 21 gave whatever they had in British pounds, U.S. dollars, South African rands, Swedish kronors – in all, fourteen different currencies. The money totalled about $5,000 Canadian. Virgin Atlantic contributed another $5,000 to Gander Academy. Captain Burgess flew back to Gander on October 11 to present the money to the school.[14]

On a typical transatlantic flight, an airplane cockpit is alive with the constant chatter of pilots in communication with each other and air-traffic control. But on this crossing there was not a word, only the dry anxious drone of the Bombardier Challenger jet cutting through the sky towards Montreal's Dorval Airport. Two governments had been asked to sign off on this emergency flight, so that the passenger at the back of the plane could return to work. The special arrangements were not for a head of state or a decorated general or an expert in counterterrorism, but for Robert Milton.

Seated with Milton at the back of the Challenger were Calin Rovinescu and his wife. The couple had been vacationing in Barcelona on September 11 and, like Milton, had been stranded in Europe. Piled around them were the September 12 editions of the Fleet Street newspapers, with their screaming headlines and blazing photographs. It all made Milton sick to his stomach. He rose from his comfortable seat and walked to the smaller third seat in the cockpit. Although he didn't have a pilot's licence, the cockpit of a jet was his favourite place to be, with its magnificent view, the bright lights of the controls, and the comforting exchanges between pilots and controllers. For an airplane junkie like Milton, the privilege of flying in the only airplane crossing the Atlantic should have been a dream to be cherished, a trip that could never last long enough. But today, Milton just wanted the journey to be over. He was still too far from Montreal and the only two places he cared about: his home, where his family was alone and frightened, and his office, where he would oversee Air Canada's uncertain future.

Rob Reid returned to his Oakville home for the first time since the terrorist attacks on Saturday, September 15. He had spent the past four nights at the airport Hilton, just two minutes from the office, and hadn't spoken to his wife in four days. When he finally returned home, it was for a brief stay. Less than twelve hours later, Reid was back out the door. He stopped at Tim Hortons and ordered his usual – two chocolate-chip cookies, medium coffee in a large cup with cream – before returning to the office to deal with the latest problem.

The world's insurance companies were cancelling war-and-terrorism coverage on airlines and airports, leaving Air Canada and the federal government scrambling to find alternative solutions. In the coming days, there would be many more crises, including inaccurate reports of anthrax and box-cutters on Air Canada's planes. "It was an interesting time," Reid reflected later. "It's a hell of a thing to say, given the tragedy, but it was certainly an interesting logistical exercise. It was gratifying to know that the system works and it was really gratifying to see how people came together to overcome what in some cases were almost impossible odds."

Sadly, if September 11 brought out the best in the men and women who ran Canada's airline industry, the days and weeks following would inspire some of the worst.

I I

FALLOUT

We determined that Air Canada, by creating Tango and targeting the routes that Canada 3000 was flying on, was undertaking an anti-competitive act.[1]
— Konrad von Finckenstein,
federal commissioner of competition

It is impossible to see how matching fares can be an uncompetitive act as alleged by the Commissioner. The role of the Competition Bureau is to foster competition in the Canadian marketplace, not to support individual competitors.[2]
— Calin Rovinescu, executive vice-president, Air Canada

On the afternoon of Tuesday, September 18, 2001, I received a call from Laura Cooke, Air Canada's media-relations manager for Central Canada, offering a telephone interview with Robert Milton. I accepted at once. Since becoming the *Globe and Mail*'s transportation reporter more than a year earlier, I had made numerous requests for a one-on-one interview and been declined every time. The company's PR staff had explained that they were intentionally limiting his contact with media, because they were worried he had become "overexposed." Milton would be made available, I was told, when he had a message to deliver.

One week after the September 11 attacks, Milton wanted to talk. Air Canada's bookings had dropped dramatically, and the carrier was burning through its cash reserves at an alarming rate. No one knew when things would get better or, God forbid, worse. There were widespread fears of more acts of terrorism and concern that a war in Afghanistan would further discourage travel. U.S. president George W. Bush had signalled that Washington would stand behind its airline industry with a multi-billion-dollar bailout package. Robert Milton had a suggestion for Ottawa in this regard, and he would happily use the media to deliver it.

At the scheduled hour, Milton was patched through by Priscille Leblanc, the airline's director of corporate communications. Milton's message was simple: Washington had indicated that it would assist its airlines, and Ottawa should do the same. Otherwise, he said, Air Canada would be "incredibly disadvantaged" in relation to the U.S. airline industry. He was confident that the Canadian government would indeed come through with financial aid for the industry. "I think the government understands that this is not a situation of our doing," he said. "They understand that an airline like Air Canada *is* the industry in Canada."

I asked how much money Air Canada was looking for. Milton was reluctant to name a specific figure, but suggested Ottawa's package should be "in line with" the $24 billion U.S. in cash, tax breaks, and loan guarantees sought by the American airline industry. He said Air Canada's compensation should match "dollar for dollar" what a similarly sized U.S. carrier might receive. Before I could ask a follow-up question, Leblanc broke in to summon Milton to a television interview. She said that, if I needed more time, they would call back a few minutes later.

The pause in the interview gave me time to do some quick calculations. The U.S. airlines were asking for roughly $35 billion in Canadian dollars. Air Canada was a little less than one-tenth the size of the U.S. airline industry, as measured by available seat miles (the number of tickets available for sale, multiplied by the average length of a trip). If Milton wanted a proportionate level of assistance, I estimated his request at between $2 billion and $3 billion. When our interview resumed, I ran the numbers by him.

"I think it would be a little more than that," he said.

"$3 billion to $4 billion Canadian?" I guessed.

"That sounds about right."

I hung up the phone and typed out my lead. "Air Canada is asking Ottawa for $3 billion to $4 billion in aid to help it recover from the massive impact of last week's terrorist attacks in the United States."

The *Globe*'s editors decided to put the story on the paper's Web site as soon as I'd written it, which allowed us to break the news immediately. As a result, the $3-billion to $4-billion figure was widely reported that night and in Wednesday's newspapers. Milton himself volunteered the numbers in an interview with Peter Mansbridge on CBC-TV's *The National*. "Right now it looks like $24 billion U.S. for the industry there and for us it would be in the range of $3 billion to $4 billion on a purely comparable basis."

The repercussions for Robert Milton were swift and severe, as critics accused him of exploiting a tragic catastrophe for Air Canada's financial gain. Clive Beddoe, the chairman of WestJet, called the request "lunacy," pointing out that Air Canada was in trouble well before September 11. Transport minister David Collenette agreed. "It was ridiculous," the minister said later. "We felt like the airlines in the U.S. – and Air Canada too, perhaps – were looking to use the events of September 11 to get assistance to reorganize and help them with their cash problems, which were long in evidence before September 11."[3]

Columnists were unanimously appalled. The *Globe and Mail*'s Eric Reguly said that, before digging "his snout into the public trough," Milton should stop paying creditors and aircraft leaseholders, slash the airline's labour costs, and sell its regional airlines.[4] *National Post* columnist David Olive called Milton "the wrong man in the wrong place at the wrong time, a growth-at-any-cost manager whose strategy is similar to that of the failed dot-coms and telecoms." He suggested that Air Canada needed a new CEO willing to abandon money-losing routes, scrap plans for a discount carrier, spin off its regional airlines, and restructure its debt.[5]

Even some of Air Canada's corporate directors – Milton's bosses – believed he had made a serious blunder. The board members were upset on two fronts. First, they were concerned that Milton's request for billions had made it look like the carrier actually needed that much money – that

Air Canada was in greater distress than it really was. Second, they believed that Milton's confrontational demands had triggered an unfortunate backlash from the public and government when Air Canada desperately needed friends. For the first time since Milton's appointment, some board members wondered whether Air Canada might be better off with a CEO who hadn't burned so many bridges in Ottawa.

The directors had expected fewer such missteps after Milton, at their behest, hired Peter Donolo as senior vice-president of corporate communications in early 2001. Donolo was the former communications chief to Prime Minister Jean Chrétien, and perhaps they expected that Donolo would be able to pick up the phone and call the prime minister whenever Air Canada needed a sympathetic ear. Donolo knew that Ottawa didn't work that way. He preferred to keep a relatively low profile on Parliament Hill, allowing the airline's government-relations team to handle the front-line work, while he offered strategic guidance behind the scenes. Contrary to his counsel, however, Milton had attached a price tag to his bailout request, a public-relations faux pas in Donolo's view.

The Air Transport Association of Canada, which represents the country's airlines, had been in discussions with officials at Transport Canada over a deal to reimburse airlines for the five days that airspace had been fully or partially closed. But after Milton broadcast his expectations, Collenette had a tough time selling the proposal in Cabinet. Some ministers looked at Air Canada's share price and wondered why they should help a private corporation with billions of dollars in aid when they could take over the company for a few hundred million. More than one approached Collenette privately to suggest that the government buy back the flag-carrier.[6] Surprisingly, the nationalist-minded minister argued against returning Air Canada to Crown-corporation status. He didn't want taxpayers to own a broken airline laden with debt. "I fought against it because I felt that the government would then be the owner of all these operational problems," Collenette said later.

On October 2, Collenette persuaded his cabinet colleagues to approve a modest $160-million bailout package for the Canadian airline industry. The program would cost $10 million to administer, with $150 million going to airlines. Air Canada, which was expected to receive about $100 million, issued a press release expressing appreciation for the funds, but at the same time hinting that it wasn't enough. The statement referred to the $160 million as "initial" and "partial" compensation, and called for a "longer-term solution" to provide stability to the industry. But instead of increasing the fund, the federal government ultimately reduced it. In April 2002, Ottawa pegged Air Canada's compensation at just $69.8 million. The initial estimate of $100 million had been based on a misinterpretation by Air Canada of how the compensation program worked, said the government. Milton and his spokespeople bit their tongues this time, accepting that further protests could trigger another backlash.

Months later, I asked Milton how he felt about the board of directors, his bosses, questioning his judgement in the matter. "They felt I should be asking for [the amount] we needed," he said. "My whole issue – and the board understands it now – was levelling the playing field" relative to the American carriers. Did he think he made a mistake in asking for billions in government aid? "For sure, the way Keith McArthur covered it led to something that was very unfortunate," Milton replied pointedly. Then he and Priscille LeBlanc conferred for a moment and decided that the mistake – if there was one – was to interrupt my interview so that I could do the math.[7]

Large international carriers the world over were thrust into crisis after the September 11 attacks. Swissair and Sabena, the national flag-carriers of Switzerland and Belgium respectively, teetered on the brink of bankruptcy, as did Ansett, the second-largest airline in Australia. American Airlines and United, each of which had lost two planes in the attacks, announced the elimination of 40,000 jobs between them. Delta Airlines intended to cut 13,000 jobs; Northwest, 10,000. Continental put 12,000 staff on unpaid leave. Canada wasn't immune: on September 24, Montreal-based Transat A.T. Inc. announced 1,300 layoffs at its airline and other operations.

On September 25, David Collenette freed Air Canada from its pledge not to lay off workers before March 2002, a condition of its takeover of Canadian Airlines. (Previously announced layoffs had been on hold until this date, unless they involved workers hired since the merger.) The next day, Robert Milton released news of the termination of 5,000 employees, bringing the total number of job cuts made on his watch to 12,500. Milton said the layoffs represented "the most difficult announcement" of his career. "I understand how many lives, children, and families will be affected by these reductions," Milton said in a recorded message to employees. "I realize how difficult it will be, and I will fight hard to get each one affected safely back to the company. But the truth is, we are in for a tough stretch, the ultimate battle, a fight for survival."

By contrast, over at Canada 3000, president Angus Kinnear was in no hurry to cut jobs. As Kinnear boarded the airline's brand-new 264-seat Airbus A340 for the inaugural polar flight to India on October 8, he said he hoped to avoid layoffs. "When I get back from India next week, we'll take another look at it," he told reporters. Kinnear's casual tone suggested that matters weren't as dire at Canada 3000 as they were at other airlines. John Lecky saw things differently. In a later letter to Canada 3000's directors, Lecky said he implored Kinnear not to go to India during "a time of crisis." Nevertheless, Kinnear "departed for the week of October 8–14, instead of downsizing Canada 3000's winter requirements."[8]

In the seasonal airline business, the third quarter is usually the busiest part of the year. The strength of the July–August–September period makes up for the losses that are routinely posted during the other nine months. But in the third quarter of 2001, during which North American air travel ground to a halt for several days, the majority of North America's airlines lost money. Air Canada lost $598 million, compared with a profit of $101 million a year earlier. American Airlines parent AMR Corp. lost $414 million U.S. compared with a 2000 profit of $313 million U.S. But the continent's discount airlines chugged along. Southwest Airlines reported a $151-million U.S. profit, down slightly from the previous year. WestJet Airlines posted its nineteenth consecutive quarterly profit, up 32 per cent from 2000. And JetBlue Airways – the industry's latest discount success story – posted a profit of $10.5 million U.S. on revenues of $82.6 million.

JetBlue was the creation of David Neeleman, whose name and reputation had helped WestJet raise its start-up capital in 1995. A five-year non-compete agreement with Southwest Airlines had given Neeleman lots of time to research and plan his next adventure. Like Morris Air and WestJet, JetBlue was based on the Southwest model. Using cheap, motivated labour, a ticketless system, and a secondary airport – New York's John F. Kennedy International Airport – Neeleman kept his costs low. But while Southwest had begun with short-haul routes, JetBlue concentrated on medium- and longer-haul flights, pushing down unit costs still further. JetBlue didn't serve meals, but did offer other frills, like leather seats and personal-entertainment screens with twenty-four channels of live television delivered by satellite. And Neeleman borrowed a page from Canada 3000, flying brand-new Airbus A320s instead of cheaper, older aircraft, in order to minimize fuel and maintenance costs.

Long before the terrorist attacks turned the industry upside down, Robert Milton had watched with admiration, perhaps even envy, as Neeleman established and grew JetBlue. Milton wanted his own low-cost brand to go up against the discounters, and he had hired Steve Smith to develop Low Cost Co., the short-haul carrier that would be based in Calgary in direct competition with WestJet. But Low Cost Co. had yet to take off. The plan depended on help from the airline's unions, who had been reluctant to grant the concessions Milton felt were required to make his discounter work. The pilots had agreed to shift twenty aircraft to the subsidiary, but other labour groups were prepared to block the hiring of new flight attendants and customer-service agents at so-called B-scale wages. And since Low Cost Co. would be a separate airline, it would have to clear various regulatory hurdles to win its operating certificate from the federal government. Milton was not ready to abandon the low cost model, but he knew it would take time. Observing JetBlue, he wondered if he couldn't create something else – and sooner – that didn't depend on co-operation from the unions or special dispensation from the federal government.

The previous June, Milton had asked vice-president Paul Brotto to spearhead an internal campaign to identify $1 billion in annual cost savings and revenue-enhancing opportunities. The initiative, dubbed "Securing Our Future," was aimed at helping Air Canada meet its low-cost competition in the midst of an economic slowdown and the disappearance of the high-fare business traveller. One of the ideas Brotto's team looked at was "unbundling" the product; that is, charging extra for "frills" like meals or connections to international routes. "The consumer was telling us that, with the slowing economy, value was important. Customers were prepared to give up on frills in exchange for value," Brotto said.[9]

It was the beginning of a concept known inside the company as JetRed – a deliberate imitation of Neeleman's JetBlue in more than name only. Leading the JetRed project were vice-president Bill Bredt and Ben Smith, a twenty-nine-year-old aviation nut who was seen by some Air Canada executives as a young Robert Milton. Like JetBlue, JetRed would use new, fuel-efficient Airbus A320s with a single class of service. The business-class section would be removed to accommodate more passengers, but there would be more legroom between rows of seats than on other discount airlines. JetRed would provide ticketless travel and focus on long-haul routes. Just as the majority of JetBlue's flights started or ended in New York, JetRed would operate in and out of Toronto. There would be no costly connecting of passengers to international flights, and there would be no meals.

Air Canada's labour contracts didn't allow it to hire new staff for new concepts, so it would have to rely on its existing expensive and highly unionized workforce. As a result, there wasn't money for JetBlue-style extras like leather seats or personal video screens. Snacks, drinks, and earphones for the audio system became profit centres, available to customers for a price. And since Transport Canada safety regulations require one flight attendant for every forty passengers, JetRed would sell just 159 seats, to eliminate the need for a fifth attendant.

Part of the beauty of the project was that JetRed wouldn't be a separate airline, but merely a re-branding exercise. For less than $100,000, Air Canada could convert an Air Canada plane to a JetRed plane by ripping out the business-class seats and giving it a quick paint job. If the economy recovered and the business traveller came back, the aircraft could be restored to a two-class configuration with ease.

On October 10, a month after the terrorist attacks, Milton was ready to unveil the JetRed project, publicly christened "Tango." The name and the image were devised by Target Marketing & Communications of St. John's, Newfoundland. Tango's aircraft would be painted a distinctive purple that would differentiate them from Air Canada's regular fleet, and service would commence in early November between Toronto and seven of Canada's largest cities, as well as some Florida destinations. "Tango is one of many initiatives that Air Canada has in the pipeline," Milton said. Referring to Low Cost Co., still on the drawing board, he said, "We continue to plan for the launch of a Western-based, short-haul, low-fare airline that will be operated as a wholly owned subsidiary."

Air Canada seemed to anticipate some negative reaction to the introduction of a fresh brand at the same time as it was asking for a multi-billion-dollar bailout from the federal government. The airline attached a question-and-answer sheet to its press release: "Why is Air Canada spending money on Tango now?" and "Should Air Canada be using taxpayer money to be launching a new product like Tango?" The answers were, first, that Air Canada needed to "aggressively promote" initiatives to stimulate travel, and, second, that no taxpayer money would be used for Tango, since the government bailout had fallen "far short" of relieving the "continuing financial impact" of the September 11 attacks.

Air Canada said it expected Tango to attract 10 to 20 per cent of the mainline carrier's traffic on routes where the two brands overlapped, as well as create new passenger demand and draw customers away from "other low-cost airlines." The airline had every intention of being "fully competitive" with its domestic discount competitors in the challenging post–September 11 environment. But industry observers suspected that Tango was actually an anti-competitive tool designed to rid Air Canada of a vulnerable competitor. They noted that Tango appeared to target Toronto-based Canada 3000, while the as-yet-unnamed discount carrier would take on Calgary-based WestJet. "You've got to step back and wonder, where's the business strategy in this? Is there a business strategy other than getting rid of the competition so they can charge whatever they want?" Jennifer Hillard of the Consumers Association of Canada asked rhetorically in the *Globe and Mail*.[10]

The people at Canada 3000's Fasken Drive offices were in no doubt. Canada 3000's airline code with the International Air Transport Association was "2T," which becomes "Two Tango" in the phonetic alphabet used by pilots. "It was *our* name," CFO Don Kennedy protested. "Because they had the excess capacity at that time, they just overlaid our schedule 100 per cent. We had a flight to Calgary, they put on a flight to Calgary, time for time, flight for flight. They matched our capacity 100 per cent on our entire domestic route network."[11]

To Canada 3000 chairman John Lecky, Tango appeared as a dangerous and immediate threat. And he was fuming that his president, Angus Kinnear, was on the other side of the world in India, unavailable to deal with the crisis. Lecky made a quick decision to file a complaint about Tango with the federal Competition Bureau, reversing a long-standing company policy of not complaining to regulators. Canada 3000 had made this a point of principle ever since protests from other airlines had delayed the carrier's launch back in 1988. Things were different in 2001. It seemed clear to Lecky that Air Canada's Tango was a fighting brand, its introduction a hostile act.

Air Canada officials claimed Tango was "fully compliant" with federal competition laws, but Air Canada vice-president Bill Bredt acknowledged that, for Tango to be successful, the brand would have to lure passengers from competitors. Inside Air Canada, he conceded, there was "certainly some expectation" that Tango would affect Canada 3000, while Low Cost Co. would draw passengers primarily from WestJet.[12]

On the day that Air Canada unveiled Tango, one plank in its post–September 11 life raft, another was yanked away. The Canada Industrial Relations Board (CIRB) – the federal labour regulator – ruled that Air

Canada appeared to have acted in "clear contravention" of a negotiated contract by sending pink slips to 1,281 customer-sales-and-service agents. Collenette had released Air Canada from its labour commitments to Ottawa, but the airline couldn't walk away from its agreements with its employees. The ruling related to a contract Air Canada had signed with the Canadian Auto Workers in 2000. In the midst of its 180-day campaign, Air Canada desperately needed to integrate workers from Air Canada and Canadian Airlines in order to reduce confusion and waits at airports. The CAW was able to extract a heavy price – an ironclad no-layoff guarantee through March 27, 2004. At the time, it hadn't seemed too much to pay: Air Canada was poised for growth, not cutbacks. But in late 2001, these no-layoff clauses looked like a terrible mistake. Pilots and some flight attendants had won similar guarantees.

Working with its unions and the federal government, Air Canada was able to avert thousands of layoffs through job-sharing and early-retirement programs. But many observers suggested it would not be enough. Transport minister David Collenette was calling for a major restructuring at Air Canada. And analysts worried that the carrier was running dangerously low on cash. After September 11, the bank that had agreed to meet with Milton and CFO Rob Peterson shied away from their remortgaging deal, and Peterson went in search of other sources of cash. "I knew we were going to raise the money," Peterson said later. "In my mind it wasn't a liquidity problem because, if there was a liquidity problem, I already had it solved. But the fact that there was so much spec-ulation in the press made it a lot harder to do what we had to do in terms of raising liquidity."[13] Among the rumours being reported was that Air Canada's executives had considered filing for bankruptcy protection.

In a series of remarkable press interviews in mid-October, John Lecky, Canada 3000's chairman, warned that, without further government aid, the airline would be out of cash by Christmas. Canada 3000 officials had been working to convince federal officials that their share of Collenette's $160-million bailout package – $7.4-million – was not nearly enough to save the troubled carrier. They had known before September 11 that they might have to borrow money to get them through the typically slow fall period, but this year – with plunging passenger bookings, the threat of war in Afghanistan, and anthrax spores showing up on Capitol Hill – no one was willing to lend Canada 3000 a dime. Lecky believed that the airline was in serious danger of collapse, and he fretted that neither the government nor his own managers understood the seriousness of the situation. On October 15, Lecky unilaterally went public with news of Canada 3000's dwindling cash resources in interviews with Reuters, the *Toronto Star*, and the *Globe and Mail*.

He blamed Robert Milton's "unreasonable" request for billions of dollars for Ottawa's reluctance to help the country's airlines. "If we go under, the public will get mad as hell, because they'll only have one place to shop for national transportation at what's bound to be higher fares," he declared.[14] And although Angus Kinnear had said that he hoped to avoid layoffs, Lecky suggested that, in fact, they were imminent. But layoffs would not save Canada 3000, Lecky said. What the airline really needed was help from Ottawa to get it through the uncertain fall period.

"We don't know the future," Lecky told the *Globe and Mail*. "We don't know whether the bookings are going to go up or down. We've got anthrax running around. We've got threatened terrorist actions. We don't know how soon the passengers are going to come back."[15]

It was a bold step for the reclusive investor, and the repercussions were immediate. Canada 3000 shares plunged 27 per cent the next day on the Toronto Stock Exchange. The morale of employees plummeted. Thousands of passengers called to cancel their reservations, and new bookings slowed to a trickle. Canada 3000 sold just 49,000 tickets the week of Lecky's warning, compared with 63,000 two weeks earlier – after the terrorist attacks but before the United States began bombing Afghanistan on October 7.

The dire warnings also forced Canada 3000 to fight a number of backroom battles to prevent suppliers from withdrawing service. There were no immediate concerns with the aircraft-leasing companies, which had agreed to reduced payments on thirty-eight aircraft. But Canada

3000 was on shakier ground with smaller creditors, including caterers, fuel companies, and airports. These creditors had no direct claim on Canada 3000's assets, and the airline was months overdue paying tens of millions of dollars in fees, including an estimated $5 million in airport-improvement fees collected from passengers on behalf of the airports.

Lecky's decision to reveal the state of Canada 3000's finances had caught Angus Kinnear, the airline's president, by surprise. Lecky and Kinnear had worked reasonably well together for more than thirteen years. In 2000, Lecky told a reporter that "the greatest part of the credit" for Canada 3000's success "goes to the management team."[16] But the tribulations of 2001 – from the unhappy merger with Royal to the terrorist attacks to Tango – had strained their relationship.

On October 23, Lecky sent a scathing letter to every company director except Kinnear, exposing the depth of the power struggle between him and the president.[17] Although Lecky began by taking personal responsibility for pursuing Royal, his five-page dispatch blamed Kinnear and his executive team for most of the airline's troubles, and accused Kinnear of ignoring directions from the board of directors. "Basically, AJK's approach to Board Governance is that, if the Directors produce ideas which he considers to be useful, he will use them," Lecky wrote.

The chairman suggested that Canada 3000 should never have gone through with its business-class program. The failure of Roots Air had made the "Big Seat" program unnecessary, he wrote. Lecky complained that he had never been able to ascertain from company executives which routes were profitable and which were money-losers. He said that, when the airline faced a problem, it tended to "throw money, outside consultants, and lawyers into the breach." He expressed concern that the airline seemed to operate without a capital budget.

> Canada 3000 spends money as needs arise. . . . Whether Canada 3000 is ok or not is measured by rolling weekly cash flow projections. Profit and loss statements are like the golf score at the end of the round. . . .
> The final strokes to all this are that even though we knew *categorically* on August 8th *'that C-3000 would run out of cash before Christmas,'*

there was no contingency plan, no cost cutting, no downsizing, and no alarm to the Board. . . . What strikes me the most is that we never lifted a finger to help ourselves with lessors, employees, cost centres, losing routes, etc. until *the Government*, of all people, told us to do so.

The letter ended with an unambiguous ultimatum.

I do not expect Canada 3000 to fail this week. However, I am worried that if we continue as we are, we will attract more debt than necessary, and finish up selling the rest of our equity in a recapitalization. In the meantime, the Chairman has lost his ability to influence the President and the President has lost his ability to manage the Company effectively. Therefore, for all the above reasons, I say to you that when we get through the current crisis, that we have to change the President. If we do not, we will never really know what goes on in Canada 3000, and we certainly will not be able to direct its affairs in a timely manner. The other alternative is to change the Chairman, which as I have indicated to you, would be as easy as asking.

On October 24, officials at the Winnipeg Airports Authority met to discuss the Canada 3000 problem. The airline was far behind on its payments, and Murray Sigler, the airport's president, was alarmed by Lecky's warnings of an imminent cash crunch. As a former president and chief operating officer of Canadian Airlines, Sigler might have been expected to show some patience with another struggling airline. Instead, Sigler's board considered the drastic step of using their powers under the Airport Transfer Act to seize a Canada 3000 plane as collateral. Such a move could destabilize the entire airline but, if Canada 3000 was almost out of cash, they wanted to act before it was too late. Halfway through the meeting, Sigler received an urgent call from Paul Benoit, chairman of the Canadian Airport Council. Benoit passed on a message from senior officials at the Department of Transport: hold off on attempts to seize planes for at least a week.[18]

The following evening, they learned why the government had asked for a delay. At 7:00 David Collenette announced a $75-million loan guarantee for Canada 3000 to help the airline through what he described as a "short-term cash crunch." He said Ottawa might backstop loans for other large Canadian carriers that were able to meet the same stringent conditions being imposed on Canada 3000. The loan guarantee wouldn't cost Ottawa a penny unless Canada 3000 defaulted on it. Nevertheless, it had been a tough sell at the cabinet table.

"Some of my colleagues in Cabinet were not in favour of a loan guarantee," Collenette said later. "They were worried about other industries coming forward – the travel industry and others. They said, 'We can't just write cheques to prop everybody up who's been affected by the events of the eleventh of September.'" But Collenette managed to convince them that Canada 3000 was a special case. In the two years since the Air Canada–Canadian Airlines merger, Air Canada's domestic market share had fallen to roughly 65 per cent from 80 per cent. If Canada 3000 went bankrupt, Air Canada's market share would shoot back to 80 per cent or higher.

At first, news of Ottawa's rescue efforts seemed to achieve the desired result. The day after Collenette's announcement, the airline's shares rose 22 per cent to close at $4.10 on the TSX, and creditors were willing to allow the airline some breathing room. Air Canada used the occasion to renew calls for an industry-wide aid package, in line with Washington's largesse to U.S. carriers.

But Canada 3000 didn't yet have the $75 million in its bank account. In order to secure cabinet approval for the loan guarantee, Transport officials had attached a number of tough conditions for Canada 3000 before they would sign the loan documents. As the company's largest investor, Lecky was asked to inject $10 million in new capital. The federal government wanted warrants entitling it to acquire one-sixth of the airline's shares. Ottawa also wanted to charge Canada 3000 an annual interest rate of 6 per cent for the loan guarantee, in addition to the rate the airline would have to pay a commercial bank for the underlying loan.

The real stumbling block was the requirement that Canada 3000 present a viable business plan for a return to profitability. The airline was dangerously low on cash by the end of October, diminishing its reserves at a rate of $700,000 a day. Revenue was down about 30 per cent and there was no way of knowing when, if ever, the forecast would improve. In other lean years, airlines simply lowered their fares and the customers came back. In late 2001, people were afraid to fly, and there was no price incentive that could overcome their fears. Complicating matters was Ottawa's insistence that Canada 3000 get smaller, cutting capacity and staff. For those employees who remained, including managers, Ottawa wanted to see pay cuts of up to 20 per cent.

Angus Kinnear wrestled with the conundrum. If the bureaucrats in Ottawa thought it was easy to downsize an airline, they were dead wrong. Kinnear knew that the only way to shrink Canada 3000 to profitability would be to retire a few aircraft of each equipment type. But pilots tended to use their seniority to fly the biggest planes they could, since paycheques are related to equipment size. If he were to lay off from the bottom of the seniority list – as labour contracts required – he would be left with too many pilots trained to fly high-capacity planes to Europe, Australia, and India, and a shortage of those capable of flying smaller aircraft within North America. His people estimated that it would take six months and $9.5 million to conduct the necessary retraining as senior crew members bumped their more junior counterparts. He didn't have the time or the money.

With revenue down 30 per cent, Kinnear figured he had to lay off about 1,400 workers, roughly 30 per cent of his 4,800 employees. As he pondered the near impossibility of that task, it dawned on him that 1,400 was almost precisely the number of workers who had joined Canada 3000 through its acquisition of Royal. Royal's 1,400 employees were trained on a mix of large and small planes. If he could shut down Royal – which had already been exposed in an unproven lawsuit as a financial disaster – he could save the rest of the airline. "It's like the doctor walking up to you in the hospital and saying, 'Mr. Kinnear, you have two choices. You either lose your limb or you lose your life, Which do you want?' "Kinnear said.[19]

On November 3, Kinnear filed what he called his "last-ditch stand," an application with the Canada Industrial Relations Board (CIRB) seeking permission to close down Royal. It was a dramatic reversal of Kinnear's efforts to merge the two carriers. Days before September 11, Canada 3000 had finalized an agreement to integrate Royal and Canada 3000 pilots into a common seniority list. Furthermore, it wasn't clear that he had the legal right to terminate Royal, and, if the move were approved, it would fundamentally alter the company. Kinnear briefed Lecky on his intentions, but he did not take the plan to his board of directors or to the federal government.

Michel Leblanc, the former chairman and largest shareholder in Royal Aviation, told reporters that he was disgusted with Kinnear's attempts to dump his former staff. Saying he could not allow Canada 3000 to shut down the airline he had built over ten years, Leblanc offered to buy back the airline and re-establish it as an Eastern Canadian discount carrier. He suggested his offer might be conditional on Canada 3000 dropping the $45 million lawsuit filed against him and another former Royal executive.

On the afternoon of November 6, Canada 3000 upped the ante. In a teleconference call, the airline's board of directors passed two remarkable motions. The first proposed to halt trading of Canada 3000 shares so that Kinnear could publicly explain to the CIRB the gravity of the airline's position. A risky second motion hammered home the point: "Unless the CIRB provides a decision which avoids the cost and the delays of retraining resulting from bumping, [the airline] will be unable to continue a viable business plan that would sustain the employment of two-thirds of its 4,800 work force, leading to the cessation of operations of Canada 3000 Inc."

Kinnear took the motions to the labour board. He explained that the airline was down to less than $1.5 million in cash and losing $700,000 a day. He read Canada 3000's motions, as a hushed crowd of reporters, labour-board officials, and dozens of uniformed staff from Royal Airlines listened attentively. Kinnear well understood the stakes. He told the CIRB that, when his comments hit the press, Canada 3000's bookings and revenues would "decrease dramatically."

Indeed they did. Travel agents urged passengers not to book with Canada 3000, caterers refused to load meals onto airplanes, and fuel companies threatened to cut off the airline until their bills were paid in full. Airport officials around the world prepared to seize airplanes to cover unpaid debts. Canada 3000 managed to hold off some of its creditors with assurances of Ottawa's imminent intervention. In an e-mail to most of Canada's major airports on Wednesday, November 7, Canada 3000 vice-president Linda Turk said the airline was "very confident" it would soon have the guarantee. "The government is planning on having all of the paperwork done by Friday. If you can bear with us for another day or two, everyone will get payment in full," the e-mail said.[20]

Union officials accused Kinnear of holding a gun to the labour board's head with his predictions of impending doom. If he was, it didn't work. On November 8, the CIRB declined Canada 3000's application to shut down Royal, saying it did not have the jurisdiction to release the company from agreements reached with its employees. The labour board urged Canada 3000 and its unions to continue their search for a negotiated solution. Union officials put forward a proposal to lay off 500 flight attendants and 180 pilots. But it was too little, too late. Canada 3000 was crumbling down around them.

The Winnipeg Airports Authority felt it had been patient long enough, and won a court order to seize a Canada 3000 jet as security for unpaid debts. In London, England, Gatwick Airport held a plane until the airline paid its overdue bills. As news of the seizures spread through the aviation community, other creditors withheld goods and services. It soon became clear that Canada 3000 would have to follow through on its threats to file for court protection under the Companies' Creditors Arrangement Act (CCAA).

Commercial-court judges grant bankruptcy protection to insolvent companies to give them time to restructure their finances without the threat of assets being seized or new debts piling up. Shareholders typically lose everything during a CCAA filing, but other stakeholder groups, such as employees, customers, suppliers, and creditors, usually come out better than they would under a bankruptcy liquidation. In theory, Canada 3000's

November 8 filing was supposed to put a halt to the aircraft seizures, so the company could continue to negotiate with its unions.

The legal work was rushed, and Canada 3000 failed to properly enforce the protection in foreign jurisdictions. Within hours, airports, maintenance companies, and air-traffic-control agencies around the world began eyeing Canada 3000 aircraft. The only hope for Canada 3000's long-term survival would be if it could maintain its schedule during the restructuring, a key condition of the judge's order to keep creditors at bay.

Hours after the filing, Canada 3000 put out a press release advising that it would continue operating and that it was "very confident" of its future prospects. The press release quoted Kinnear as saying the CCAA filing would allow the airline "to continue serving the travelling public" to ensure "the long term viability of Canada 3000." Kinnear says he did not authorize the release, and, in fact, circumstances had changed by the time the release went on the wire at 5:00 in the afternoon of November 8. In a telephone conference call at about the same time, Canada 3000's board passed a motion approving Kinnear's painful recommendation that the airline bring its aircraft back to Canada and cease operations. With threats of airplane seizures at airports in Canada and abroad, he felt he could no longer operate the airline safely. The move came as a shock to managers across the country, who had been advising local officials that it would be business as usual. Even the company's court-appointed monitor, Deloitte & Touche, had not been advised that Canada 3000 was grounding its planes.

David Collenette was in Toronto, waiting for a delayed Air Canada flight at Pearson, when he received a call from an aide, advising him of Canada 3000's decision. Despite his best efforts, the minister's rescue package could not be delivered in time to reverse the company's fortunes. His government's loan conditions were necessary to protect the public purse, but they proved too onerous for an airline that had waited too long before trying to save itself.

Konrad von Finckenstein, who had been probing Air Canada's Tango brand for weeks, did not learn of the airline's demise until the next morning. Astoundingly, von Finckenstein said his officials had finished their investigation the previous night and had concluded that Tango was indeed an anti-competitive tool designed to target Canada 3000. With Canada 3000 gone, however, the order to shut down Tango became moot, and was never signed.

Air Canada claimed the allegations were unfounded. The company pointed out that Tango had operated only a few flights by the time Canada 3000 closed its doors. But von Finckenstein believed that Air Canada had hurt Canada 3000 not just in the week that it operated Tango flights, but throughout the month it was selling flights against it. He said he had satisfied himself that Tango was a "large contributing factor" in Canada 3000's failure.

Canada 3000's former executives are skeptical of the commissioner's claims that he was hours away from issuing a cease-and-desist order when Canada 3000 grounded its planes. Kinnear says the problem with competition law is that it's virtually impossible to do anything until it's too late. "You were like roadkill. You could stand in the middle of the 401 and say, 'There's an eighteen-wheeler truck coming down the centre lane, and I'm tied to the road here, and this thing's going to kill me.' And their response would be: 'Give us a call when it's happened and we'll investigate it. They haven't broken the law just because they're driving towards you at eighty miles an hour and you can't move," Kinnear said later. "They've only broken the law when they've hit you.'"[21]

There remained some hope that Canada 3000 might be able to get its planes back in the air. Von Finckenstein suggested that he could resurrect the cease-and-desist order against Tango if the airline flew again. But it was not to be. On Saturday, November 10, John Lecky, Angus Kinnear, and the rest of the company's directors and officers resigned en masse. And on Remembrance Day, November 11, Canada 3000 went bankrupt.

Why did Canada's second-largest airline fail? The competition commissioner blamed Air Canada and Tango. Analysts said the company tried to grow too fast. Shareholders question whether management did enough research before buying Royal Aviation. Former board members accuse the airline's unions of failing to make the necessary concessions.

Former executives faulted Ottawa for attaching onerous terms to its loan guarantees. Federal officials derided the airline for assuming the government would have no choice but to save the troubled carrier. Everyone had a different explanation, and everyone was right.

"It shouldn't have happened," former CFO Don Kennedy said. "It was an incredible waste, an absolutely incredible waste. I've replayed everything in my mind many times over. I can't tell which individual event would actually have played different to change the course of the thing."[22]

Angus Kinnear says that, in the end, there's only one explanation for the disappearance of Canada 3000: the September 11 terrorist attacks. "You can live on either side of the fault line for a long time, but if the world moves, you get a situation where it's difficult to survive, purely and simply because the earth moves that much," he said. "That's what happened to Canada 3000."[23]

With Canada 3000 dead, Air Canada's domestic-market share leaped to over 80 per cent, as expected. Investors warmed to the airline's fortunes and to Canadian carriers generally. Air Canada shares rose 6 per cent on the day Canada 3000 grounded its planes, while shares in Transat A.T., the parent of Air Transat, jumped 29 per cent. Observers speculated that Air Canada would kill its Tango brand now that its main competitor was vanquished. But Milton had a different idea. He spoke of expanding Tango and proceeding with plans to launch another low-cost airline in Western Canada.

Robert Milton wasn't the only airline veteran hoping to capitalize on the gap left by Canada 3000. The usual suspects were soon at it again – Michel Leblanc of Royal Airlines, Ken Rowe of CanJet, and Angus Kinnear of Canada 3000 – as if there were nothing more natural to do than start up another airline.

12

RE-REGULATE, RELAUNCH, RE-BRAND

Just because something doesn't work out the first time doesn't mean to say you give up.[1]

— Ken Rowe, founder, CanJet I and CanJet II

Once you get hooked on the airline business, it's worse than dope.[2]

— Ed Acker, former president,
Braniff, Air Florida, and Pan Am

On November 16, 2001, five days after Canada 3000 went bankrupt, transport minister David Collenette held a press conference at Toronto's Union Station to crow about Ottawa's $402-million capital investment in VIA Rail, a Crown corporation. "The federal government is fully committed to the revitalization of passenger rail," Mr. Collenette said after driving one of VIA's speedy new locomotives into the station. "It makes good economic sense. It makes good environmental sense. And it expands the range of options available to Canadians in the transportation marketplace with more trains, faster trains, and better facilities across the country." The television clips of a smiling Collenette shaking hands with VIA Rail president Jean Pelletier stood in sharp contrast to the grim faces of Canada 3000 workers who had lost their jobs less than a week earlier, when Collenette had been unable or unwilling to deliver on his pledge to provide $75 million in loan guarantees to the troubled carrier.

Months later, Collenette explained that VIA's capital funding was given in "an entirely different context" from the bailout money promised to

Canada 3000. Collenette accurately pointed out that governments around the world subsidize passenger rail service but not airlines. If Canadians valued rail service as an efficient, environmentally friendly mode of transport with important links to their past, then they had to be willing to pay for it, the minister said. Collenette deplored VIA's neglect at the hands of his own government and that of the previous Progressive Conservative regime. He would right those wrongs. "I'm damn proud that I was able to convince the prime minister – over the opposition of a lot of people in government – to reinvest in the railway and recommit," Collenette said later.[3]

In the months after September 11, VIA's volumes surged as travellers opted to stay on the ground, either out of lingering anxiety or to avoid the time-consuming new security measures at the country's airports. Collenette hoped that VIA might become an alternative to Air Canada in the busy Quebec City–Windsor corridor, now that Canada 3000 had collapsed. But VIA was only part of the answer to Air Canada's new stranglehold. Collenette was concerned about service between Toronto and Ottawa, Montreal, Halifax, and St. John's. On some of the country's most heavily travelled routes, Air Canada suddenly had a virtual monopoly.

Milton hated the monopoly label and always challenged it, pointing out that his airline still faced intense competition on the vast majority of its flights, including those into the United States and overseas. By playing with the numbers, Milton could demonstrate that Air Canada's domestic market share was closer to 50 per cent, rather than the 80 per cent routinely cited by government and the media. Since market share is measured by the percentage of units sold, it came down to how one defined a unit. When Milton defined a unit as a passenger trip instead of a passenger mile, Air Canada was no monopoly, nor even a near monopoly. WestJet flew shorter trips on average than Air Canada, so Air Canada lost ten to fifteen points off its reputed market share right there. By eliminating the domestic portion of trips originating in Europe, Asia, or the United States, its share fell further still.[4]

Milton's case might have been compelling if not for the fact that, in presentations to investors, who prefer hefty market-share numbers, he returned to the industry's standard unit of measurement. In February 2002, for example, in a slide presentation to investors, he displayed an estimate of the airline's domestic market share that projected 78 per cent in 2002, compared with 73 per cent in 2001 – based on passenger miles.

Economists, newspaper columnists, and the federal competition commissioner reacted to the death of Canada 3000 with renewed calls for the opening of Canada's skies to foreign competition. Despite his unhappiness with Air Canada's dominance, however, the transport minister was not prepared to turn to the Yanks for a solution. His inclination was not to deregulate – by eliminating the government's foreign-ownership restrictions – but to re-regulate.

In late November, Collenette summoned Robert Milton and board chairman Jack Fraser to his Ottawa office to warn them that, unless Air Canada took steps to reduce its market share, he would do it for them. He said he would consider limiting Air Canada to the most heavily travelled domestic routes or capping the number of seats the carrier could sell on individual routes. Government officials, he revealed, were working on a plan that would restrict Air Canada to a single city in each province, with the exception of Ontario, where it would be allowed to fly to Toronto and Ottawa. The minister said he was especially disturbed by Air Canada's plans to launch a Western-based discount airline. In his view, what Air Canada really needed was a major restructuring to become smaller and more focused – perhaps even to file for bankruptcy protection while it underwent this reorganization and regained its financial footing.

Collenette's proposals were shocking. They seemed diametrically opposed to the minister's previously stated goals of greater consumer choice and the assurance of regional service to small markets.

"I was operating from the point of view that the government was just tired of the posturing that was coming from Air Canada," Collenette explained later. "They really had to behave in such a way that their main goal was to run a business, not put others out of business, quite frankly."[5]

Milton was furious at Collenette's presumption. When Onex launched its hostile takeover bid in 1999, the government appeared to have no objections to a merger that would have resulted in one company dominating the market. If 80 per cent of the domestic market was acceptable for Onex in 1999, why wasn't it tolerable for Air Canada in 2001? Furthermore, some government officials were spinning his plea request for billions in aid against him, portraying him as personally greedy and opportunistic. At the same time, Collenette had been prepared to selectively bail out Canada 3000, to the detriment of the rest of the Canadian airline industry.

"This was a very difficult time, when we needed government support. What we had instead was a minister of the Crown saying Air Canada should go bankrupt," Milton recalled in 2002. The way he saw it, the government wanted Air Canada to fail.

Jack Fraser was so concerned about the minister's threats that he convened an emergency meeting of the company's board of directors. On Milton's recommendation, the directors decided that Air Canada's proposed low-cost carrier should be put on hold, at least until Air Canada could repair its damaged relationship with Ottawa.

When Collenette appeared before the Standing Senate Committee on Transport and Communications on December 4, he again raised the possibility of re-regulation. "We have said to them that the present situation is untenable and that we must find ways to reduce their domestic share," Collenette said. "Otherwise, Parliament will have to re-regulate the entire industry. You cannot have one operator out there without competition; you need to have some balance." Asked if re-regulation was a serious option, Collenette replied, "Anything is possible. We could nationalize; we could take a controlling piece of Air Canada. We could fire all the management. We could fly 747s to Windsor, Ontario, or to Chicoutimi. We could do all those kinds of things."

Collenette was before the committee to answer questions on Bill C-38, a short but profound piece of legislation that would scrap the limit on the number of Air Canada shares an individual investor could own. The 10-per-cent cap had been the critical factor preventing Onex

Corporation from taking control of Air Canada in 1999. In 2000, Collenette had raised the limit to 15 per cent. He had never been fond of the restriction, which effectively protected management, since no shareholder had the clout to put new people in charge. In 1999, Air Canada officials had gone to court to ensure that the ownership cap was respected. But in late 2001, they were so hungry for new capital that they asked Collenette to eliminate it altogether.

A gaggle of Air Canada executives appeared before the Senate committee, among them general counsel John Baker and Steve Markey, vice-president of government relations. Markey was one of the few executives from Canadian Airlines who had survived the takeover. Leading the group was Peter Donolo, senior vice-president of corporate communications. In one of his few public appearances as an Air Canada executive, Donolo told the senators that Air Canada was not wedded to its overwhelming industry pre-eminence, noting that in the *New York Times* a few weeks earlier Robert Milton had described Air Canada's dominance as a curse. "In many ways, it is," Donolo said. "We are so big that any complaint, no matter how large or how picayune, is directed at us because Air Canada is a large target."

As if on cue, the senators began to pepper Donolo and his colleagues with picayune – and self-serving – grievances. Senator Len Gustafson noted that he had made over eight hundred trips to Saskatchewan on Air Canada, and suggested some areas of customer service that could be improved at very little cost. He referred to his customary late-night flight to Regina. "A dinner used to be served on that flight, but the dinner has been cancelled," Gustafson said. "It is a difficult situation for the passengers. I heard many complaints on that flight. I do not think the cost of a meal would break Air Canada's budget."

Senator Laurier LaPierre had recommendations for Air Canada's snack choices.

Lapierre: I would say that peanuts are not good on the airline. There are children who are allergic to peanuts and merely touching them might create a problem. Furthermore, pretzels are no good for anyone's health. I think that you should give them cookies or chocolate. That is the best thing to do.

Baker: We discontinued peanuts three years ago.

LaPierre: I got them.

Markey: You probably had almonds or cashews.

The Chairman: Let's return to Bill C-38, please.

While the senators debated Air Canada's snack policy and Bill C-38 (which would become law on December 18), the House of Commons industry committee approved amendments to the Competition Act designed to enhance Ottawa's ability to prevent predatory pricing. The new legislation allowed the competition commissioner to extend cease-and-desist orders while he completed his investigations. It also gave the Competition Tribunal the authority to levy fines of up to $15 million on airlines found guilty of engaging in anti-competitive behaviour. Air Canada lobbied aggressively against the amendments before the Senate Banking, Trade and Commerce Committee; vice-president Calin Rovinescu condemned them as "a form of selective regulation of one private-sector company indirectly through the Competition Act." Collenette was convinced that Air Canada's opposition to the tougher guidelines was a sign that the airline intended to abuse its dominance, and therefore the amendments were all the more necessary.[6] Air Canada's campaign did achieve some success, however, when the government agreed that the laws would automatically expire in 2004, unless they were renewed.

On December 6, Robert Milton unveiled his own plan to address Air Canada's dominance. He sent letters to David Collenette and U.S. secretary of transportation Norman Mineta, urging them to establish a common aviation zone between the two countries, one that would allow Air Canada to fly between U.S. cities and U.S. airlines to do the same in Canada. As a first step, Milton proposed that Canada allow U.S. carriers to shuttle passengers between Canadian cities via a U.S. hub – Vancouver–Chicago–Montreal, for example. In exchange, he wanted the right to fly between U.S. destinations via a Canadian city, perhaps Boston–Montreal–

San Francisco. Milton was clear that he preferred this approach to the re-regulation being touted by Collenette. He said he was confident that Air Canada would be able to hold its own against the larger U.S. carriers on their own turf.

Collenette was quick to dismiss Milton's proposal, saying he didn't think the Americans would agree to it. Even if there were support for the idea in Washington, it could take years to negotiate an agreement, and the minister wanted a quicker fix to Canada's competition woes. He also pointed out that the proposal would not help Canadians in small communities. "I don't think American Airlines or Delta is going to service Chicoutimi or Moose Jaw or Prince George," he said.[7] Officials at WestJet were not enthusiastic about Milton's plan either, despite their free-market roots. They feared that U.S. discounters like Southwest or JetBlue would enjoy unfair advantages, such as access to cheaper fuel in the United States and more lenient U.S. regulations on the number of flight attendants required.

A few days after Milton attempted to get the federal government off his back with the cabotage proposal, he lost the man who was supposed to help mend Air Canada's relationship with Ottawa. Peter Donolo had been caught completely off guard by Milton's open-skies proposal, one more indication that his advice was not being taken seriously at Air Canada's head office. Milton had called for a major government initiative without briefing the vice-president in charge of the government-relations file. Donolo decided Air Canada wasn't the right place for him, and in mid-December he quietly left the company.

On December 10, Ottawa dealt another blow to the industry when finance minister Paul Martin announced that the federal government would levy a $24 surcharge on every return ticket to pay for improved security at airports and in the skies. The money would be used to buy new bomb-detection equipment, to provide better pay and training to airport screeners, and to put armed RCMP officers on select flights. The airlines were glad they weren't on the hook directly for these costs, but they didn't want their customers to pay for the improved security, either. They complained that the surcharge would make it more difficult to lure passengers back to the skies, and that it was particularly harmful to low-cost and regional carriers, for whom it would represent a greater share of the total ticket price. WestJet drove home this point with a "ridiculous fares, ridiculous fees" promotion, whereby it sold short-haul tickets for $3 each way. When the security surcharge, airport-improvement fees, and other charges were added on, the price of a $6 round-trip Calgary–Edmonton ticket rose to $89.27, while a $6 Hamilton–Ottawa ticket sold for $81.78. Once imposed, the surcharge's impact was dramatic. Air Canada claimed traffic fell by 30 per cent on its shortest regional routes, while WestJet yanked planes off short-haul routes and redeployed them to longer-haul markets, where the fee wasn't as evident. A year later the new finance minister, John Manley, reduced the surcharge to $14 from $24, citing the benefits of a new accounting system and optimistic estimates that passenger air travel would grow by 20 per cent between 2002 and 2005.

On January 15, 2002, at the University of Waterloo, Robert Milton made a rare speaking appearance. He told his audience that, for the first time in the history of aviation, worldwide revenue was expected to shrink in 2002. But Milton said he was "decidedly bullish" about Air Canada's prospects. He boasted that there had been far fewer empty seats in the airline's planes in December 2001 than a year earlier, and that Air Canada was one of the few airlines in the world that had been able to improve its load factor – its percentage of occupied seats – in December. He credited the airline's "aggressive capacity reductions" – that is, taking seats out of the market after the September 11 terrorist attacks. He neglected to mention that Air Canada had benefited significantly from the November failure of Canada 3000.

Milton also took aim at government regulators who were putting limits on Air Canada's ability to set prices. "It's like operating a business on a roller coaster where high prices are considered gouging, low prices are considered predation, and matching prices is considered … suspicious," Milton said. "I have never seen more sinister motives and malicious intent ascribed to a company simply trying to recover from an international, industry-wide crisis. I feel like I'm Dr. Evil in an Austin Powers movie."

Like most of Milton's speeches, this one was written by his assistant, Duncan Dee, a former aide to federal cabinet minister Sheila Copps. Some of Milton's advisors were unsure about the Dr. Evil reference, but he went with Dee's recommendation. After the speech, a staffer presented Dee with an Austin Powers poster in which the faces of Dr. Evil and his diminutive assistant Mini Me were replaced with those of Milton and Dee.

On February 7, Milton had the nasty task of announcing that Air Canada had lost $1.25 billion in 2001, roughly a million dollars every seven hours. It was the greatest twelve-month loss in the company's sixty-five-year history, but Milton promised shareholders that good things were on the way. He couldn't guarantee that Air Canada would post a profit for 2002, but he did vow that the company would return to profitability in the "seasonably stronger" second and third quarters, and that, when the economy recovered, Air Canada would emerge as a more cost-efficient airline in a market with less competition. In the company's annual report, Milton wrote that he viewed 2002 as a new beginning. "After wrestling with the special issues posed by the merger, global economic slowdown, and September 11, we can finally focus all our energies on making Air Canada the best and most-profitable airline it can be."

Milton was hopeful, even exuberant, but he was cautious not to jinx himself. Air Canada always seemed to be on the verge of a major breakthrough to clearer skies, only to hit another pocket of turbulence. "I've been saying over the past couple of years that it can't get any worse, and then it keeps getting worse," Milton told a reporter in February. "So now I don't say it any more."[8]

They were all at it again – Michel Leblanc, Ken Rowe, and Angus Kinnear – each trying to build a new domestic airline to fill the gap left by the collapse of Canada 3000. As Valerie Dufour, director general of air policy for Transport Canada, said in a 2002 speech at an airports conference, "Same fishbowl. Same water. Same fish."

Leblanc was the first to go public with his plans. He had tried to resurrect Royal Airlines even before Canada 3000's demise, when Kinnear made a last-ditch attempt to save his airline by sacrificing the Royal division. Leblanc's offer to buy back some of Royal's assets and rehire its workers had gone nowhere, while Canada 3000 spiralled into bankruptcy. Now that the airline was dead, Leblanc believed there was an opportunity to revive Royal, but only if he acted quickly. The new Royal would be based in Montreal or Toronto, use eight to twelve jets, and fly as far west as Winnipeg. Leblanc entered into negotiations with U.S. Airways Group to take over leases on seven Boeing 737s from the Canada 3000 fleet. He talked to Canada 3000's trustee in bankruptcy about buying such assets as computer systems and baggage-handling equipment, even trucks used to empty airplane toilets.

Leblanc wasn't the only one interested in that equipment. At Canada 3000's Fasken Drive offices, Angus Kinnear and Don Kennedy were quietly working on a scheme to return Canada 3000's planes to the skies. The plan would put 1,200 of the airline's former employees back to work using ten Airbus A319s and A320s. One of Canada 3000's largest share-holders was willing to bankroll Kinnear in his efforts to resuscitate the carrier. John Mullen, a Pennsylvania businessman who controlled Apple Vacations Inc., had once owned as much as 15 per cent of Canada 3000, before his holdings were watered down when the company paid for Royal and CanJet by issuing new shares. Mullen liked the Canada 3000 business model so much that he had started a similar airline in the United States under the name USA 3000. Mullen would have been willing to fund the whole start-up, but as an American citizen, his investment was limited to 25 per cent.

In Halifax, Ken Rowe was inundated with calls from former employees, local businessmen, and politicians urging him to restart CanJet. Having sold only CanJet's assets, he still owned the name. There were sound business reasons to relaunch CanJet. Back in 2000, Rowe had used his well-capitalized corporate holding company, IMP Group Ltd., to secure cheaper aircraft leases. As a result, he was still on the hook for the planes, despite Canada 3000's bankruptcy. "There's a lot of people who would like to see IMP restart CanJet, in particular the employees and the travelling public who used it," Rowe said in late November. "My answer to you is that we would not consider starting any airline again unless the government made severe penalties for the monopoly carrier if they were found guilty of predatory practices or abusing their dominant position."9

There were others, too. Bob Deluce – who became the titular president of Canada 3000 after regulators told Angus Kinnear he was too British for the job – had dreamed of introducing a regional carrier out of Toronto City Centre Airport ever since Onex unveiled its plan to merge Air Canada and Canadian Airlines. Despite its convenient downtown location near the CN Tower, the island airport was not well used by Torontonians. Air Canada's regional subsidiary, Air Ontario, offered a few flights to Montreal and Ottawa out of the airport, but the number of passengers had fallen from 400,000 in 1987 to just 114,000 in 2001. Deluce felt that one of the reasons more people didn't use the airport was that they had to take a ferry to get there. He predicted that as many as 900,000 would use his airline each year if a bridge connected the airport to the mainland. When he publicized his plans in early February 2002, Deluce said he had identified sources of up to $550 million in equity and debt for the construction of a bridge, a new terminal, and the purchase of turboprop aircraft from Montreal-based Bombardier. Deluce said the airline would serve routes between Toronto and such destinations as Ottawa, Montreal, New York, and Boston, and would appeal especially to business travellers. He initially projected a start date of September 2003, but opposition from local politicians and community groups would stall that timeline.10

Ted Shetzen, the garrulous ideas man behind Roots Air, was still dreaming of an airline just for business travellers. He thought it possible to send his next airline venture aloft in late 2004, using small or medium-sized aircraft that would link some of Canada's biggest cities, as well as international destinations, through partnerships with foreign carriers. "There is room for another major full-service airline in this country that targets corporate travellers and premium travellers who will obviously get a lot more for less," Shetzen told the *Globe and Mail* in 2002. If it sounded like the same pitch he had made for Roots Air two years earlier, it was.

The first person to fill the vacuum left by Canada 3000 was Russ Payson, the CEO of Skyservice Airlines. Within weeks of the Canada 3000 bankruptcy, Skyservice had taken over the leases on five of its aircraft and hired hundreds of its former workers. Payson went after the business generated by Sunquest and Conquest, the tour companies that had relied on Canada 3000 for air transportation to southern climes. Payson rushed in so quickly that he had to attire his flight attendants in the barely used blue-and-purple uniforms that had been designed for Roots Air.

Robbie Goldberg, the president of Conquest, similarly appreciated that the failure of Canada 3000 offered a huge opportunity in the domestic market. On February 21, 2002, Goldberg announced that Conquest would vastly expand its domestic program over the summer, flying up to seventy-four flights a week between Victoria, Vancouver, Calgary, Edmonton, Winnipeg, Toronto, Halifax, Moncton, St. John's, and Gander. Conquest's best fares would be comparable with Tango, but he promised to offer more seats at the lowest published fares. Conquest was a virtual airline, with no planes of its own. Instead, Conquest handled marketing and sales, using chartered aircraft for the flights. The windfall charter contract went to Skyservice. For Russ Payson, it was a sweet irony. He blamed Canada 3000's "Big Seat" program for the failure of Roots Air; now Canada 3000 was gone and Skyservice was picking up its business.

In late February, after three months of long days trying to bring back Canada 3000, Angus Kinnear gave up. Days before, in a quarterly conference call with analysts, Robert Milton had said that Tango would be expanded to 10 per cent of Air Canada's domestic capacity in the summer of 2002, with sixteen aircraft serving twenty-one cities. "Certainly the investors were very concerned about the effects that Air Canada's increase in Tango capacity would have over all on the marketplace," Kinnear told the *Globe and Mail*. "And they were very concerned that there were no defined guidelines in policy from the government and therefore nobody was aware of what the rules would be. I think Air Canada has won this game."[11]

Kinnear, who had spent the last thirteen years of his life at Canada 3000's Fasken Drive headquarters or at his suite at the airport Hilton, said he needed some time to consider what to do next. He didn't think long. Within weeks, Kinnear had moved to Philadelphia and assumed the role of president of USA 3000. He settled into a nearby Hilton.

In the meantime, Leblanc and Rowe were in a race to launch their respective discount carriers. Each hoped the other would drop out, but both were in too deep to retreat. Leblanc's enterprise, Jetsgo Corporation, began service on June 12, 2002. By going with a fresh brand name, Leblanc ensured that Royal's former unions had no claim of successor rights. He hired an entirely new team of workers, paying flight attendants below market wages and requiring pilots to put up a $30,000 training bond, which would be repaid over two years. He opted for a new type of aircraft as well, using Boeing MD-83s. These large planes, configured for 170 passengers, would give Leblanc the lowest unit costs in the business, but analysts predicted he would have difficulty filling all those seats.

CanJet returned to the skies on June 20, retaining the same brand name, the same planes, the same marketing campaign, and most of the same executives and staff of its original incarnation. Mark Winders, the one-time chief operating officer, returned temporarily to help get CanJet II off the ground, but he declined an offer to stay on permanently. That responsibility would go to Julie Gossen, Rowe's daughter.

Analysts warned that the resurrected carriers were in danger of introducing too much capacity at cut-rate prices into the fragile air-travel market. Ben Cherniavsky of Raymond James said there were substantial elements stacked against the new airlines, including the fact that many leisure travellers had already booked airline tickets for summer travel. "For these guys to enter the market now, with fuel prices where they are, with prevailing economic uncertainty and high insurance premiums and no apparent excess of demand – all this puts the odds against them being around for very long."[12]

The most fundamental rule of successful business management is that income must exceed expenses. It is a rule that has never really applied to Air Canada, especially since Robert Milton took over as CEO in 1999. By 2002, it was obvious to anyone studying the airline's books that Air Canada was headed for bankruptcy unless it could boost revenue or lower costs. With a prolonged travel slump, the disappearance of the business traveller, and increased competition from low-cost carriers, there was little chance of increasing income. Milton knew that, if Air Canada were to fix itself, it needed to ruthlessly slash expenses.

Air Canada took in $9.6 billion in revenue in 2001, but spent $10.3 billion on the airline's operations and hundreds of millions more on debt interest. Its biggest cost item – roughly 30 per cent of the operating budget – was salaries, wages, and benefits. This was clearly an area where the company had to cut expenditures, but it would take time and careful handling. The next-largest item was jet fuel, accounting for about 15 per cent of Air Canada's costs. This expense was largely outside the airline's control, but it has since implemented fuel surcharges to help cover rising fuel prices. The airline also paid $1 billion a year to lease airplanes, about 10 per cent of its operating costs. This was one of the fastest-growing expense items, because Milton's team had been selling aircraft to cover operating losses. The move helped resolve the airline's imminent cash shortfalls, but pushed up operating costs in later years. Air Canada's three largest expenses – labour, fuel, and aircraft leases – represented more than 50 per cent of its annual costs, and none was easy to control. Robert Milton needed a quick hit, an expedient way to cut hundreds of millions of dollars from the airline's operating costs. One obvious target presented itself: the $476 million Air Canada had paid to travel agents in 2001.

Traditionally, travel agents have sold the vast majority of airline tickets, taking a commission off the top of every ticket sold. But the Internet has made it much simpler for consumers to bypass agents altogether. Airlines had been cutting back on commissions paid to travel agents for some years, and Marc Rosenberg, Air Canada's vice-president of sales and product distribution, had warned that the time would come when airlines would eliminate conventional commissions altogether. That day arrived in March 2002, when Air Canada followed the lead of U.S. carriers and eliminated most commissions paid to travel agents. It would continue to pay commissions for tickets booked on its Tango brand, and it promised to enhance its incentive-based commission program by giving rewards for overall booking patterns rather than for each ticket booked. WestJet, now the country's second-largest airline, maintained its allegiance to travel agents, saying it had no intention of gutting its commissions.

The Association of Canadian Travel Agents (ACTA) warned that the sharp reduction in commissions would cause a number of travel agencies to close shop. "We've been waiting for this, dreading this moment," said ACTA spokeswoman Louise Crandall.[13] Most travel agencies implemented service charges billed directly to consumers to make up for the loss of commissions, a move that might encourage even more consumers to book over the Internet. Commissions paid by Air Canada fell by 22 per cent in 2002, representing a saving of $107 million.

A few weeks after the March announcement, Air Canada angered travel agents once again with the inauguration of Destina.ca, its own on-line travel agency. Destina allowed Air Canada to take advantage of the popularity of Internet bookings, and to compete with established players like Expedia and Travelocity. In addition to selling Air Canada tickets, Destina offered hotel rooms, car rentals, package tours, even tickets for travel on rival airlines. Travel agents and third-party computer-reservations systems filed lawsuits and registered complaints, arguing that Air Canada was abusing its dominance by offering low fares on Destina that weren't available to other retailers. An internal deal giving Destina exclusive rights to award bonus Aeroplan miles didn't help matters. Most of the complaints against Destina were soon dismissed, but the tensions between Air Canada and the industry's travel agents would continue.

Having taken on the people who sold his product, Milton geared up for a battle with the people who delivered it. The key to transforming

Air Canada, he believed, lay with the company's workers. They had to be persuaded that the airline's very survival depended on a lower cost structure. For years he had tried to secure the unions' co-operation in starting a discount airline with lower pay and more flexible work rules, but the unions had been unwilling to throw their support behind his call for concessions. Now the aggressive Air Canada boss was starting to think that his airline needed not one discount brand, but many.

Milton found his inspiration in Marriott International, a name familiar for its hotels. What intrigued him was that, within the Marriott empire, there were nineteen different enterprises: a conference centre, a food-services centre, and *no less than seventeen* hotel and residential brands. Founded in 1927 as a Washington, D.C., root-beer stand, Marriott operated more than four hundred hotels under its own name in 2002. But that was just the tip of the iceberg. Through its various brands, Marriott offered something for everyone. There were forty-five Ritz-Carlton hotels for customers who demanded luxury and could afford to pay for it. At the other end of the spectrum were nearly five hundred motel-style, budget-priced Fairfield Inns. For extended stays, guests could choose the Residence Inn or TownePlace Suites chains. There was a brand catering to executives posted away from home and another that comprised 156 retirement homes. It didn't matter that the average guest might not know that Ramada and Renaissance hotels were also Marriott brands. What was important was that Marriott generated revenue from every type of customer by offering every style of accommodation.

Milton wondered if he could reinvent the airline industry along the same lines. Gone were the days when full-service airlines could be all things to all people. By offering different classes of service and playing with the yield-management curve, Air Canada had offered cheap, restricted tickets with few frills and expensive, unrestricted tickets with lots of frills, all on the same flight. The rise of the discount carrier and the disappearance of the big-budget business traveller had destroyed that traditional airline model. And Milton confronted the additional headaches of high labour costs and poor public image. He came to believe that he could solve all three problems with branding. Carving the airline into a number of different brands was the way to reach a wider range of passengers, to seem less monolithic in the minds of government and critics, and to squeeze concessions from labour unions.

Air Canada's first foray in re-branding was Tango, which had taken off just days before Canada 3000's bankruptcy. Tango had arisen out of what Milton called his "incredible frustration" with the unions, who would not allow him to launch a separate discount subsidiary with lower labour costs. As he studied the Southwest model with vice-president Bill Bredt and Ben Smith, Tango's managing director, they realized that, while labour costs were a big factor, they were not the only factor. "It was distribution efficiency," Milton told *Air Transport World* in 2003. "It was efficiency in the use of real estate on the aircraft and it was efficiency in product delivery."[14] Tango was designed to reduce unit costs by putting more seats on each aircraft and keeping the planes in the sky for more hours each day.

On the day before Tango was scheduled to launch, Air Canada announced its next brand. Jetz aimed to fill a void left by Sport Hawk International, a sports charter business that had filed for bankruptcy protection shortly after the September 11 terrorist attacks. By removing the 120 seats on a regular Boeing 737 and replacing them with 48 executive-class seats, Air Canada was able to pick up Sport Hawk customers such as the Toronto Maple Leafs, the Toronto Raptors, and the Edmonton Oilers. The 737s carried a dedicated team of flight attendants, who could familiarize themselves with the whims of every athlete, as well as an on-board mechanic to ensure timely departures and arrivals.

The next move came in March 2002, when Air Canada re-branded its various regional carriers – Air Ontario, Air Nova, Air BC, and Canadian Regional – under the single name Jazz. The regional subsidiary flew smaller planes into smaller markets and paid lower wages. The Jazz brand was developed by the same virtuosi who had named Tango: Target Marketing & Communications. Noel O'Dea, the company's director of strategic and creative planning, said the moniker was intended to suggest that Jazz workers were more friendly and flexible than those at the main Air Canada brand.

Then, on April 19, Steve Smith finally unveiled Zip Air Inc., formerly known as Low Cost Co., Air Canada's own discount carrier. Like Tango, Zip would reduce costs by doing away with meals, using planes more efficiently, and eliminating business class to accommodate more seats. Zip would also have the benefit of lower wage scales. Consumers were surprised to hear Smith admit that Zip's fares would be no lower than Air Canada's. He pointed out that, on the routes where Zip would operate, Air Canada's fares were already quite low after years of competition against WestJet. Instead, Zip was a tool to lower Air Canada's costs in order to make those low fares profitable – or at least less of a drain on resources. He made no secret of the fact that the intent was to squeeze more out of workers. "For the employees, they have to understand that they will be working for zip," Smith joked tactlessly. While some observers suggested that Zip could take a toll on WestJet,[15] Clive Beddoe predicted Zip might actually drive loyal Air Canada customers to WestJet. "If Air Canada's main line disappears in the West, then those people that have traditionally flown only Air Canada will look at Zip, I think, as something essentially less than what WestJet provides," Beddoe told analysts. "And we may well see a migration of these traditional Air Canada passengers onto WestJet." The Air Canada brand would not disappear from the West, but it would be replaced by Zip on key money-losing routes – Calgary–Winnipeg, Edmonton–Vancouver, Edmonton–Winnipeg, and Vancouver–Winnipeg. The plan called for Zip to add cities in Eastern Canada as it grew from six to twenty planes.

The announcement that Zip would go ahead marked a significant milestone after two and a half years of planning and fighting with Air Canada's pilots and with the federal government. Days before the announcement, transport minister David Collenette had been briefed on Zip and had given his qualified blessing. Air Canada emphasized that the Boeing 737 planes that would be part of Zip's fleet did not constitute additional seats, but would replace mainline capacity. In other words, Air Canada promised not to use Zip to flood the market with low fares and extra flights – the "dilution" strategy described by an internal Air Canada document back in 2000. Collenette felt that the proposed amendments to the Competition Act, allowing the commissioner of competition to renew cease-and-desist orders and to levy fines of up to $15 million, was additional insurance against Air Canada's competitive tendencies. "I think it's essential that we have these changes in place as soon as possible," Collenette said, "but certainly these amendments go a long way in dealing with my concerns that I had originally with the low-cost discount carrier for Air Canada."[16]

The irritations with the government had been soothed for the moment, but the fight with employees was just heating up. Although Air Canada had reached a deal with its pilots, the carrier had not secured agreements with its other employee groups. Air Canada wanted new flight attendants and customer-service workers for the discount subsidiary, hired outside existing union contracts, but the unions maintained their contracts wouldn't allow it. "We want Air Canada to be successful and we will continue to do all we can to make that happen, but we are concerned with the direction this airline is taking with Zip," said Pamela Sachs, who represented flight attendants at CUPE. "Air Canada gives Zip by zapping its employees. They are hurting the very people who have worked so hard for them for so long."

It was the latest in a series of attempts by Air Canada to undermine its own collective agreements. Under Milton's command, Air Canada's approach to labour relations was to put pressure on the unions by trying to break the contracts it had signed. It would worry about the legal consequences later. Air Canada had used the technique successfully with its pilots in 2001. By announcing a deal to make Roots Air its discount carrier – an apparent violation of its contract with the pilots – Air Canada was able to push the pilots to agree to fly twenty planes at B-scale wages, instead of the six they had originally agreed to. The tactic had been employed again after the September 11 terrorist attacks, when Air Canada tried to get rid of workers it had previously promised not to lay off. Even though federal labour regulators told the airline this was illegal – because it had negotiated no-layoff clauses – Air Canada used the crisis to wrest concessions from its unions to mitigate the job cuts, which were unlawful in the first place. Now Air Canada wanted concessions to hire outside of its existing union contracts for Zip. Once again, the tactic worked. By hiring new staff for Zip before it had the requisite consent of the unions, Air Canada was able to push them into negotiating. Air Canada did not dispute that the new hires would be represented by one of its unions. But the company's starting position was that it wanted these new employees to work some shifts as customer-service reps and others as flight attendants. This would keep costs low by maintaining maximum flexibility. It also raised questions about which union would get the members – the CAW, which represented workers on the ground, or CUPE, which represented them in the skies. The threat of losing the work to the other union made both more responsive to Air Canada's demands. Days before Zip's scheduled launch date, Air Canada reached a deal with CUPE to hire new, unionized workers at B-scale wages for Zip.

Zip launched service on September 22, 2002, on three Western routes: Calgary–Winnipeg, Edmonton–Vancouver, and Edmonton–Winnipeg. The inclusion of Winnipeg prompted a call to Robert Milton from chairman Jack Fraser.

"Robert, I've gotten several phone calls in just the last twenty-four hours from friends of mine who fly business class Winnipeg to Calgary and they are very upset that there's now no business class."

"Jack, obviously you know the business leaders in Winnipeg, and I'm sure they're upset. Our design is not to upset anybody. Let me look into it, and I'll call you right back."

Milton would often call low-level managers directly when he had a question, rather than wait for the chain of command to respond. Managers reported quickly when Milton had a request, sometimes scribbling "RWI" – short for "Robert wants it" – on documents, as a proxy for "URGENT." Milton contacted the airline's marketing department, asking staffers to find out how many passengers had paid for business-class service before the aircraft were converted to Zip planes. A few minutes later, he was armed with the statistic he needed.

"Jack, I've got the answer for you. There are four business-class passengers on the Winnipeg–Calgary route per day."

"Four per flight?"

No, Milton replied, four paying passengers *per day*. Anyone else in the business-class cabin had received a free upgrade.[17] To Milton, this was a perfect illustration of why Zip was necessary and why it would work. If no one was paying for business-class service, there was no need for a business-class cabin. Rivals at WestJet mocked Steve Smith's new airline, which often had more empty seats than passengers. But Milton knew the passengers hadn't been there even when Air Canada's higher-paid workers were operating the flights. Zip didn't have to make money to be successful in the dismal post–September 11 environment. It just had to lose less money than Air Canada did when it was operating the routes.

Air Canada, Tango, Jetz, Jazz, and Zip. There were now five airline brands in Milton's stable – as well as Air Canada Vacations for package tours – and he felt there was room for more. Executive vice-president Montie Brewer, who had been hired away from United Airlines in 2002, headed up the team charged with developing new brands. The next, scheduled for 2003, was an international leisure airline, a sort of Tango for overseas flights. It was expected to specialize in reuniting Canadians with their roots, carrying recent immigrants back to Europe, the Middle East, and Asia to visit relatives. Milton's own roots at Midnite Express encouraged him to pursue a cargo brand with a dedicated fleet of freighters for transpacific and transatlantic cargo. Perhaps the most radical of the proposed new brands was known internally as Elite, a carrier designed specifically for business travellers. Elite would use a standard Airbus A319, but replace the 120 regular seats with some 40 spacious business-class seats. In late 2002, Milton said Elite was fully designed and could be rolled out in mid-2003. Ted Shetzen suspected that Milton wasn't serious about Elite, but had simply floated the idea to frighten investors away from Shetzen's proposed start-up.

On August 1, 2002, Robert Milton accomplished a feat that none of his counterparts at U.S. carriers had been able to achieve: he posted a tidy quarterly profit less than a year after terrorist attacks threatened the economic viability of every full-service airline on the continent. "Clearly, we're on the right track," Milton said in a conference call with reporters and analysts. "Clearly the track we're on is radically different from our North American peers." While analysts cautioned that Air Canada remained a high-risk stock, some were praising Milton's multi-branding strategy. Air Canada didn't provide segmented financial statements, but Milton insisted that Tango was performing better than the rest of Air Canada's domestic operations. Analyst Ben Cherniavsky was an early skeptic. He argued that, instead of re-branding and expanding, Air Canada should focus and shrink. Analysts also put a figurative asterisk beside Air Canada's $30-million second-quarter profit, noting that the company was benefiting from the failure of Canada 3000 and a stronger domestic economy than its U.S. counterparts. But they agreed that it was an accomplishment, one that augured well for the Montreal-based carrier. Investors were happy to buy into Air Canada's turnaround story. The stock, which had fallen below $2 in late 2001, was now trading at almost $8 a share, the level it had debuted at back in 1988.

Air Canada continued to outperform the wretched U.S. industry in the third quarter. The major U.S. carriers were all in the red for what is usually the strongest period of the year, but Air Canada posted a $125-million profit. "I'm thrilled to pieces about the progress our people have made," Milton said. "If you look at our peers in this industry in North America, they've effectively done nothing and their results are horrific. We have seen a tremendous reversal of fortune here." Things were looking up for Milton, who had been hard-pressed to score a win since acquiring Canadian Airlines in early 2000. The merger was supposed to bring handsome profits, but Air Canada had lost money for the past two years because of merger difficulties, an economic slowdown, and the terrorist attacks.

In November 2002, *Globe and Mail* columnist Eric Reguly declared Milton "the comeback boss of the year . . . well on his way to becoming one of the best CEOs in the land." Reguly boldly predicted that Milton's re-branding strategy would be the salvation of the airline. While there were many challenges ahead, the columnist wrote, Milton had two things going for him: audacity and a massive domestic market share.[18]

But while Milton's audacity was unshakeable, his market position was not. An analysis by the *Globe and Mail* found that the airline's domestic market share plunged in 2002 from 83.2 per cent in January to just 70.5 per cent in December. The analysis was based on revenue passenger miles, passenger traffic data disclosed monthly by Air Canada, WestJet, and Jetsgo. RPMs are the total number of passengers flown multiplied by the average length of flight. Air Canada officials said they weren't concerned, that Air Canada's dominance made market-share loss inevitable. But it was already clear that the outlook for 2003 was not as optimistic as it had been a few months earlier. There was the threat of a war in Iraq, which was pushing up fuel prices and keeping customers at home. And WestJet, CanJet, and Jetsgo continued to grow, making more and more domestic routes less and less profitable.

At the end of 2002, Air Canada was again running dangerously low on cash, despite continued attempts to cover operating losses by selling aircraft and engines. In late December its reserves had fallen to $558 million, down from $717 million at the end of September. Most of that – $506 million – represented liabilities for advance ticket sales. In other words, the airline was frighteningly close to insolvency. But the senior executives at Air Canada's Montreal head office weren't spooked yet. Talks were under way for a deal that could bring some desperately needed cash into the airline, help that would come from a most unlikely source.

13

EMERGENCY LANDING

The airline business has always been run by guys with big egos, and they compete to have the most flights, the most airplanes, the biggest market share. The problem with that philosophy is that you can win all those little games and still come out losing money.[1]

— Gordon Bethune, Chairman, Continental Airlines

Gerry Schwartz likes to think of Onex Corporation's downtown Toronto headquarters as a "theatrical set," designed to inspire confidence, if not awe, in any visitor. "When a guy comes up to your office who wants to sell you his company for $600 million," Schwartz told Peter C. Newman, "it helps to be in surroundings where he can implicitly assume that we can pay for it — and he kind of understands we don't need to buy his business."[2] The curtain rises when the elevator doors glide open on a well-appointed wood-panelled foyer, the most arresting feature of which is a small carved beaver standing sentry above the Onex logo. This is no sterile business environment, but a Georgian-style country house painstakingly recreated forty-nine floors above Bay and Front Streets. Large, double-hung windows spill sunshine onto a floor covered in 150-year-old chestnut planks imported from Alabama. "If God were a capitalist," Rod McQueen once wrote in *National Post Business* magazine, "this would be heaven."[3]

Robert Milton and Calin Rovinescu stepped into Schwartz's theatre for the first time in September 2002, three years after the Onex boss had tried to take over Air Canada. The offices — imagined as the enemy's lair in 1999 – now represented hope to the two executives. They intended to solve Air Canada's cash and debt problems by selling the airline's under-valued assets, hidden deep within the balance sheet. Financial analysts had told them that Aeroplan – the country's top customer-loyalty program – was worth $500 million to $1 billion. But the stock markets valued all of Air Canada's shares at just $500 million. This made no sense to Milton, even though he recognized that most of Air Canada's capital base was in the form of debt, not equity.

Few had studied Air Canada's hidden assets more carefully than Onex. Schwartz and his team knew that Aeroplan represented a huge opportunity. Onex was ready to buy a stake in the scheme, and Air Canada clearly wanted to sell. The only question was whether the hostilities of the past would sour a working relationship in the future. The fight had been personal, after all. Schwartz had told reporters that Milton showed "immaturity" in his handling of the Onex bid, while Milton had accused Schwartz of trying to "steal" Air Canada from its shareholders.[4] Schwartz invited his former foes to a gourmet dinner in Onex's luxurious executive dining room to see if they could bury any hard feelings and construct a deal that was beneficial to both sides.

A smiling Schwartz, accompanied by his chief strategist Tony Melman, greeted Milton and Rovinescu with handshakes and flattery. "So these are the guys who made my life so difficult," Schwartz said.[5] He was full of compliments for their tactical craft during the takeover fight and praised their handling of the rough seas in the years since. Over veal chops, wild rice, and steamed vegetables (like Milton, Tony Melman is a vegetarian), the four men joked and laughed as they relived the drama of the battle. By the end of the evening, there was no doubt they could work very well together. All that remained was an agreement on amicable terms for the sale of part of the Aeroplan unit.

Schwartz's fortunes had taken a turn for the worse after his withdrawal from the Air Canada contest in 1999. Onex was on its way to posting a $145-million loss for 2002, compared to a $798-million profit in 2001 when it made extraordinary gains by selling its remaining stake in Sky Chefs. But the takeover king who had never quite been able to close the big deal had finally acquired a visible Canadian company. In 2001 he purchased Chapters, the bookstore giant, which his wife, Heather Reisman, added to her Indigo chain. As with Air Canada, the war for Chapters was fought on many fronts: in court, in front of the Ontario Securities Commission, and before shareholders, with a rival white-knight bid from Future Shop Limited, the Vancouver-based electronics retailer. Schwartz stayed out of the limelight in this contest, handling all communications through press releases, and he prevailed. This time it was Schwartz and Reisman who won dominance in a protected industry – there are foreign-ownership restrictions in the bookselling business as there are for airlines – but he has been unable to turn that dominance into meaningful profits. As of July 2003, the power couple owned 75.8 per cent of the shares of Indigo Books & Music Incorporated.[6]

Back in November 2001 Schwartz had sent an investment advisor to inquire if Air Canada would be open to an Onex offer for Aeroplan. But any discussions were put on hold when an internal squabble erupted at Air Canada over how to save the airline in the aftermath of the terrorist attacks. Everyone agreed that the company had too much debt and not enough equity, but there was a difference of opinion over how to fix its balance sheet. One option – advocated by the carrier's financial advisors, BMO Nesbitt Burns and Goldman Sachs – was to issue more shares on the stock market. After Air Canada posted strong results in 2002, the advisors offered a bought deal, through which they would have assumed all the risk. Another possibility was to bring in cash by selling off pieces of Aeroplan, the regional airline Jazz, or other assets.

Milton and Rovinescu were keen on a third option, one involving Texas Pacific Group, a U.S. investment company with an interest in aviation. Air Canada's senior executives and board members were well acquainted with TPG and one of its founders, David Bonderman. Under Hollis Harris, Air Canada had teamed up with TPG to acquire the insolvent Continental Airlines in 1992. Both Texas Pacific and Air Canada had done extremely well on the venture. Air Canada had paid roughly

$55 million U.S. for a one-third interest in Continental and realized a gain of more than $350 million U.S. when it sold its stake in 1996. Air Canada's former chairman, Claude Taylor, had worked closely with Bonderman on Continental's board of directors, and officials from the two companies maintained close relations for more than a decade.

Bonderman still owned a piece of Continental in early 2002 when he proposed to take an equity interest in Air Canada. Airline stock had never been as cheap as it was in the months after September 11, and Bonderman was willing to gamble $250 million in the expectation that Air Canada's financial fortunes were about to turn. He was convinced that an investment in the company could lead to Continental-style profits.

Over weeks of negotiations, Air Canada's executives sketched out the framework with TPG officials. BMO Nesbitt Burns and Goldman Sachs advised them to hold off, believing the airline's shares were about to soar. Milton took the arrangement to his board anyway. The debate was tense and divisive and ended with the board voting down management's recommendation. They preferred to wait until the stock markets rose to sell shares, so that they wouldn't have to give up so much of the company. Moreover, they believed that, while it was essential that Air Canada address its balance-sheet woes, increased equity was not the answer. If Air Canada was to survive the onslaught of WestJet and other low-cost rivals, it must radically lower its costs.

With the TPG deal off the table, Milton and Rovinescu had to look at the other options, among them asset sales and the Onex overture. Through the fall of 2002 into January 2003, officials from Air Canada and Onex fashioned a deal that would see Onex acquire 35 per cent of Aeroplan for $245 million. They called the negotiations "Project Delta." (In mathematics, delta represents a change to a variable, and the Onex–Air Canada relationship had changed dramatically.) At Air Canada's headquarters, Onex's involvement was known to only a few senior individuals. Most of the company's vice-presidents had to be content with references to a mysterious "Group B." Those participating in the negotiations were almost giddy with anticipation; they knew the media and the business community would be blown over by this unlikely alliance.

Milton saw the sale as a way to bolster the airline's cash reserves in anticipation of another war in Iraq; in January and February 1991, during the last conflict there, Air Canada's passenger traffic fell 14 per cent from the previous year. Over the longer term, Milton knew Onex had the resources to turn Aeroplan into an even more abundant cash cow, by transforming it from a frequent-flyer program into a frequent-buyer program, one that would allow members to earn and redeem points with a wider variety of partners, including retail stores.

The agreement was announced publicly on January 27 in a conference call with reporters and financial analysts. Representatives of both companies gushed over their new relationship. Onex vice-president Andrew Sheiner promised that consumers would benefit too, because Onex would be sure to free up more reward seats. On Flyertalk, an on-line discussion board for frequent flyers, some of Air Canada's most frequent customers – the points-rich Elite or SuperElite Aeroplan members – discussed the pros and cons of the Onex deal. They liked the idea of more available seats, but they worried that partnering with retail stores could turn Aeroplan into a program that rewarded customers with toasters rather than free flights.

Neither Milton nor Schwartz participated in the conference call. In a press release, Schwartz referred to Aeroplan as a "gem" within Air Canada. In a recorded telephone message to employees, Milton raised the issue that was at the front of their minds. "Given our history, I know many of you will be asking why we chose Onex as our partner. Onex is well known and highly respected as one of the country's most experienced and knowledgeable investor groups with a solid track record of successfully investing in divisions of companies and creating tremendous value for all stakeholders in the process." He didn't try to explain why, if Onex was so wonderful, he hadn't tried to work out an accommodation with the investment company three years earlier.

Air Canada said the deal, a complicated agreement that included side transactions involving debt, valued Aeroplan at $900 million – almost double the stock-market capitalization of the entire company. While the valuation was good news, it was also a clear reminder of Air Canada's dire straits. The company's stock had fallen to about $4 a share; the company's debt outweighed the market capitalization of its shares nineteen to one. Just a few days earlier, analyst Nick Morton of RBC Dominion Securities had issued a warning of a cash shortfall at Air Canada. "Some major U.S. airlines that are not yet in Chapter 11 are now hiring bankruptcy lawyers as they prepare for the consequences of a potential war in Iraq. In our view, Air Canada faces similar problems and must raise cash or face a possible liquidity crisis," Morton wrote. During the Aeroplan conference call, Calin Rovinescu dismissed speculation that Air Canada might file for bankruptcy protection as "hysteria."

Milton had never much enjoyed the labour-relations aspects of his job. He wanted to treat his people well, but he believed that the airline industry was burdened with overly generous and anachronistic labour contracts, an unhappy legacy of the days when government regulation ensured that airfares and labour costs rose together in predictable harmony. Milton's paternal grandfather had been a shop steward with the Teamsters. According to family lore, it was the stress of trying to please both labour and management that resulted in his untimely death by heart attack. "Don't let these labour issues get the best of you," Robert's father reminded him frequently. "Your health is the most important thing."[7]

It was hard to focus on his personal health when his company was so sick. Milton recognized that Air Canada was dying a slow death. Without major reductions in operating costs, the company would not pull through. At his highly unionized airline, Milton couldn't cut costs at will; he desperately needed the co-operation of the airline's labour leaders.

On the morning of February 6, 2003, he met with representatives of the various unions in a crowded meeting room at Air Canada's Montreal headquarters to deliver an urgent message. Among those present were Don Johnson, president of the Air Canada Pilots Association; Gary Fane, the director of transportation for the Canadian Auto Workers, which represented customer-sales and service workers; Pam Sachs, who represented flight attendants at the Canadian Union of Public Employees;

and Jean Jallet, president of the transportation component of the International Association of Machinists and Aerospace Workers.

Milton outlined the realities of the company's position, and asked for the unions' help in reducing the airline's annual $3-billion labour costs by $650 million. Contrary to rumours circulating before the meeting that Air Canada intended to axe ten thousand jobs and slash wages and benefits, Milton assured the union bosses that this was not his objective. Instead, the exercise was about productivity. If Air Canada's workers were subject to WestJet's more flexible scheduling and work rules, for example, Air Canada could reduce its labour bill by 44 per cent, or $1.3 billion a year. Milton was looking for half of that – $650 million – roughly 20 per cent of Air Canada's labour expenses. If costs came down, Milton vowed, the airline would be able to grow. Marginal international routes would become profitable, and Air Canada would be able to expand in the low-fare market within North America. "The low-cost carriers are eating our lunch . . . ," read one of the overhead slides that animated Milton's presentation. "We need to become a low-cost carrier."[8]

Other slides summarized Air Canada's difficulties in unflinching point form: "Revenue picture isn't getting any better. Uncontrollable costs keep increasing. Going through too much cash." Labour and management must "share the same sense of urgency." Air Canada's cash reserves had fallen 50 per cent in a single year, one slide noted, and the company had fewer assets left to sell. In 1997, Air Canada owned 51 per cent of its aircraft fleet. By 2003, the percentage had fallen to 4 per cent as a result of dozens of sale-leaseback arrangements. Air Canada had to repay $373 million in debt in 2003, and $300 million to $700 million annually over the next several years. The implication was that, without labour-cost reductions, there would be no funds available for these payments, since Air Canada had accumulated just $193 million from operations over the past eleven years. "We cannot afford to wait," declared yet another slide. Milton told the unions that the large U.S. airlines were also hastening to slash costs, but they didn't face the immediate pressure Air Canada did because most had "deeper pockets."

South of the border, US Airways and United Airlines parent UAL Corp. had both filed for Chapter 11 under the U.S. bankruptcy code. Don Carty, chairman of American Airlines parent AMR Corp., had frequently threatened to file for Chapter 11 if his unions didn't deliver significant concessions. The CEOs of full-service airlines around the world were grappling with the same problem: the rise of discount air-lines and the disappearance of business travellers willing to buy full-fare, unrestricted tickets had undermined their revenue projections. Yet they could not shrink their operating budgets in response because of entrenched high labour costs. When one union leader asked Milton if Air Canada might file for protection under the Companies' Creditors Arrangement Act – Canada's equivalent of Chapter 11 – Milton would say only that such a decision was for the company's board of directors. His response left the union leadership with a sinking feeling.

Milton was quick to say that labour-cost reductions were only part of the solution. Air Canada was planning to bolster its dwindling cash reserves by selling stakes in assets besides Aeroplan. Jazz, its regional airline, was a candidate for a partial sell-off, as was Air Canada Technical Services, the aircraft-maintenance division, and Airport Ground Handling Services, which was involved in checking in passengers and loading their baggage. These operations were seen as ideal spinoffs; all had the poten-tial to boost revenues dramatically by providing services to other airlines.

Despite the alarm of his message, Milton came across as gracious, patient, and forthcoming. It was a refreshing change for the union leaders, who were accustomed to a far more combative approach. Milton had been straightforward about the scope of Air Canada's problems, laying out the issues and humbly asking for their assistance to overcome the crisis. It seemed that Air Canada's top executive was willing to regard them as allies instead of adversaries; he suggested they work together to lobby the federal government for lower airport and Nav Canada fees.

The labour leaders appreciated that, instead of telling them how he intended to cut costs, Milton invited them to reflect on the problem and come back with their own proposals. Most union bosses already had plenty of ideas; they believed the company could save tens of millions of dollars by reducing middle management and empowering front-line employees to deal with issues on their own. Milton's labour-relations staff had also prepared their own detailed lists quantifying hundreds of millions of dollars in potential savings, items which would be brought into the negotiations at the appropriate time. Milton requested their responses by March 15, but there was confusion among the labour leaders present about what was supposed to happen by that date. Some were left with the impression that Milton wanted to have the labour-cost savings finalized by mid-March, while others thought they had until March 15 to get back to him with their ideas.

Milton's outlook was distinctly more upbeat in a conference call with analysts and journalists later the same day, when he presented Air Canada's $428-million loss for 2002, an improvement over 2001's $1.3-billion loss.[9] Asked by a reporter if the company was facing a cash crunch, Milton claimed the airline had $2.5 billion in assets that could easily be sold to raise cash. He said Air Canada needed to reduce its labour costs to compete with low-cost carriers, but he emphasized that the airline was not facing an urgent financial crisis. "It's a lousy environment in the airline industry in North America, and Air Canada is doing better than anybody else, and I intend for us to continue to do that." When questioned on whether he had hired bankruptcy lawyers, as his U.S. counterparts were doing, Milton said Air Canada was much better off than its American peers. "We're playing in a completely different game." Milton said he had "no interest" in going to court to seek bankruptcy protection; it would mean having changes "shoved down" his throat by judges.

Pundits were divided on the merits of Milton's plans to slash costs and sell assets – and on the question of how close Air Canada was to running out of cash. Fadi Chamoun, an analyst with UBS Warburg, warned that labour unions rarely co-operated with airline management, and suggested that the crucial cost reductions might not be possible without a court filing. Citing formidable competition, pension-fund concerns, an unsustainable cost structure, and a lack of cash, he advised clients to reduce their holdings in Air Canada shares. But Claude Proulx, an analyst with BMO Nesbitt Burns, maintained his neutral "market perform" rating on the stock. Accepting Milton's figures, he reminded clients that Air Canada had $2.5 billion in unencumbered saleable assets, and said the airline was not likely to face a financial crisis in the foreseeable future – barring another disaster on the scale of the September 11 terrorist attacks.

Some Air Canada watchers suspected that asset sales would do little to fix Air Canada's long-term problems. Douglas Reid, a professor at the Queen's University School of Business, wrote in the *National Post* that the proposal appeared to be "born of desperation" rather than being a well-executed divestment strategy. "Given the deterioration of Air Canada's cash position and the very high likelihood that further borrowings will be needed to fund current operations in 2003, the disposition of these assets is much akin to selling one's furniture to pay the rent – good only as long as you don't need the furniture, and viable only as long as there is some furniture left to sell."[10]

In early March, the Competition Tribunal wound up the first stage of hearings into allegations that Air Canada had engaged in predatory pricing against WestJet and CanJet in 2000. The purpose of this phase was simply to define avoidable costs – to establish which of Air Canada's expenses could be spared by not operating a flight – and to determine whether revenue from connecting flights should be included in the equation. To do so, the tribunal focused on just two of the seven routes where Air Canada was alleged to have abused its dominance: Toronto–Moncton and Montreal–Halifax. It planned to look at the other five routes in the second segment, when it would rule on the fundamental question of whether Air Canada had in fact abused its dominance with illegal predatory behaviour.

In closing arguments, Air Canada's lawyers maintained that the Competition Bureau's definition of avoidable costs was, in itself, anti-competitive. Almost half of its domestic flights would constitute illegal predatory behaviour under rules being proposed by the bureau. "Any test that leads to a monthly average 'failure rate' of 42 per cent of Air Canada's domestic flights, irrespective of the state of competition, is patently wrong," the airline argued in its legal brief. "Any test that would have the result of forcing Air Canada not to respond to competition, but to sit by and watch as its financial position erodes further is clearly anti-competitive." The hearings wound up on March 5, with both sides anxious for the tribunal's ruling.

A few weeks earlier, Air Canada had won a round against the commissioner of competition. In a unanimous decision issued on January 16, the Quebec Court of Appeal struck down the provision that allowed the commissioner to order Air Canada to raise fares when he suspected it of predatory behaviour. Parliament had granted the commissioner these unprecedented powers in an effort to rein in Air Canada's monopoly power after it acquired Canadian Airlines in 2000. The airline had always argued that the legislation violated "principles of fundamental justice," because the commissioner was not required to hear the airline's position before imposing a cease-and-desist order. In July 2001, a lower court had upheld the provision. Mr. Justice Kevin Downs ruled that, although the commissioner's powers might infringe on Air Canada's rights, they were necessary to protect consumers and to give smaller airlines a chance to compete. But the Quebec Court of Appeal ruled that Section 104.1 of the Competition Act was in conflict with Air Canada's rights to due process of law under the Canadian Bill of Rights, because it made the commissioner both investigator and judge. "At first glance, any reasonable, sensible and well-informed person would note a confusion of roles," Mr. Justice André Rochon wrote. "While pursuing his investigation, the commissioner-investigator becomes judge when he issues a temporary order."

By mid-March, Robert Milton felt he had waited long enough for co-operation from labour. It had been six weeks since his presentation to the union bosses, and there were as yet no firm agreements on how to save even a fraction of the $650 million he had requested. On March 14, Milton sent an ominous-sounding letter to the union leadership, with copies to the airline's forty thousand employees, in which he hinted for the first time at filing for bankruptcy protection. Milton commended some union leaders (he didn't name them) for engaging in serious discussions. But he lamented that, just one day before his March 15 deadline, none had reached definitive agreements on cost reductions. He said it was an "inability on the part of unions to agree to cost relief on a timely basis" that led United Airlines and US Airways to file for protection under Chapter 11. "Employees of those two companies have been hurt far more severely subsequent to their bankruptcies, and their futures are now largely out of their hands," Milton wrote. "So as leaders we face two questions: do we act decisively and do what it takes to avoid a fate none of us wants, or do we stand frozen staring at the oncoming headlights waiting for some miracle to happen."

Union officials were caught off guard by the letter's dire tone. Although Milton had expressed a desire for immediate action on February 6, some labour leaders had been given a different signal by his subordinates. CAW officials had been eager to arrange timely negotiations, but were told that company officials were not available until March, after they had travelled the country to sell the cost-cutting plan to rank-and-file workers.[11] Other unions found that financial data – requested in order to confirm management's dire predictions – was slow in coming or did not arrive at all. They wanted to be sure they weren't being asked to make long-term sacrifices to solve a short-term cash crunch. If Air Canada was serious about cutting operating costs, the unions reasoned, company officials should do everything possible to process information requests quickly. There was also the confusion as to what was expected by March 15. Milton's March 14 letter implied it was set as a firm deadline by which labour-cost negotiations were to have been concluded. But Air Canada spokeswoman Isabelle Arthur told Canadian Press on the same day that the deadline delivered in February had been "merely intended to convey a sense of urgency" to unions in order to hasten discussions.[12]

Earlier in March, Milton had made a special plea to the airline's pilots, urging them to accept a temporary and immediate pay cut of 15 per cent while they hammered out the more flexible work rules that would boost productivity in the long term. He hoped the pilots might be more receptive than the other unions, since they had the most to lose if Air Canada went bankrupt. Not only were their skills the least transferable, but they also had a generous supplementary pension plan that would likely be erased if Air Canada were forced to seek bankruptcy protection. But even the pilots had been unwilling to move with the haste Milton required.

The leaders of the various unions just didn't see the urgency. They generally regarded Air Canada as a company unlike any other, still more of a state institution than a private business. The federal government, they believed, could not allow Canada's flag-carrier to fail. At the same time, many thought it was inevitable that Air Canada would be forced to go to court to seek bankruptcy protection from its creditors. That scenario might be preferable, since other stakeholders – from lenders to suppliers to non-unionized workers and executives – would be required to share the pain. And if bankruptcy protection was inevitable, they didn't want to agree to pre-filing concessions only to be asked to take more hits later.

CUPE, which represented flight attendants, was particularly reluctant to negotiate further concessions. In December 2002, the company had agreed to a new four-year contract with the union, which had extracted a no-layoff clause for its members in exchange for dropping its grievance over Air Canada's outside hiring of new flight attendants for Zip at B-scale wages. CUPE administrator Ken Hopper wasn't about to relinquish that gain. In a February letter to flight attendants, Hopper said the union wasn't willing to amend a contract that had been ratified just five weeks earlier. "To now attempt to get more outside of regular bargaining is to make a mockery of our new contract and the collective bargaining process," Hopper wrote. "A deal is a deal."

With $1.7 million in cash being devoured every day, Air Canada's reserves were quickly evaporating. Analysts who followed the airline were contemplating the possibility that its shares would be wiped out with a court filing for bankruptcy protection. On March 13, the *Globe and Mail* asked five analysts to quantify the likelihood and timing of a potential filing. The most pessimistic put the odds at 65 per cent and predicted a filing as early as April.

Some of Air Canada's own board members were pushing for a court filing, but Milton hoped to avoid that scenario. He was in no doubt that his team had done a remarkable job under extraordinary circumstances, but he knew that a filing would be seen by others as a symbol of their ultimate failure. Furthermore, restructuring under court protection would be exorbitantly expensive, with tens of millions of dollars flowing to lawyers, accountants, and other consultants. Milton feared he would become a lame-duck leader, having to submit his every decision to the scrutiny of the judge and the court-appointed monitor. Besides, Milton wanted to be remembered as the CEO who had fixed a broken company, not the guy who had piloted Air Canada into insolvency.

Milton acknowledged the need for a major financial restructuring, but he believed it could be accomplished without filing for court protection from its creditors. If Air Canada were to survive, it had to persuade its bank lenders and bondholders to forgive hundreds of millions of dollars in debt and its aircraft leasers and other suppliers to accept reduced payments. The airline had to find new equity investors, a move that would significantly dilute the holdings of its current shareholders. Milton's plan had all the features of a court-supervised restructuring, except that management would retain control of the company.

American carriers had an incentive to restructure under court supervision, since Chapter 11 of the U.S. bankruptcy code gave courts some authority to nullify labour contracts. It was not at all clear that Canadian courts had this authority. Air Canada had nothing to gain and everything to lose by filing for bankruptcy protection.

Milton asked Calin Rovinescu to lead the restructuring team. Working with Rovinescu were Paul Brotto and Montie Brewer, a well-respected executive who had surprised many of his peers the previous spring by leaving United Airlines to accept a job at Air Canada. Brewer had long advocated the abandonment of the outdated fare structure used by full-service carriers, but he understood that such a radical move would not be possible in the highly competitive U.S. market. Air Canada's restructuring would give him a chance to test his ideas. Kevin Howlett, the airline's vice-president for labour relations, was designated the point man in the crucial talks with union leaders. The legal strategy would be handled by Stikeman Elliott, the firm that had so impressed Milton during the takeover battle in 1999. Heading the legal team was Marvin Yontef, who took over as lead external counsel when Rovinescu joined Air Canada's executive. There was no obvious candidate for financial advisor. The conflict aroused by the Texas Pacific proposal having soured management's relations with BMO Nesbitt Burns, Milton turned to Seabury Group, a boutique U.S. investment bank specializing in airlines. Seabury president and CEO John Luth, a former CFO at Continental Airlines, was engaged in a court-supervised restructuring at US Airways which appeared to be going extremely well; he had also gained valuable experience in an out-of-court airline restructuring with America West Airlines in 2002.

There remained the possibility, however, that Air Canada would run out of cash before it could complete an out-of-court restructuring, in which case the company had to be ready with the less-palatable backup plan. Marvin Yontef's colleague Sean Dunphy would be the litigator preparing for a possible filing under the Companies' Creditors Arrangement Act.

Whenever it seemed Air Canada's circumstances could not become any worse, they did. On the morning of Saturday, March 15, the weekend newspapers carried alarming headlines about a new virus that was killing people in Air Canada's hub city, Toronto. Two deaths there were attributed to a mysterious illness that had struck hundreds across southeast Asia and killed at least six people. The early reports referred to the disease as "atypical pneumonia." It would soon be familiar as severe acute respiratory syndrome, or SARS. The *Globe and Mail* reported that health officials believed air travel was spreading the disease; SARS was moving "at the speed of a jet," according to one expert. Health Canada recommended that passengers consult with doctors before travelling to China or Hong Kong. Later on the same Saturday, the World Health Organization issued an emergency global travel advisory. The United Nations agency urged passengers to be aware of the symptoms of SARS – a high fever, shortness of breath – especially if they had recently travelled to a country affected by the disease. There was no explicit recommendation to avoid travel at that point, but the words "emergency travel advisory" would surely affect Air Canada's bookings, especially on key Asian routes.

If that weren't enough, a war in Iraq now appeared inevitable. U.S. president George W. Bush and his hawkish defence secretary, Donald Rumsfeld, had been threatening invasion for months, amid speculation that a narrow window of military opportunity would present itself in the spring. North American carriers had already experienced a drop in bookings simply because of the talk of war. The 1991 U.S.–Iraq conflict had cost the world's airlines hundreds of millions of dollars, as passengers delayed travel plans or cancelled altogether. The consequences threatened to be more severe in 2003, according to the Air Transport Association, the industry group representing airlines in the U.S. In a March 11 report, "Airlines in Crisis: The Perfect Economic Storm," the ATA outlined various scenarios. The most likely would result in 70,000 job cuts and "sequential airline bankruptcies." The worst-case scenario – war, plus an airplane-related terrorist attack – would lead to the loss of 98,000 jobs and "total industry collapse."

Once again, U.S. airlines received more support from their government than did Canadian carriers from theirs. On March 18, U.S. transportation secretary Norman Mineta told an aviation conference that Washington would move quickly to support its airlines in the event of war. Although he declined to elaborate, the announcement was enough to bolster the share prices of many major American carriers.

While the beating of war drums kept customers away from European routes and the deadly SARS outbreak threatened Asian traffic, Air Canada continued to be pummelled at home by WestJet, Jetsgo, and CanJet. Robert Milton had a cargo-hold full of lemons; now he wondered if he couldn't make a little lemonade. With his unions no closer to granting the necessary $650 million in cost reductions, Milton signed off on a plan to use the pending war in Iraq to get around the company's restrictive no-layoff clauses.

Since acquiring Canadian Airlines in 2000, Milton had announced a total of 12,500 job cuts, representing roughly 28 per cent of the pre-merger workforce of the two airlines.[13] Yet remarkably, Air Canada employed the equivalent of 40,238 full-time workers on December 31, 2002, down just 9 per cent from 44,267 full-time equivalents before the merger. Milton had made a lot of tough-talk announcements about job cuts, but most had never been implemented. Robert Milton was not about downsizing; he was a growth-oriented manager who held to the conviction that an airline couldn't shrink itself to profitability. He believed the key to long-term profitability was to reduce costs and boost yields by adding more routes and growing market share. Time after time, however, Milton was forced to concede that paring down might be a short-term necessity. And one of the impediments to even temporary weight loss was the no-layoff clause in many of Air Canada's union contracts.

Hours after the bombardment of Baghdad began on March 20, Air Canada put out a press release advising that it was hastening its cost-cutting program and chopping another 3,600 jobs, 800 of which were from the management ranks. "The outbreak of war confirms our pressing need to achieve our target of $650 million in labour-cost savings in addition to the job reductions announced today," Milton said in the release.[14] "I regret the impact of this decision on the many loyal employees affected, but we need to accelerate our transformation into a leaner, lower cost carrier." With the invasion under way, Milton said the airline would invoke the *force majeure* clauses in its contracts to circumvent its job guarantees. In fact, not all of the union contracts included *force majeure* language. And while the threat of layoffs would force the unions to the table once again, it would also taint the discussions.

Union leaders had given Milton credit at the February 6 meeting for his honesty and humility. Now they were furious that he had undermined what they saw as their constructive efforts to help the airline reduce its labour costs. "This is not a *force majeure*," CUPE president Pam Sachs said. "Canada is not at war. Jean Chrétien has made that very clear." CUPE promised to challenge the layoffs before the Canada Industrial Relations Board, along with the CAW and the IAM.

Meanwhile, Air Canada had presented CAW officials with a controversial proposal to trim $200 million from its share of the labour bill. The airline wanted to close call centres in Toronto and Calgary, eliminating 661 jobs. It proposed automating services in call centres in Winnipeg, Montreal, and Saint John in order to eliminate 30 per cent of the remaining workforce. Those with enough seniority to keep their jobs would see wages cut to $16 an hour from $22, along with less vacation time, the loss of paid parking, and a reduction in the uniform-cleaning allowance. In presenting the list to a hundred call-centre agents in Toronto on March 18, Gary Fane, the CAW's director of transportation, made it clear that the union would never agree to the company's demands, but said he was hopeful that a compromise could be reached. "They shot for the moon and the stars," Fane said. "With bargaining we can reach something that we both agree on, but they're not getting this list."[15]

By the end of March, Air Canada's cash reserves had fallen to $360 million. The airline would hit the wall in less than six months at its pre-SARS depletion rate; after SARS, its life expectancy was no more than three months. Typically, cash flow became positive as summer approached, but there were no guarantees for 2003. The airline needed to finalize the Aeroplan sale and secure Onex's $245 million, but Gerry Schwartz was concerned about the security of his investment in the event that Air Canada filed for bankruptcy protection. Schwartz still regarded Aeroplan as a great investment, but he wasn't in the same hurry as Robert Milton to close the deal. On March 12, the companies jointly announced that the arrangement would not take effect at the end of March as initially planned. The contract to continue negotiations was extended by a month.

Air Canada's anemic cash reserves came under pressure again on March 21, when the airline received a letter from the Office of the Superintendent of Financial Institutions (OSFI) ordering the immediate injection of $135 million into the company's pension plans. This federal regulator alleged that Air Canada had violated the Pension Standards Benefits Act by underfunding its pensions. In a notice to Air Canada vice-president Susan Welscheid, OSFI assistant superintendent John Doran cautioned that "by taking contribution holidays, Air Canada is committing or is about to commit or pursue an act or course of conduct that is contrary to the safe or sound financial or business practices in respect of the plans."

Air Canada wasn't the only Canadian company with a massively underfunded pension plan, but reports of the airline's near insolvency had attracted OSFI's watchdogs. Pension funds are protected in the event that a company goes bankrupt or files for protection under the Companies' Creditors Arrangement Act. But OSFI officials were worried that there wasn't enough money in Air Canada's plans to pay employees and retirees in the event of a bankruptcy.

Through the late 1990s, the pension funds of many large North American firms had benefited from the heady returns of soaring stock markets. The companies were able to take "contribution holidays" from pension-plan payments: while they continued to deduct pension premiums from employees' paycheques, they were not contributing the employer share. By 2003, markets had tumbled, leaving most plans with massive shortfalls. But a legislative loophole allowed corporations to stay on the sidelines. Under the Pension Benefits Standards Act, Canadian companies are allowed to enjoy contribution holidays as long as their most recent actuarial reports show a surplus in the plans. Air Canada's last evaluation, completed in 2001, had shown a surplus of more than $915 million.

By January 1, 2003, however, the funds had a deficit of $1.3 billion, according to OSFI's estimates. The regulator insisted that Air Canada pay its contributions for 2002 and 2003 without delay. The order made no sense to Air Canada officials, who maintained that the best way for OSFI to protect the company's pensioners and employees was to work with the airline on a long-term plan to recapitalize the funds, not make demands that threatened to push Air Canada into bankruptcy.

After being briefed on the OSFI directive, David Collenette weighed in on Air Canada's prospects on March 21. He told journalists that the federal government was committed to ensuring a viable Canadian airline industry, and he refused to rule out federal aid for the troubled airline. "Air Canada will survive," the minister said. "We are committed to the survival of the nation's flag-carrier. But in what form and in what shape is to be determined." Collenette thought it inevitable that Air Canada would file for bankruptcy protection, in which case he felt it was important to signal that the government didn't want the flag-carrier to disappear altogether. Air Canada officials could only shake their heads in disbelief when Collenette's comments crossed the wire. The alluring possibility of federal aid would surely stymie their efforts to extract the necessary wage reductions from labour.

If Milton and Rovinescu were annoyed by Collenette's comments, they didn't say so when they met him the following Monday in Ottawa. It was the first face-to-face meeting between Milton and Collenette in a year, although their deputies had convened regularly during the previous twelve months. Milton thanked the minister for his public declaration of support, then asked him in effect to put his money where his mouth was. He explained that the airline had tried to restructure its costs and debt out of court, an effort that now appeared impossible in light of the OSFI directive. Air Canada's board of directors would meet the following Sunday, the minister was informed, where they would discuss whether to file under the Companies' Creditors Arrangement Act. Milton said he needed Collenette's help to navigate through the murky waters of bankruptcy protection.

Milton and Rovinescu had two requests. They were scrambling to arrange debtor-in-possession (DIP) financing from private lenders, but those negotiations could take weeks. Before a company files for bankruptcy protection, it usually tries to arrange for a DIP loan so it won't run out of cash during its restructuring. Generally, a commercial-court judge will give the DIP lender first claim over an insolvent debtor's assets as security. Nevertheless, DIP loans are considered extremely risky and generally come at a high price. Milton and Rovinescu needed time to win terms that weren't too onerous, and they asked the government to provide short-term bridge financing of about $1 billion for the interim period. This could be either a straight loan or a federal-government guarantee of a bank loan.

The second request was more problematic. Milton explained that, while Air Canada intended to clean up its balance sheet, writing off liabilities and injecting capital, the most critical component of its restructuring was a reduction in operating costs. The centrepiece of that offensive was aligning its labour costs with the new industry reality. The company had been urging the unions to agree to concessions for six weeks, with no success. An article in that morning's *National Post* quoted a number of union leaders saying it would be folly for the unions to grant concessions in advance of a CCAA filing, since they would only be expected to bleed again later. "If CCAA is inevitable for this company, it probably is to our advantage not to do anything until we get there," said Don Johnson, president of the Air Canada Pilots Association. "Because then everyone takes a hit."[16] The story helped Milton and Rovinescu press their case. A court-ordered restructuring would be more likely to succeed if the government amended the Companies' Creditors Arrangement Act to allow Canadian courts to suspend pre-existing labour contracts.

Without making specific commitments, Collenette assured the executives that Ottawa would participate if necessary. He promised to consult with the prime minister and his cabinet colleagues and get back to them as quickly as possible. On Friday, March 28, Collenette secured the approval of key ministers to make an offer to Air Canada. The government would provide a loan guarantee of $300 million, fully secured against the carrier's assets, for up to sixty days. Collenette said the government might be willing to go as high as $500 million, but the $1-billion request was almost certainly out of reach. Ottawa insisted on having an observer at Air Canada's board meetings, as well as a veto over the choice of the airline's chief restructuring officer. But the government was not prepared to amend the Companies' Creditors Arrangement Act to help Air Canada extract itself from its union contracts. Collenette gave the airline until the end of business on Monday to accept his offer.

While Air Canada officials considered this disappointing option, they looked to other sources of cash. Talks were under way with two of the largest U.S. lenders of DIP financing. Milton was reluctant to surrender to the federal government until he had no alternative.

On the morning of Monday, March 31, CAW officials travelled to Ottawa for urgent meetings with David Collenette and other senior Transport Canada officials. They had caught wind that Air Canada wanted Ottawa to modify the CCAA, and Buzz Hargrove intended to remind Collenette that such a move would erode the principles of free collective bargaining. At the same time, he would encourage the minister to help Air Canada avoid a bankruptcy filing. Shortly before the first meeting, the CAW's Gary Fane received a telephone call from a senior Air Canada executive. "That thing we've been desperately trying to avoid is happening tomorrow," the executive said.[17] Aware that cellphones aren't secure, the executive wouldn't be explicit, but Fane got the message: a CCAA filing was imminent. He begged his source for one final attempt at bargaining between the unions and the company, citing reports that AMR had reached an eleventh-hour deal with its unions on the courthouse steps that very morning, minutes before it was to file for protection under Chapter 11 of the U.S. bankruptcy code. Coincidentally, US Airways emerged from eight months under bankruptcy protection the same day.

The idea of a last round of talks was put to some of Air Canada's directors and the company's legal and financial advisors. None had much confidence that further negotiations would lead to a resolution, but they couldn't hurt. Besides, the company had yet to finalize a deal for a DIP loan. They suggested Milton go ahead, on condition that he try to extract even greater concessions. They had already determined that, under bankruptcy protection, they would seek much more in labour-cost savings than the $650 million Milton had initially proposed.

Air Canada's directors had scheduled a meeting for 6:00 the next morning, where they would have one final debate on the question of whether to file for bankruptcy protection. A courtroom had been set aside in Toronto, booked under "X versus Y." Although Air Canada was based in Montreal, Toronto was the logical venue for the filing. Toronto was Air Canada's major hub, and the city boasted the largest population of corporate lawyers and the most sophisticated commercial court in the country. As well, Air Canada hoped that an Ontario Superior Court judge would be more likely to break new legal ground than a Quebec judge. In January, the Quebec Court of Appeal had overturned a lower-court decision which allowed a court-appointed monitor to circumvent collective agreements at Jeffrey Mine Inc.

When reporters asked Collenette that afternoon whether the government was prepared to rescue Air Canada, he knew that a bankruptcy filing was imminent and that the airline might turn up its nose at Ottawa's funds. "We are not interested in a cash bailout of Air Canada. However, if we can assist in its restructuring efforts, we will do so," the minister said. Canadian Alliance transport critic James Moore warned Collenette against extending "corporate welfare" to the airline. He said the minister had to decide once and for all if Air Canada was to be a Crown corporation or a private-sector company. "If it's a private sector, then let them organize and compete on a level playing field."[18]

After huddling with Collenette, Hargrove called a press conference in Ottawa for 5:00 p.m. to announce that the CAW would agree to the concessions deemed necessary to save the airline. His public declaration put pressure on the other unions to follow suit, and it ensured that the company couldn't blame the CAW if it went ahead with the bankruptcy-protection filing.

At the same time, Air Canada contacted the union holdouts to inform them that the company would file the next morning unless they agreed to immediate cuts. Jean Jallet of the IAM hopped on a plane from Washington, while the CAW's Gary Fane and Anne Davidson, president of the Air Canada local, rented a car to drive to Montreal. Others negotiated by telephone. While Milton's officials maintained direct contact with each union's representatives, the CEO went from group to group to try to broker new deals.

The union leaders were stunned to hear that the company had raised its concession demands. Milton had been clear on February 6 that the cost-cutting exercise was not about layoffs or wage reductions. Now he insisted he had no choice but to ask for across-the-board pay cuts of 22 per cent. Furthermore, the company wanted to lock the cuts into new collective agreements for eight years. Union officials considered these terms extortion. By requesting such drastic pay cuts over eight years, Air Canada was obviously trying to do more than relieve its short-term solvency headaches; this was a deliberate attempt to get out of the agreements it had signed as recently as three months earlier.

CAW officials felt used and manipulated, and they refused even to consider the new demands. When Milton's subordinates insisted, the CEO stepped in to say that Air Canada would be willing to revert to the list of cost-saving measures it had tabled weeks earlier.[19] The CAW agreed in principle to an arrangement that saved the airline $65 million. Then Air Canada wanted assurances that it would have eight years of labour peace, with no chance of a strike. Fuelled by adrenalin and a sense of urgency at last, negotiators on both sides reached consensus on a long-term contract with built-in provisions for boosting salaries if Air Canada's fortunes turned around. They shook hands on a tentative agreement at 2:00 a.m.

There was less progress with the other unions. Representatives from the IAM and the Air Canada Pilots Association both said they might be willing to accept a 22-per-cent wage cut – at least temporarily – as long as it also applied to the company's senior executives and not just unionized staff. Milton told the pilots that he personally would be willing to accept the cut, but an across-the-board management salary reduction was a non-starter. "I'll lose all my best people," he said candidly.

By about 3:00 in the morning, it became clear that Milton would not be able to secure the necessary labour deals before the board meeting scheduled for 6:00. The personnel negotiating for a DIP loan were having better luck. At about 3:30, with the key players approaching twenty-four hours without sleep, Air Canada finalized a deal with GE Capital for a $700-million U.S. line of credit.[20] Air Canada already had an important relationship with GE Capital's aviation-services division; GECAS had an interest in 106 of Air Canada's aircraft, either leasing them directly or financing leases from other owners. This was one of the largest DIP loans ever extended to a Canadian firm, but it came at a price. The interest rate was set 2 percentage points higher than the DIP loan obtained by United Airlines parent UAL (relative to a floating benchmark rate) and 3 percentage points higher than the loan US Airways had secured from other lenders under bankruptcy protection. In addition there was $40 million U.S. in other fees – charges which would have to be paid whether Air Canada borrowed off the line of credit or not. In the *Daily Deal*, the weekly bible of investment banking, reporter Jonathan Berke pointed out that those fees were higher than those charged to scandal-ridden companies such as Adelphia Communications Corp. and WorldCom Inc.[21] Finally, Air Canada had to pledge its unencumbered assets against twenty-two of its leases with which GE Capital was involved. The *Daily Deal* said it made little sense for Air Canada to face such onerous terms, since it appeared to be in better operating shape than UAL. The publication suggested it may have had to pay a premium because Canadian banks don't typically extend DIP loans and because the Companies' Creditors Arrangement Act does not address them.

In the 6:00 a.m. conference call with the airline's board of directors, Milton confirmed that he had been unable to obtain all of the labour concessions he had sought. Sensing that he might be close to a breakthrough, Milton asked for more time. The directors weighed the alternatives for nearly three hours. Shortly before 9:00, they voted to halt trading on Air Canada's shares so that the airline could go to court as an insolvent debtor, unable to honour its commitments. It was April Fool's Day, 2003.

Stikeman Elliott lawyers were pleased to see the case on the April 1 docket of Mr. Justice James Farley, a no-nonsense commercial-court judge, reputed to be hard on litigators, but skilled at keeping complex restructurings on track. Farley was also expected to be innovative on the question of labour contracts, should it prove necessary.

In a cramped courtroom on Toronto's University Avenue, Judge Farley stressed that the restructuring must be a team effort between labour and management. "Both sides will have to look at themselves in the mirror to see if they are truly pulling their own load," Judge Farley said. A separate motion was filed simultaneously under Chapter 11 of the U.S. bankruptcy code, to ensure that the order was honoured wherever Air Canada had planes. The U.S. filing, which had been prepared in advance, cited the order from OSFI for Air Canada to inject money into its pension funds as the motivating factor behind the decision to file. But the Canadian paperwork had been updated to point the finger at unions for refusing to bow the day before.

In a conference call with reporters and analysts, an exhausted Milton lashed out at the labour leaders, accusing them of "burying their heads in the sand." The unions had their own version of events. "This company has always pretended that the problem has been the employee group and we simply don't see it that way. We believe that this company has been mismanaged and that, together with federal mismanagement, are the root causes of Air Canada's problems," CUPE's Pam Sachs told a reporter.

Milton showed no sign of abandoning the growth strategy he had pursued for the past three and a half years. While analysts and creditors said Air Canada should use the restructuring to downsize, Milton continued to hold the opposite view. He told analysts that, even if the airline shrank during the CCAA process, he was hopeful that Air Canada could eventually grow still larger by lowering its costs. "If you get your costs right, run the airline right, offer a good product with good value," he said, "you will grow."

After the conference call, he went back to his office and recorded a sobering message to the airline's 40,000 employees. "This is a day which none of us wanted for Air Canada or our people but which became inevitable as a number of factors contributed to this outcome," Milton said. Without mentioning the union leadership, Milton was magnanimous towards the airline's workers. "This filing is not the fault of our employees. You have done tremendous work against a backdrop of unprecedented upheaval in our industry. But despite our best efforts,

CCAA became our best option to transform Air Canada to confront the new realities in the marketplace today."

On the morning of Wednesday, April 2, when Air Canada stock resumed trading, 43 million shares changed hands – more than a third of the airline's common stock. The shares traded down as much as 67 per cent below the previous day's close. Savvy investors knew that, while Air Canada would probably emerge from bankruptcy protection, the stock would almost certainly be rendered worthless. Less-knowledgable investors were eager to snap up the shares of a national institution; after all, they had heard Collenette say he wouldn't let the airline fail.

Among those selling were Robert Milton and Calin Rovinescu. The court-appointed monitor, Ernst & Young, said the two executives sold their shares to prevent any real or perceived conflict of interest during the restructuring period. And the monitor revealed that the two were donating the proceeds to Dreams Take Flight, a charity sponsored by Air Canada employees, which took physically, mentally, or socially chal-lenged children to Walt Disney World and Disneyland. The proceeds were a paltry $21,700 – $14,000 from Milton's shares and $7,700 from Rovinescu's.

Milton's personal ownership stake in Air Canada had fallen to zero. He knew well that there would be little, if anything, left for shareholders after the restructuring. The stock sale highlighted the fact that Milton had failed at the primary responsibility of any CEO – to create value for shareholders. Despite his many triumphs, despite his unquestioned gift for airline operations, despite the challenges from WestJet and September 11 and SARS, and no matter how successful an airline Air Canada might be in the future, history would likely judge Robert Milton as something of a disappointment, the man who won – and then lost – control of Canada's skies.

14

PARADISE RESTRUCTURED

*I don't dwell on mistakes. You learn from them and get on and make sure you
don't do them again.*[1]

— Robert Milton

*I*n the days following Air Canada's filing for bankruptcy protection, one
question was asked with embarrassing frequency: How could a monopoly fail? For many Canadians, the court filing was proof of mismanagement at Robert Milton's Air Canada. Milton was still well respected in
international aviation circles, but he had lost his credibility with customers, government, employees, and investors. Pundits doubted Milton
would long occupy the corner suite at Dorval Airport – and wondered
why he would want to. Some critics gleefully pointed out that few CEOs
survive court-supervised restructurings. Even Calin Rovinescu, Milton's
right-hand man, conceded in an interview with the *Globe and Mail* that
Milton might not stick around. "He's a guy who likes to have his way. He
has many opportunities, so I don't really know."[2] Anti-Milton sentiment,
which had peaked in the summer of 2000, surfaced again. Daniel Mullen,
a Canadian consultant living in Germany, established an on-line petition, <www.miltongottago.com>, calling for the resignation of Air
Canada's senior executives and its board of directors. The petition boasted
more than one thousand signatories, including such dubious names as
Osama bin Laden, Britney Spears, and Robert Milton himself.[3] "I'm
doing this because I see things going wrong that shouldn't be going

wrong and someone has to call them on it," Mullen said. "I know that the company has its back against the wall. It's in a bad position. But it got put there by its management."[4]

Not according to Milton, who consistently focused his blame on the familiar villains. Gerry Schwartz and American Airlines had tried to steal his company. The federal government had pressured Air Canada to buy Canadian Airlines. Low-fare carriers had broken Air Canada's business model. The news media had exaggerated Air Canada's failings, and regulators had interfered in its corporate affairs. OSFI had made demands Air Canada couldn't possibly satisfy. And then there were the unco-operative labour unions.

Weeks after the September 11 terrorist attacks, when it appeared Air Canada was on a flight path to bankruptcy, Milton was asked by a reporter if he, the CEO, had made any mistakes. "I am comfortable with everything we've done," he replied. "We've done it with conviction and we just fight on." He was adamant that Air Canada's management had done better than most airlines' executives in weathering the turbulence that had rocked the airline industry since late 2000.

Hindsight allows an exploration of what might have been if the key players had made different choices. Who's really to blame for Air Canada's failings: the government, the unions, or Milton himself? Or did they all do their best to struggle through the most challenging period in the first century of aviation history?

Team Collenette: There's a persistent myth at Air Canada's headquarters that transport minister David Collenette forced Air Canada to buy Canadian Airlines. The story goes something like this: Collenette suspended the Competition Act in August 1999, either because he wanted to prevent a bankruptcy at Canadian Airlines, or because he wanted to do a favour for his pal Gerry Schwartz. His meddling precluded the natural free-market solutions: either Canadian would have had to merge on Air Canada's terms, or Canadian would have failed, enabling Air Canada to pick up its pieces at bargain prices. Instead, Air Canada faced a below-market hostile bid from Gerry Schwartz. Air

Canada says it had no choice but to fight back with a bid of its own.

The minister readily admits that his main goal was to avoid a bankruptcy at Canadian Airlines. To a self-described interventionist, it would be ludicrous to stand by and allow the airline to fail, putting thousands of employees out of work and stranding tens of thousands of passengers, if there was an alternative end-game. The free-market solution might have been better for Air Canada, but it wasn't better for the country. Collenette insists that he had no favourite in the takeover battle. His true feelings may never be known, but the suggestion in the media at the time – that Collenette was in bed with Gerry Schwartz – was certainly overblown. Collenette and Schwartz were both Toronto Liberals, but they weren't buddies. Schwartz was a well-known Paul Martin supporter, while Collenette was squarely in the Chrétien camp. More importantly, Collenette the nationalist had misgivings about AMR's involvement in the Onex bid.

Milton had cried foul at Collenette's decision to suspend competition rules. In retrospect, the move was probably a mistake, but not one that damaged Air Canada in any way. Onex would almost certainly have proceeded with its bid, even if Collenette had not invoked Section 47 of the Competition Act – and Air Canada still would have won. The minister's decision to do so actually benefited Air Canada, since Konrad von Finckenstein was unable to negotiate with Robert Milton when there were two bids on the table. By the time von Finckenstein was able to set the terms of the merger, his position had weakened considerably.

Milton was also annoyed that Collenette had not thwarted the Schwartz bid early on by stating unequivocally that it was illegal and that the government would not change the law. But it would have been folly for Collenette to take a stand on an issue before the courts or to step into a takeover battle between private companies, however tempting that might have been.

What about Collenette's response to Air Canada's dominance? Despite calls from many quarters to open Canada's skies to foreign competition, the minister took the opposite tack, responding with new regulations specific to the airline industry that were panned by all sides.

Air Canada argued that it had a right to match fares, and suggested that any limit on that right was in itself anti-competitive. The airline's smaller rivals complained that the rules were ineffective, because they made it so difficult and time-consuming to prove predatory pricing. In fact, the rules probably struck a reasonable balance between the interests of a potential predator and its prey. But what about the interests of consumers? The unfortunate irony of a near-monopoly is that in order to maintain healthy competition, it is sometimes necessary for the state to order a dominant firm to raise its prices.

The federal government deserves more criticism for its overall handling of the airline industry since the September 11 terrorist attacks. While U.S. officials quickly rallied behind their industry, the Canadian government was more hesitant. Washington offered its carriers a $15-billion U.S. aid package, combining $5 billion in cash with $10 billion in loan guarantees. In April 2003, Congress approved another $2.4-billion cash bailout to help American airlines recover from the war in Iraq. Robert Milton has correctly pointed out that, if his airline were based in the United States, it would have received about $1 billion (Canadian) in cash from the two payouts. Instead, Air Canada was granted $69.8 million by the Canadian government, about 7 per cent of that amount. Collenette has defended the minimalist bailout with the argument that U.S. airlines were far more seriously affected by the terrorist attacks than were those in Canada. In addition, the U.S. industry was well organized, with all the airline CEOs united in their pleas for corporate welfare. In Canada, the airlines were sharply divided, with Milton seeking help and WestJet's Clive Beddoe arguing against it. Milton says the U.S. carriers were able to use their subsidies to dump capacity on trans-border routes where they competed against Air Canada. He claims it was a matter of maintaining an equal playing field. Once Washington offered its bailout, Ottawa should have done the same.

An extra billion dollars may well have been enough to prevent, or at least delay, Air Canada's CCAA filing. But that doesn't mean it would have been the right thing to do. The U.S. decision to prop up its industry was motivated largely by emotion, a belief that the airlines had been victimized by terrorists who, in the words of President George W. Bush, hated America for its freedoms. Washington was probably too generous, and the government of Canada was correct not to match this largesse. No European or Asian governments felt compelled to follow the U.S. example, even though their carriers competed against subsidized airlines like United and Northwest on international routes. But Ottawa may well have made the right decision for the wrong reasons: animosity towards Air Canada and its unpopular CEO likely contributed to Ottawa's stinginess. After Milton asked for more than $3 billion in government aid, some Liberal backbenchers approached Collenette to say they would not support a bailout of Air Canada unless it involved a change in management.

Ottawa could also have done better in its handling of loan guarantees. Canadian officials are quick to remind critics that most of Washington's loan guarantees were never claimed, and that the conditions were quite similar to those that Ottawa specified for Canada 3000. Indeed, transport bureaucrats in Washington and Ottawa compared notes regularly on the terms of their respective programs. There was, however, a fundamental difference in the all-important optics of the two programs. The U.S. government declared it would be there to help any airline that could meet its stringent conditions. Collenette intervened selectively with an aid package tailor-made for Canada 3000, and only after airports threatened to seize its planes. Collenette said the package would be made available to other Canadian carriers who needed it, but it stank of a bailout of a broken company, not of an ailing industry.

Air Canada has identified OSFI's demands as the final blow that forced it to abandon out-of-court restructuring attempts. The regulator claimed it moved to protect Air Canada's pensioners and employees, but in fact the directive pushed Air Canada closer to the brink, endangering the livelihoods of the very people OSFI was trying to safeguard. If the regulator had shown greater patience, Air Canada might have been able to delay its filing. The trip to bankruptcy court would have become inevitable, however, when SARS peaked in April and May.

Team Buzz: Milton and Rovinescu have frequently railed against organized labour for refusing to bend. On the contrary, Air Canada's unions have shown a remarkable willingness to do whatever was necessary to save the airline. Yes, the unions made a fuss whenever Air Canada tried to break its contracts, and they rarely met the company's aggressive timelines. Yes, the labour contracts were too rich, the products of a previously highly regulated industry. Certainly they bargained hard for their members, sometimes more effectively than Air Canada bargained for its shareholders. And the unions were guilty of blowing too much hot air, bashing management while feigning steadfast resistance. But when push came to shove, the unions acted responsibly. After the September 11 terrorist attacks, the CAW worked around its job guarantees and agreed to job-sharing and other measures to reduce Air Canada's labour bill. And even though the pilots gave up potential raises in 2000 to limit Low Cost Co. to just six planes, they later agreed to allow it to grow to twenty aircraft.

The unions played along primarily because they saw the Air Canada–WestJet fight as a battle between a union shop and a company that profited off non-union labour. Milton's pitch to the union leaders had been consistent: every plane WestJet added to its fleet took one away from Air Canada. Even before the company filed for bankruptcy protection, most union leaders recognized that the jobs they were entrusted to protect would not survive without concessions.

Team Milton: Smart business people at successful companies like Texas Pacific Group and GE Capital threw their full support behind Milton in the early stages of the restructuring. Others were less convinced that the man who had brought the company to the edge of collapse was the right person to guide it to safety. The three weaknesses that hobbled Air Canada when Milton became CEO in 1999 – spotty profits, a sagging share price, and poor employee morale – were significantly worse by 2003.

Shareholders were right to wonder what might have been if Air Canada had consummated a friendly merger of some kind, instead of fending off Onex with a $1.1-billion-share buyback. The first opportunity for such a consensual agreement came in early 1999, when Air Canada was in tripartite talks with Canadian and American Airlines. The second arrived later that year, when Gerry Schwartz unveiled his takeover bid. The initial Onex offer, at less than the market price of Air Canada's shares, was clearly inadequate. But if Milton had tried to negotiate with Schwartz, instead of digging in his heels, he might well have been able to achieve an acceptable price. A marriage with Onex might have meant switching to the oneworld alliance, paying Canadian Airlines shareholders more than they deserved, or a change in management and the board of directors. Even so, it's quite possible that Air Canada's shareholders would have been better served.

It is tempting, too, to consider the outcome had Canadian Airlines accepted Air Canada's proposal to acquire its international routes and related inventory for $525 million. Air Canada would have also assumed $1.4 billion of Canadian Airlines' debt and lease obligations, and Canadian would have become a purely domestic carrier and a feeder for American's oneworld alliance. That deal would have preserved domestic competition and spared Air Canada its merger headaches. But former Canadian executives say the airline would not have lasted long under such an arrangement. The subsequent crises which led to the bankruptcy of Canada 3000 and Air Canada's CCAA filing appear to confirm that view.

When Air Canada prevailed in the takeover battle, Milton agreed to a number of conditions demanded by the federal government: there could be no merger-related layoffs before March 2002 and Air Canada had to maintain service to small communities in its route network until the end of 2002. These onerous pledges played as large a role as any in Air Canada's insolvency. They denied Milton the flexibility he needed to deal with subsequent crises. But Collenette didn't pull such conditions out of thin air. At the height of the takeover bidding, Milton himself had promised the union heads that there would be no merger-related layoffs at either airline. And he sealed the pledge by giving some of his unions ironclad no-layoff guarantees in 2000. At the time, it was clear skies ahead, and Milton was not thinking about layoffs; he believed the merger would allow Air Canada, and its profits, to prosper and grow. In retrospect, the company should never have agreed to conditions that prevented it from rationalizing its business when the environment changed.

And what about lost opportunities to sell equity? When Air Canada's prospects appeared bright and shiny in early 2000, the airline was offered a chance to issue new shares for which the proceeds would be guaranteed by a group of investment banks. The move would have allowed the company to clean up its balance sheet, debt-heavy after its share buyback. "Should we have done a deal? Of course, but at time it didn't look like a good idea," chief financial officer Rob Peterson said in 2002. "It was too soon, quite frankly."[5] Air Canada was in no immediate need of cash then, and analysts were predicting the stock would continue to soar. Peterson figured that if Air Canada were patient, it would be able to raise even more. The economy was strong, and nobody could ever have guessed at the grim near-term future.

The airline again passed up a chance to raise cash in 2002, when the board rejected management's proposal to issue $250-million worth of new shares to Texas Pacific Group. The proceeds – which represented just two weeks' worth of operating expenses – would not have been enough to escape filing for bankruptcy protection. Of course, the purchase would have been a disaster for TPG, unless the company ensured that its money was used to undertake a rapid and dramatic restructuring of Air Canada's operations. As the board realized in 2002, equity was only part of the solution; the fundamental problem was that Air Canada's costs were too high for its revenue.

Instead of raising equity, Air Canada was continually mortgaging its future. Rob Peterson was once described by a colleague as a "magician" who was always able to tap another source of ready cash to meet the airline's latest crisis. But Peterson's magic came at a cost. By the time Air Canada filed for bankruptcy protection in early 2003, it had mortgaged almost all its aircraft and engines and was preparing to sell off its last remaining assets. Air Canada paid $1.1 billion in aircraft rent in 2002, up 55 per cent from $713 million in 2000, not because the airline was flying more planes or paying increased rates, but because it was forced to lease back the planes it had once owned. Selling assets allowed Air Canada to fund its operating losses and delay the inevitable bankruptcy filing. Shareholders might not have fared any better under an earlier filing, but there would certainly have been more assets left for the creditors, and employees and suppliers might have suffered fewer losses.

Milton himself has been portrayed by his enemies as the worst kind of growth-at-all-costs CEO, more interested in beating the competition than in pursuing consistent profits. After September 11, some airline analysts said Air Canada could have returned to profitability more quickly by shrinking its operations. Milton countered that argument with another: the airline that flies into the most cities, with the highest frequency, will be able to charge the highest fares. In other words, market share is directly tied to profitability. Historically, that was true, but by 2002 Milton was trying to transform Air Canada into more of a discount airline, and the Southwest clones retreated from routes that weren't profitable, surrendering them to a competitor if necessary. Milton was rarely prepared to do the same. While he preached the discount gospel, he continued to manage like the CEO of a network carrier. Moreover, his bold attempt to reinvent the airline based on the Marriott model has yet to be realized. Milton's experiment with Tango clearly helped Air Canada outperform its U.S. rivals in mid-2002, but the jury was still out on the long-term merits of multi-branding when the company filed for bankruptcy protection in April 2003.

Much of the criticism levelled at Milton has been personal. Self-confidence, superciliousness, or arrogance – whatever it was, Milton had it, and it didn't play well with the Canadian public. Milton appeared to believe that he alone had the answers to Air Canada's problems, and perhaps he did. But he couldn't implement the fixes on his own. He needed help from government and unions, yet he seemed almost bereft of the humility that would have swayed politicians and labour leaders to buy into his vision. Some workers speak about him with real venom, as if Milton alone were responsible for Air Canada's problems. Pam Sachs of CUPE once said Milton had "managed to create an airline in his image – arrogant, insensitive, and unable to deal with passengers, the government, and employees." Those who work most closely with Milton say he is an inspiring leader who cares passionately for his airline and its employees. Some say he may be the most creative airline CEO in the world, others, that he is well suited to be a chief operating officer, but isn't diplomatic enough for the top job. Even his strongest allies admit that Milton's confidence borders on smugness.

Milton's personality arouses both love and loathing, never indifference. When he wins, as he did during the 1999 takeover battle, he wins big. When he loses, he falls hard. Every CEO must deal with unexpected external calamities, and Milton has had more than his share. Would another CEO have performed better? It's impossible to know. A more conciliatory executive might have been able to wring more cash out of Ottawa or more generous concessions from the unions. But Milton's stubborn single-mindedness kept the airline intact through crisis after crisis. He flew Air Canada during the toughest years in its history; it was no time to be nice.

By mid-May 2003, Robert Milton had little choice but to downsize his airline. Bookings and revenue were in free fall thanks to SARS and uncertainty over Air Canada's future. The company was devouring $5 million in cash a day, roughly $3,500 a minute. Passenger traffic through its Toronto hub was down 25 per cent, while Asian travel had fallen 60 per cent. On May 13, Air Canada responded with what it called "immediate, aggressive" steps to reduce operating costs, cancelling a dozen transborder and transpacific routes, slashing capacity by 17 per cent and grounding forty aircraft. Milton did not expect international travel to Canada to recover in the near term.

For the first time since the company filed for bankruptcy protection on April 1, it appeared that a successful restructuring might elude Milton and his loyal advisors. There was a very real chance that, if the airline could not reach immediate agreements to cut labour costs, Canada's flag-carrier would permanently ground its planes. A company can remain insulated from its debts under the CCAA only as long as it has a reasonable chance of reorganizing itself to emerge from bankruptcy protection. When that hope fades, a company usually places itself into bankruptcy, ceasing operations and surrendering its assets to creditors.

Mr. Justice James Farley, the Ontario Superior Court judge over-seeing the restructuring, was justifiably concerned. On May 9, Farley took what he called an "extraordinary" step, appointing a facilitator to help broker a deal between Air Canada and its unions. Warren Winkler was a respected judge who delivered no-nonsense orders with a folksy charm. He held preliminary talks with the various union leaders and with Milton's intermediaries. On May 13, he was ready to meet with Milton himself. After his assistant patched him through to the company's Montreal headquarters, Winkler summoned Milton and Rovinescu to Toronto – at once. The executives weren't accustomed to complying with someone else's agenda. When they protested that they were in the middle of an important board meeting, Winkler told them to cancel it. When they suggested that it might be tough to get a flight out of Montreal on such short notice, Winkler retorted, "You just grounded forty planes. Why don't you take one of those?"[6]

Milton and Rovinescu arrived at 10:00 p.m. at Winkler's makeshift headquarters on the thirty-second floor of the Hilton Hotel in down-town Toronto. Winkler asked Milton what he needed from his unions, and received an extensive list of demands. The facilitator instructed him to stop dreaming, to put aside the wish list, and reduce his items to the bare minimum the airline required to survive and prosper. "It has to be about needs, not wants," Judge Winkler scolded, "need, not greed."[7] At the end of a four-and-a-half-hour meeting, the Air Canada executives agreed to take Winkler's advice.

A week later, on May 21, Robert Milton stood at a podium at the Fairmont Royal York hotel before an audience of some sixty representa-tives from the airline's labour unions. Judge Winkler was in attendance as Milton laid out the minimal concessions that he regarded as critical to Air Canada's recovery. He asked for 7,800 job cuts, pay cuts of 10 to 15 per cent, a wholesale rewriting of work rules to enhance productivity, and a 10-per-cent reduction in pension benefits for all active workers. His delivery was solemn, but there was no mistaking his anxiety. He urged his listeners to take the company's future seriously. "Every employee from Pan Am or Eastern Airlines remembers who the CEO and union heads were on the day those airlines grounded their planes," Milton said. "But nobody remembers the people who work together to save an airline. I don't want to be remembered for the wrong reasons and neither should you."

Seabury president John Luth and Murray McDonald, the airline's court-appointed monitor at Ernst & Young, also addressed the crowd. They wrapped up the meeting briskly, without taking questions from the floor. Milton said he needed the unions' answer by 5:00 p.m., May 27. Few observers thought the airline could accomplish in a week what it had failed to achieve over three and a half months.

On May 23, the union leaders met privately with Judge Winkler and put forward a united position. They said they would be willing to discuss concessions, but only if Air Canada withdrew its demand for reduced pension benefits. They asked the judge to take that message to the company. Winkler agreed. He called Milton and told him that his list was still too onerous. He urged him to preserve pensions, to treat his current and retired workers with the respect they deserved. Milton reluctantly acquiesced.

With the pension issue resolved, Winkler began brokering in earnest. There was a constant stream of management and union reps in and out of his "chambers" on the thirty-second floor. Winkler thought nothing of calling in officials in the middle of the night, or of surprising an airline executive by suddenly contacting his union counterpart to rebut the company's position on an issue. He indulged in long-winded anecdotes from his childhood in Pincher Creek, Alberta, and stories about his dogs, Maggie and Gretzky, to make his point. If he felt one side was wasting time on an irrelevant matter, Winkler would chide that Maggie and Gretzky wouldn't "chase a rabbit down that hole."

Then, a breakthrough. On May 24, Jazz president Joe Randell announced that the regional carrier had reached new agreements with its pilots and dispatchers. More followed in quick succession: with the CAW, representing employees at Jazz and Air Canada proper, on May 26; with the IAM on May 27; and with the flight attendants represented by CUPE on May 28, shortly after Milton's deadline. Later that day, Air

Canada announced that it had secured agreements with all of its unions except the Air Canada Pilots Association. Notably, the pilots had made a decision early in the process not to use the services of Judge Winkler. They had expected a court-appointed facilitator to slow matters, not accelerate them.

While the various deals had similar components – most included the sacrifice of holidays and sick days, for example – no two were precisely alike. The CAW was able to avoid pay cuts by agreeing to layoffs and reduced staffing levels that would save the company tens of millions of dollars annually. The Air Line Pilots Association (ALPA), which represented pilots at Jazz, agreed to pay cuts of 7.5 per cent, with the promise of a profit-sharing arrangement.

Still, the mainline pilots, represented by the Air Canada Pilots Association, remained outside the tent. At the heart of the matter was a turf war with the regional pilots. The ACPA contract, in place since 2000, limited Jazz pilots to aircraft with turboprop engines and just a handful of 50-seat aircraft with jet engines. But the new Jazz contract gave the regional pilots the right to fly any jet with up to 75 seats, and to bid against the pilots at Air Canada for jets with up to 110 seats. In other words, Air Canada had promised the same planes to two groups of pilots, and was now insisting that the mainline pilots give up their claim to the jets. For Air Canada and its consultants, this would be a positive development, since every flight that could be transferred to the lower-paid Jazz pilots represented reduced costs.

For the mainline pilots, however, such a shift could mean a significant loss. Air Canada was planning a major fleet change as part of its restructuring, hoping to retire all its Boeing 737s and even Milton's cherished 747s, the bread and butter of ACPA's members. It would replace these aircraft with 85 new jets, each carrying between 70 and 110 seats. The smaller jets would allow Air Canada to cut back on capacity while maintaining frequency. The airline could then offer its frequent customers the range of departure times they expected, without having to discount a lot of otherwise empty seats. And, by using smaller jets with lower operating expenses, Air Canada could launch service to new destinations on a profitable basis.

ACPA chairman Rainer Bauer feared the revamped Jazz contract would result in hundreds of layoffs as Jazz grew larger than Air Canada's core airline. "To put this in perspective, if Jazz is successful in capturing the 110-seat aircraft, then by 2009, using the company's projected fleet plan, Jazz would have 219 aircraft and Air Canada mainline would be reduced to 132 aircraft," he wrote in an urgent dispatch to the airline's 3,150 pilots. "To say this is unacceptable is . . . an understatement."

Neither the airline nor the ACPA was willing to budge. With a critical court session before Judge Farley scheduled for 10:00 on the morning of May 29, it seemed that Air Canada would have to choose between the two groups of pilots and renege on either the contract it had signed with its mainline pilots in 2000 or the one it had signed with the Jazz pilots the week before.

Appearing before Judge Farley on May 29, Air Canada's top litigator, Sean Dunphy, did his best to paint the airline's situation as desperate, pointing out that Air Canada had become "double-insolvent." In other words, the airline had been insolvent on April 1 when it was granted protection from debts owing prior to that date; now the airline did not have enough cash to cover debts that had arisen since. Dunphy referred to the latest report from the airline's court-appointed monitor, who said that these post-filing liabilities exceeded its cash on hand by $237.9 million. A cash-flow statement showed Air Canada would have just $187.9 million in cash available at the end of the summer, even if it drew down a $350-million advance from the Canadian Imperial Bank of Commerce for the purchase of about a year's worth of Aeroplan points for distribution to Aerogold cardholders. "This cash balance would be well below the minimum cash the company advises it needs to operate," the monitor's report stated bluntly.

The situation was indeed serious, although not quite as dire as Dunphy and the monitor were suggesting. It is not uncommon for a company under bankruptcy protection to be double-insolvent, which is why it will arrange a DIP loan to cover ongoing liabilities. Air Canada had access to $700 million U.S. from GE Capital Canada Limited, but its board of directors had opted not to touch the cash until they had won the concessions they wanted from all the unions. In fact, they hoped never to have to use the loans.

Dunphy berated the pilots for their intransigence. "Eight bargaining units participated in the process and gave 100-per-cent effort," he told Judge Farley. "One of the bargaining units chose to stay on the sidelines." He said a board meeting scheduled for the following weekend had been moved up to that evening so Air Canada's directors could immediately spend time "reviewing the situation and providing guidance" on how to proceed. Judge Farley, who was fond of sending messages to the parties through their lawyers and the press, said he found it "very puzzling" and "very troubling" that Air Canada had been able to reach tentative agreements with all of its major unions except the pilots. He urged both parties to take a "sober second look at the situation." "One must look at what the alternative will be," Farley warned. "I think that the natural, logical, practical inevitability of night-follows-day is that there will be a crater."

There was much speculation about what might emerge at the board meeting. Murray McDonald of Ernst & Young reduced the board's decision to the simplest of terms. "The board will have to decide if it carries on with the business," he told journalists. "They have some tough decisions to make."

While negotiators talked circles around the impasse, Air Canada's directors dialled into their conference call that night. Milton advised that his people were working on a plan to protect passengers in the event the airline spiralled into bankruptcy. They would attempt to spool down operations over three weeks rather than ground planes overnight.

None of the options before the directors was ideal. One was to ask the Jazz pilots if they would reconsider the deal they had just signed, so the company could offer something more palatable to the mainline pilots. But if they reached an agreement with one union that put another agreement in jeopardy, they were no further ahead. Some directors pushed for a more hardline approach. They were familiar with the course taken by Crossair, Swissair's regional affiliate, which had effectively taken over its insolvent parent after the September 11 terrorist attacks. Would it be possible to bankrupt Air Canada and allow Jazz, with leaner costs, to assume all of its routes? Or could they simply impose concessions on the pilots and deal with the consequences later? Another possibility was to ask Judge Farley to nullify ACPA's contract, thereby establishing the very legal precedent the judge had hoped to avoid. Another key question for the directors was whether they should quit, and when. If the company was really about to crater, the directors had to push their eject buttons in advance to limit their personal liability. In the event they bailed, Murray McDonald of Ernst & Young might take charge of the company.

The directors adjourned for the night, hoping there would be good news from the negotiation table when they resumed their conference call the next morning. There wasn't. The talks were deadlocked, and the morning's newspapers offered only grim headlines. "Air Canada on verge of chaos," the *National Post* declared, while the Montreal *Gazette* reported that "Air Canada could be grounded." The game of brinkmanship would prompt a further decline in bookings, with customers persuaded that the failure of Air Canada was a real possibility. Management had to resolve the crisis one way or another. Unsure how to proceed, they decided the best course of action was to throw up their hands and see if Judge Farley could do it for them.

Back in court on the afternoon of Friday, May 30, Sean Dunphy told Judge Farley there was still no deal and asked for a rare Sunday court session to determine the next step. During a recess, ACPA lawyer Richard Jones told reporters that, in his opinion, any talk of shutting down the airline was pure bluff. "I think there's a certain amount of posturing in these things," he said, suggesting that a change in management might help.

Farley returned to the bench following the recess. Air Canada was in a "perilous and ultra-precarious" position, he said. "There is no time to reach a leisurely resolution on this. Otherwise, what we will have will be an academic debate over the bones once the buzzards have picked it over." He ordered the pilots, who had so far shunned the facilitator, to meet with Winkler at 6:00 that night. If a compromise could not be reached within thirty hours – by midnight Saturday – Judge Farley would hold an emergency court session on Sunday morning to discuss Air Canada's future. He told the dozens of lawyers involved in the case to prepare submissions on three questions: first, whether he had the authority to impose a settlement on the pilots; second, whether Air Canada should be assigned into bankruptcy; and third, whether there was some other reasonable alternative. "I'll remain on standby to deal with the issues," Farley concluded. "I trust that there will be no game playing." In effect, Farley was giving Air Canada the stick that Collenette had refused to grant. By hinting that he might be prepared to reject the ACPA contract, he signalled the union that it had to negotiate. Consigning the company to bankruptcy was no better.

In a media scrum outside the courthouse, Dunphy walked a tightrope, seeking both to assure customers that they could book with confidence and caution the pilots that, unless they co-operated, the end was nigh. "We are flying today. We will keep flying until the court orders otherwise," Dunphy said.

Robert Milton had spent years cultivating his tough-guy persona, but on the night of May 30 he was worried sick. He sat in his office jotting notes for what might well be his final communiqué to employees. If no deal could be reached, there was a very real chance Air Canada's directors would elect to resign en masse before Sunday's hearing in order to reduce their personal liability. Whoever replaced the board might keep Milton on, but there were no guarantees. He was angry that the ACPA leadership had scuttled the efforts of those who had worked so hard to save the company – including the pilots themselves. But he played the statesman in his message. "Today is unquestionably the most unsettling day any of us will have ever spent at Air Canada," Milton began. "The fact that our existence as a corporation sits in the balance is a sobering thought." He asked his employees to stay focused on safety and customer service, and he asked them to be patient with each other.

Our company's existence is not being challenged by the failures of our employees but rather we face a radically different marketplace than we faced when we came into being 65 years ago, or even a decade ago. Beyond the advent of low cost carriers and the Internet, we face a world exposed to SARS and the constant threat of terrorism and so we must change, and change in a permanent, structural fashion. But, as we go forward, we need to do it together and so I would ask you today to be understanding of our pilots. They too want to come to an arrangement which will enable this airline to prosper. Over my eleven years at Air Canada, I have met hundreds of our pilots and they are true professionals who share in our view of a successful future for this company. So when you see them remember, inside they are feeling every bit of uncertainty and emotion that we all are.

Lawyers for Air Canada, its unions, and its creditor groups worked around the clock in preparation for the Sunday-morning court session, while Judge Farley waded through the weighty submissions that had been delivered to his Toronto home. Warren Winkler wrapped his head around the pilots' issues. He saw that the mainline pilots had cause for concern, but only if their worst-case scenario materialized. With Farley's midnight deadline approaching, Winkler dropped in to one of the pilots' meeting rooms. He reminded them that they were bickering over the right to fly aircraft that would not be part of the Air Canada fleet for years, if at all. He cut to the chase: Did the pilots really want to bankrupt the company over hypotheticals? Maggie and Gretzky wouldn't be so foolish. Winkler proposed a stop-gap solution whereby Air Canada would promise the mainline pilots the same jets it had already committed to Jazz. When the planes began arriving in 2005, an arbitrator would decide which contract would be honoured. Such jurisdictional disputes were common in the construction industry, where, for example, the Carpenters Union and the Labourers' International Union might both be granted the right in principle to dismantle a wood frame. The final decision was made by an arbitrator.

"Guys," Judge Winkler told the mainline pilots, "this is your deal."[8]

Down in the lobby, a dozen journalists waited to find out whether the deadlock had been broken. If not, they would be outside the court again at 8:00 the next morning. One minute past the midnight deadline, lawyer Ken Rosenberg held a press conference in the lobby of the Hilton, where he declared that the Jazz pilots had a deal that guaranteed they would fly all jets with fewer than 75 seats and have the opportunity to bid on the bigger regional jets. Rosenberg gleefully produced ALPA's agreement for the cameras. Reporters who were new to the story went live with the bulletin of a breakthrough, without realizing that the Jazz pilots had signed their deal a week earlier. Rosenberg's grandstanding was ALPA's way of reminding company officials that they had been the first union to sign a reworked contract that included the jets. Earlier that night, they had reluctantly agreed to Judge Winkler's proposal as a way out of the impasse and they hoped that being the first to sign would be favourably remembered when it came time for the arbitrator to rule on the matter.

The mainline pilots were also hoping to strengthen their hand ahead of any arbitration. They had agreed in principle to Winkler's proposal, but wanted Milton himself to guarantee that the sought-after jets would be theirs alone. Their tentative agreement included a letter from Milton in which he committed that all aircraft with 76 to 110 seats acquired or leased by Air Canada or any of its affiliates would be flown exclusively by the mainline pilots.

With the deal-breaker resolved, negotiators turned their attention to the remaining issues. They quickly agreed on a 15-per-cent pay cut in exchange for profit-sharing, plus a host of other cost savings. Uniforms would be dry-cleaned less frequently, for example, and the company would accommodate pilots at airport hotels instead of at the more expensive establishments downtown. Half an hour after the midnight deadline, the pilots signed a tentative deal. The Sunday-morning court session was cancelled.

By the end of July, all of the company's Canadian unions had ratified new collective agreements. Air Canada estimated that these, plus across-the-board pay cuts of 3 to 15 per cent for non-union personnel, would eliminate $1.1 billion from the company's annual $3-billion labour bill. Now the airline could turn its attention to other challenges, including its ongoing debate with OSFI over its pension plans, and negotiations with aircraft lessors, suppliers, and potential new investors. These parties grumbled at the aggressive tactics employed by Air Canada and its lawyers, but most agreed that Milton and Rovinescu performed impressively during the restructuring, accomplishing so much so quickly. The airline would not meet its publicized objective of emerging from bankruptcy protection before the end of 2003, but with labour deals in place and progress on other fronts, it was almost certain to do so some time in 2004, with dramatically lower costs and a solid capital structure. Robert Milton could almost taste the profits that had eluded him since he became CEO in 1999. Now he just had to make sure that he would be around to savour the rewards.

On July 22, 2003, the Competition Tribunal released the first part of its long-awaited decision on allegations that Air Canada had abused its dominance by offering cut-rate fares against CanJet and WestJet in 2000. The tribunal stopped short of saying that Air Canada had broken the law, but the ruling was a clear setback for the larger carrier. It concluded that Air Canada had indeed priced below its avoidable costs on the Toronto–Halifax and Montreal–Moncton routes. The tribunal's seventy-seven-page decision read like a dry economics textbook, with few specifics of Air Canada's actions, but elaborate details on cost and pricing theory. The goal of the first stage was simply to come up with a definition of "avoidable cost" and apply it to two test routes. The premise was that there was no sound business reason for operating flights below avoidable cost – except perhaps to prey on smaller, more vulnerable competitors. During hearings the previous spring, Air Canada had argued that few of its costs were avoidable, and that the avoidable-cost test should incorporate revenue from connecting flights. Instead, the tribunal generally accepted the commissioner's arguments that Air Canada could have avoided most of its labour and equipment costs if it hadn't operated the questionable flights, and that revenue from connecting flights should not count in the equation. Air Canada had previously suggested that, if the tribunal accepted the avoidable-cost test proposed by the commissioner, roughly 42 per cent of its domestic flights would constitute illegal predatory behaviour. On the two routes it evaluated, the tribunal found that an even higher percentage of flights operated below avoidable costs: 69 per cent of monthly schedule flights on the Toronto–Moncton route, and 65 per cent on the Montreal–Halifax route.[9]

Because of the CCAA proceedings, the tribunal ruled its decision would not take effect until Air Canada emerged from bankruptcy protection. Neither the airline's appeal period nor the second phase of the hearing would start until after the restructuring was completed. If the ruling stood, it threatened to seriously impair Air Canada's ability to match cut-rate fares offered by lower-cost competitors if that meant pricing below its avoidable costs.

By lowering its costs through its restructuring, however, Air Canada would be able to match fares offered by its discount rivals without losing money – something that was sure to please its shareholders as well as the Competition Bureau. But it was not clear that would be enough. Air Canada had been matching on price all along, yet had been unable to stop a massive loss of market share to the discount airlines. An analysis by the *Globe and Mail* found that Air Canada, Canadian Airlines, and their regional affiliates held a commanding 87.5-per-cent share of the market in the third quarter of 1999. Four years later, Air Canada's domestic share had fallen to 64.8 per cent, while WestJet held 22.8 per cent and Jetsgo 6.5 per cent.[10] Air Canada was still the country's dominant domestic carrier, but it was no longer a virtual monopoly. Consumers, however, continued to think of Air Canada in those terms. All the problems faced by its customers – from cancelled flights to rude attendants to long lines at the check-in counters – were routinely blamed on the airline's perceived monopoly.

At the start of the millennium, the world's airlines fell into two categories: Air Canada–style carriers that were able to charge a premium because they offered an extensive route network and two classes of high-frequency service, and airlines like WestJet that were able to offer cut-rate fares because their costs were so low. By 2004, the lines had blurred. Air Canada was slashing costs to become more of a no-frills carrier. And WestJet had grown so quickly that it provided an extensive domestic route network and regular service to twenty-four cities from coast to coast. Business travellers recognized what many leisure travellers had known for years – WestJet often offered better service than Air Canada, even if it didn't always deliver the same frills. The general impression was that its staff were more friendly, its planes arrived on schedule more often, and its flights were seldom overbooked. At the same time, the discounters were starting to add frills. In 2003, Jetsgo and CanJet initiated Jetsmiles and SmartRewards, their own frequent-flyer programs, while WestJet offered its customers points in the Air Miles program. Air Miles, operated by the Loyalty Management Group, offered loyalty points through a number of retailers, including grocery chain Canada Safeway, Shell Canada gas stations, and Holiday Inn hotels. WestJet also borrowed a page from JetBlue, announcing in July 2003 plans to install video screens with twenty-four channels of live TV for every passenger on its Boeing 737-700s.

Both WestJet and Air Canada were evolving into the industry's ultimate ideal: airlines with low operating costs, but an extensive enough route network to charge higher fares. WestJet was poised to add to its fleet, increasing frequency on domestic routes and expanding into the United States for the first time. Assuming faster economic growth and barring any unforeseen surges in the price of fuel or further aviation-related terrorist attacks, both carriers might have a chance to reap decent profits. And both should have the wherewithal to defend their turf against other carriers with ambitions of growing too quickly. This didn't mean that the Canadian aviation market was returning to the duopoly that existed in the 1990s, with two similar-sized titans trying to be all things to all people. Despite its restructuring, Air Canada's costs would never fall as low as WestJet's, while WestJet's route network would never be as extensive as Air Canada's. Although the airlines were becoming more alike, each needed to focus on its particular niche – Air Canada as a high-margin international carrier with enhanced service offerings for business travellers and WestJet as an ultra-low-fare carrier. Rather than a duopoly, the near-term market appeared to favour two distinct monopolies, with Air Canada remaining the only choice at the top end of the market and WestJet gaining a stranglehold on the discount side.

As WestJet grows in size and frequency, its ability to raise prices – its monopoly power – increases. But it will use that power at its peril. Any move by WestJet to capitalize on its added frills and expanded route network by raising fares will drive customers to ever smaller, scrappier airlines with lower fares. WestJet will continue to reap profits as long as it takes every opportunity to lower fares instead of raising them.

If it does, WestJet may well become a larger player than Air Canada in the domestic market – a feat that seemed impossible to imagine in 1999. In the third quarter of 2003, WestJet carried more domestic passenger traffic than Canadian Airlines and Canadian Regional did in the third quarter of 1999. With about 40 aircraft in its fleet in early 2004, WestJet planned to have 63 by the end of 2005. The airline still had options to purchase more than 35 additional Boeing 737s, and was separately considering a purchase of 100-seat Embraer jets. This would be a deviation from one of the central tenets of WestJet's business model, which stipulated that low-cost carriers should stick to a single aircraft type. In June 2002, David Neeleman's JetBlue placed an order for 100 Brazilian-made 100-seat jets to supplement its fleet of Airbus A320s. Neeleman said the mixed fleet would allow JetBlue to serve markets of all sizes across the United States. Southwest and WestJet were looking at doing the same. The plan was to retire some of the older 737-200s as the newer aircraft arrived.

The trend lines in market share suggested that WestJet's domestic operations could grow larger than Air Canada's some time in 2005. While such conclusions are speculative at best, WestJet's founders are convinced that the future is theirs – that they will overtake Air Canada some time in the next few years. Their challenge is that, the larger WestJet becomes, the more difficult it will be to maintain the underdog reputation that has contributed so much to its success.

Air Canada, meanwhile, will suffer if it deludes itself that it is a true low-cost carrier, abandoning the frills that differentiate it from WestJet. An increasing share of passengers are choosing the airline with the lowest fares, and that's a contest Air Canada can never win, since its costs will never be as low as its smaller rivals. While Air Canada was lowering its operating costs through its restructuring, WestJet's costs continued to fall, largely because it was using newer, more fuel-efficient jets and operating longer average flights.[11] The key to Air Canada's success will be to use its new lower-cost structure to become profitable, without forgetting that it needs to spend money on meals, frills, and service. It must also confront the fact that its front-line employees – who have suffered through a merger, seniority disputes, cuts to pay and benefits, and a customer base irate over Air Canada's performance – do not provide the same quality of service as their younger, less experienced counterparts at WestJet. Part of the problem could be remedied with a change in policy, giving Air Canada's workers more authority to resolve difficulties on their own. But the more challenging issue is cultural: the majority of Air Canada employees simply do not believe that Robert Milton and the rest of the company's executives care about or understand what they're dealing with on the front lines.

If there's one lesson Robert Milton could learn from the discount carriers, it is that all airlines must be prepared to retreat from unprofitable routes. Air Canada is no longer subject to government dicta that it maintain service to small Canadian communities. If the company can't serve a route on a consistently profitable basis, then it has no business being there. Instead, it should surrender the market to WestJet or other lower-cost carriers and focus on the routes where it can make a difference: the largest markets in Canada and around the world. When Air Canada pulls out of a small community, other airlines will fill the gap, sometimes offering more-frequent service than Air Canada could afford, and making a profit at it.[12]

By the summer of 2003, it was clear that the restructuring had knocked the lustre off Milton's ballyhooed multi-branding strategy. On August 14, Air Canada issued a disingenuous press release trumpeting a "major expansion" of the airline's Tango brand. In fact, Air Canada was turning

Tango from a quasi-airline into nothing more than a fare class. The discounted fares would now be available on flights around the world, but instead of flying dedicated Tango jets, Air Canada would sell a few seats on each airplane at "Tango" fares. This shift back to the way airlines had sold discount seats since deregulation was a remarkable retreat – after all, Milton had once described Tango as limitless. But the announcement received little attention. Minutes after the press release crossed the wires, a massive power blackout hit Ontario and the northeastern United States, carrying Air Canada to its next crisis. While other airlines returned to regular service on August 15, Air Canada's operations were grounded for most of the day, because it didn't have backup power at its Systems Operations Control centre near Toronto Pearson Airport.

Why didn't Tango work? Because there is one fundamental difference between Marriott and Air Canada. It is widely understood that market share is of paramount importance in the airline industry, since customers will pay a premium to travel on the airline that offers the greatest frequency of flights. If Air Canada offers twelve flights a day between Toronto and Vancouver, but Jetsgo offers only four, then Air Canada will be more attractive to the business traveller. But when Air Canada divides its twelve flights among three brands – say four flights a day on each of Air Canada, Tango, and the proposed business-class airline Elite – then it loses its market-share advantage. For this reason, Milton's attempt to offer multiple brands on the same routes, in order to cater to different passengers, was a doomed experiment.

Marriott-style multi-branding might be more successful when each route is limited to just one brand. There will always be room for a separate Jazz, a regional brand flying little planes into smaller markets. Zip, too, has been used in isolation, replacing the Air Canada brand, rather than competing against it. These may survive and thrive because they are being used, first and foremost, as mechanisms to lower costs through B-scale wages on specific routes, not to cater to the needs of a specific type of customer. In 2002, Milton acknowledged that Zip's lower cost structure is more important than the type of service it provides. "I think it could work with or without first-class. The real difference is what you actually get accomplished from a wage standpoint," he said.[13]

As Air Canada laboured to emerge from bankruptcy protection in early 2004, the competitive landscape was healthier than it had been in years. Air Canada's market share was falling, while WestJet's and Jetsgo's were on the rise. But it wasn't enough. As long as the global transportation industry clung to outdated protectionist policies, Canadian consumers would pay the price for rules that benefited only shareholders.

A growing number of observers, from economists to government officials to the federal competition commissioner, have argued that the way to ensure competition is to free the industry from the foreign-ownership restrictions, which do little more than protect airlines in Canada from true competition. Robert Milton had called on governments in Canada and the United States to eliminate some of these regulations, on condition that foreign carriers be allowed to compete within Canada's borders only if Air Canada receives reciprocal rights in other countries. Even Milton's moderate push for change was considered too radical by many. WestJet executives liked the government's protectionist policies and didn't want anything changed. They claimed that, were the domestic market opened up, foreign airlines might come in to serve the country's most profitable routes, but might not provide competition where it was most needed.

David Collenette was opposed to freer trade in aviation. Although he clashed regularly with Air Canada's management, Collenette took pride in the notion of a strong national airline; he believed a Canadian flag-carrier was a symbol worth protecting. He regarded Canada's airlines as instruments of nation-building, successors to the railways that underpinned Canada in the late 1800s. His answer to monopoly dominance has been to add regulations to a heavily regulated industry. Instead, it is time to move in the opposite direction, eliminating artificial barriers to competition, whether the United States reciprocates or not. It is inevitable that other nations will follow suit, clearing the way for such revolutionary notions as cabotage and international airline mergers.

It is worth speculating how things might have turned out in 1999 had the airline industry not been hampered by foreign-ownership restrictions. It is reasonable to assume that American Airlines' parent, AMR Corporation, would have taken over Canadian Airlines – without any help from Onex Corporation – and either merged it with American or operated it as a subsidiary. This would have preserved sustainable competition, at least until September 11, 2001. Canada 3000 and Royal Airlines would not have felt the pressure to expand so quickly, and could have remained viable players in the charter market. It is conceivable, however, that an American Airlines–Canadian Airlines merger would have left Air Canada vulnerable, forcing it to pursue a merger with UAL Corporation.

International airline mergers, unthinkable in 1999, may not be far off. Members of the European Union have already established a common aviation zone that allows cabotage across the continent for European airlines. In late 2003, Brussels and Washington held historic preliminary discussions on such radical concepts as cabotage and cross-border ownership, a shift towards multilateralism and away from the bilateral approach that had governed aviation since 1944. And in September 2003, Air France announced plans to acquire KLM, the Dutch flag-carrier, for about $900-million U.S. Italy's Alitalia said it also wanted to be part of the merged carrier. The national brands were supposed to survive the ownership change, at least over the short term. But the merger proposal marked the end of the sacred notion that every nation needed its own flag-carrier.[14] It was likely the beginning of a trend that would see the more than 250 international carriers consolidate into perhaps a dozen or so mega-carriers. The global airline-marketing alliances – Star (Air Canada, United Airlines, Deutsche Lufthansa), oneworld (British Airways, American Airlines, Cathay Pacific), and SkyTeam (Air France, Delta Air Lines, Korean Air) – may form the foundations for the largest of these merged international carriers. After all, these alliances were established as a way of adapting to the globalized economy in an industry that did not allow cross-border ownership.

Assuming that the world's competition regulators do their jobs, carefully scrutinizing all proposed mergers, such cross-border marriages will not result in less competition. After all, airlines have never really competed within their alliances. In most parts of the world, the competitive situation will stay about the same. For Canadians, however, such mergers could lead to enhanced competition, since each of the new mega-carriers will want to serve Canada's biggest cities. As alliances, oneworld and SkyTeam have no access to Canada's domestic routes, but as merged entities in a world without foreign-ownership restrictions, they would be able to provide competition to Air Canada's Star. Currently, Canadians wanting to fly from mid-sized Canadian markets to international destinations have just one choice – Air Canada – unless they are prepared to make numerous aircraft changes. But a day will come when Canadians living in Victoria or Sault Ste. Marie or Fredericton will have a choice of international carriers, say Star Airlines, oneworld Airlines, or SkyTeam Airlines, offering one-stop service to New Delhi or Santiago or Brussels or Nairobi.

Air Canada's days are numbered. Despite its efforts to reinvent itself with multi-branding and a restructuring through bankruptcy protection, the airline that was born of the duelling visions of C.D. Howe and James Richardson will not survive as an independent Canadian airline. Whether in two years or twenty, the protectionist policies that have been a central tenet of the airline industry since the 1944 Chicago Convention will fall away. In time, the airline industry will be treated like any other business in a free and global economy. Countries around the world will face the harsh reality that not every nation can support its own independent flag-carrier. When the shackles come off, Air Canada will be forced to merge with foreign carriers, or risk becoming marginalized as a fringe player in the international market.

EPILOGUE

It's personally gratifying that the folks at Trinity – and, for that matter, Cerberus – made it a condition of their investment that Calin and I stay on to execute the plan that has been developed and become their partners.

– Robert Milton[1]

Robert Milton and Calin Rovinescu had several reasons to smile on the evening of Saturday November 8, 2003. Earlier that day, the airline's board of directors had approved a deal to sell nearly one-third of Air Canada to Hong Kong businessman Victor Li for $650 million – cash that was critical to the airline's efforts to reinvent itself. The deal eliminated any lingering doubts about whether Air Canada would be able to emerge from bankruptcy protection; it also solidified the future of Milton's team. A key condition of the investment deal was that Milton and Rovinescu would stick around to run the airline. The investor also insisted on keeping five other top executives: Rob Peterson, the chief financial officer; Montie Brewer, vice-president commercial; Paul Brotto, vice-president of planning and cost management; Rob Giguere, vice-president of operations; and Aeroplan president Rupert Duchesne. They would be well compensated for sticking around. The investor promised to set aside up to 5 per cent of the airline's new shares for management stock options.

Milton and Rovinescu, in particular, had a chance become very, very rich. In addition to options, the investor promised to give each of the executives 1 per cent of the company, over four years, from his own holdings. Unlike stock options, which only had value when the under-lying shares rose, these restricted stock grants would be valuable even if Air Canada's shares tanked after the airline emerged from bankruptcy protection. Li's offer – $650 million for 31 per cent of the company – valued Air Canada at $2.1 billion. At the price that Li was paying, the management-retention bonuses for Milton and Rovinescu were worth about $21 million each. If the shares lost half their value, each grant would still be worth more than $10 million. And the upside potential was significant. The New York investment funds that were snapping up Air Canada's debt estimated that the company's stock-market capitaliza-tion would soar to around $4 billion to $5 billion soon after the company emerged from bankruptcy protection. That would value the executive stock grants at something in the range of $40 million to $50 million each – over and above whatever Milton and Rovinescu would receive in salary, bonuses, and stock options.

In an internal newsletter, Milton said he was pleased that Li wanted to keep him around and grant him stock. "In essence, our shares will make us small partners with Mr. Li and their value will be directly related to how well the company performs. It's his way of doing business, and is in line with a successful investment policy," Milton said.

But it was more than money that made Milton feel good about the Victor Li investment. He saw the Stanford-educated businessman as someone who could help Air Canada achieve its true potential, growing the business to profitability instead of shrinking it. If governments ever allowed international airline mergers, Li might be expected to use Air Canada as a platform to acquire a major U.S. carrier. With his back-ground in Asia and in air cargo, Milton must have felt some affinity with Li, whose family controlled some of the world's biggest cargo ports. Victor's father, Li Ka-Shing, was known as "Superman" in Hong Kong because of his success in such industries as telecom and energy. At thirty-nine, Victor Li was the heir apparent to the Li family empire, which involved controlling interests in Cheung Kong (Holdings) Limited and Hutchison Whampoa Limited.

He also had other important credentials: a Canadian passport and a business history in Canada. After earning degrees in civil and structural engineering from Stanford University, Li had lived in Vancouver in the 1980s. Like many wealthy Hong Kong nationals, he took out Canadian citizenship as a sort of insurance policy – hedging his bets against what might happen after communist China reclaimed Hong Kong in 1997. In Vancouver, Li convinced his father to acquire two hundred acres of land that had been the site of Expo '86. Then they paid $320 million to develop the site for condominiums. Many of the condos were snapped up by Hong Kong residents who were also looking for insurance against Hong Kong's uncertain future. The development raised concerns that valuable Vancouver property was falling into "foreign" hands. There were similar criticisms about the Li family's best known Canadian investment: a controlling interest in Husky Oil (now Husky Energy). Despite his Canadian credentials, Li did not come to Canada during the Air Canada investment talks. After having been kidnapped at gunpoint in 1996, Li kept an extremely low profile and rarely travelled. To win his son's freedom, Li Ka-Shing had paid a $134-million U.S. ransom to a group led by Hong Kong gangster "Big Spender" Cheung Tze-Keung, who was sentenced to death in 1998 for smuggling arms out of China.

Air Canada had begun the process of selling $1.1 billion in shares in the new Air Canada on July 16, 2003. Calin Rovinescu worked closely with Seabury chairman John Luth, and with Murray McDonald, the court-appointed monitor, contacting dozens of potential investors in North America, Asia, and Europe. On October 24, the company announced a deal with Deutsche Bank AG, a large financial creditor, to administer a $450-million rights offering, which would give all the airline's creditors a chance to buy shares in the new Air Canada at the same discounted rates as the new majority investor. Deutsche Bank would buy any shares not taken up by other creditors. Although one group of bondholders had proposed putting up the whole $1.1 billion through a rights offering, open to all creditors, Air Canada made it clear that it wanted a controlling shareholder – someone who could be a driving force going forward. Because they were asking both bidders to invest $650 million, the richer bid would be the one that required the lowest percentage of shares in the airline. About a dozen groups expressed interest, but only three submitted non-binding letters of intent by the September 16 deadline: Li; Cerberus Capital Management LP; and a partnership involving Texas Pacific Group and Onex.

All three groups were well known to Air Canada's top executives, but for different reasons. Milton and Rovinescu were probably most comfortable with the third group, having hammered out deals in the past with both Onex and TPG. Unfortunately, that group asked for a far greater percentage of Air Canada's stock than did either Li or Cerberus.

The Li family was also well known to people in and around Air Canada. Eva Kwok, an Air Canada director who ran a private investment firm in Vancouver, had arranged for Milton and Victor Li to meet in the summer of 2003.[2] Years earlier, Kwok and her architect husband, Stanley, had worked with Li to develop the Expo '86 lands in Vancouver. Both were also Li appointees on Husky's board. In order to avoid the appearance of any conflict, Kwok resigned from Air Canada's board after Li was identified as a finalist in the investment auction.

But Kwok wasn't the only connection between Li and Air Canada. Peter Donolo, Air Canada's former vice-president, was hired by the Li team to work on the deal. And former Stikeman Elliott lawyers were in charge of the negotiations on both sides of the deal: Calin Rovinescu at Air Canada and Frank Sixt, the chief financial officer of Hutchison Whampoa, for Li. Remarkably, Rovinescu and Sixt both attended the same Montreal high school, earned undergraduate degrees at McGill University, and graduated with top honours from the law class of 1978 at the Université de Montréal, before being recruited by Stikeman. Investment banker Sonny Gordon, another former Stikeman lawyer, was also working for Li on the deal. The Li family – like Air Canada – had long been a top Stikeman client.

Some creditors complained that these connections gave Li the inside track, but Marvin Yontef, Air Canada's top legal advisor at Stikeman, said it would be impossible for any one group to influence the outcome, considering the involvement of the court, the monitor, and the board of directors. "I'm surprised and flattered that anyone would think that

Stikeman Elliott or I personally could have any material influence in this process," he told the *Globe and Mail*. Yontef said the connections simply reflected that Canada was "a small country with a small business community [in which] you keep running into the same people all the time."[3] Just how small the business community was became clear when Li set out to find Canadian lawyers other than Stikeman who could represent him. Li enlisted the help of Osler, Hoskin & Harcourt LLP – a firm that already had its share of clients involved in the restructuring, including Onex, GE Capital Canada Inc., and the Greater Toronto Airports Authority. Osler made arrangements to ensure it could represent all of its clients without conflict.

And then there was Cerberus. Named after the three-headed dog in Greek mythology that guards the gates of Hades, Cerberus had a reputation as a vulture fund – a company that preyed on dying companies. Cerberus had made millions by buying up debt in distressed companies, then fighting to maximize recovery. Cerberus's initial involvement in Air Canada had been through the purchase of bonds, but it agreed to sell the debt in order to participate in the equity auction. Cerberus spent more time than any of the other bidders on due diligence, and impressed the board's restructuring committee with its presentation. But Brett Ingersoll, who led the Cerberus team, also asked tough questions about why Air Canada had been forced to file for bankruptcy protection, coming close to suggesting that it was something management might have been able to avoid. In fact, Cerberus's vision for Air Canada was the restructuring plan that came the closest to the one that Milton and Rovinescu had spelled out back in January: spinning off assets like Aeroplan and technical services to unleash value. Cerberus saw the airline itself as a high-risk investment made palatable by the tremendous potential in these undervalued assets.

Cerberus enlisted the help of former prime minister Brian Mulroney, who had developed a friendly relationship with Milton. Mulroney was a partner in the Montreal offices of Ogilvy Renault, the firm that was handling the legal work for Cerberus. Like Milton, Mulroney was a member of Montreal's Westmount crowd. He could identify with Milton, who always seemed to be getting what he saw as an undeserved bad rap from the public and the media. During the equity talks, Brian and Mila Mulroney dined at least once with Robert and Lizanne Milton. Cerberus said that if it won the contest, it would install Mulroney on Air Canada's board of directors.

On September 26, Air Canada announced that it had narrowed its search to two potential investors: Cerberus and Trinity Time Investments Limited, a company controlled by Victor Li.[4] A few weeks earlier, financial advisor Seabury had sent letters to potential investors outlining the issues they were to address in their preliminary bids. One of the items was management-retention bonuses. Potential bidders were asked to "identify all relevant proposed compensation principles, equity ownership and any other incentive plans for management, if any." In the initial letters of intent, Cerberus had been the only bidder to have proposed management-retention bonuses but, when the final bids came in on November 7, Cerberus and Trinity proposed identical retention bonuses. However, Air Canada's top managers weren't sure that Cerberus could be trusted to ensure that the executives would retain their jobs. One rumour had it that Cerberus had lined up Don Carty, the ousted former American Airlines CEO, to step in as Milton's boss and, unlike Mr. Li, who wanted to keep all of Milton's top executives, Cerberus insisted on keeping just Milton, Rovinescu, and Brewer. Cerberus proposed paying $650 million for 29 per cent of the airline, while Li wanted 31 per cent for his $650 million.

Air Canada's board of directors ultimately concluded that the bids were nearly identical in economic terms, but selected Li because they believed that he brought more important qualitative factors to the table. One was his international connections. The other was that he had a key asset that the owners of Cerberus did not – a Canadian passport. Canada's foreign-ownership laws stated that foreign investors could not control or own more than 25 per cent of the voting shares in a Canadian airline. Cerberus hoped to abide by the regulations using non-voting shares and control provisions that had already been approved by Canadian regulators. When Air Canada had first announced its short list of investors on

September 26, it emphasized in a press release that both proposals were structured to take foreign-ownership laws into account and did not require "any change of legislation for implementation." But Trinity officials went out of their way to pitch Li's bid as the most Canadian. "He reckons that Air Canada has a lot of potential, and also, being a Canadian himself, he would like to keep it in Canadian hands," said Wendy Tong Barnes, a Li spokeswoman. "He's Canadian and we're pro-Canada. His wife is Canadian; his three kids are Canadian. He met his wife in Canada so [there are] definitely strong ties."[5]

Also, with the deals being so similar economically, the board didn't want to take the chance that the Canadian Transportation Agency might turn down Cerberus's ownership, so they went with the deal the regulators would be more likely to approve. Cerberus officials felt an injustice had been done. As far as they were concerned, they had lost despite having submitted a richer offer. Ingersoll met with Sixt to see if Trinity would cut Cerberus into its agreement. The implied threat was clear: Cut us in or we'll come back with a richer offer and steal the deal. It was a tough, ballsy move, and it almost worked. Li and Sixt knew Cerberus represented the only real risk to completing their deal, since it was the only investor that had done the due diligence necessary to submit a better offer. Sixt and Ingersoll even met in New York to discuss a possible partnership. But the talks fell apart when Cerberus refused to make an agreement that would prevent it from selling its shares for a period of time.

Instead, Ingersoll followed up on his threat. On November 20, Cerberus officials met with Murray McDonald, the monitor, and presented a revised investment proposal. This time, Cerberus said it was willing to accept just 27 per cent of Air Canada's shares for its $650 million. It also proposed boosting the rights offering by $100 million. The next day, Cerberus volleyed in yet another offer, $250 million for 12 per cent of the airline, and a rights offering of $850 million. Cerberus knew that the rights offering was critical for the creditors, who would see that their debts would be paid out through shares in the new Air Canada, at a fraction of face value. The creditors were buying debt based on estimates of where they thought the shares would trade after Air Canada emerged from bankruptcy protection. The more those shares rose, the more valuable the rights offering would become. Mizuho International PLC, a key creditor, filed an affidavit, estimating that the Cerberus proposal would result in a further $962 million for the company's unsecured creditors.

Milton and Rovinescu were livid that Cerberus had come back with richer offers at the end of what they saw as a fair and comprehensive process. They were also disturbed that details of the Cerberus bid were being leaked to creditors and the media, despite Cerberus having signed extensive confidentiality agreements. What was worse, the financial creditors were now rallying behind Cerberus, raising questions about whether the process had been slanted in Li's favour all along. Mizuho hired Harvey Strosberg, a well-known class-action lawyer, and threatened to sue the airline's directors for breach of fiduciary duty unless they abandoned Li for Cerberus. Bondholders thought management and the company's board should be thrilled to have received a richer offer, because it would allow them to maximize the company's value.

Milton and Rovinescu saw things differently. They had an agreement with Trinity – an investor they could trust – and a deal was a deal. They also felt that Cerberus's persistence was getting in the way of other pressing issues, such as how to address the pension deficit, thus delaying Air Canada's emergence from bankruptcy protection. Air Canada and its advisors reacted by beginning to dig up dirt on Cerberus and leaking examples to creditors and the media of past investments where they thought Cerberus had been overly aggressive and untrustworthy.

The tensions between Air Canada and Cerberus came to a head in early December, when the airline threatened to seek an injunction preventing Cerberus from discussing its bid publicly – and preventing the monitor from making it public. On December 4, Judge Farley interrupted a vacation in Florida, where his wife had recently bought some vacation property, to fly back to Toronto to mediate the dispute. That afternoon, the judge brokered a deal whereby Cerberus agreed to withdraw its bids and said it would not oppose court approval of the Trinity agreement. In exchange, Air Canada and Li agreed that Cerberus would have a chance to submit one final bid, which would be considered by Air Canada's board of directors. If Cerberus won, it would have to pay a $19.5-million fee to Trinity for spoiling its deal. Farley also imposed a formal gag order on Cerberus, which prevented distribution of its previous bids.

Farley later agreed to allow Trinity to improve its offer as well, thus giving the board two new options to consider. In its final offer, Cerberus proposed replacing the stock grants with cash bonuses worth a total of $10 million, to be split between Milton and Rovinescu. Trinity's last bid promised to reward the two executives with at least 1 per cent of the airline's stock, through a combination of grants and stock options. Cerberus proposed two investment alternatives, both of which valued the airline at $2.6 billion: one included a substantially richer rights offering; the other asked for just 25 per cent of Air Canada's equity for $650 million, while Trinity's bid still insisted on 31 per cent for $650 million, valuing the company at $2.1 billion. Nonetheless, the directors decided to stick with Trinity. Relying on an analysis from financial adviser Seabury, the board concluded that the bids were similar in economic terms, because Trinity had struck side deals with two key creditors – Deutsche Bank and GE Capital Aviation Services – that improved creditor recovery by about 15 percentage points. Cerberus believed it could have struck the same deals, but Air Canada's board declined to speculate.[6] This allowed the board to use qualitative factors – such as Li's Canadian citizenship – to affirm Trinity. A stubborn group of bondholders continued to fight for Air Canada to abandon Li for what they considered a much better deal with Cerberus, but on January 16, Judge Farley approved the final Trinity deal, eliminating almost any hope for Cerberus and the creditors.

That a Canadian passport could make an investor living in Hong Kong (12,000 kilometres away from Montreal) so much more attractive than an investor living in New York (500 kilometres away) highlighted the folly of Canada's foreign-ownership laws. Yes, Victor Li was Canadian, but that didn't mean that he would run the company from Canada – or in a way that was in the best interests of Canadians. This issue was underscored when Judge Farley, in a December 16 hearing, needed an urgent response from Li about how quickly he could improve his offer, and Trinity lawyers said it would not be easy to reach the key decision-makers, since it was the middle of the night in Hong Kong. "I was under the impression that this was a Canadian operation," Farley quipped.

By early 2004, many of the familiar faces in and around the Canadian airline industry had changed. Former Canadian Airlines CEO Kevin Benson had landed as CEO of Laidlaw Inc., the insolvent Burlington-based conglomerate that was in the process of reinventing itself as an American company under bankruptcy protection. Since leaving Canadian, Benson had also worked briefly in senior management for B.C. tycoon Jim Pattison, and as president of the provincially owned Insurance Corp. of British Columbia. After arriving at Laidlaw, Benson recruited Doug Carty, his former lieutenant from Canadian Airlines, as Laidlaw's chief financial officer. Angus Kinnear, the former Canada 3000 president, had moved to USA 3000, while his chairman, John Lecky, had died on February 25, 2002. WestJet's Clive Beddoe and the other three founders remained firmly in control at WestJet, while Michel Leblanc and Ken Rowe, the proprietors of Jetsgo and CanJet, held on at their fast-growing discounters. But analysts looked at the crowded domestic market and predicted that some form of bankruptcy or consolidation was becoming inevitable.

Despite begging David Collenette to extend his appointment for a third year, Bruce Hood was replaced as Air Travel Complaints Commissioner in September 2002. The new commissioner was Liette Lacroix Kenniff, the former manager of corporate travel at the International Air Transport Association. In August 2003, Konrad von Finckenstein stepped down as commissioner of competition, taking a post as a federal court judge. His successor was Sheridan Scott, the former regulatory officer at Bell Canada. Collenette also found himself replaced when Paul Martin became Canada's twenty-first prime minister on December 12, 2003. Martin selected Tony Valeri, a former insurance broker from Hamilton, as the new transport minister. Industry insiders hoped that, as a right-leaning MP who had served as Martin's parliamentary secretary, Valeri would be open to ideas like cabotage and international airline mergers — concepts that had been taboo when Collenette was minister.[7]

Days after Air Canada filed for bankruptcy protection, the airline had announced that former Bombardier boss Robert Brown would become its new chairman. Brown, a former federal bureaucrat who had joined the transportation giant and worked his way up to president and CEO of Bombardier in 1999, took over on May 13, 2003. Outgoing chairman Jack Fraser continued to sit on Air Canada's board and its restructuring committee. It was likely that Brown's appointment wouldn't stick. Victor Li was expected to replace most of the directors and to assume the role of chairman himself or name a well-trusted lieutenant to the post.

As Air Canada prepared to emerge from bankruptcy protection, it appeared that Milton would remain in place. By maintaining control of an airline he had flown into court protection, Milton had certainly defied the odds. Friends said the fact he would retain his position was testament to his vision and the impressive job he had done despite impossible challenges. Others said it spoke more of the way his team had deftly used the rules of the Companies' Creditors Arrangement Act to maintain control of the airline.

That Air Canada now had a controlling shareholder for the first time since privatization meant that things would be different at the Montreal head office. In an interview published in an internal newsletter, Milton said he didn't expect that Li's team would take an active role in running the company. "As long as we perform financially, I don't expect them to look over our shoulder over the long term, but it's only reasonable to expect Trinity Time to work closely with us over the next few months until we complete the restructuring," he said.

The Li family has had a history of maintaining experienced technical managers to run the operations, while at the same time slotting in at least one loyal deputy to be Hong Kong's eyes and ears on the scene. Some pointed to Husky as evidence that things would now be different for Milton. When the Lis took control of Husky in 1987, they initially expressed support for the executive team that had delivered them the company. But early in 1992, they inserted John Lau, a loyal Hong Kong accountant, into executive ranks. Eighteen months later, Lau took over as chief executive officer, while Arthur Price, the man he replaced, was named special advisor on international investments to the board of directors of Hutchison Whampoa. "From the Husky experience, we learned that management has to be perfect," Li Ka-Shing has said. "The management was really a bit slack at the beginning."[8]

Can Robert Milton be perfect in an industry known for its grim surprises? Victor Li appears willing to give him the benefit of the doubt. But Milton and his colleagues know that Li's loyalty is not unconditional; if they don't perform, they will be replaced. Milton needs to move quickly to repair the airline's damaged relations with employees, the government, and the travelling public. Most importantly, he needs to show that he can deliver more for the airline's new shareholders than he did for the old lot. The airline, after all, has not posted a profit since 1999, the year Milton was appointed CEO.

Despite the hundreds of millions of dollars in concessions that Air Canada has realized through the restructuring, a profit in 2004 is far from certain. Air Canada is still facing intense pressure from expansionist discount carriers in domestic markets, while its international and transborder routes suffer from a lack of business travel. There are renewed fears of aviation-related terrorist attacks and new cases of SARS in China. The CCAA filing kept Air Canada alive and had the potential to make Milton and Rovinescu very rich. But it is no guarantee of future profitability, little protection from the stormy weather that seems to constantly hammer the national carrier.

NOTES

PROLOGUE

1. Gordon McGregor, *The Adolescence of an Airline* (Montreal: Air Canada, 1970), p. 239.
2. Robert Milton, as quoted in Bernard Simon, "For Air Canada, Dominance is a 'Curse,'" *New York Times*, Nov. 20, 2001.
3. Buffett has used this line, or one like it, many times. This quote comes from an interview broadcast on CNBC on Dec. 20, 2001.
4. Interview with Ted Shetzen, Oct. 8, 2002.
5. "Canada's Not So Open Skies," *The Economist*, Sept. 2, 2000.

Chapter 1: THE RED TEAM AND THE BLUE TEAM

1. Gordon McGregor, *The Adolescence of an Airline*, p. 238.
2. Grant McConachie, as quoted in Ronald Keith, *Bush Pilot with a Briefcase* (Vancouver: Douglas & McIntyre, 1972), p. 309.
3. C.D. Howe, as quoted in Philip Smith, *It Seems Like Only Yesterday: Air Canada, the First 50 Years* (Toronto: McClelland and Stewart, 1986), p. 34.
4. C.D. Howe, as quoted in Susan Goldenberg, *Troubled Skies: Crisis, Competition & Control in Canada's Airline Industry* (Whitby: McGraw-Hill Ryerson, 1994), p. 5.
5. The Canadian Government Trans-Atlantic Service would officially become a subsidiary of TCA in 1947, when it would assume the job of transporting civilians and mail as well as troops and government officials.
6. A complete list of the freedoms of air travel: The first freedom is the right to fly over another country without landing. The second allows a plane to stop in a foreign country for fuel or repairs without boarding or dropping off passengers or cargo. The third and fourth allow a plane to carry passengers between its home country and a foreign country. The fifth is the right to take passengers or cargo from the home country, drop them off in a foreign state, then pick up more passengers to transport to a third country. Other freedoms

were added later. The sixth is the right to carry passengers or cargo between two foreign countries via the airline's home country. The seventh is the right to carry passengers between two foreign countries without touching down in one's home country. The final two freedoms are almost never granted; they are more theoretical than practical. The eighth is the right of an airline to carry passengers between two points in a foreign country, on a flight which originated in the airline's home country. And the ninth, cabotage, is the right for an airline to carry traffic between two points in a foreign country without having set off from the home country.

7. Stephan D. Krasner, *Structural Conflict: The Third World Against Global Liberalism* (Berkeley: University of California Press, 1985), pp. 197–98.

8. Daniel Yergin, Richard H.K. Vietor, and Peter C. Evans, "Fettered Flight: Globalization and the Airline Industry," Cambridge Energy Associates Report, 2000.

9. *Ottawa Journal*, as quoted in Susan Goldenberg, *Troubled Skies: Crisis, Competition & Control in Canada's Airline Industry*, p. 13.

10. C.D. Howe, as quoted in Gordon McGregor, *The Adolescence of an Airline*, p. 1.

11. Gordon McGregor, as quoted in Philip Smith, *It Seems Like Only Yesterday: Air Canada, the First 50 Years*, p. 144.

12. Allan Levine, *Scrum Wars: The Prime Ministers and the Media* (Toronto: Dundurn Press, 1993), p. 209.

13. Gordon McGregor, *The Adolescence of an Airline*, pp. 247–48.

14. Russell Baker, as quoted in Susan Goldenberg, *Troubled Skies: Crisis, Competition & Control in Canada's Airline Industry*, p. 16.

15. Max Ward, *The Max Ward Story: A Bush Pilot in the Bureaucratic Jungle*, (Toronto: McClelland & Stewart, 1991), p. 12.

16. Max Ward, *The Max Ward Story: A Bush Pilot in the Bureaucratic Jungle*, pp. 166–67. In a June 24, 2002, interview, Air Canada executive Paul Brotto told a similar story about his first flight in the late 1960s. For $10, Brotto received a membership as a Dieppe War Veteran so he could buy a ticket on a cheap Air France flight to Europe. He was seated near some very legitimate war veterans, who asked if his father had fought for the Allies at Dieppe. "I don't know," the Italian-born Brotto replied. "He might have been on the other side."

17. Thomas Petzinger, Jr., *Hard Landing: The Epic Contest for Power and Profits That Plunged the Airlines into Chaos* (New York: Times Books, 1995), p. xxi.

18. Jimmy Carter, as quoted in Thomas Petzinger, Jr., *Hard Landing: The Epic Contest for Power and Profits That Plunged the Airlines into Chaos*, p. 105.

19. George F. Will, "Always a Bumpy Ride," *The Washington Post*, May 9, 2002, p. A31.

20. Thomas Petzinger Jr., *Hard Landing: The Epic Contest for Power and Profits That Plunged the Airlines into Chaos*, p. xix.

21. Claude Taylor, as quoted in Ken Romain, "Air Canada Now Felt Ready to Fly Without Government Protection," *Globe and Mail*, Feb. 2, 1979, p. B5.

22. Interview with Claude Taylor, Montreal, June 27, 2002.

23. Interview with David Collenette, Toronto, July 12, 2002.

24. Lawrence Martin, "PM says CBC, Air Canada Not for Sale," *Globe and Mail*, Jan. 15, 1985, p. A1.

25. Quoted in Peter Pigott, *Flying Canucks III* (Madeira Park, B.C.: Harbour Publishing, 2000), p. 149.

26. Peter Pigott, *Wingwalkers: A History of Canadian Airlines International* (Madeira Park, B.C.: Harbour Publishing, 1998), p. 310.

27. Coincidentally, the carriers had been somewhat red and blue right from the start. James Richardson's first planes were unpainted aluminum, but there was a hint of dark blue on the engine cowlings. TCA's first planes – also aluminum – sported a red stripe and a maple leaf logo.

Chapter 2: THE PLANE-SPOTTER

1. Telephone interview with Robert Milton, Dec. 11, 2002.

2. Telephone interview with David Milton, Sept. 11, 2002.

3. Telephone interview with Doug Green, Sept. 5, 2002.

4. Hollis Harris, as quoted in Terry Maxon, "Continental Fires Harris as Chairman," *Dallas Morning News*, Aug. 22, 1991, p. 1D.

5. Interview with Robert Milton, Montreal, June 28, 2002.

6. Interview with Claude Taylor, Montreal, June 27, 2002.

7. Geoffrey Rowan, "Air Canada Recruits New Chief," *Globe and Mail*, Feb. 20, 1992, p. B1.

8. Hollis Harris, as quoted in Geoffrey Rowan, "Air Canada to Try to Stop Rival's Deal," *Globe and Mail*, March 31, 1992, p. A1.

9. Rhys Eyton, as quoted in Cathryn Motherwell, "PWA to Merge with Air Canada," *Globe and Mail*, Sept. 10, 1992, p. A1.

10. Kevin Jenkins, as quoted in Peter Pigott, *Wingwalkers: A History of Canadian Airlines International*, p. 320.

11. Susan Goldenberg, *Troubled Skies: Crisis, Competition & Control in Canada's Airline Industry*, p. 127.

12. Telephone interview with Don Carty, Dec. 20, 2002.

13. The description of Milton's experiences in Air Canada's cargo division are based on his account in his June 28, 2002, interview in Montreal. Geoff Bridges, who was Air Canada's vice-president for cargo at the time, said in a

Oct. 29, 2002, telephone interview that, while he does not recollect the events Milton has described, he does not refute them.

14. Interview with Robert Milton, June 28, 2002.

15. Telephone interview with Hollis Harris, Oct. 23, 2001.

16. The TriStar anecdote is based on accounts in interviews with Harris (Oct. 23, 2002) and Robert Milton (June 28, 2002).

17. Telephone interview with Hollis Harris, Oct. 23, 2001.

18. Kevin Benson, as quoted by Doug Carty in telephone interview, Aug. 16, 2002.

19. Kevin Benson, as quoted by Doug Carty in telephone interview, Aug. 16, 2002.

20. Interview with Robert Milton, Toronto, Sept. 9, 2002.

21. Interview with Robert Milton, Sept. 9, 2002.

22. Derek DeCloet and Sean Silcoff, "Be Nice for a Change," *Canadian Business*, Oct. 8, 1999, p. 37.

23. This anecdote is based on an account in an interview with Paul Brotto, Montreal, June 24, 2002.

Chapter 3: PROJECT PEACOCK

1. Interview with Don Carty, Dec. 20, 2002.

2. Interview with David Collenette, July 12, 2002.

3. Interview with David Collenette, July 12, 2002.

4. Jacquie McNish, Heather Scoffield, and Steven Chase, "Airline Merger Maelstrom," *Globe and Mail*, Sept. 18, 1999, p. B1.

5. Interview with David Collenette, July 12, 2002.

6. Kevin Benson, as quoted by Steven Chase, "Canadian Dismisses Merger Rumour," *Globe and Mail*, Aug. 14, 1999, p. A10.

7. Don Carty, as quoted by Robert Milton in Christopher J. Chipello, "Air Canada's CEO Milton Says Nation Shouldn't Give Industry Control to U.S." *Wall Street Journal*, Oct. 8, 1999.

8. Izzy Asper, as quoted in Peter C. Newman, *Titans: How the New Canadian Establishment Seized Power* (Toronto: Viking, 1998), p. 221.

9. Gerry Schwartz, as quoted in Peter C. Newman, *Titans: How the New Canadian Establishment Seized Power*, p. 225.

10. This telephone conversation is based on an account in an interview with Robert Milton, Sept. 9, 2002.

11. Peter C. Newman, *Titans: How the New Canadian Establishment Seized Power* (Toronto: Viking, 1998), p. 220.

12. Interview with David Collenette, July 12, 2002.

13. Interview with Rob Peterson, Toronto, Aug. 15, 2002.

14. Rob Peterson, as quoted by Paul Brotto in interview, Montreal, June 24, 2002.

15. The warrants expire in 2004, but lost any potential value when Air Canada filed for bankruptcy protection on April 1, 2003.

Chapter 4: DOGFIGHT

1. Interview with Calin Rovinescu, Montreal, June 28, 2002.

2. Angus Reid, as quoted in Murray Campbell, "68% Support Single Airline for Canada," *Globe and Mail*, Sept. 18, 1999, p. A1.

3. Milton has a somewhat revisionist memory of Air Canada's profitability. The airline lost $16 million in 1998 because of a two-week pilots' strike, and managed to squeeze out a $3-million profit in the first quarter of 1999 only because of the well-timed sale of its investment in Equant NV, a Netherlands-based telecommunications company. Air Canada posted a profit of $73 million in the second quarter, down from $91 million in the same period a year earlier. The airline's third quarter was strong at $124 million, especially when compared with the weak third quarter of 1998, when the pilots' strike resulted in a loss of $61 million. This gain in the peak summer season was largely attributable to Canadian Airlines' well-publicized troubles as consumers booked with the more secure carrier.

4. Interview with Buzz Hargrove, Toronto, May 28, 2002.

5. *La Presse* cartoon, as quoted in William Walker, "Flak Flies Fast for Collenette Over Handling of Airline Deal," *Toronto Star*, Oct. 28, 1999, p. A1.

6. Interview with David Collenette, July 12, 2002.

7. Interview with David Collenette, July 12, 2002.

8. Andrew Willis, "Onex Scraps Airline Merger," *Globe and Mail*, Nov. 6, 1999, p. A1.

9. Calin Rovinescu, as quoted in Jared Mitchell, Jacquie McNish, and Trevor Cole, "Rare Air: How the Airline Smarts of Robert Milton Saved Air Canada from Gerry Schwartz," *Report on Business Magazine*, Nov. 26, 1999, p. 46.

10. Gerry Schwartz, as quoted in Rod McQueen, "Reflected Glory," *National Post Business Magazine*, Nov. 1, 2001, p. 38.

11. Interview with Robert Milton, Sept. 9, 2002.

12. In retrospect, some pundits have suggested that a third option was available – that Canadian Airlines could have tried to return to profitability by filing for bankruptcy protection under the Companies' Creditors Arrangement Act, cutting its operating costs and reducing its indebtedness. But after having completed two restructurings in less than a decade, it seems unlikely that the

airline's employees or creditors would have endured the severe cuts that would have been necessary to fix the country's number-two carrier without a merger with Air Canada.

13. Interview with David Collenette, July 12, 2002.

14. David Collenette, as quoted in "Collenette Trims Air Canada's Wings," *Toronto Star*, Feb. 18, 2000, p. D1.

15. Four of these airlines would never get off the ground: Great Plains, Regional Airlines, London Air, and Branson's carrier; Capital City Air would disappear before the end of 2001.

Chapter 5: FOOLS RUSH IN

1. Interview with Ted Shetzen, Toronto, May 16, 2002.

2. The story of Virgin Atlantic's launch relies on Richard Branson, *Losing My Virginity: How I've Survived, Had Fun, and Made a Fortune Doing Business My Way* (New York: Three Rivers Press, 1998).

3. Telephone interview with David Tait, Oct. 18, 2002.

4. In a letter to the editor, one *National Post* reader pointed out the irony of dressing a group of prepubescent girls in hockey sweaters emblazoned with the word "Virgin." "Mr. Branson's excuse is that he's a donkey," Valerie Smith wrote, "but what was the coach of this girls' hockey team thinking?" Dec. 1, 2000, p. A19.

5. The minister acknowledged this in Keith McArthur and Mark MacKinnon, "Branson Plan Won't Fly in Canada: Transport Minister Says He Won't Open Skies to Foreign Airlines Any Time Soon," *Globe and Mail*, Dec. 1, 2000, p. B3.

6. Telephone interview with John Gilmore, Nov. 29, 2002.

7. Ken Rowe, as quoted in Keith McArthur, "N.S. Businessman Determined to Make CanJet Fly," *Globe and Mail*, Sept. 18, 2000, p. B1.

8. Ken Rowe, as quoted in Oliver Bertin, "Investor Says Air Canada Snuffs His Airline Plans," *Globe and Mail*, Nov. 24, 1999, p. B9.

9. Don Green, as quoted in John Heinzl, "How Roots Plants Its Products," *Globe and Mail*, May 28, 1998, p. B10.

10. Ted Shetzen, as quoted in Keith McArthur, "Roots Air Takes Flight in March," *Globe and Mail*, Jan. 27, 2001, p. B6.

11. Jonathan Gatehouse, "Day One: Roots Lives Up to the Hype," *National Post*, March 27, 2001, p. A1.

12. Daphne Bramham, "Roots Air: Not Quite Flight of Fancy," *Vancouver Sun*, March 27, 2001, p. F1.

Chapter 6: MILTON'S PARADISE LOST

1. Scott Feschuk, "Stealing Lucien's Lines," *National Post*, June 17, 2000, p. B2.

2. The shares would peak one week later. On May 25, 2000, the shares briefly traded above $21, before closing the day at $20.95 on the Toronto Stock Exchange. The stock price has fallen ever since.

3. Robert Milton, as quoted in Keith McArthur, "Air Canada Set for Global Expansion," *Globe and Mail*, May 31, p. B1.

4. Kevin Benson, as quoted in Peter Pigott, *Wingwalkers: The Rise and Fall of Canada's Other Airline*, revised edition (Madeira Park, B.C.: Harbour Publishing, 2003), p. 389.

5. Interview with Paul Brotto, Montreal, June 24, 2002.

6. Raymond Hall, as quoted in Peter Kuitenbrouwer, "I Win, You Lose," *National Post*, Sept. 27, 1999, p. C1.

7. Peter C. Newman, "Giving Air Canada the Finger," *Maclean's*, Sept. 18, 2000, p. 14.

8. Jennifer Hillard, as quoted in Lisa Wright, "Canada's Airlines Swamped by Beefs," *Toronto Star*, July 18, 2000, p. A1.

9. Interview with Robert Milton, September 9, 2002.

10. Telephone interview with Luc Lavoie, Dec. 2, 2002.

11. Robert Milton, as quoted in Jacquie McNish, "This Is Something I Never Wanted for Air Canada," *Globe and Mail*, Oct. 21, 2001, p. B1.

Chapter 7: THE THREAT FROM THE WEST

1. Interview with Clive Beddoe, Calgary, June 11, 2002.

2. The story of WestJet's birth is based on accounts in interviews with Mark Hill, June 10, 2002; Clive Beddoe, June 11, 2002; Tim Morgan, June 11, 2002; and Don Bell, June 12, 2002. All interviews were conducted in Calgary.

3. In a February 2002 interview at a Toronto restaurant over a double helping of smoked salmon.

4. The story of Southwest Airlines relies on Thomas Petzinger Jr.'s *Hard Landing: The Epic Contest for Power and Profits that Plunged the Airlines into Chaos*.

5. Interview with Clive Beddoe, June 11, 2002.

6. Judy Fahys, "Tough but Tender," *Salt Lake City Tribune*, Apr. 4, 1995, p. A1.

7. Wendy Zellner, "Bringing New Air to New York: David Neeleman Is Set to Pilot His Second Discount Airline," *Business Week*, May 3, 1999.

8. Barry Lapointe, as quoted in Paul Waldie, "Federal Agency Grounds Greyhound Air," *Globe and Mail*, Apr. 13, 1996, p. B1.

9. Terence Corcoran, "Let Greyhound's Buses Fly," *Globe and Mail*, Apr. 19, 1996, p. B2.

10. David Anderson, as quoted in Scott Feschuk, "Greyhound Air Gets Cabinet Nod for Up, Up and Away," *Globe and Mail*, June 8, 1996, p. A1.

11. This account of Flight 592 relies on the work of Ken Kaye, a pilot who covered the story for the *Sun-Sentinel Times*. "Following the Deadly Path of Flight 592," Dec. 12, 1996.

12. As recounted by Clive Beddoe, June 11, 2002.

13. Interview with Mark Hill, June 10, 2002.

14. Clive Beddoe, as quoted in Matthew Ingram, "WestJet's Troubled Skies." *Globe and Mail*, Sept. 19, 2002, p. B2.

15. Kevin Freiberg and Jackie Freiberg. *Nuts! Southwest Airlines' Crazy Recipe for Business and Personal Success* (New York: Broadway Books, 1996), pp. 3, 10.

16. Dave Arnott, *Corporate Cults: The Insidious Lure of the All-Consuming Organization* (New York: AMACOM, 2000).

17. Clive Beddoe, as quoted in Peter Verburg, "Prepare for Takeoff," *Canadian Business*, Dec. 25, 2000, pp. 94–95.

18. These documents became public when they were submitted as evidence by the Competition Bureau in 2003 in a hearing before the Competition Tribunal.

19. Interview with Robert Milton, Sept. 9, 2002.

20. Steve Smith, as quoted in Steven Chase, "WestJet Slams Budget Carrier Plan," *Globe and Mail*, Oct. 20, 1999, p. B12.

21. Interview with Mark Hill, June 10, 2002.

22. Interview with Steve Smith, Toronto, Oct. 23, 2002.

Chapter 8: THE FIGHT FOR THE EAST

1. Ken Rowe, as quoted in CanJet press release, Nov. 15, 2000.

2. Calin Rovinescu, as quoted in Air Canada press release, Oct. 12, 2000.

3. Dave Barry, "The Unfriendly Skies," *Miami Herald*, June 12, 1998.

4. Pat Hanlon, *Global Airlines*, 2nd ed. (Oxford: Butterworth-Heinemann, 1999), p. 183.

5. Michael Trethaway, Expert Witness Statement of Dr. Michael Trethaway, Feb. 8, 2001. This was prepared for a hearing in which Air Canada sought to overturn the commissioner's cease-and-desist order.

6. Interview with Calin Rovinescu, Montreal, June 28, 2002.

7. Jacques Kavafian, as quoted in Karen Howlett, "Air Canada's Profit Fallout," *Globe and Mail*, Oct. 7, 2002, p. B1.

8. Interview with Rob Peterson, Aug. 15, 2002.

9. Telephone interview with Angus Kinnear, Dec. 7, 2002.

10. Canadian Press, "Intair Already Profitable," *Globe and Mail*, Feb, 23, 1990, p. B8.

11. After its restructuring, Intair would be carved into pieces, with the Quebec regional division retaining the Inter-Canadian name but with the French spelling, Inter-Canadien.

12. Ben Cherniavsky, as quoted in Keith McArthur, "Canada 3000 to Acquire Rival Royal Aviation in All-Stock Deal," *Globe and Mail*, Jan. 30, 2001, p. B1.

13. Mark Winders, as quoted in Peter Fitzpatrick, "CanJet Halts Expansion, Blaming Tough Rivals," *National Post*, Feb. 15, 2001, p. C1.

14. Pat Hanlon, *Global Airlines*, 2nd ed., p. 204.

15. Under the competition regulations introduced in February 2000, the federal Cabinet specified that Air Canada cannot operate or increase capacity on a route or routes "at fares that do not cover the avoidable cost of providing the service. Neither can the dominant carrier create a fighting brand – that is, create a second low-fare carrier – to operate below avoidable cost.

16. Interview with Dave McCallister, Ottawa, June 21, 2002.

17. Andrew Reddick, as quoted in Keith McArthur, "Air Canada Rapped Again over Pricing Policies," *Globe and Mail*, March 8, 2001, p. B1.

18. Angus Kinnear, as quoted in Peter Fitzpatrick, "Canada 3000 Closes In on CanJet Airlines," *National Post*, March 23, 2001, p. C1.

19. Interview with Angus Kinnear, Dec. 7, 2002.

Chapter 9: A BROKEN INDUSTRY

1. Found at <skygod.com>, a Web site of great aviation quotations.

2. Mark Pazner, as quoted in Colin Freeze, "View from Pearson," *Globe and Mail*, Dec. 22, 2000, p. A9.

3. Bruce Hood, as quoted in Keith McArthur, "Complaints Referee Knocks Air Canada," *Globe and Mail*, Dec. 28, 2000, p. A1.

4. Interview with Bruce Hood, Ottawa, June 19, 2002.

5. Howard Wilson, as quoted in Peter Fitzpatrick, "'Appearance of Conflict Exists,' Says Air Ombud," *National Post*, March 31, p. A1.

6. Bruce Hood, as quoted in Keith McArthur, "Airline Referee Gets Quite an Earful," *Globe and Mail*, March 30, 2001, p. A3.

7. On Oct. 23, 2001, Lecky sent copies of this letter and four other pieces of correspondence to Canada 3000's board of directors along with a new letter summarizing his concerns. The communications were later leaked to financial analysts and the media.

8. Michel Leblanc, as quoted in Bertrand Marotte, "Ex-Royal Executives Sue Canada 3000," *Globe and Mail*, Sept. 21, 2001, p. B3.

9. Canada 3000's Notice of Annual Meeting of Shareholders, Aug. 8, 2001.

10. Lecky's letter to Canada 3000's board of directors, Oct. 23, 2002.

11. These quotations were found at <skygod.com>.

12. Pat Hanlon, *Global Airlines*, 2nd ed., p. 52.

13. Keith McArthur and Heather Scoffield, "Air Canada Cuts Fares on Rival's Route," *Globe and Mail*, March 7, 2001, p. B3.

14. Ted Shetzen, as quoted in Keith McArthur and Heather Scoffield, "Air Canada Cuts Fares on Rival's Route," *Globe and Mail*, March 7, 2001, p. B3.

15. Interview with Russ Payson, Toronto, June 6, 2002.

16. David Collenette, as quoted in Les Wittington, "Air Canada Needs New Rivals, Watchdog Urges," *Toronto Star*, May 9, 2001, p. A1.

17. Keith McArthur, "Pilot Opposition Delays Launch of Skyservice," *Globe and Mail*, July 5, 2001, p. B1.

18. Peter Verburg, "Dogfight," *Canadian Business*, Sept. 17, p. 23.

19. Peter Verburg, "Dogfight," p. 23.

20. Gordon Bethune, *From Worst to First: Behind the Scenes of Continental's Remarkable Comeback* (New York: John Wiley & Sons, 1998), pp. 17, 48–49.

21. Interview with Don Kennedy, Toronto, Nov. 21, 2002.

22. Robert Milton, as quoted in Jacquie McNish, "Air Canada CEO Won't Back Down in Onex Dogfight," *Globe and Mail*, Oct. 2, 1999, p. B1.

23. Interview with Rob Peterson, Aug. 15, 2001.

Chapter 10: THE DAY THE WORLD CHANGED

1. Interview with David Collenette, Toronto, Sept. 12, 2002.

2. Interview with Robert Milton, Toronto, Feb. 5, 2002.

3. David Collenette in Transport Canada, "11-09-2001 Four Days in September," 2002.

4. Interview with Rob Reid, Toronto, July 30, 2002.

5. Telephone interview with John Creighton, Nov. 14, 2002.

6. Interview with David Collenette, Sept. 12, 2002.

7. This account of Flight 85 relies on two reports: Alan Levin, "Korean Air Jet May Have Narrowly Missed Disaster," *USA Today*, Aug. 13, 2002; and Andrew Duffy et al., "Empty Sky," *Ottawa Citizen*, Sept. 11, 2002, p. D7.

8. Telephone interview with Robert Burgess, Oct. 27, 2002.

9. Interview with John Creighton, Nov. 14, 2002.

10. Interview with David Collenette, Sept. 12, 2002.

11. Details about the new security regulations and the phone-line gaffe rely on Transport Canada, "11-09-2001 Four Days in September," 2002.

12. Jean LeCours, as quoted in Transport Canada, "11-09-2001 Four Days in September," p. 20.

13. Interview with Robert Burgess, Oct. 27, 2002.

14. A year later, Captain Burgess flew some children from Gander to England, where they had dinner with the Canadian high commissioner and Virgin Atlantic chairman Richard Branson. Other airlines made similar overtures to thank their Canadian hosts. The German airline Lufthansa renamed one of its planes the Gander-Halifax.

Chapter 11: FALLOUT

1. Konrad von Finckenstein, as quoted in Keith McArthur, "Tango Judged Anti-Competitive," *Globe and Mail*, Nov. 10, 2001, p. B1.

2. Calin Rovinescu, as quoted in Air Canada press release, Nov. 9, 2001.

3. Interview with David Collenette, Toronto, July 12, 2002.

4. Eric Reguly, "Once Air Canada's Gutted, Then Mr. Milton Can Beg," *Globe and Mail*, Sept. 22, 2001, p. B8.

5. David Olive, "Air Canada Chief Should Be Grounded: Robert Milton Has Dropped the Ball Too Many Times," *National Post*, Sept. 25, 2001, p. B4.

6. Interview with David Collenette, July 12, 2002.

7. Interview with Robert Milton, Sept. 9, 2002.

8. Lecky's letter to Canada 3000's board of directors, Oct. 23, 2002.

9. Interview with Paul Brotto, June 24, 2002.

10. Jennifer Hillard, as quoted in Keith McArthur, "Air Canada Plans Two Discount Brands," *Globe and Mail*, Oct. 13, 2001, p. B1.

11. Interview with Don Kennedy, Toronto, Nov. 21, 2002.

12. Bill Bredt, as quoted in Keith McArthur, "Air Canada Could Easily Undo Tango," *Globe and Mail*, Oct. 20, 2001, p. B1.

13. Interview with Rob Peterson, Aug. 15, 2002.

14. John Lecky, as quoted in Susan Pigg, "Canada 3000 Heading for Cash Crunch," *Toronto Star*, Oct. 16, 2001, p. C1.

15. John Lecky, as quoted in Keith McArthur, "Canada 3000 Could Run Out of Cash," *Globe and Mail*, Oct. 16, 2001, p. B1.

16. John Lecky, as quoted in Carol Howes, "Canada 3000 and the Man Behind It Go Public," *National Post*, July 24, 2000, p. C3.

17. The five-page letter was sent along with ten pages of previous correspondence sent to Kinnear through 2001. The communications were later leaked to financial analysts and the media.

18. Keith McArthur and Jacquie McNish, "On a Wing and a Prayer: Canada 3000's Bet," *Globe and Mail*, Nov. 19, 2001, p. B1.

19. Kinnear made this statement Nov. 6 at a hearing before the Canada Industrial Relations Board.

20. Keith McArthur and Jacquie McNish, "On a Wing and a Prayer: Canada 3000's Bet."

21. Telephone interview with Angus Kinnear, Dec. 7, 2002.

22. Interview with Don Kennedy, Nov. 21, 2002.

23. Angus Kinnear, as quoted in Keith McArthur, "Airlines Still Suffer 9/11 Aftershocks," *Globe and Mail*, Sept. 10, 2002, p. B7.

Chapter 12: RE-REGULATE, RELAUNCH, RE-BRAND

1. Ken Rowe, as quoted in Keith McArthur, "CanJet to Be Resurrected in Early June, Rowe Says," *Globe and Mail*, May 14, 2002, p. B5.

2. Ed Acker, as quoted on skygod.com.

3. Interview with David Collenette, July 12, 2002.

4. Milton took me through the math during an interview at his Toronto office on Sept. 9, 2002.

5. Interview with David Collenette, July 12, 2002.

6. Interview with David Collenette, July 12, 2002.

7. David Collenette, as quoted in Keith McArthur and Steven Chase, "Air Canada Chief Calls for Open Skies to Spur Competition," *Globe and Mail*, Dec. 7, 2001, p. A1.

8. Robert Milton, as quoted in Keith McArthur, "Air Canada's President Rides Out the Turbulence," *Globe and Mail*, Feb. 5, 2002, p. B1.

9. Ken Rowe, as quoted in Keith McArthur, "Ottawa Told to Toughen Anti-competitive Rules," *Globe and Mail*, Nov. 22, 2001, p. B2.

10. On Nov. 10, 2003, David Miller was elected mayor of Toronto on a platform of not building a bridge to the island airport. Miller convinced city council to follow through on his promises, effectively killing Deluce's plans.

11. Angus Kinnear, as quoted in Keith McArthur, "Discount Air Battle Heats Up," *Globe and Mail*, Feb. 22, 2002, p. B1.

12. Ben Cherniavsky, as quoted in Keith McArthur, "CanJet to Be Resurrected in Early June, Rowe Says," *Globe and Mail*, May 14, 2002, p. B5.

13. Louise Crandall, as quoted in Keith McArthur, "Air Canada Scrapping Most Commissions," *Globe and Mail*, March 23, 2002, p. B1.

14. Robert Milton, as quoted in Perry Flint, "The World Has Changed Forever," *Air Transport World*, March 1, 2003, p. 22.

15. Steve Smith, as quoted in Patrick Brethour and Keith McArthur, "Air Canada Unveils Zip Discount Carrier," *Globe and Mail*, Apr. 20, 2002, B1.

16. David Collenette, as quoted in James Stevenson, "Air Canada's Low-Fare Zip Air Faces Challenge from Unions, WestJet," *Canadian Press*, April 19, 2002.

17. This anecdote was told by Robert Milton in a telephone interview, Dec. 11, 2002.

18. Eric Reguly, "Divide and Conquer?" *Report on Business Magazine*, Nov. 29, 2002, p. 39.

Chapter 13: EMERGENCY LANDING

1. Gordon Bethune, *From Worst to First: Behind the Scenes of Continental's Remarkable Comeback* (New York: John Wiley & Sons, Inc., 1998), p. 52.

2. Gerry Schwartz, as quoted in Peter C. Newman, *Titans*, p. 240.

3. Rod McQueen, "Reflected Glory," *National Post Business Magazine*, Nov. 1, 2001, p. 38.

4. Interview with Robert Milton, Sept. 9, 2002.

5. Gerry Schwartz, as quoted in Jacquie McNish, "How Two Feuding Titans Learned to Play Together," *Globe and Mail*, Jan. 28, 2003, p. A1.

6. As measured on a fully diluted basis, that is, if any stock options, warrants, and convertible bonds were converted into equity. In its fiscal year ended March 28, 2003, Indigo Books & Music Inc. eked out a profit of $1.4 million, compared with a loss of $47.9 million a year earlier. If you purchased *Air Monopoly* in Canada, there is an excellent chance it was sold in one of the stores controlled by the Schwartz–Reisman powerhouse – Indigo, Chapters, Coles, or SmithBooks.

7. Interview with David Milton, Sept. 11, 2002.

8. The slide show, titled "The Model is Broken . . . Dealing with the New Reality," was presented to Air Canada's unions Feb. 6, 2003.

9. In May, Air Canada would write down a $400-million future tax asset, resulting in a restated loss of $828 million for 2002.

10. Douglas Reid, "Air Canada Flies to Bailout City," *National Post*, Feb. 7, 2003, p. FP11.

11. This according to Gary Fane, CAW's director of transportation, in a sworn affidavit filed in court.

12. Isabelle Arthur, as quoted in Allan Swift, "Air Canada Deadline for Union Concessions on Saturday," Canadian Press, March 14, 2003.

13. Air Canada had announced 3,500 job cuts on Dec. 21, 2000, 4,000 more on Aug. 1, 2001, and an additional 5,000 on Sept. 26, 2001. There had been other smaller announcements, too. On Aug. 21, 2001, Air Canada announced 1,300 temporary job cuts, and in Nov. 2002, it announced 390 job cuts at Jazz.

14. The release did not mention SARS, which would prove to be a much more serious blow to Air Canada's revenue than the four-week war in Iraq.

15. Gary Fane, as quoted in Peter Brieger, "Air Canada 'Not Getting This List,'" *National Post*, March 19, 2003, p. FP4.

16. Don Johnson, as quoted in Derek DeCloet, "Unions Dig in at Air Canada," *National Post*, March 24, 2003, p. FP1.

17. Telephone interview with Gary Fane, Sept. 3, 2003.

18. James Moore, as quoted in Keith McArthur and Steven Chase, "Air Canada, CAW Reach Deal," *Globe and Mail*, Apr. 1, 2003, p. B1.

19. Affadavit of Gary Fane, sworn Apr. 14, 2003.

20. Sandra Rubin, "Air Canada Deal Flew on Adrenalin," *National Post*, Apr. 2, 2003, p. FP11.

21. Jonathan Berke, "DIP Dimensions: Air Canada Corp," *Daily Deal*, Apr. 24, 2003.

Chapter 14: PARADISE RESTRUCTURED

1. Interview with Robert Milton, Dec. 11, 2002.

2. Calin Rovinescu, as quoted in Jacquie McNish and Keith McArthur, "At 5 a.m., the Clock Ran Out on Robert Milton," *Globe and Mail*, Apr. 2, 2003, p. A1.

3. As I was the first reporter to write about <www.miltongottago.com>, my name was also posted numerous times to the Web site by pranksters.

4. Daniel Mullen as quoted in Nicolas van Praet, "Air Canada Labour Bares Claws," Montreal *Gazette*, July 8, 2003, p. B1.

5. Interview with Rob Peterson, Aug. 15, 2002.

6. Warren Winkler, as quoted in Susan Pigg, "How a Judge's Plain Speaking Saved Air Canada," *Toronto Star*, June 2, 2003, p. A1.

7. Interview with Warren Winkler, Toronto, June 1, 2003.

8. Warren Winkler, as quoted in Keith McArthur and Jacquie McNish, "The Air Canada Deal," *Globe and Mail*, June 2, 2003, p. A1.

9. These conclusions relied on data provided by Douglas West, an economist called as a witness by the commissioner. West concluded that Air Canada operated 43 of 73 monthly schedule flights on the Toronto–Moncton route and 72 of 111 monthly schedule flights on the Halifax–Montreal route below its avoidable cost. A schedule flight compares aggregate monthly revenue with aggregate monthly costs for a set of flights with a similar departure time.

10. Keith McArthur, "Change in the Air for Canada's Carriers," *Globe and Mail*, Nov. 11, 2003, p. B8.

11. In the third quarter ended Sept. 30, Air Canada's unit costs fell 2 per cent from the same quarter in 2002, excluding restructuring costs and other non-operating items. WestJet's unit costs, meanwhile, fell by 16 per cent, because of its newer, more fuel-efficient jets and longer stage lengths.

12. After Air Canada pulled out of Yarmouth, Nova Scotia, for example, an Ontario airline filled the gap. Wild Country Airways of Red Lake, Ontario, planned to operate eleven flights a week into the community, instead of the seven that had been provided by Air Canada Jazz. (Keith McArthur, "Small Airlines Fill Void Jazz Leaves Behind," *Globe and Mail*, Jan. 8, 2003, p. B4.)

13. Interview with Robert Milton, Dec. 11, 2002.

14. Previously, there were only a handful of countries that shared their flag-carrier. SAS Scandinavian Airlines represented Sweden, Norway, and Denmark, while British West Indies Ltd. acted as flag-carrier for a number of Caribbean nations.

EPILOGUE

1. Robert Milton, as quoted in "A Conversation with Robert About the Victor Li Investment," *Horizons Online* <www.achorizons.ca>, Nov. 2003.

2. Jacquie McNish and Keith McArthur, "Air Canada Connections Run Deep at Stikeman Elliott," *Globe and Mail*, Oct. 14, 2003, p. B1.

3. Jacquie McNish and Keith McArthur, "Air Canada Connections Run Deep at Stikeman Elliott."

4. Li's financial advisor, Goldman Sachs, was also expected to put up a piece of the $650-million investment through Trinity.

5. Wendy Tong Branes, as quoted in Keith McArthur, "Li's Bid Said to Keep Air Canada Canadian," *Globe and Mail*, Oct. 1, 2003, p. B4.

6. Under pressure from some financial creditors, the board hired Merrill Lynch Canada Inc. to provide the directors with independent advice on the Li and Cerberus offers. Merrill did not evaluate the deals but reported on Seabury's analysis. According to the board, there was "no significant component of the financial methodology, assumptions and calculations" on which Seabury and Merrill Lynch were divided.

7. But it wasn't clear that Valeri would be a long-term fixture in the post. Because of a redistribution of ridings, he first had to fight Sheila Copps, the former deputy prime minister, for the Liberal nomination. Even if he held on to the riding, there was speculation that Martin had bigger things in mind for Valeri, which would leave room for another transport minister to set out the future of air-transport policy.

8. Li Ka-Shing, as quoted in Joanne Lee-Young, "Victor Victorious," *Report on Business Magazine*, Jan. 2004, p. 51.

BIBLIOGRAPHY

No one has written more about Canadian aviation history than former diplomat Peter Pigott, who has published detailed corporate histories for both Air Canada and Canadian Airlines. *Wingwalkers: A History of Canadian Airlines International* (Madeira Park, B.C.: Harbour Publishing, 1998) was republished in 2003, with new material on the carrier's final months, as *Wingwalkers: The Rise and Fall of Canada's Other Airline*. Pigott's first book in a multi-volume history of Air Canada, *National Treasure: The History of Trans Canada Airlines* (Toronto: Harbour Publishing, 2001), tells the story of Canada's flag-carrier through 1965, when TCA became Air Canada. The well-illustrated histories, which are popular with aviation buffs and employees, include such details as early aircraft inventories and staff lists.

Philip Smith's *It Seems Like Only Yesterday: Air Canada, the First 50 Years* (Toronto: McClelland & Stewart, 1986), is another good book on the early history of Air Canada, while Shirley Render's *Double Cross: The Inside Story of James A. Richardson and Canadian Airways* (Vancouver: Douglas & McIntyre, 1999) makes the case that Richardson was hoodwinked by C.D. Howe. Susan Goldenberg's *Troubled Skies: Crisis, Competition & Control in Canada's Airline Industry* (Whitby, Ont.: McGraw-Hill Ryerson, 1994) provides a quick overview of the history of the Canadian airline industry – a good reminder of why the country wasn't big enough for two full-service carriers.

For more detail on PWA founder Russ Baker, there's John Condit's *Wings Over the West: Russ Baker and the Rise of Pacific Western Airlines* (Madeira Park, B.C.: Harbour Publishing, 1984). Gordon McGregor's *The Adolescence of an Airline* (Montreal: Air Canada, 1970) is a thoroughly readable autobiography on his years at TCA. For the Blue Team perspective on the same time period, try Ronald A. Keith's *Bush Pilot with a Briefcase: The Incredible Story of Aviation Pioneer Grant McConachie* (Vancouver: Douglas & McIntyre, 1972). Another legend tells his tale in *The Max Ward Story: A Bush Pilot in the Bureaucratic Jungle* (Toronto: McClelland & Stewart, 1991).

It is surprising there are no biographies of Gerry Schwartz, one of Canada's most intriguing businessmen. Peter C. Newman's *Titans: How the New Canadian*

Establishment Seized Power (Toronto: Viking, 1998) includes a good chapter on the man ("The Onex Juggernaut," pp. 219–241). Also useful is Rod McQueen's "Reflected Glory" in *National Post Business Magazine* (Nov. 1, 2001, p. 38).

The most dramatic book ever written on aviation history may be Thomas Pertzinger, Jr.'s *Hard Landing: The Epic Contest for Power and Profits That Plunged the Airlines into Chaos* (New York: Times Books, 1995). *Hard Landing* is also a good source for the story of Southwest Airlines. A more glowing corporate history can be found in Kevin and Jackie Freiberg's *Nuts! Southwest Airlines' Crazy Recipe for Business and Personal Success* (New York: Broadway Books, 1996). For the more critical take, Dave Arnott uses Southwest as a case study in his book *Corporate Cults: The Insidious Lure of the All-Consuming Organization* (New York: AMACOM, 2000).

Two autobiographies by international airline heads are also worth noting: Gordon Bethune's *From Worst to First: Behind the Scenes of Continental's Remarkable Comeback* (New York: John Wiley & Sons, 1998), written with Scott Huler, and Richard Branson's colourful *Losing My Virginity: How I've Survived, Had Fun, and Made a Fortune Doing Business My Way* (New York: Three Rivers Press, 1998), which focuses as much on Branson's daredevil exploits as on his business ventures.

With the airline industry changing so rapidly, books on airline economics tend to be almost out of date by the time they are published. Two relatively recent books that I have found useful are Pat Hanlon's *Global Airlines: Competition in a Transnational Industry*, 2nd ed. (Oxford: Butterworth-Heinemann, 1999), and Rigas Doganis's *The Airline Business in the 21st Century* (London: Routledge, 2001).

There are reams of government and academic reports with recommendations on how to fix the airline industry. I'll mention just three. Fred Lazar, a professor at York University's Schulich School of Business, makes a persuasive argument for the relaxation of foreign-ownership restrictions, but says Canada should not open up its skies unilaterally in *Potential Market Impacts of Liberalization Options on the Commercial Canadian Aviation Industry* (April 2001). Debra Ward, the independent airline observer appointed by David Collenette, goes further, suggesting that Canada should be prepared to act alone if there are obvious advantages for Canadians and consumers. Her final report on *Airline Restructuring in Canada* was released in September 2002. And B.C. economist Michael Trethaway makes the case that airlines are particularly vulnerable to predatory pricing in an expert witness statement prepared for the Competition Bureau (Feb. 7, 2001).

For fun, I'll finish by mentioning two Web sites. The "Airline History" site <www.afriqonline.com> features illustrated histories of 650 airlines, as well as photographs of virtually every commercial aircraft model, indexed by the decade. <skygod.com> is an on-line encyclopedia featuring hundreds of aviation quotes, as well as a page on aviation books and writers.

ACKNOWLEDGEMENTS

David Milton chuckles when he tells the tale – recounted at the start of Chapter 2 – of how his four-year-old son Robert packed a suitcase and announced he was going to fly away from home. We all have stories from childhood that won't die. My father doesn't let me forget how I told him in my early teens that I didn't want to follow him into newspaper journalism. I said that, instead, I wanted to be a "serious" writer. By this I meant that I intended to write novels and, presumably, be angst-ridden and poor. Nevertheless, I completed a journalism degree in 1997 and joined him at the *Globe and Mail* two years later. With a passion for learning, a deep sense of compassion, and a zest for life, Douglas McArthur worked for three decades as Canada's top travel journalist at trade publications and the *Globe*. He was writing about airlines when I was still in diapers. This book is for him.

Air Monopoly is also for my best friend and loving wife, Laura Williams, who put up with much grief as I toiled on the book, while she was working, finishing a master's degree, and struggling with the trials of pregnancy. She is truly the wisest and most generous person I have ever met. Laura and my dad gave invaluable feedback on my early drafts, as did my good friend Jon Shell.

I could not have started the book without the support and guidance of my agent, Dean Cooke, and could not have finished it without the careful eye of my primary editor, Jan Walter. Thanks also to Pat Kennedy and everyone at Macfarlane Walter & Ross and McClelland & Stewart, who helped get the book to its readers. I am deeply indebted to my editors at the *Globe* – Cathryn Motherwell, Michael Babad, Colin McKenzie, Richard Addis, Edward Greenspon, and publisher Phillip Crawley – who allowed me to take several months to work on this project and who have supported me in my daily reporting on the airline industry. Thanks to *Globe* reporter Steven Chase, who has helped cover the Ottawa side of the airline story. I'm also grateful to the country's other talented transportation reporters – Peter Fitzpatrick and Paul Vieira at the *National Post* and Susan Pigg at the *Toronto Star* – who have set a worthy benchmark against which to judge my own reporting every day.

Thanks to the industry experts who acted as sounding boards for my ideas and theories, including Ben Cherniavsky, Sam Barone, Fred Lazar, Fadi Chamoun, Debra Ward, and Douglas Reid. I am also grateful for the assistance of my primary contacts: Laura Cooke and Renée Smith-Valade at Air Canada, Siobhan Vinish at WestJet Airlines, Angela Saclamacis at Canada 3000, and Anthony Polci in the office of David Collenette. Priscille Leblanc at Air Canada and Caterina Trotto in the Air Canada archives were particularly helpful. So were Paula Wilson at the *Globe* and Kerri Button at Canada's Aviation Hall of Fame, who helped with photo research. Thanks to Peter and Mary Calamai, who housed me when I was doing research in Ottawa, and to Joe Paraskevas and Marni Kagan, who fed me when I was doing interviews in Calgary. I am especially grateful for the support of my families and friends; you know who you are.

Finally, *Air Monopoly* is much richer thanks to those who made time available for me. There are too many to name them all, but the list includes Robert Milton, Calin Rovinescu, Rob Peterson, Paul Brotto, Rob Reid, Rob Giguere, Doug Port, Rupert Duchesne, Marc Rosenberg, Hollis Harris, Claude Taylor, Steve Smith, Clive Beddoe, Mark Hill, Tim Morgan, Don Bell, Rob Winter, Dick Huisman, Angus Kinnear, Don Kennedy, Michel Leblanc, Ken Rowe, Mark Winders, John Gilmore, Philippe Sureau, Russ Payson, Ted Shetzen, Don Carty, Doug Carty, Stephen Sibold, Jeff Angel, Roland Dorsay, Geoffrey Elliot, Peter Lougheed, Buzz Hargrove, Cliff MacKay, Warren Everson, John Creighton, Konrad von Finckenstein, Richard Annan, Dave McAllister, Louis Ranger, Valerie Dufour, Peter Gregg, Randall McCauley, Bruce Hood, and David Collenette.

This is not quite the book any of them would have written, but I hope all will see it as constructive, informative, and fair.

Keith McArthur
October 2003

INDEX